9⁵⁰, 6B/VS

A1040
BF10

FOREPLAY

CATHERINE ROMAN

FOREPLAY

🏠 RANDOM HOUSE   NEW YORK

Published in Canada as *Bang for a Buck* by Somerville House, Publishing, a division
of Somerville House Books Limited, Toronto.

Library of Congress Cataloging-in-Publication Data
Roman, Catherine.
    Foreplay / by Catherine Roman.
        p.   cm.
    ISBN 0-394-56579-7
    I. Title.
    PR9199.3.R583F6   1990
    813'.54—dc20   88-43208

Manufactured in the United States of America
98765432
First Edition

TO THE ORDER OF D KIDS OF THE 1990'S:

THE BIGGEST DICE ROLL OF ALL
IS YET TO COME.

A bladder, a blade of straw, and a shoe went to chop wood in the forest. They came to a river and did not know how to cross it. The shoe said to the bladder, "Bladder, let us swim across it on you." The bladder said, "No, shoe, let the straw blade instead stretch itself from shore to shore, and we will walk over it." The blade of straw stretched itself across the water; the shoe walked on it and the straw broke. The shoe fell into the water, and the bladder laughed and laughed until it burst.

—A RUSSIAN FAIRY TALE

"I can only make direct statements, only 'tell stories.' Whether or not the stories are 'true' is not the problem. The only question is whether what I tell is my fable, my truth."

—CARL JUNG

Aperte mala cum est mulier,
tum demum est bona.
[When a woman is openly bad,
she is then at her best.]

While the following story is based on fact, I have used full creative license in the reproduction of some scenes. The sequence of events has been slightly altered to lend order to an otherwise disorderly life. With the exception of major cities, all place names have been changed. The names of the people here have been changed and in some cases, where I felt necessary, their physical representation altered to protect their privacy and my ass.

—CATHERINE ROMAN

FOREPLAY

PROLOGUE

ociety would like the world to believe that the street is an amoral holding tank of poverty, criminal stereotypes, and lower working-class anachronisms. Instead, it is a half-melted pot where the overflow from all classes come to set up a class system and laws all their own. It is a subculture where the riotous rabble of one generation eventually ferments into the ravaged rubble of the next. Sometimes the fermentation takes minutes; sometimes years. The street mirrors the conscience and the temper of the times in all its extremes and colors. It can give an accurate forecast today of what will be on the agenda tomorrow in the House of Commons or the Congress. The truth is that society is afraid of the street because many of its best-kept secrets ultimately end up there. The street is as cruel as it is truthful. It spares no one.

PART I
COMING
INTO IT

'm supposed to be a Christmas baby named Holly but I defy the gods and emerge kicking into the nightmare of cold and light, upside down and one month early. I know outrage. I'm born . . . early enough to be a 1955 tax write-off, too late to enjoy the Thanksgiving turkey. . . .

Shot out of the increase-and-multiply baby-boom barrage of the mid-1950's, coffee sells for ten cents a cup; black leather jackets, greasy ducktails, poodle skirts, and saddle shoes are the rage, Hula-Hoops and Davy Crockett dolls the craze, and everybody's rocking to "Hound Dog" and "What Will Be, Will Be."

Love makes the world go round.

Charlottesburg, Ontario, is a workingman's ghetto, a factory town squatting like a knocked-up centipede on an island in the St. Lawrence River. The bottom line is, Your ass might be your own, brother, but your soul belongs to Canada Cement, Inc.

We rent an apartment over a funeral parlor. My father doesn't believe in home ownership and can't afford a change of opinion. The whole place smells of ash-ridden new ghosts drowning in formaldehyde. My teen-age parents married because they didn't know any better. I came along to punish them for it.

Coming from lower working-class stock, my father never expected to progress in life beyond his parents' place, so when he was kicked out of school at sixteen for fighting, he went right into the factory to be processed and labeled like a can of dog food. He wanted to be an artist. Now that he is an assembly-line monkey see monkey do, he has stopped dreaming, too.

My mother, on the other hand, comes from those god-fearing Pennsylvania Dutch. While my father remains a mixture of soot, sweat, and Old Spice, a presence exuding warmth and earthiness, my mother remains an emotional iceberg, an enigmatic, brilliant, unmaternal matriarch, a blond blue-eyed German princess cured in Palmolive soap and aged in remoteness, practicality, scrubbed floors, and hiding a soul striving to evolve.

So here I am at the crossroads of two isms, half salt of the earth peasant and half working-class stiff. This probably explains why I hate being tied into chairs and harnessed up to the same clothesline as the dog and why I'm constantly Messerschmitting out of my crib at night, cracking my head open and being rushed to the hospital by the undertaker in a part-time hearse.

A retired English nanny lives downstairs. Nan not only looks after me but names me after a Hebrew prophetess at my baptismal as well. I have baby pictures taken with her holding me and it takes me a couple of years to figure out that Nan has really been minding my mother while my mother has been minding my father and the family dog has been minding me. I don't get the tit either. Breast-feeding is considered dirty and unhygienic. It seems to pain my mother to touch me. My father rolls across the Axminster carpet with me instead.

In the middle of the night I pad down the stairs to the room of the sleeping people laid out in beds of flowers. I don't understand why they refuse to respond when I pull their arms, so one night I crawl in with one of them to keep warm. I'm hauled out in the morning with a horrified smack and scold and told I've committed a sin. To my mind, this must have everything to do with toilet training. As soon as I learn to talk better, I have only the one eternal question to ask: "When can I get off the pot?"

My Grampy is my savior. Angularly provocative in a pinstriped black woolen suit, he often takes me to the track, lifts me up to one of the stalls, and slips sugar cubes into my sweaty little paw. Lucky Joe's hot breath tickles my hand. This horse is a winner. Since everybody loves a winner, a winner must be a good thing to be. "I want him to be mine," I announce.

"Then he's yours whenever you want him," Grampy says.

From this day forward I'll never equate what I have in my pocket with what I have in my hand. Ownership of anything will be a fleeting illusion. Years later when I become a gypsy I will understand why Grampy, too, rented houses his entire life instead of buying one. Trust not, want not.

In the tack room my Grampy sits down, knocks his pipe against the wall, fills it with a plug of tobacco, and smokes in a studied slump. I crouch nearby on a wooden stool feeding on the bitten faces, the dirty yellow light, the sweet aromatic resin of leather and stale tobacco filling my nostrils with warmth, comfort, and security, which I will always associate with the company of men.

Grampy says I have horse sense.

When I take an afternoon nap Grampy tells me that sleep is a gift from the gods, the only part of yourself you'll ever be able to deny the world. I don't yet realize, you see, that denying the world a piece of my butt is to be the greatest challenge of my life.

My mother's ahead of her time in a time when there aren't supposed to be any alternatives for women outside the tedious employment of spit, polish, and elbow grease. Turning her back on the family compact and taking strength from the Book of Ruth and a college curriculum that came in the mail, she borrows money and goes back to the books. What does she care if she's the only girl in the class?

An irreparable rift between my parents occurs, mainly because of my mother's pursuit of an education. They don't have time for me so I'm farmed out with relatives for the next few years and shunted around from pillar to postmark. I don't mind. I love the change of scenery and faces and simply transform myself into a turtle, learning to carry my memories and dreams on my back.

I have fond memories of summers spent on the road with a favorite uncle as we traveled from sunup to sundown through the farm belt, selling housewares from the back of a truck. I remember living with my Grampy on the other side of the blanket, spending hours with him in the kitchen of the greasy spoon where he worked fifteen hours a day. I remember the eczema that had forced him to leave the farm he loved and how the disease made him cry with pain every spring. I remember how he pretended not to be sad and how I pretended not to notice.

The towns along the waterfront were rich then. The building of the St. Lawrence Seaway had made them rich. Whole towns were dismantled, brick by numbered brick, and reassembled farther inland to make way for the river. There was new money by the millions, new blood by the thousands, and old values that wouldn't let you go.

Then came the day when the Seaway was finished and little by little the money dried up and the people left. And there was a feeling of displacement and disenchantment. And the towns died.

Every year until I'm nine years old I'm stricken with pneumonia and rheumatic fever and confined to bed from October to April. Meanwhile, on holiday weekends I visit my parents. I'm in awe of my mother, her terrible strength, her quick changes of moods, her books. Proud of her and a little afraid of her too. She talks to me only when she's scrubbing floors. Knowing I'll never get closer to her than a block of worn linoleum, I always grab a cloth to help, hoping she'll regard me as the son she always wanted. Secretly I dream of someday creating dirt worthy enough for her to clean up.

At seven, I'm packed off to my great-uncle Jack's farm for the summer. A new species on the family breadboard, he emerges from the shadows of the barnyard, tall, gangly, a condor, with big callused hands, inspiring fear in the world around him and insecurity within himself.

On hot afternoons he hoists me up onto the hay wagon beside him and we rumble out to the yellow burnt fields, littered with row upon row of straw tepees. Armed with a pitchfork, he jumps down and loads the tepees onto the wagon. I'm instructed to drive the horses and whenever I mess up the reins he curses thickly at me over his shoulder. After supper he takes me to the outer pasture to watch him shoot rabbits and groundhogs and then calls me a gutless little heller because I'm not impressed with his marksmanship. If this's what a summer vacation on the farm is all about I'll stay to hell at home next year.

My uncle's crude tauntings hit me in the quick. I'm getting to know my bad angel on a first-name basis. Her name's Spite. To get even I throw stones at his prize bull, Bernard, the meanest son of a bitch I've met so far, next to my uncle. Then I crawl under the legs of the wild stallions in the corral—I do love those horses—until he chases me up into the mow of the barn with a crazed fury. "I'll get you yet, daughter of Judas!" he shouts.

Isolated from the environment of his violence outside the house, my uncle transforms into the lamb incarnate inside, burying his thoughts in his plate of spuds, pretending that I don't exist. Even the hired hands are afraid of him. Now, after the episode with Bernard the bull and the stallions, I know that we're not at loggerheads. We're at war.

The next morning he orders me into the barn and locks the door. I wait for the ax to fall, shaky and ready to sprint on cue. He lifts a bullwhip off a nail in the tack room. Then he lays it across the back of one of the horses until she's neighing in a falsetto and twisting her rump and doing a crazy two-step and I realize that Uncle Jack is trying to get to me through hurting that horse. I run for the aisle between the wildly whinnying animals, and they stamp their hooves and kick the sides of the stalls and bite at the air, and I hear his footsteps and run again and then he stops and I stop, knowing we're not only still circling each other in that same Jesus-to-Judas corral we've been jiving in—but in the same aisle, and we're still miles apart from each other because neither of us is willing or trusting enough to square off. Now he's waiting for me to lose the advantage and move again and I move back to the horses because I'm seven years old and only believe in my feet but at the end of the darkened aisle his shadow is already standing at twelve o'clock on mine and the whip is cracking again off the backs of *my* stallions, his nostrils flaring, his sweat beading on my forehead, his arm moving mechanically like a piston pump as he screams in anguish, "Lay down! Lay down, Lucifer!"

Now he's mistaken me for another devil. But I don't notice. The sour sweat and the deep bloody slashmarks and rearing, ramping horse-flesh sear my senses like fire as man and beast groan in pain, locked in some cruel pagan sacrifice. Hysterically, I grab my uncle's arm and he throws me up against the barn wall and I slip to the floor stunned and crouch in the corner beside an empty milk can with my hands over my head and ears to block out the sound but I find that my hands have cracks called fingers which can see and hear and remember. . . .

Finally he's worn himself out and stops for the moment. Noticing me again, he unlocks the door and I run to the house and nearly rip the screen door off its hinges trying to get into the kitchen. "Help, Aunt Isabelle, he's killing the horses!" I grab the hem of her apron and run with it to the window.

She pulls me up short, her hands floured to the elbow. "What nonsense—let me go!"

"But Uncle Jack is lost and you have to bring him home!"

More impatient than angry, she keeps pounding a mountain of dough into the board, hoping it'll disappear. "What he does to his horses is his business. I'll have nothing to do with it!"

Her attitude is inconceivable to me. These two are my first real experience with the injustice of the outside world and it stinks. White with fury, I charge around the kitchen, issuing war cries and throwing myself against the oak furniture, trying to destroy the pain in my head with the pain in my body and when the one subdues the other, the bubble in my brain bursts and I pass out cold on the floor.

I wake up in my little iron bed in the dark little guest room, smelling of linseed oil because it cries for guests and of mildew because it can't round up any, and the coldness of a strange house without a furnace. Sometimes in the night, the incoherent cries of my great grandmother who's bedridden and closeted away in one of the many rooms down the hallway come to me. I'm not allowed to see her because she's busy dying.

Then, I suddenly hear my uncle's steps on the stairs below. At once I hope he comes in and I hope he doesn't.

The door squeaks open and with a labored sigh he sits down on the sagged side of the bed, his face lacquered with sweat and his hair matted in a fur ball to his forehead. I'm afraid for myself until I remember that the corral outside will have no place here. For him the house is like a church, the permanent residence of his good angel. At the moment, I'm safe. So, motionless I watch, now afraid for him and the devils who possess him, suddenly afraid that they might secretly try to possess me. Finally, I'm not able to hold back any longer.

"You killed my horses—for nothing you killed them!"

"I didn't kill them, I saved them. And they aren't yours."

"Yes, they are. Every horse in the world is mine—if I feel for it."

"You have a fever in the brain. That's why you talk and act so crazy," he concludes, changing the subject. "How about staying here and living with me?"

Now that I know how he plays the game . . . how sweet can he make the pot? I've got to find out.

"What about a pony of my own?"

Though he nods at me I can tell by his east-to-west, firmly pressed preacher's smile that I could never trust him with any living creature.

Come Sunday night Aunt Isabelle makes me up with my blue velvet dress, lace ruffled at the neck and sleeves, and my black patent-leather shoes. Taking my hand, she guides my party-perfect self into that off-limits vault down the hall to visit my great grandmother. I was afraid of her before because I couldn't see her—only imagine a witch in a hooded shroud. When the shrunken frame in the large iron bed peeps at me over the covers, rasps yellow phlegm, and extends a thin transparent hand, I realize that reality is one step down from my worst dreams. She looks at me awhile and I wither awhile under her stare and she rasps again and whispers something to my aunt, who plays interpreter while ushering me out. Apparently, I remind my great grandmother of her husband, Wyatt. He deserted his young wife and seven children to roam across the province on horseback, hawking sheet music and stories. From other members of the family I was told he was a demon who lived "selling bullshit by the pound." On his way home one night, for one of his short, sporadic visits, only a mile from the farm, he was killed. In the morning they found him in the shallows of the Nation River, his body crushed underneath his horse, who had slipped and fallen on top of him. Wyatt died with a bottle of whiskey in his hand and a Bible in his saddlebag. For insurance.

Of all Wyatt's sons, only one always hated him with religious zeal— my great-uncle Jack. Now I understand his resentment against me. It doesn't help the situation at all . . . because now I know his weakness and will learn to play on it.

Glad to have the interview over, I race along the hall and thump down the stairs. In the kitchen, Aunt Isabelle collars me and sets me Little Miss Muffet-style in a chair by the window.

Eventually, if not sooner, Uncle Jack and the hired hands clump in after milking and take chairs at the table. A bottle of whiskey is uncapped and goes the rounds. Aunt Isabelle grasps her knitting bag and retreats to the parlor. "Now you be a good girl."

Suffering Jesus! Why must adults leave the onus of the untoward at a child's door as if we've got a voice in Parliament? I'm scared. I'm scared of women who protect the devil by playing the lamb. I'm scared of men who protect the Lord by playing the devil. I'll never take Sunday school seriously again. Somehow this day I realize I can expect help from no one. Grown-ups are fakers who can't slay dragons they can't see. This little dragon is on her own.

The radio is snapped on and soon the jamboree music gets up to full throttle with that foot-stamping, knee-slapping, seesawing fiddle and the barnyard yodeler sitting on the back fence with a horny rooster. Uncle Jack grabs my hand and dances me around the kitchen until

I'm dizzy and the smell of whiskey makes me sick. Then he stands me on the table and lets me play centerpiece while he plops into a chair and becomes as unintelligible as I've heard him. "Boys, here you have Adam's impossible punishment. She's wrought from anger and pain and doomed to lose as much through negotiation as through the violence of the wooden spoon." I prefer a rolling pin myself.

Their raw, brute laughter scratches at the frail, fragile fiber I am and I pray to control the violence of the wooden spoon (if I'm able to get it out of the drawer of the hutch) and to stop him I pull my dress up to my waist and suddenly they stop laughing and I stop feeling afraid and, released, I run out of the room, laughing.

All summer long the war continues. I'm not sure whether it's a complete difference of opinion or of blood but I do know I'm part of this family madness and I'll always be watching my hand for signs of a weapon.

At departure time I see relief on my aunt's face. She no longer has to lie to me or herself and it's all because of the devils my uncle saw in his father and imagined he saw in me and made the whole house suffer for. We don't exchange a word in the pickup on the way to the train depot. When he kisses me good-bye, there's a comet tail blazing in his eyes. I'll never see him again. One day I will hear that he's in an asylum and I will think of him. But for now I'll try to forget I ever met Jack. He knows why. I know why. And that's enough.

I'm eight years old. My mother's strongly fixed personality and independence are too much for my father to handle. Taking the remedial step from separation to divorce, I move with my mother to another town and get to visit my father on weekends, when I can become wild and woolly.

First I was a social outcast because my mother wanted to become an educated breadwinner and took courses; now she's turned her back on the precious state of marriage to boot. Uncle Jack taught me I was born into a family that was on the left hand of something—so when will I start to enjoy it, too?

My mother's indifference or nervous impatience gives me withdrawal symptoms. About this time my body starts to rumble with a vile nervous condition. I stutter, roll my eyes, twitch, and at night lie in bed kicking like mad as if trying to expel a live-in demon. The doctors can do nothing but prescribe a tonic for worms. I can do nothing but masturbate more regularly.

At school I'm given constant tongue-lashings. I get psychological testing because I write in two completely different scripts, one a back-handed hen scratch, the other a right-handed lazy scrawl. My note-books look as if they're shared by a pair of kids with opposing personalities.

For moral upbraiding I'm enrolled in the CGIT—Canadian Girls in Traction, official caretakers of the Protestant female psyche, who meet in a ghoulish church basement to dissect brain cells. It's a dandy place to pick up lockjaw and heresy. On initiation night the girls throw a blanket over my head and tell me to remove everything I don't need. Being abnormally normal I start with my shoes, planning to end at the fillings in my teeth, and hiccuping tears. "Stupid, stupid, stupid! Take off the blanket, dumb, dumb, stupid!" they chant and taunt, closing in for the kill with snickers and goo-goo sneers. As the blanket is zipped from my head, I'm wearing nothing but a horror-stricken look. I manage to grab a corner of it and hang onto the primitive mantle for dear life, kicking and punching, ripping one girl's glasses from her moony face and pulling the buttons off the blouse of another. I'm prodded and pushed and end up half wrapped under a pile of these heartless harpies with not enough tit to fill a training bra. The fat horn-rimmed troll in charge orders the girls off of me until I calm down and let go of a girl's teeth braces. Then she gives me a blast of shit for not being "sporting." Give me a gun and I'll show her how sporting I can be.

The only animal I'll ever despise more than a man will be a woman. Up to now I haven't been thinking high enough on the barometer of human malice.

3

W hile pilfering lost balls from the county golf course down the street and selling them back to golfers at a fraction of their original cost, I meet and fall in with some French-Canadian kids who just moved into the tenements next door. Gabrielle, their mother, a professional shoplifter, who has only one arm, is a warm, generous earth mother and treats me like the gold bracelet she filched from Birks Jewellers and hid up her fake left arm, which means I'm lost goods in search of a receipt or a store detective. Now I'm part of a gang, signboard news to me since I've never been accepted as part of anything but a tax bill. Gabrielle barely exists on welfare handouts as her husband is crippled and can't work, but she knows how to sow and reap in a sandbox economy. In short order I'm hooked on the world's second-oldest profession—with nickel and dime incentives. There's nothing quite like the hype of stealing, the gutfuls of guile, the expectation of being caught, the ecstasy of making it out the door, your pockets loaded with trust. Every Thursday and Friday night we hit the mall downtown to score. Payday pockets yawn and so do store clerks under the pressure. But our fingers itch. Later, we hit any houses under construction for lumber, gardens for anything eatable, and cars for anything easily disassembled. Then we divide the booty on Gabrielle's kitchen table over cake and ice cream and I usually give my share to her, asking only that she let me pretend that she's my mother and continue to telephone my mother to say that I'm sleeping over. Since she always sends me home with a few trinkets to keep me in drive, I always bury them in the field out back. I can't bear to have

Trust and me sleeping in the same room. It's enough to cause nightmares. My criminal tendencies might prove terminal.

My eccentric grandmother Gerty, a sister of my great-uncle Jack, moves in to "watch and look over me." Everything's a game with her. Every morning I wake up with Oral Roberts satanizing from the radio by the bed and my grandmother's false teeth biting my ass.

During tourist season she dons her shades, ties a kerchief around her head, and loads a big red wagon with perfume, soaps, jewelry, and all kinds of junk she has hidden in a trunk in my room. Then, like gypsies, we pull it downtown and set up shop without a hawker's license or a booth.

Sometimes she wakes me up in the middle of the night, sneaks me down the back stairs to the garden, and we sit in the moonlight for hours beside the lilac bushes, pulling our garbage apart and organizing it into piles—cans here, peelings there, newspapers we save. Then, while expounding on the wastefulness of society, she digs a hole for each pile and buries it. No wonder she always has the Bible open at Revelation. Everything gets recycled. Even the worms get a feed.

One night she inadvertently digs up one of my caches of stolen jewelry and wallets. I stand by speechless while she shaloms the earth. "There, child. Now you see how bountiful the earth is. It never stops giving."

Eventually my mother catches us in the act. Grandma bursts into tears and I'm beaten up the stairs to the bathroom with the broom handle. I can't understand why she's being punished—just because she's different? The next day I'm lost in a crying jag while helping Grandma pack her bags. She's just been committed to an asylum.

I'm eleven years old when my father decides to keep me for good. But an Ontario Provincial Police officer busts up his plans and drags me screaming right out of the school classroom into a cruiser with my mother and I'm moved away by car across the country all the way west to Vancouver.

My mother lands a peach of a job working for a West Coast newspaper. I'm dumped off in the suburbs to live with her sister, my auntie

Lil, the Ice Queen, a tall, green-eyed redhead. To me she's a movie star with all the props. Her clothes have New York and Paris labels on them, she only wears her dresses twice, and she cha-chas around in bikinis, black silk negligees, and gold lamé pajamas.

The house is my dream come true, too, a splashy two-story white edifice with green shutters, swamped by trees and surrounded by a high hedge. Inside, a complicated kitchen, a maze of bedrooms, a den, a bar, and a living room wallowing in white sheepskin, studded with statues of naughty Nubians and scattered with delicate glass tables. Outside, the patio, swimming pool, kenneled German shepherds, borzois, and Siberian huskies keep me occupied. I love it all. It's like staying at the animal Ritz.

While I tear around unsupervised, men come and go via a revolving door which has no time restrictions or special favorites and includes construction magnates, doctors, politicians, lawyers, and Royal Canadian Mounted Policemen (without their horses). They're her Johns and my uncles. She uses them to pay the mortgage, stock her wardrobe, and baby-sit me.

Sometimes I creep inside the house from the patio and watch her turn on a man friend in the living room. First they sip martinis in their underwear while he snaps *Playboy* layouts of her against the snowscape panorama of fur on marble. Then he feeds her an olive on the end of a toothpick and she feeds him a grape from her toes. When they start panting twitchy I sweat from the eyes, a throbbing pain pounds in the pit of my pelvis, and I expect the indoor sprinkler system to snap on. I hightail it outside, shaking with fear and excitement, and release the dogs from the kennels and wrestle with them until my clothes are in threads and there are teeth marks all over me. This is some kind of love. . . .

A new John pulls up to the front gate in a shiny red MGA. In response to my usual interrogation procedure which includes a dollar toll fee, he grins and whips out a badge. Impressed, I raise the toll to two dollars and let him in. Alex is one of the Royal Canadian Mounted Police officers using German shepherds to help subdue those hell-raising Russian immigrants called Doukhobors who'd rather sacrifice their clothing to bonfires and be arrested for indecent exposure than change their dinner etiquette. Instead of giving me a social conscience, Alex teaches me where to kick a masher and how to train the dogs to heel.

Then my aunt Jane moves into the house—for added bounce. Fun, voluptuous, and warm, she's not only my favorite person but everyone else's, too. Blond and always on the verge of chuckle, she's the one I'm supposed to take after if genes are any determining factor. Her steady flame is a Brit nearly twenty years her senior, an ex-Mackenzie Papineau Brigadier who fought in the Spanish Civil War and is now a professional con man with an incurable ulcer called gambling.

Round and boyish, Uncle Teddy is charming, gentlemanly, mischievous, and once did time in jail with the brains behind the famous Canadian bank robbers called the Boyd Gang. Uncle Teddy, too, is wanted by the constabulary. They sure as hell can't be all they're cracked up to be if he's not afraid of them.

I'm farmed out with him one weekend while my auntie Lil has a house party. It's strictly off limits for me because I don't have peekaboo underwear and can't spell orgy backward. Uncle Teddy picks me up in a junker and we drive into Vancouver. "Is this your car?" I ask. Every time I see him he's driving a different set of wheels.

"Not bleedin' likely." He grins. "I wouldn't own a piece of crap like this. It's not my style."

"Whose piece of crap is it then?"

"Haven't the foggiest, kid. But I'll bet yeh ten to one that the sod is thanking me right now for taking it off his hands. What a pity that the city will be giving it back to him tomorrow."

We ditch the junker on a side street and leg it up to a cream-colored Buick nearby. He puts me into the driver's seat and props me up on my overnight bag. While he pushes the bumper from behind, I steer along the curb. Slowly we cruise to the top of a hill overlooking a mile-long stretch of here-today gone-tomorrow butcher car lots known as Running Board Alley. Then he takes the wheel and we glide down, veering right into a car lot. "Wait here," he says, passing me a racing form. "Pick a winner and make us rich." He gets out and shakes the hand of a sour-pussed car salesman and the heated bargaining session begins.

When the deal's struck and the cash and ownership papers have exchanged hands, he grabs my arm and hauls me out of the driver's side. Soon we're lost in the pedestrian traffic and a block away from the strip of used-car dealerships. Suddenly he halts and I stumble against his leg. He's spied a blue Dodge at the curb and the windows are rolled down.

He pushes me through to the passenger side, reaches under the dash, hot-wires it, and we're off. For lunch we pull into an A & W for burgers and shakes. "Gosh, we must be rich now that we've got money for the car," I admit on an all-time high.

"Three hundred dollars is nothing to sneeze at, mate."

"Is that a good price?" I ask, wanting to sound very knowledgeable.

"Well, there wasn't any bloody motor in the bugger so I guess you could say it was a steal."

He shoves our cardboard empties onto the tray and pulls my feet into his lap. The laces on my runners are running all over the place. "Don't want to go around with your tathles disengathed, do you?" he chants merrily.

"Huh?"

"Tathles." He grins. "Dithengathed tathles can make you thumble."

He crosses his eyes and I believe him.

We cruise around for a while. He stops twice to call his bookie to place a bet on Irish Eyes and Snazzy Sally. Since I appreciate only heroes both evil and medieval he buys me a handful of Thor comics. We're passing an apartment building when we spot a TV sitting outside on the sidewalk. The poor thing looks abandoned. "H-e-l-l-o, what've we got here?" He whistles. Applying the brakes, he backs up to the curb, slips her into park, and has the TV loaded in a jiff. "That'll make a nice present for your auntie Jane. What do you think of it, mate?"

"I think that maybe you got a deal."

"That's what life is all about, kid—getting a deal when the odds are against you."

Soon things get hot for my uncle Teddy. The R.C.M.P. have a

bead on him and he and Auntie Jane have to bugger off to Mexico in a flash.

Why do I keep losing people without even posting want ads? Worse, why do they want to be lost from me in the first place?

A gala event: my auntie Lil is taking me out for a night on the town. She's dolled up in a cotton-candy-colored body hugger with heels, gloves, and a white picture hat to match. I'm in a seersucker print trying to hide my boy's haircut under a straw pillbox.

Soon, as usual, she's driving her white Cadillac along the freeway like a rocket. When a cop pulls us over she gives the virgined virtuoso the thirty-second come-on that includes an eye-batting drill, cleavage lifts, and a damp line still pegged with yesterday's laundry: "Why not let me write you out a ticket instead?" She scribbles her telephone number on the back of his ticket book and blasts off into the traffic. Uncle Teddy used to say that no man was safe with her unless he wore a leaded jockstrap. (Instead of asking him what a jockstrap was, I asked him if he wore one.)

It's neato to be with someone who's such a knockout that you're always in the limelight even if you do have the figure of a stick and the face of Harpo Marx. We have dinner at a posh Italian restaurant that is early braggadocio and late Dino Ferrari. I expect an organ grinder with his pet monkey to appear at the table anytime—and pay *us* for the privilege. The staff fawn over us presto zesto during the meal and after a short tête-à-tête at the bar with Luigi, the owner, we walk out without paying.

Fifteen minutes later we're at the drive-in with our feet up on the dash, munching popcorn and downing Cokes through three hours of *Ben-Hur*. Right out of the blue she comes out with a brain beveler. "You like your Uncle Alex, don't you?"

"Sure. He bought me a boomerang. I can get it all the way around to the kennels already."

"He's an asshole."

"But why?"

"He can't think past small, that's why. He's nothing but a two-bit flatfoot with biceps for brains. He thinks he's reached the big time because he can buy a piece of my ass instead of having to beg for it like any other cheap son of a bitch. He'll never be anything but a loser like Teddy—in the slow lane going nowhere fast." She pauses. "When you grow up don't go for anything but the bucks or you'll wind up in the gutter under a pile of promises."

I've got a lot to remember for eleven. By the time I'm twenty I should be a regular walking library of wash-and-wear wisdom.

Uncle Bill, a surgeon, takes me under his wing at his research lab when he gets stuck playing Father Goose without custody papers. He ties a white muzzle around my face and together we watch a dog die and neuter a cat. I wish to hell we could have neutered his wife instead. I always seem to be cleaning shit out of a cage when she comes up with her standard Sunday school stinger, "Aren't you related to *that* woman?" Then she explains herself and I'm surprised. I've never heard my aunt openly referred to as a whore before.

I nod as always and am angry as always wishing that when I was born they had stuck a sign around my neck saying WHAT I'M NOT GUILTY OF I'M NOT CAPABLE OF—YET. PLEASE ADD ALL FURTHER BILLS TO THE ACCOUNT OF EVERYMAN. AMEN.

One day at home I'm putting Cheevers, a big brown boxer, into the kennels when Dixie the cat strolls by, malicious intent dripping from her wanton whiskers. Cheevers knocks me down and, yelping and yodeling, penetrates the shrubbery. Auntie Lil appears at the door, flagging her arms and toning her tonsils. "He belongs to a rich muck-amuck—catch him!"

Adrenaline pumping in every vein, I chase Cheevers into the bush and streak along a stitch of railway tracks. In the swimming heat the boxcars look like melting slugs and smell of molten tar. Sure I'll never catch the bugger, I'm turning on the tears and choking on the suds when I get lucky in my laments. Cheevers hesitates while trying to nose out a groundhog hole and I leap onto his back. Not having even a rope to tether him with, I make a leash by sheepshanking my halter top to my shorts.

Fifteen minutes later I'm completely lost, stumbling along the freeway in my underpants and the passing motorists are hooting, hollering, and honking their hosanna-hyped horns. Finally I'm met by my hysterical aunt and the calmly hostaged Uncle Bill; they've been patrolling the area for the last hour in her Caddy. To complicate matters, Uncle Alex screeches up to the shoulder in his cruiser.

Uncle Bill puts Cheevers in the backseat of the Cadillac and my aunt stamps her Italian heels on the smoldering pavement. "What the hell are you doing waltzing around showing your ass?"

"I was told to catch him," I counter curtly. "You didn't say how."

"What'll people think of you?"

"Pipe down," Alex charges, coming between us.

She turns on him with both claws flexed. "Don't tell me to shut up, you son of a bitch. If you like the brat so much you can damn well look after her. I'm busy for the rest of the day so drop her off tomorrow."

Before he has time to object to being left with The Dogcatcher of the Year, she jumps into the driver's seat and is gone. Cursing her, Alex puts me into the cruiser and orders me to get dressed before he gets arrested as a pervert.

Minutes pass. Now that he's relaxed enough to smoke a cigarette with his teeth, I have a question—as usual. "If you hate Auntie Lil so much, why do you bother to see her?"

"She's available—I guess somebody has gotta be."

"Is that why she's so popular?"

"No. She's popular because she plays at being unavailable."

He drops me off at the station for the remainder of the afternoon. While he's out finishing his shift I play crazy eights with a baby-faced constable named Glenn who has a watermeloned weakness for wards of the state. He buys me sweets and pop out of a machine to keep me from complaining about police brutality. If he was a bird he'd be a parakeet.

Two hefty officers, aping John Wayne blotting out a sunset, drag in a cuffed and manacled hood and fire him into a chair nearby. He's a wolf-faced punky pariah, parceled in a black leather jacket. Too bad somebody pounded the piss out of his face. Now he's a dead ringer for the Roadrunner's pet coyote—after the bomb went off and the bridge gave way.

A hullabaloo at the front desk involving another hood who's just been trucked in sends Glenn into grumbling action. In the interim I offer the new ruckabutt in the chair part of my Milky Way.

"Thanks, kid," he says restlessly, parboiling. "But I'd rather have a weed. Say, do yeh know where I could get a weed? I could sure use a weed."

Figuring Glenn won't mind giving to charity, I filch a pack from his desk, light one, place it between the guy's blue lips, and watch him work it to the corner of his mouth. "I'm Ty," he croaks after one puff. "What're you going up for, kid?"

"Walking a dog along the highway in my underwear."

"No kidding? Shit, I didn't know that one was on the books."

"It is now. What'd you do?"

"Pulled a mail heist. Swiped one of their trucks. I got away with it, too. If it hadn't been for that fucking dumb broad I was shacked up with I'd be doing beach time in Hawaii right now. But she just *had* to go back to the apartment for her goddamned cat. We couldn't find the son of a bitch when we were moving out. When we got there the cops were inside waiting. I'll betcha anything that goddamned cat turned us in. If there's anything I can't stand it's a dumb broad with a goddamned cat that's smarter than she is."

"What happened to your face?"

"It took three of the fuckers to get me into the cruiser."

"Why?"

" 'Cause I tried to kick their rocks off, that's why. You've gotta kick the system in the balls, kid, when you've got the chance. It'll always be kicking you."

"You must know lots about the system, huh?"

"Fuck, yes. Up till noon today I worked for the post office."

Constable Glenn stomps back and drops his load behind the desk like he's ready to write his last will and testament. "Hey, leave the kid alone!" he barks at Ty. "And who gave you the smoke?"

"I talk better with a butt in my mouth and a burr under my ass," Ty chisels. "Mind?"

With a guttural gurrr, Glenn takes down Ty's vital information while I quietly keep lighting his cigarettes.

Alex blows in like an urgent all points—tired, sweaty, and belligerent. Before I carom off, Ty puts a buzz in my ear. "Hey kid—do yourself a favor. Don't grow up to be stupid. Nobody likes a dumb broad."

Figuring it's high time I advertised my feelings in *True Confessions*, I hit up my auntie Lil one day at the bar. "I want to stay here forever," I blurt out.

She slaps me across the face. "Don't ever say a thing like that to me again! How can I make money with a kid hanging around the house?"

I wish Uncle Teddy were here. He'd say, "Buck up, kid. It's not the end of the game. There's always a fresh deck of cards in somebody else's pocket."

So I try a different approach on Lil. "Can I go and live with Uncle Len? He's always asking me to." Uncle Len's a religious fanatic with an excellent driving record and a construction company and I sometimes hang out at his building sites, watching Indian steeljackers defy the laws of gravity.

"You don't belong to my Johns—you belong to your parents!" she shrills, shooing me outside to play with the dogs.

The rudiments of a resolve begin to form in my brain. When I grow up I'll have a stable of Johns to belong to, too.

My father responds to my keep-in-touch telephone call by flying to Vancouver and kidnapping me back to Ontario.

The spring of the year, the smell of the earth, and the wild stallions my cousin Cat and I have quartered in a corral in the woods are suddenly responsible for the fact that I'm paying for the rental on the body I inhabit. Cat is the same age, lives on a farm twenty miles away, and one afternoon he ignites a heated puppy passion in me. I entice him up to the mow in the barn, and kiss him. I insist he respond.

He does—by struggling to get away. Frantically I leap on him, pushing him down in the straw, and he hits me and I think he's mad and hit *him* and realize *I'm* mad and he's *afraid*.

Having suspected that I was in season, his mother soon finds us and pulls me off of him and we're both treated to Rock of Ages Lecture on something called incest. I'm sent home in disgrace. Cat and I are kept apart for two years so we have time to find out what it is we missed in the first place.

Now that I know about my horny hormones, I'm anxious to try them out on the world for size. I join an all-girl gang in one of those isolated pockets of morbid mulligan north of town where the two main social diseases are interbreeding and illiteracy. It's populated with crazy Irishmen (crazier Canukies) and third-generation ex-Yankees who still call mudpout *catfish*, white trash *truck*, and speak with a southern drawl.

At night we trucky toughs tear around with half-breed Indians and hillbilly ploughboys, smoking, drinking bootleg liquor, fighting, playing road hockey, and learning the details about the more functional features of the anatomy. When a boy unzips his fly and asks me to hold something for him for a dollar I figure it should be worth two dollars to hold any animal that bites.

Fred's bait shop pays for frogs by the bucket. One night I'm froggin' with the gang in the swampsuck, my overalls bunched up above my knees, when Roberta, the hefty Irish leader, calls me into a weed warren nearby for a powwow. They've decided to initiate the smallest pea in the pod. Sensing trouble, I make a sloshy run for it toward the trees but they fan out, close the noose, and surround me.

I'm wrestled down into the soggy abyss of stagnant water and slippery slimerot and one takes an arm and another takes a leg and then I'm spread-eagled split into an X and I know what will happen next but I can't won't can't believe no, no, no, please, no. goddamn, no, twisting, jerking, because my screams are lost in the whooping, squealing laughter struggling to remove the T-shirt, ya fuckheads, over my head and yank my overalls, goddamn ya ta hell, over my rubber boots and I can hear their oooing, ahahing warbling shrieks as they prod, pinch, pull, poke at my scrambled tits shriveling into points and their picking, pricking plucks at the chick-down hairs on my cunt, ya daughters of a poxed whore, and I can see the end of a hockey stick for Chrissakes no Jesus no breaking me in half dead center as it scrapes, jimmies, jumps, jams flesh that must stop it and doesn't and I'm skewered bloody and bawling the fuckers to hell and spitting shitting mad screaming mad, mad right up to the CCM trademark on the busted stick and the gaping, gummy, grubby vulnerability of my own sex measuring the immeasurable stretchstroke into blind seething rage and dumped at last curled up like a clenched fist into a mudhole.

"Not so tough now, are yeh?" Roberta phoohs, saliva dripping from her mouth. "Mush—pure mush, that's you!" And so out of the mouth of my defilers springs my nickname: Mushy. The guilt will stick.

Poor innocence . . . poor truth. I refuse to be a good sport about the outrage especially when the poop gets all over town. The power of the press is small potatoes in comparison to the human voicebox at work.

Next day at school I call Roberta out. The bitch blackens one of my eyes and kicks my knee to pieces. The day after, I call her out a second time, intent on pounding her to pieces with one of my crutches, and she decks me again. The doctor doesn't believe I fell down the same flight of stairs twice in two days. I'll spend the rest of my life spitting and praying that eventually the wind will shift and send it all back into the face of my enemies.

Tabbed as crazy, I go all out to support the publicity. My special confidant is a cricket named Fred which I carry around in a matchbox in my pocket. Fred's smarter than anybody I know, including God, and God would do well to have a cricket of his own. Blackballed at school, I become wolverine mean. At night I ride around town on my bike like a maniac, kicking over garbage pails and thumbing providence. I stuff rotten eggs up the tailpipe of the only police cruiser in town, then flatten the tires. I smash streetlights, make obscene telephone calls, and mail dead rats to people who offend me.

My rangy reputation provokes the gang into taking me back into its felonious fold—and I go willingly. One enemy in the sun is worth two in the shade. And now they treat me with kid gloves.

4

know my problem—I'm overdeveloped and undernourished. I've got everything but roots in a specimen bottle. I've got to get down to basics. I've got to find out where to hell I'm going. But first I've got to find out where I came from. What tree did I get shaken out of? And who in hell did the shaking in the first place? Too bad Show and Tell, unlike cod-liver oil pills and the rap on the knuckles, isn't on the Anglo-Saxon Snakes & Ladders School Agenda. Tradition in this hamburger kultur comes without the bun and amounts to the fizz in your nose when putting back a bottle of Classic Coke. When I ask questions concerning my ethnic origins, nothing . . . nobody wants to know nothing. That's right, folks, I came koshered right out of a can of beans and that's all there is to the hunger problem in the world. So, here I am—a bucket of multicultural possibilities—an anthropological missing link. Emotionally, I'm white, without prejudice, black, without roots, red with riotous reasoning, and purple with vulnerability. I'm just where the sons of bitches running this country from that Corn Mill in Ottawa wanted me in the first place—in the last seat in the back of the bus called Nowhere Bound, except for one minor detail . . . while they've got the power, I've got the rage. And all because of a bucket with a leak. I don't know whether to empty it, fill it, or bury it. Is it any wonder that power is a blow*out* and rage is a blow*through?*

More and more I think about the promised land and every day at six o'clock Walter Cronkite assures me that it's America, the lady holding the torch to light the way to paradise on the roadside. Bucking for space and acceptance, I decide to emigrate to Fort Drum, that military camp Stateside, to sign up as a nurse, guerrilla fighter in Nam, before it's too late and I'm over the hill—and thirteen—and a Communist.

In the middle of the night I pack a bag, crawl out my bedroom window, steal a boat from the canal, and using a board for a paddle and my finger for a rudder, manage to elude the border patrol boats, lakers and tankers, and cross the St. Lawrence in a thunderstorm. It takes me almost two hours. Then, after beaching myself on a sandbar, I climb the cliffs above and my pilgrimage begins.

The night's a wipeout in search of dry land. A rangy farmer, believing I'm Billy the Kid with a letter from Internal Revenue, shoots a twelve-gauge at me and shatters the light over the door on his chicken house instead. His muddy garden swallows my sneakers and his mangy dog eats the denim jacket I leave in the fence I'm scrambling over to escape them both. Then—salvation! I hit a main highway with one broken line and no yield signs. I hitch it and a slick hick in a Chevy picks me up. He's so sugary I figure he's part of the welcoming committee from Washington until he pulls off onto the shoulder and tries to feel me up for operative parts. Wrecking yard yahoos have always given me the creeps. I hit the bum with my jug of orangeade, yank the door open, and promptly fall fifty fathoms into a hole, designed by fate to catch saps in their early prime.

When I kneewalk it out of the ditch with underwear squishy, the bum has already split and burned rubber for parts unknown. Before I have time to lick a finger and get my bearings, a state trooper screeches up to the shoulder in a blaze of light and dust. Knowing my soggy underwear could never hold up under a stiff interrogation by a textbook cop, I make a run for it. He shouts for me to stop, and of course I don't, so of course he shoots into the air, and figuring he just added another notch to his gun I fall down face first in a field of couch grass—and he gets me—and that's how pigs always get yeh—with a blast of bullshit.

My capture makes the morning news both sides of the 49th parallel. I'm confined to a hospital Stateside, to recover from exposure—from what, I wonder? Yankee paranoia or Canadian indifference?

Back home I'm treated as both a celebrity and a misfit—because I made it through enemy lines but not to the Gulf of Mexico. Unable to progress in life, I can only regress. Slipping into mental and physical inebria, I lie on the couch all day watching TV. The church, school, and family friends can do nothing to help. It's Operation Shutdown in a suitcase.

Despite my antisocial tendencies and incapacity to function socially, the backup systems in my head are operating at above capacity. I demand to be segregated from society entirely and be institutionalized. My father finally calls in a psychologist who suggests that I be hospitalized for temporary observation and psychoanalysis.

At twelve, I'm the youngest patient interned in a unit attached to the big provincial asylum fifty miles up the river.

Since my grandmother Gerty is here, too, we're keeping up a family tradition—here in Squirrel City where the doctors are the squirrels and the patients are the nuts the squirrels can't remember burying.

I'm put on a schedule that includes pill popping, meals in the canteen, communal showers, and meditation and recreation in the craft shop, where I make clay idols in my own image which have the perfect tendency to crumble when touched and crack when left to dry.

We sleep in a six-bed unit which belongs on a boxcar doing the coast-to-coast midnight shuffle. At first I respond to the complaining, crying, and groaning of my middle-aged roommates with sympathy. Then I'm told by an intern it's menopausal megalomania so I try to avoid them—I don't want to catch anything.

Quickly I learn that self-degradation is the yellow brick road to a shrink's good nature. He's society's dope pusher who mistakes "a degree of sensitivity" with a "degree of lunacy." Trying to veto their school-book attempts to psychoanalyze me, I read the ink splashes on the cards upside down and think up far-out dreams for them to dissect. They love me, how can they love me not? I'm such a lay-me-down in the palm of their hands.

Freddy's a black-leather jacketed greaseball who hasn't uttered a word in over a year. He's always staring into a mirror, slicking his hair back into a ducktail or firing a red ball off the walls of my unit, and I'm the running target trying to avoid his volleys. And every day Freddy and I talk through that bouncing red ball and I wonder when he'll start throwing it at open windows.

My best friend is Jason, a Korean veteran and, according to a book on Greek mythology in the library, an Argonaut in the true sense of the word. Forty-five, he could be taken for seventy. His hair is snow white and his eyes electric blue. Like Moses, Jason saw a burning bush, too, but he won't talk about it. Once a week the interns take him down to the Red Room for shock treatment and later I creep into his room to keep him company. Motionless and incapable of speech, Jason watches a fly circle the ceiling, knowing that the insect carries the germ of his own life and must soon pass it on.

Once a week I'm taken with the other women to the hair salon in Kook Central, where the windows are barred, the interns are part Doberman, and the patients are the saints, satyrs, and gargoyles of the human imagination—all come to life. There's a secret war going on in Ward 6, I'm told. The doctors are sending electric rays through the walls, the food has been poisoned, the bedding sprinkled with radioactive dust, aliens in the guise of Ben Casey have taken over the dispensary, and Jesus Christ has been cut down from the pipe in the recreation room and locked in a padded cell in solitary. Who is *my* enemy? Who?

I'm signed onto the work detail at the agricultural farm attached to the hospital and every day for a week we're taken out in a truck to plant thousands of evergreens. Then I'm transferred to the gardens, where we play with soft tomatoes and hard cabbages in the greenhouses and crazy Sypes gets me down behind the potato sacks and slides his hand down my panties and cries, "Let me f-i-d-d-l-e! Nobody will ever let me f-i-d-d-l-e!" And I let him because making music is not a sin.

I return to civilization enlightened but not less enraged.

At thirteen, I'm bused to the big county high school nine miles away, the roughest in the belly of the province. Bloody fights between pig farmer and no-account hick, and working class lords-in-waiting and teacher-in-the-raw, keep the halls bouncing on a daily basis. Now *I'm* the one in the fishbowl—looking out, an extra shoelace in a cast of thousands. Right away I'm outnumbered, outmaneuvered, and gone fishing. Deciding to dump the gang in favor of the bigger, the gamer, and the smarter, I go solo, hanging out with everybody and nobody.

Sooner or later we've got to have it out with the Bumfuckers, that truckload of Wops, Micks, Polacks, Frogs, and other European riffraff that blew into the county with the construction of the St. Lawrence Seaway and stayed past the duration. It's enough they don't come from our little acre of Lean, Green, and Mean. Do they have to make it worse by giving us the gears, by trying to screw us up the ass with a brand-new recipe for another kind of social disease? Keyed up to a prejudicial frenzy, we have it out with a boatload of them behind the school one afternoon and there's more than the paranoic phenomenon known as rape-with-race on the psychological debating table. According to them the upshot is, *we're* not good enough to play soccer in the halls with the math teacher's lunch. That's enough of a sty in the eye of hope to launch a shoving, shouting, cursing rumble.

The bumfucking fascists got their lines down pat. According to them *we're* muckraking mongrels without a documented pedigree. We don't know who we are or care. *We're* medieval—we don't count apples out in kilograms. *We're* stupid—we speak only one language and that one, fractured. *We're* amoral—we wiggle our buns to African drumbeats on Sunday instead of Siegfried's Funeral March on Monday. *We've* got no respect—we won't lick the hand that feeds us. *We're* old-fashioned—we come with a queen instead of a Texan president, South American dictator, Italian pope, East Indian swami, party chief, or a jolly French chef with a nose like a rutabaga. Yeah, *we're* high-grade chickenshit and we smell pretty good, too. But *we've* got one redeeming quality—*we're* disgracefully easy.

Don't worry. Just because their credits are rolling on prime time doesn't mean they'll last the season. We've got some rocks and rawhide to pelt them with, too. According to us *they* only took a banana boat here because their own country can't afford to educate any more street cleaners. *They* only come here because nobody else can afford the bill either. *They* only come here to get rich quick and pay lip service to a constitution they can't understand and we can't spell. *They* only come here to finance a revolution back home and when that one hits sand they'll transport it back here. *They* only come here because they can't be first-class citizens in their own country without a gold-plated ration card but here they can run a lottery. *They* only come here because Canuckies always come up to them with a wagging tail, a friendly smile, and legs spread so wide they encompass the whole northern hemisphere. Yes, it's open season for foreign domination, armed G-men, and genetic insemination. Fuck us and get the government to write out a check for the privilege. No, and don't bother to say please anymore because now we're the ones with immigrant status, shoved to the bottom of the low-rental housing list. *We're* the ones who have to learn to be pleased every time we're bumfucked.

A few noses get bloodied, a few eyes blackened, somebody gets kneed in the nuts and our adolescent hormones have got the jump on us. We'll teach them that the promised land comes with more than promises in an open hand and make them pay up! Then switchblades are drawn and two high-spirited Trojan warriors dance each other around the pavement, lunging and ducking, and one nicks the other's arm. At the sight of blood, one soft-core sap runs inside the school and pulls the fire alarm while we're pulling our Trojan back and away and they're pulling their Trojan back and forward and everyone's screaming and running, trying to find a way out of the school yard fast because the sound of police sirens just broke the sound barrier.

We thought we wanted amnesty, not blood, but it turns out that we wanted both.

One day while lunching in the Catholic cemetery across the street, I take up with a brother-and-sister team of lightning bugs who just blew in from Dinkhole Downs, Ontario, in a beat-up Chevy with their parents, twelve brothers and sisters, and two hens who won't lay. With their dark curly hair, alabaster skin, and gypsy good looks I suspect Byron and Vicki have a Black Irish horse thief running around in their family photo album. They live five miles down the line in that squalid anthill back in the sticks known as Glitter City. After we're summoned to the principal's office, given a lecture, and nearly expelled for "intruding on the sanctity of the dead *and* lunching with Saint Peter," we become a heady threesome. In no time flat they're my number-one boon buddies and share my lusty interests in history, crime, war, and things that bite toes in the night. While the world is responding to social injustice in the hands of an overpopulated, overturned, and overhauled lower class using the primal mating calls of the Beatles as its theatrical agent, we laugh our way through horror films, trade dirty books, dodge cars, steal horses for midnight rides, run bootleg liquor to chums at school, hot-wire cars for cruising, shoplift, and dress up like gargoyles to terrorize parked couples at Lover's Lock. It's a rioting good time to be alive.

On Halloween we help transfer Joe Ferguson's shithouse to the top of Joe Ferguson's barn with Joe Ferguson bellowing inside like a poked pig, thanks to the tenacity of four strong horses on one side of the barn connected to the five thousand feet of rope slung over the roof and attached to the shithouse on the other side and the blessed law of gravity.

In a joyous spirit of all for one and one for what he can get, we form the Order of D—for dispossessed, displaced, disturbed, despondent, destructive, dogged, and ultimately damned. For our headquarters we use a network of caves hidden under the jumbled-up rock piles slated into the sides of the river. Then we hunt and kill the fat rats that live down there, using them as sacrifices to the pagan gods. As an initiation rite, we wash in snakeberry juice, sit naked beside a roaring fire, and draw blood Indian-style from our veins with a hunting knife, rubbing each other to seal our friendship, and making it legal in the eyes of the boogies, Martians and Government Yes Men, who're probably hiding overhead taking notes. Our prime obligation is toward each other. And the first one to kick the bucket gets to pave the way for the next. The second obligation is to flush out pseudo-Christians wherever we may find them, and turn them away from The Great Pretender, old J.C. himself.

Although our provincial outpost seems permanently on the layaway plan, we do receive regular transmissions of world events from Poop Central, the roost of the CBS Peacock. The ripples don't amount to much until the mid-1960's. Ever since John Kennedy's assassination, everything has been nicely falling to pieces like a line of dominoes. The good ship *Lollipop* is going down with one magnificent blurp to the tune of "I'd rather hold the hand of the Man from *Mad* magazine than the thumb of Uncle Sam—ya! ya! ya!"

Then it happens. One day at high noon in the hottest day of the summer, we're sunning ourselves on truck tire tubes in the canal. Somebody's transistor radio onshore switches from the Turtles to a freak announcer narrating The War of the Worlds—Martin Luther King has just been shot! Our tubes go over and we're suddenly caught in a current we can't fight our way out of.

Now we can not only read the writing on the wall, we can expand on the philosophy. Everyman has finally found his place on the mantel alongside Abraham Lincoln, Malcolm Muggeridge, and the Little Tramp. Now that he's discovered that he's the poet of his own soul and the master of his own destiny, Everyman has put down the hammer, the shovel, and the gun and taken up the pen, the knitting needles, and the microphone and developed a social conscience. Like Bob Dylan says, the times they are a-changing.

Visiting Byron and Vicki on their own home turf is an ecological dig. The land itself seems invincible yet immobile. Nothing moves forward in a plumb line but as shadows in a shapeless, sordid mass like heat rising from asphalt. No wonder the kids who live here can't get their hormones into drive and would rather deny than defy.

A bullet-ridden stop sign pokes its nose out of goldenrod and tansy and a sprinkling of shacks knock about on the greensleeving flats, shingled in tile and tar paper with newspapers, soft-drink signs, and creased plastic ballooning from the windows. Ragtag mongrels tear across the mucked-up yard scattering the chickens and the cows and the dirty-faced children and the pigs. The only prop missing is a honky-tonk hamburger stand with a wrinkled-up hound dog playing the Jew's harp.

In a field out back, the hoods of wrecked cars and trucks are thrown up in uproarious laughter, thumbing the gods of graft and gravy, the seats spilling out the open doors with foam on their lolling tongues after an act of silent ejaculation, their last. This graveyard of aerials, windshields, and hubcaps glinting in the sun has earned this diamond in a garbage heap its name, Glitter City.

And sitting on the stoop of a veranda eaten by neglect and apathy is Ketch O'Connell, the local hack-hustler and cutup, cut off from his peers by intrigue and petty larceny and cut off from himself by a bitter disposition which leaves no stone unturned in its constant search for maggots and the unrequited. "Huzzit goin', kids?" he hollers, searching his hairy face for a nose to blow and then a sleeve to blow it on.

His protuberant plug eyes chisel away at the smartalecky coat of veneer on my grinning face, put there so that disgracefuls like him will feel so guilty about pushing bootleg liquor to minors, he'll spit in his hand and straighten the part in his hair—and not notice that I've got my hand in his pocket. But the ploy doesn't work on Ketch. In his eyes, screwing the powers that be should earn him a pat on the back, not a reprimand from The Little Horrors Committee. As far as pockets, Ketch doesn't have any. He uses them to patch the hole in the arse of his pants.

As Ketch knows, Vicki, Byron, and I are always trying to wangle a few extra fishing days out of the *Farmer's Almanac*—or filling our pockets with Whatchamacallit. So when he gives us a new pitch in his rusty rascible voice, it's not surprising that we take the bite. He cons us into buying a beat-up boat with an 18-horsepower Johnson Seahorse motor for two hundred dollars. Now we're free to cruise the Canadian shoreline at night to scavenge booty from the docks and boathouses of the mightier-than-might muckamucks, a mixture of old money from the established British gentry and new money made from Canadian blood, sweat, and illegal whiskey for the last hundred years. We'll also have the luck to be working for Ketch's refugee-running service.

Strategically placed on the 49th parallel border between Canada and the United States, the St. Lawrence River has always been an international black market zone of trade and commerce. It was used by Blacks, before and after the Civil War as an underground railroad into Canada. It was used during Prohibition by Capone to ship bootleg liquor into the United States. Now it's being used by draft dodgers fleeing that American Woman who stands in New York Harbor holding a torch that transforms into a broom when it's ignited and also by illegal immigrants from third- and fourth-world countries trying to get Stateside for a piece of the Rock.

We've heard all about it from the locals, we've dreamt about it. Now we're doing it—all for the tinkly and the crispy. It's getting complicated to transport illegal immigrants and draft dodgers in either direction in sealed containers hidden under and behind false floors and walls in trucks and vans. Not only are the border police hip to the scam and giving all big vehicles the twice-over, but word is leaking out that the illegals run the risk of suffocating to death for lack of oxygen in the two-by-four–foot cubbyholes they're stashed in.

On the night of our first run, Ketch meets us at the river with his contraband: two adolescent black men from the Caribbean in jeans and tie-dyed T-shirts, and a middle-aged Chinese couple with their teen-aged daughter, dressed in black tunics and matching pants. Right away Vicki and I know something's gone wrong but we leave it to Byron to iron out. "Hey," he yips at Ketch, drawing him into our circle. "What're yeh trying to pull? I keep counting and coming up with five. I was told there'd only be two."

"So they got relatives I didn't know nothing about." Ketch shrugs lamely, tugging on his pants because they won't stay up because he can't afford a button. "Can I help it if they breed faster than they talk? This's the cargo that rolled into the yard this morning. So if I get five, you get five. That's how it goes, kid."

"But we only have room for five," Byron argues. "And there's three of us already."

"Ah, c'mon—yeh can always squeeze in extra niggers and Chinks. Just lay them on top of one another to distribute the weight."

"I'm telling yeh that the boat can't handle it!" Byron shouts. I've never seen him so hot.

"So leave the girls behind and take them across yourself."

"No way," Vicki pipes up excitedly. "Either we all go or none of us goes."

I wonder if the kids who ran bootleg liquor for Capone during Prohibition ever had this problem. Ketch shrugs emptily with finesse and hops in the cab of his pickup. "Youse do what the hell yeh like. But I'm telling yeh one thing, kid. You might be able to convince me yer not going across tonight—but try convincing them." Stepping on the gas, he leaves us standing in a dustball at the end of a road with no name.

There's no doubt about it, Ketch hit it on the nose. We've been ditched in a no-littering zone with five illegals. Winston and Reginald, the two Blacks, are as fidgety as hell, toeing dirt with their sneakers, trapped animals waiting for a door to open. We don't understand the conditions they live under since to us the world is a candy store waiting to be robbed. Also, it's the first time we've ever seen a Black up close without the lights and shades of a TV tube to give him soul—and remoteness. We didn't verbalize on the novelty before because we didn't want our ignorance double-exposed. The Blacks who left the U.S.A. via the underground railroad a hundred years ago entered Canada through the eastern provinces. To complicate the issue, the Chinese are staring at us helplessly with hollow expectation bordering on a cliché. For the first time in our lives we're really frightened.

Winston, the more talkative of the Blacks, approaches Byron, speaking for all of them. "Dass wind is getting high, mon. We bess be going now."

Byron looks at him vacantly, expecting applause or confirmation from the audience at large, and receiving none, merely nods dumbly, speaking for the three of us who seemingly matter because we're transporters. As we load, we don't even have the headache of fitting everyone in. They seem to have a natural instinct for packing sardines, Hong Kong style. Vicki takes the bow and Byron the stern. I take the middle seat with Winston and Reginald. The Chinese prefer to curl up in blankets on the bottom of the boat between Vicki and me.

The storm clouds overhead don't look encouraging; neither do those whitecaps rioting on the river. Byron pulls the starter on the motor and we putt-putt out from the shore. In a few minutes the sky opens up and drenches us to the skin. "Lord above," Reginald wails. "Dis is a night for de fish." Then he strikes up a tune under his breath and starts singing and Winston joins in. All the way across, all we can hear is the monotonous gurrr of the engine, the sloshing water, and a Caribbean soulwringer dragged through a coral reef.

"What're yeh gonna do when yeh get Stateside?" I ask Winston, noticing the gold doubloon on a chain around his neck.

"I work on de billboards and dat's no lie," he confesses, rolling his eyes. "Everyone in New York City will see Winston's work every day of the week, dass for sure. Can you juss picture dat? I be rich in no time, darling."

We're only a quarter of a mile from the American shoreline when the friggin' motor conks out. Frantically, Byron keeps yanking the starter but the bugger refuses to catch.

"Shit in a bucket!" Vicki shrieks, pointing westward.

"Is dat the FBI, mon?" Winston moans with alarm. "I saw dem on de television back home. Dey is bad news, huh, mon?"

"No—it's the Coast Guard!" I fire, giddy with fear.

"Woooo, mon!" Reginald echoes. "Dass a night for de shark."

The Coast Guard's lit-up cruiser is edging toward us at a crawl about a half-mile up the river. Thankfully we haven't been spotted yet. But there's no way we can outrun them, nor can we turn back.

"We're drifting—do something!" Vicki's voice is a shriek.

"I can't!" Byron snaps back. "The son of a bitch has seized up!"

"Where's de can of oil, mon?" Winston rallies, crawling to Byron's side. "I'll put it on de motor. Dat will get it for sure." Byron hands him a can from the bottom of the boat and Winston pours it into the spout. Byron gives the starter another few tugs. Nothing.

Meanwhile, we're cursing at Ketch, each other, and the gods in general. We should have left earlier. We shouldn't have left at all. We should have hired a professional to do the job right.

Then Winston makes the decision for all of us by lifting himself over the side. "Juss scuttle de skiff, mon. Dat's de only ting we can do."

"We no go back!" the Chinese woman insists, standing up and rocking the boat. Reginald grabs her before she upsets us and lifts her and then himself over the side. The rest of us follow suit with the help of Winston and Reginald. In minutes, *The Black Boot* is lost to sight and we're bobbing in the water, letting the current carry us downstream while we stroke it like mad on an angle for the U.S. shoreline.

Choking on water, the Chinese woman suddenly slips beneath the surface and her husband hysterically calls her name and waves his arms. Byron, fatigued and strained himself, goes after her. Reginald and Winston do a synchronized flip dive and bring them both to the surface, sputtering and coughing. Vicki and I turn Byron on his back and float him between us. Reginald and Winston take care of the Chinese.

When our feet touch the soft sandbar Stateside, we catch our breath and crouch in the water under the projected shadow of the cliff overhead, watching the blurred lights of the approaching Coast Guard. They cruise right by without cutting their speed by a knot.

As soon as they've gone, we stumble out of the shallows, cold and fatigued, ready for a whore's breakfast of a cup of strong coffee and two cigarettes. Since we landed about a half-mile down of the pickup point, we have to crawl up the steep cliff and follow the shoreline until we spot the camper truck on a laneway with its headlights shut off and its engine idling.

It's here that we leave our contraband. In parting, the Chinese make small humble bows, thanking us, Winston shakes our hand and says, "I'm dry of de spit and piss poor. Juss like dat, I'm a celebrity," and Reginald responds with "Dass a night for de flying fish."

So there we are, three Canuckies on alien shores, stuck in the mud. Byron wants a beer, Vicki can't find a dry cigarette, and as usual my bladder is full.

Byron suggests that we hike toward Fredericksburg and steal a boat. Having no better alternative, we leg up the shoreline until we spy a motorboat tied to a dock. Surreptitiously, we slip into the water, cut her loose with a hunting knife, and belly-crawl in. It takes us only fifteen minutes to reach our pew of the river. Then we scuttle her about a quarter of a mile from shore and stroke it from there.

We crawl ashore at a lighthouse for an illicit powwow. In no time flat we're huddled around a fire, trying to thaw out.

"One of them almost drowned tonight," Byron confesses, jittery as hell and trembling from the cold. "Shit, I almost drowned tonight. This is the last—no more—it's not right, yeh know it's not. I'm not going out again so don't bother asking me."

Vicki and I are inclined to agree. This is our first and last fling with international intrigue. You've got to be born with four legs, not two, in order to run in a sitting position. The gods are definitely on the payroll of the Department of Immigration. What else is new?

Like religion, school is for me just another institution comparable to international banking. If you never intend to make a withdrawal, why make a deposit? It's something to be feared and ultimately denied. Not for any particular reason other than because "it is" and "I'm not." The system beats me at the start by rating me a slow learner and throwing me into an inferior course, where, it's hoped, I'll learn to get pregnant. I'm already one up on them: I already know.

The fix is in but I beat it by skipping classes regularly and crawling off to the library to feed my cerebral or other cortex and catch up on the things that are really important—Al Capone and his fight with the boys in the Treasury *and* Karl Marx and the emancipation of the proletariat. Once the teachers know where to find me, they just follow the smoke. Then, as punishment, they give me detentions after school—*in the library.*

At thirteen, I've developed a sort of social conscience and found a flag to wave. I can recite the Communist Manifesto by heart and track Che Guevara from the Bay of Pigs to Bolivia. After writing the party for an application form I get a letter back to the tune of, Wait until you're sixteen. Too young. But I can't wait until I'm sixteen. The world can't wait until I'm sixteen. By the time I'm sixteen I may be a borderline Liberal, I may be too *rich* to have a conscience, or, I may just be plain dead.

By fourteen, I'm off the kick of world revolution. It doesn't need me. It doesn't need another mouth to feed and another bone to pick. Revolution starts at home. Why catch the bandwagon when I can take a bus? Why take a bus when I can take a private car with a coat of arms on the door?

While I'm busy selling my soul to slave labor in the guise of world politics, Byron and Vicki are busy trying to buy it back with the Order of D. Sometimes my friends and I become hotwalkers on the lam, trying to do the cakewalk to the watusi, and looking for trouble.

One warm summer night we decide to give our adolescent genes an airing with an old standby—stealing a horse from a nearby farmer for a midnight ride. The plan starts off according to schedule until we're in the barn and Byron is fitting the halter on Black Beauty. Then a dog starts barking and a bullet zings off the barn door. Byron and Vicki are well on their way to winning the Boston Marathon while my runners are cycling in horseshit and I'm competing with Black Beauty for the race. Outside, I'm halfway over the barnyard fence when a hand grabs me by the seat of the pants and I'm suddenly trying to kick myself out of the grasp of Farmer Brown.

Being caught at doing *any*thing is my idea of panic in the big time. Before I can properly detonate, Byron appears from a hole in the darkness with Vicki sauntering behind and faces Farmer Brown, employing his best bad-boy smile. "May as well let her go, mister. She didn't do nothing I didn't tell her to do. We didn't mean no harm."

Farmer Brown is so surprised by the confession he lets me go. I'm so incensed with love, I'm unavailable for comment. Byron got clean away yet he came back for me.

Happy to be free, we shoot off like rockets into the night, pull our bikes out of the ditch, and breeze down the lane. That road's so shiny it looks like a plastic membrane whirling in and around the trees. We only get a couple of licks when we breeze right into a mass of headlights—a police roadblock, courtesy of Farmer Brown. Convinced they've just nabbed the rustlers who've been working in this end of the county, they treat us to an interrogation at the house of Glitter City's major landowner and self-professed mayor. Then, unable to find any cross-Canada warrants on three midgets with dirty faces, they give us a sermon on the hazards of Little League crime, Baptist style, and release us.

Having won the second round of the evening, we bike it back to the ninth concession and take refuge in the ditch to dodge the cars and trucks returning from the dances and bars in town. At sight of the first pickup, we play chicken until the headlights are only a few hundred yards away, then leg it across the road on a thrilltide. The startled driver frantically wheels to the left to avoid hitting us and plows into the ditch, narrowly missing a telephone pole. Screaming obscenities, the drunked-up hick chases us back into the fields, where Vicki, sensing the romantic vibes between Byron and me, splits for home.

Byron takes my hand, and accompanied by the lone beep of a nighthawk we cross the sand dunes and wind up at the spring-fed quarry we call The Big Dip. Skinny-dipping is a midnight sport for mudlarks and water babies out strictly for the play and not the plunge. Playing it safe, I peel down to my underwear and dive in. Bashful Byron refuses to join me. He's sucking up false courage from a beer bottle. To get his attention, I have to initiate a fake drowning episode into the evening's program. Then he's climbing all over my body in the water, trying to drag me out while successfully pushing me under. In the end *he's* the one who needs saving and somehow we wrestle each other to the slate-shelved shore where I gash my knee on a jagged piece of limestone.

Then he's Byron the hero again—letting me bleed on his shirt sleeve and share his cigarette. I sit waiting for my hero to make the plunge. He's trembling, afraid that in losing childhood he'll lose its symmetry. I flinch, watching him struggle against that splendid frailty in himself. Both of us know there's no road back.

The cigarette between us hasn't even been smoked down to the fingertips when he's on me, maneuvering my lips toward a kiss. "You ever do this before?"

Byron the Profound has turned into Byron the Prophetic. He wants me to teach him how. He wants someone to blame if he strikes out. I want somebody to blame, too.

"Sure. Lots of times. I'm an ace."

Comforted by my self-professed experience, he gropes for the on switch, and finding it between his legs, not mine, becomes Byron the Protagonist, the role he wanted to assume in the first place. "Ah— c'mon. It's nothing."

I'm more than a little afraid of being so excited. Byron's no longer the puppy I could pacify with a scratch behind the ear. Byron's little nothings are adding up to a big hot something and it's tearing away at that sense of security I always get from riding bicycle seats over a bump on the road. And I know he can't accommodate the squeeze and I can't accommodate the shame of my body denying him and before he can retaliate and I can pretend to let him he comes on my leg and not even noticing he's missed the mark, he says "I'm a man! I'm a man!" in my ear and what we're left with is "Sex on the safe."

The following fall the worst happens. Vicki, Byron, and I tramp into the bush to stalk the hunters stalking the deer in hopes of blowing their cover and preserving wildlife from the disciples of *Field and Stream*. Vicki is accidentally shot in the head by a disoriented hunter and our world is thrown into limbo. We can't accept waste. We never had enough of anything that we could afford to lose anything. We pay her a visit in the hospital. Though she has tubes in her nose and arms, she seems genuinely cheerful and pleased to see us. The doctor says she's a real fighter and Vicki smiles and says she'll see us tomorrow.

But she dies in the night.

At her funeral she's all laid out in white lace, her long auburn hair dressed with flowers. In her coffin, she looks like one of those virgins the natives in the South Seas used to sacrifice to the fertility gods. Vicki was a virgin, too. But what was she sacrificed for?

Following the dictates of our Order of D to the letter, I smoke a package of Players over her grave, drink what I can of a 26-ouncer of rye, and pour the rest into the ground before passing out.

I promise Vicki that the gods are gonna have one hell of a time catching me. I'm gonna be quicker and meaner than the average victim. I won't cover my butt with dust and soft grass but with good honest mud and horseshit. I swear I'll enter hell dirty with enough coats of grime to protect me from the heat.

Now suddenly I'm sixteen and living for two—one for the pot, two for the glory. Vicki got the pot. Now I'm stuck with the satisfaction of kicking the lid off of it for the glorification of the goddamned.

5

My teachers have joined a coven and that Prince of Darkness known as the principal has politely asked me to leave school at the end of term. My academic performance is below standard. My creative performance in the abstract is above boiling. I can't fight a herd of stampeding buffaloes. I don't even want to try. It's time I left this groundhog hole to seek my misfortune elsewhere. After kissing my dad, who doesn't know me, and relatives, who pretend not to know me, I put my Order of D show on the road. With a knapsack on my back and fifty dollars in my pocket, I hitch it with a lard-arsed trucker who's got a week's supply of bennies (to keep awake) and Alka-Seltzer tablets (so he won't run out of gas), and so many tattoos I'm sure he's a cartographer by profession. He's hauling televisions all the way past Teronna, the nickname of Toronto if you plan on pitching a tent and staying a while. The jump-off point for this suckered skidkid is the end of the line, Niagara Falls, honeymoon city, with its cute corny cameo shots of smooching couples sacrificing themselves to the Maid of the Mist. Personally, I think God made a better blacksmith than he did a shoemaker. People have a natural leaning toward being forged and not cloned.

Low on bread, I have a three-course meal in a family restaurant and crawl out the bathroom window to avoid cops, revolving doors, and dishpan hands. Then I crash on credit at the two-star Flamingo Motel with my sleeping bag, whoopie cushion, and outdated copy of *According to Hoyle*. The decor is candy-coated chintz on the *Sugarland Express*: teddy-bear furred chairs, gold-trimmed hurricane lamps, a mirror on the ceiling, and a heart-shaped bed with a red satin spread. I'm surprised it doesn't come with lips.

The Italian cleaning lady calls her brother and gets me a job at Valentino's, a chicken factory on the outskirts of the city. So, bright and early the next morning I board a bus for work, the sole Canucky in a tapestry of foreigners with their three-story garlic sandwiches and punchy homemade wine.

My feisty boss, Joe Juggernaut, is a four-foot-eleven sweetie with hairy eyebrows, fat cheeks, and tight underwear. His pre-work pep talk is inspirational. "Nica place here. People nica, chickens nica, I nica. Much bigga money here."

Wearing a white smock and mosquito netting over my hair, I stand at an assembly line and pluck feathers off chickens as they pass by on hooks.

Within the month I'm working my way up the ladder of commercial chicken success. I've graduated to a gutter and am scheduled to advance to a cleaner next month. Already I can't stand the sight of fowl, on or off the plate, with or without their clothes on.

It's Joe's job to unload the crates of live chickens from the truck, hang them up by the feet on the hooks, and penetrate their necks with a needle to stun them. This one morning Joe's shirt sleeve accidentally gets caught on one of the hooks and he's lifted right up in the air, screaming "Fucka duck!" Punching and kicking, he's shot along the conveyor and instead of being dipped in the four-foot tub of cold water like any other stunned bird, his shirt sleeve is torn right off his arm and he's dumped with a thump in one squealing, sputtering splash. And that's how to drown a chicken-hustler!

Sherry is the dippy blond bombshell with the insincerity complex and the 38 jugs in the room next door at the motel. We get along mainly because there's no reason on earth why we should. The only phobia we have in common is a horror of being taken seriously. Her sole preoccupation in life is finding a twenty-year-old virgin with the facial structure of Ricky Nelson so he can violate her Girl Guide principles and she can drag him to the altar in a straitjacket and suffer a life of perdition with him. The vulgarity of the scheme sickens me.

"Hey—wanna go barhopping?" She's banging my door down one Friday night.

"Maybe some other time," I chirp back. "I'm broke," knowing she wants me as a stalking-horse.

"What do you dooooo with all your money?"

"I burn it and eat the ashes. It's called sacrifice with a smile."

She rallies. "I've got enough to cover us. Besides, smart girls don't pay for anything but the first drink."

Knowing I'll never get rid of her Heartbreak Hotel routine, I'm presentable in ten minutes, which is why she banged in the first place—I'm fast.

Half an hour later, we're gawking at the Friday night crowd on the street in front of the local hot spot, the Rendezvous. Muscle boys with shaggy hair in cut-off T-shirts and flowered bell-bottoms, smelling of dime-store cologne and body grease, are putting the make on girls with microdotted miniskirts and wingy hairdos.

Inside, the lounge slumbers in burnt burgundy, polished mahogany, and gilt candelabra. Fancy schmantzy—for a Neapolitan funeral parlor.

We slide into a velvet-upholstered booth. Sherry orders a sling for her and a Bloody Mary for me. Mellow torch songs supported by weepy mandolins thrum in the background. A suited crooner from The Al Martino School of Smooth Knocks and Polished Tonsils takes the stage and belts out a tearjerker that grinds at my bone marrow and puts my genes to sleep.

Now the trick is to appear nonchalant, an unresolved contradiction in pursuit of the unattainable. Jack your skirt up past the Cape of Good Hope and pray for stormy weather at the Horn.

Personally I haven't got the patience for this trip. I'd just as soon throw a mean baseball at their heads with an obscene limerick printed on it. Absently Sherry toys with the gold cross around her neck and I pull out a pen and draw a maze of triangles on the damp coaster, waiting for the arrival of the pallbearers and the chorus of monks. I'm well on my way to getting the froggie to the fly when a tall lean suave swarthy boy presents himself at our table.

"My name's Mario." He grins with bared teeth. "Mind if I join you?"

"Lovely," Sherry whimpers on the warm.

Eyeing her bustline, Wonder Boy slides into the booth. He's old news from my school days in a box gift-wrapped by Saks Fifth Avenue, a polished smoothie. He's nice—too nice to be believed, not my type at all. But I smile sweetly as if my knickers are in a knot and kick Sherry under the table. She's just hooked a hot number for the night.

To make light conversation, he turns to me. "From around here?"

"No, I'm from everywhere else."

"I haven't seen either of you around before. If you come here often you'll be seeing a lot of me."

"Why? Is there more than one of you?"

"My father sometimes thinks so," he says, offering us a cigarette from a gold case. "He owns this place. I'm only working here for the summer. Then I'm going back to law school."

"Oh, isn't that groovy," Sherry coos, juicing up her Marilyn Monroe mating call. "Don't you think that's groovy, Mushy?"

Though I'd like to gag her and stuff her under the table so the mice would have a playmate, I'm impressed. "What kind of law are you gonna practice?"

"Criminal law."

"Good for you. That's just what the system needs, another legal criminal to practice on the law."

He laughs and Sherry looks like she might eat her glass. Knowing I've goofed, I lie low and listen to her dish-sink drivel about how groovy this joint is in comparison to another beer keg she swung inside of last week. It's worse than flying a kite in a monsoon. I'm ready to pack it in and leave for the graveside of Lost Friday Nights.

Mario snaps his finger and a waiter materializes. He orders another round. "Where do you work?" he asks Sherry.

"I'm a waitress down at the Evergreen."

"And you?"

"I'm a pluckeress down at Valentino's."

He and I crack up, unrestrained. Poor Sherry. The trussed-up hen looks petrified, not knowing whether to laugh or cry. She wanted to appear so *Harper's Bazaar* and I just bounced her from Broadway to the Bronx.

Now she's eating ice cubes and trying to strangle the tip of her finger with her straw. Mario ignores her. "I can get you a better job than that. Let me talk to my old man. He has a friend who owns a bakery and they always need extra help."

"No guff?"

"No guff. Give me your number and I'll call you tomorrow."

I jot my telephone number down on the back of the coaster and make a feeble excuse to exit. "Sorry, but I'm noctivagant, a night wanderer, and I'm already getting itchy feet."

Outside on the street, I zip through the crowds like a zephyr trying to make the second showing of *Clockwork Orange*. At the next intersection a horn beeps repeatedly. It takes me a minute to realize it's meant for me. Rough-and-ready Jeffrey, a plucky ploughboy from the motel, pulls up to the curb in a red bug with a JO-JO'S PIZZA PALACE sign up top. "Hey, dollface. Wanna go vetting?"

"No, I'm going to see a filthy movie."

"Ah, c'mon. We'll deliver this load and take in the all-night show at the drive-in."

"I'll think about it."

I'm always thinking about everything, waiting for somebody with a magic key to take me out of park and put me into drive.

"I don't have all night," he fires impatiently. "Hop in!"

"Finally got a job, huh?" I ask after slamming the door.

"Yeah, this's my first night." He turns the radio up full blast and thumps the steering wheel as the Rolling Stones belt out "I can't get no satisfaction."

For the next hour we zip from one address to another and he picks up some fat tips en route. I have the city map spread out in my lap. We've got only two more orders to deliver when a siren whirrs up two cars behind us.

Jeffrey throws a harried-hare glance in the rearview mirror. "Oh, fuck!" he gulps, shifting from first to second gear. "Hold on, dollface!"

He guns it through a yellow light and swerves in and out of the traffic so quickly I'm hanging onto the dash for dear life, my stomach doing somersaults. Thankfully we're on a one-way street with three lanes of traffic to fishtail in.

"Jesus H. Christ!" I wail. "Pull over—a lousy ticket isn't worth getting cracked up for!"

"I can't. I don't work for Jo-Jo's. I just borrowed their wheels for a few hours to make some fast bread."

"Can't you drive any faster?"

"Shut up and let me drive!"

"Don't tell me to shut up, buzzhead. I'm about to go up for car theft *and* transporting cold linguini. I don't even know what the hell linguini is."

The pig is still hugging our ass with hot intent. Jeffrey spins the wheel to the right. We jump the curb and take the sidewalk, attacking a petunia bed, a lawn sprinkler, a basset hound having a leak, and a dune buggy parked in a driveway before bump-a-dumping down off the curb into the traffic again. Then a carload of drunked-up yippies in New Testament disciple rags swoop up beside us in a station wagon. The driver salutes us with a bottle of beer and hollers out the window, "C'mon, man, let's drag!"

Suddenly another pig pulls out of a side street with his cherry on top flashing and the fun starts all over again.

"Grab some linguini out of the back!" Jeffrey shrieks.

"This's a fine time to develop an appetite!"

"Do what the fuck I tell yeh! And throw it at the pig!"

I pull a tinfoil tub out of a paper bag, pry off the cardboard lid, shuffle up on my knees, and lean out the window in a studied pose on the slide. Constable Buckbuzzard slips up to our right. The snarling snipe is smacking his lips and signaling us to pull over as Jeffrey closes the gap between the cars.

Then the pig is too far ahead, then veering away from us. Finally we're almost kissing metal and Jeffrey cries, "Let her rip!" I do and the pig's windshield is suddenly wearing a coat of linguini. Losing control of the wheel for a split second, he changes lanes and rear-ends The New Testament disciples in the station wagon. As we pass them, the yippies yip yip yahoo, and screeching their tires, take up the chase to perform a hallowed citizen's arrest.

I'm still hanging out the window, laughing so hard I haven't got the strength to haul myself back in.

Jeffrey cuts off a laundry van, loses the other pig, and whipping down a dark side street, relieved, we suddenly crash through a yellow construction barrier and plunge into a ten-foot trench. By some miracle we're okay but our kidney stones are shaken. Jeffrey crawls out the driver's side, climbs onto the roof, and pulls me out, cursing. Then we notice headlights sharking down the street in a search-and-destroy mode. Quickly, Jeffrey yanks me into the bushes just as Constable Buckbuzzard sees the roof of Jeffrey's hot car, jams on his brakes, and loses his front wheels to the Panama Canal.

We leave him rocking over the abyss and leg it through a rash of backyards with gardens and swing sets, climbing over fences and tripping over toys and lawn furniture. Breathless, we finally crawl under a veranda obscured by a flower bed. Fagged and fearful, my heart beating out of my chest on silver wires, I light into Jeffrey. "If we ever get out of this mess I'm gonna have you stuffed and sent to an archery range."

Then, scared shitless, I break out in giggles and Jeffrey claps a hand over my mouth.

The animal closeness is a lethal combination. Pulling a dirty, he slides his hand under my dress and up my leg, covering my angry threats with his whistle-whirring mouth. Figuring that the best defense is an all-out offense, I unfasten his fly, take him soundly by the handle, and with a pet, a squeeze, and a tug he's equally horned up.

Enclosing me in his arms in the confined space, he fiddles with the fasteners on the back of my dress. "Shit!" he pants impatiently. "My watchband's caught. Do something before I go soft."

Without thinking, I pull my dress up and get it halfway over my head when I'm suddenly stuck, the embroidery on my pocket caught on one of Sherry's earrings. "If there's anything I can't stand it's an amateur," Jeffrey curses, high on his genes, while I go off in a gale of suppressed giggles. I can't take boys my own age seriously at all. Jeffrey's funnier than the Chinese puzzle we're messing in. He flips on his back, pulls me on top of him and with his free hand yanks at my dress-over-head Chanel original. Everything else uptop comes off with it. When I'm virtually strangling on my bra strap and my clothing is swathed around my face like a Sikh in disgrace, we hear a pig scouring the yard. "Shshshsh!" Jeffrey rolls me over and pins me to the ground, slobbering on my shoulder while the pig's squeaky shoes are squashing vegetables in the nearby garden. I feel like I'm trapped inside an overturned pizza box with the sauce stuck to the lid and the crust on the bottom looking for a face.

Though sex's probably the best answer for anything volatile and ticking, it's clear that Jeffrey has no intention of wasting his hard-on. The made-to-order mummy under him is in no position to argue or to advertise her lack of experience. From hanging out with the boys in the swamp, I learned where everything is and where everything is supposed to go—the rudiments of the grab and the gab, country-style. From Byron, I learned that while lust is a must, mutual consent is no simple answer to the Cold War. Hip on Jeffrey—and improving my education, I let Jeffrey go for the brass ring right then and there. Feeling a little like a clogged drain I let his plunger plunge until the pain is excruciating and I know that he'll never break into Mecca. I shift a little, letting him believe the drain's free and the plunger's disappeared in me, while holding onto him with both hands as hard as I dare between my legs. And throughout, he's asking me how great it feels and I'm thinking about how great it might have felt, wishing he'd drop me off at the next bus depot.

Later, when I've managed to transform my head bandage back into a ball of clothing and dressed and the pig is nowhere to be seen, we emerge, hightailing it to the main drag, and hail a cab back to the motel. I have a quickie shower, change my clothes, and we're off to the movies.

Jeffrey doesn't own a car. Instead, he drives a broncobuster part submarine that could only have come out of the combined imaginations of Jules Verne and General Custer (before, during, and after

Little Big Horn). It's a souped-up blue '58 De Soto with a wingspread like a rocket. Mag wheels, dice, a Kewpie doll dangling from the rearview mirror, furry seat covers, a raccoon tail tied to the aerial, and a set of horns on the hood. The first time I saw it I wanted to break into a barn dance on the roof.

There's a horror festival playing at the drive-in, a twenty-sixer of whiskey I'm not equipped to handle as hard alcohol always sends me into the advanced stages of schizophrenia, a three-quart bucket of buttered popcorn, and a buzzed-out bronco rider who almost got thrown once tonight. To top it off, we're right in the middle of a bumper heat wave.

Jeffrey and I get lost altogether in the love-in of physical and metaphysical forces which follows. What with the Gravedigger's Opera drumming from the speaker box, the monsters, devils, and body parts that ride horses better than Nickabob Crane on the screen and the high voltage of too much warm booze and a hot libido, it's a Fantasia's Freeforall. Count Dracula leaps on my neck and I bite his ear and he rips my clothes and I think he's cute and wrench his nose until his fang comes off in my hand and then Dr. Strangelove is dissecting me over the steering wheel and loses his glasses and I'm coming coming apart in pieces with the popcorn and I've no sooner discovered Dr. Strangelove's glasses on the One-eyed Cyclops between my knees when I'm hot hot hot and writhing on a horn that won't stop blowing until it's disconnected by Lon Chaney in a bubble suit and when the graves around us open up and we're attacked by an army of killer tomatoes I dive into the backseat of a hearse beside a corpse that looks just like me and before I can kill it before it eats me, Godzilla is goring me with his tail and all I can hear is the organ from the Phantom of the Opera pumping, bellowing, and feel the Blob slithering hungrily down the insides of my legs.

What respite there is occurs after this Lost Faces and Fallen Graces, as grim Peter Lorre in a rented suit rises like a mail-order butler on a monolith out of the abyss of empty bottles and discarded clothing, soberly carrying before him a plate of severed heads. And I can identify every one.

I keep crawling out the window to kiss him and Jeffrey keeps pulling me back into the Land of Living Gore. . . .

In the morning we have a heavy breakfast of piggies in a blanket—or sausages and pancakes if you aren't hip. I have dark shades on my eyes to remove the chlorophyll from the surrounding foliage, hoping it'll soothe the carpenter pounding in my head. Jeffrey gives me a lengthy account of my behavior last night. "I don't do things like that . . . do I?" I sizzle on the rebound.

"Would I lie?"

"Yes, you're the biggest liar I know."

I kiss him and hop out of the broncobuster before it bucks again. I must never see Jeffrey again without a priest, an exorcist, or Wild Bill Cody.

True to his word, Mario, the smoothie from the Rendezvous, gives me a telephone call. I have a new job starting a week from Monday.

When I tell Joe Juggernaut at the chicken factory that I'm moving on to bluer pastures he throws a tantrum and spits out his words in machine-gun blips. "Why you go? You not lika? Why you not lika? Nica place here. People nica. Chickens nica. I nica. Mucha bigga money here. You stay, ehhhhhh?"

I explain to him that spending the rest of my life with my hand stuck up the arse of a chicken isn't my idea of romance.

His eyebrows jet and jive in the midst of a frazzled frown. "You wanna romance you be a nun, you wanna be a martyr you be a wife, but you wanna make bigga money you gut chickens."

He'd make a hell of a lot of sense to a rooster. Still, I'll miss Joe terribly. See, I don't yet realize that you don't pick people off the street, put a brand on their rumps, and claim them. I make family out of strangers, fondle them, tease them, hug them, and then when I feel the noose tighten slip out the window in the middle of the night with a note taped to the pillow. I feel like an absolute sewer rat but I can't stand good-byes.

The bakery's a leavened switch, hygienic, cheery—and no feathers. I'm constantly in stitches at the birthday-party banter of my coworkers.

Though I can't understand a word I can curse in Italian like an ace. I learn how to mop my education off the floor, scrape it off the walls, and all by my lonesome I can burn cookies, drop cakes, and make a mound of dough explode in the oven. Not even the head baker can manage that one. I do better at the cash, where I can play with the crispy and the damp and make them shake hands with the balance on the tab.

From time to time Mario pops in for a chat. He's still playing beach-party bingo with Sherry. She's still trying to bury him on Blueberry Hill. Vito, Mario's father, drops in every morning to pick up a bag of fresh baked goods and has a coffee with his cronies in the restaurant next door. Short, portly, and Roman-nosed, with gray-flecked black hair, he's always immaculately turned out in designer suits, his manners very continental-charm. The first time I meet him I'm wearing a grin, a big apron, and about five pounds of green icing. He asks me how I'm doing. I tell him that one day I'd like to come out of a cake instead of falling into one.

"You mustn't worry about such things, little one." He smiles. "At least you chose a color to match your eyes, eh?"

He has a point. I might be clumsy but I'm not color-blind.

We have a few inspiring conversations. He turns me on to *La Bohème* and buys me the record. I try to predict the hour when Venice will drop through Italy and ask him how his kinsmen will adapt to speaking Mongolian and gondoliering around the rice paddies in Chinese junks.

"I'll teach them how to say General Motors in Italian," he says with a wink.

For lunch each day, I jump on Boris, my bike, and pedal a few blocks over to Rollo's, the local greasy spoon and hangout, getting lost between the pages of Harold Robbins over a coffee and a hamburger. Rollo's is a smoky home to a rolling-hipped hairy clientele from Patagonia, boys in dirty denim disposables, tattooed T-shirts, and holey sneakers, girls in peasant sacks in Aztec colors, love beads, and buffalo-hide thongs. A jukebox is writhing in the corner to the J's, Jimi Hendrix, and Janis Joplin.

One day a blond ploughboy with the face of a horse en route to a dog-food factory slides into the seat opposite me without even being invited and gives me the once-over slippery. "Hey, I saw you around here before, didn't I?"

"Might've," I mumble. Ignoring him is bliss.

"I'm Joel. Who're you?"

"Mushy."

"You're kidding."

"Fine, I'm kidding."

"Where do you work?"

"None of your beeswax."

"Oh, I get it—you don't wanna talk, eh?"

What with his vocabulary of about twenty-five words prefixed with the third-person syndrome of "He goes, she goes, and I go," and my attention span, that of a well-fed mosquito, we have a fun five-minute station break waiting for Led Zeppelin to blow the jukebox through the roof. But I hang in there hoping for a button to pop somewhere. Eventually he gets to the meat. "How'd you like to go into business for yourself?"

"I don't have anything to sell."

"You don't have to, baby. All you need is a little investment capital to start the ball rolling." He goes on to explain that I'll start drawing a regular salary as soon as the business starts turning over a profit.

"You didn't say *what* business," I remind him.

"Oh, didn't I? Sorry, baby. I run a courier service. See, I've noticed you riding your red bike almost every day so it's a natural line of work for you." He hands me his business card.

"J. C. Roxley Associates Limited," I repeat out loud. "Financial Consultants." Then I catch a blurb at the bottom. *Joel Stanley, Consultant.*

"That's me," he pipes up. "I work for them on a commission basis." I hand the card back.

"Keep it." He grins. "I've got a pocketful of them."

"But I've already got a full-time job."

"That's the beauty of this one, baby. It takes only a couple of hours every Saturday afternoon—yeh can't lose." He takes a slug of Coke and lets the information sink in.

"Go on, I'm listening," I volunteer, wanting to hear at least a little more.

"Two hundred bucks up front—for expenses—and you're in. That's how it is. Meet me here tomorrow same time with the bread."

"Is that all?"

"What the fuck more do yeh want, baby? The key to my heart?"

o see if he's legit, the next morning I call up J. C. Roxley Associates Limited. I don't trust business plunderbunds who advertise the fact that they're limited. Joel works there all right but he's not in and I don't bother leaving a tidy message. Let the bum sweat it out.

According to the magazines that are youth-oriented and bullshit-provoked the world is theoretically my oyster, so why not indulge? Boris and I could use the extra capital. He's always throwing a shoe and his gears jamming up. I'm as hard on machinery as I am on people. Everything I touch seems to break in my hand.

After work I hit the bank, make the necessary withdrawal, and show up at Rollo's hip on the big time with a hundred and fifty dollars cash and every conceivable excuse to explain the missing fifty. I was robbed. My dog ate it for breakfast. I lost it down a sewer grate. But I'm not draining my bank account for any business venture no matter how lucrative it's supposed to be. Joel ignores the discrepancy entirely and gives me my instructions.

On Saturday morning I meet him at a phone booth on Second Street at ten o'clock. He pulls up in a souped-up beige Dodge, gives me an address, and hands me a brown paper package tied up in heavy cord. "Get it there between two-thirty and three o'clock. Got it, baby?"

Committing the address to memory, I fire the package into my carrying basket with a copy of *Lord of the Rings* and a packed lunch. Then I zigzag it all over downtown, having a hell of a good time sightseeing and deepening my summer tan. For lunch, Boris and I pull into a park and picnic on smoked salmon, cream cheese on bagels, and a cheap bottle of Baby Duck. I arrive at the boardinghouse on Bleaker Street at two forty-five on the button.

A long-haired freak in a Mexican poncho with a red nose and buzzy eyes opens the door a sliver, grabs my wrist, and pulls me inside. "Any problems?"

"No—with what?" I start, a little confused.

"That's okay, baby. Coool it. You did good—real good." Then he paws the package to make sure it hasn't been tampered with. The room stinks of sour smoke, urine, sweating armpits, and beer, the table littered with bottles, overflowing ashtrays, and cardboard food containers ravaged by vultures. Three grubbies with beads, beards, and headbands in the cut of Jesus Christ Superstar after he was cut down from the cross are lounging about doing make-believe potshots at a cheap autumn scene on the wall with .38's. Figuring I just might be the next leaf to take the plunge, I can't get out of here fast enough.

When I run into Joel again on the street I question him about the heavy hardware and he calms me with "Don't worry about it. They're security men, licensed to carry them."

"But what's in the packages?"

"Valuable stocks and bonds. That's why everything is so hush-hush."

The moonlighting continues like a quilting bee. Four more runs and I'm in a cozy little routine of working at the bakery through the week and on Saturday bombing all over the city on Boris, having lunch in the park with my latest bookstore acquisition, and then delivering the packages to different drop-off points. On the fifth run I simply dump the parcel off at a locker at the bus terminal and the key through the mail slot of a rooming house on Tenth Street.

Up to now Joel's only slipped me a lousy twenty-five bucks after every delivery. Figuring it's high time I consulted him about the bookkeeping, I have it out with him at Rollo's. "We ought to be showing a profit by now," I blurt out. "How about giving me my cut—for incentive?"

He sticks two fifties in the front of my dress. "Don't worry, baby. A bigger percentage will be coming later. Keep up the good work."

* * *

The next Saturday afternoon I'm blasting down Ferry Street on Boris with the sixth package in my carrying basket when I notice Joel's car pulled over to the curb by two police cruisers. And it's not a traffic ticket. The backseat of his car has been ripped out and he's being shaken down and handcuffed as well. I brake in fast, funny little prickles sliding up my spine. I sense a benchmark rising on the horizon. To cool down my brain I buy a Fudgsicle from a passing Dickie Dee Wagon. Then Joel gives me the once-over, burning, and I split on greased wheels. What the Christ is going down?

Desperate to either reach a climax or run down a bagman with all the answers, I bomb it all over downtown for an hour—I'm that high on riding the downside of a silver dollar—and I've never been a poker player. Finally, I cash in my chips and race it over to the drop-off point, another seedy rooming house. Nobody answers number 6 on the second floor. For two hours I wait in the dimly lit corridor making friends with the cocker spaniel down the hall. What the hell do I do now? Weighing the odds, I decide to take the package back to the motel and stash it in my dresser drawer under my spare set of underwear.

Jumpy as hell, I stay in all evening waiting for a call for any omnipotent power with a dialing finger. Shortly after midnight the phone rings. I let it go a nerve-wracking few more times before picking up the receiver.

The voice is unfamiliar, gruff, and snappy. "Meet me at Rollo's in an hour. Sit down in one of the booths and wait."

"Who's this?"

"Stewy to you, sister."

"Where's Joel?"

"In lockup. The pigs busted him today. But don't worry, his lawyer is getting him bailed out tomorrow. Now you're dealing with me, see. So don't ask questions and don't be late." Suddenly the dial tone is nurring in my ear.

At Rollo's, a fat hermaphrodite with earrings, shades, and shaggy blond hair slides into the booth next to me. "There's a shopping bag on the seat beside me," he says without even turning his head. "Get up, walk by, and drop it in."

I do exactly what he wants and buzz off. Shit, I'm getting cold feet and wet pants. Somebody's watching me . . . or should be watching me . . . through a zoom lens.

A couple of full moons later Joel and his gang of goonies pluck me right off the street in front of the library. They whisk me off to a farmhouse on the outskirts that's early demolition dump, late bomb shelter. The furniture is ratty, consumed with rot and vermin, candles flicker in every room, dust motes mingle in every corner, and posters are plastered on the walls, even on the fridge in the kitchen which's trying to roll its way out of dirty dish alley. The room referred to as "the lab" is out of bounds entirely.

In that cosmic cornfield of dying brain cells and outer galactic stardust everyone's riding, the only two girls present are so spacy I'm sure they just glanced back toward Sodom and saw St. Peter's Square on Easter Sunday. I have a beer to blasé down and blend into the warped woodwork. A wild rap session is in progress around the kitchen table. The hairy-faced Weasel with the black tam and green shades is chewing up a storm. "The goddamn pigs grabbed me outside of Woolworth's yesterday. They frisked me and tore open the box I was carrying. And guess what—out comes a toy helicopter. I was shopping for my sister's kid. Yeh should have seen the look on their stupid faces."

A baby-sized bazooka on the end of a bobby pin is making the rounds. I pass it on to Joel and he passes it right back. "Smoke it!" he cusscoughs. "Yeh don't wanna spit on my hospitality, do yeh?" he threatens, squeezing my arm until it hurts. From the trafficker-to-buyer lingo I overheard at Rollo's, I'm pretty sure it's grass but it smells like rolled elephant dung. Having not been tried I can't be true but I can be testy-pesty. On the other hand, if millions of plainclothes dicks worldwide can't get stoned on it, what can it possibly do to one undersized overexuberant Canucky?

This's my first tango with dope in the round—and it's scary. I've heard too many news flashes about kids flying out of ten-story windows on LSD. Except for the fur balls growing on the inside of the irises in my eyes and the start-stop-start motor in my head, it seems to have little effect on my body bank. I still show a balance on the debit side.

"Wanna hear a winner?" quips the spidery-legged, fruity-fingered Tricks with his pimply sense of playball. "The R.C.M.P. broke into my pad last night and tore the goddamn place to pieces. No warrant—nothing. I should have had the fuckers charged."

"What were the pigs looking for?" I burst out, wheezily.

Joel gives me a sharp nudge. "The goods, baby. The packages you've been running for us."

"Do you mean those stocks and bonds were *hot?*" I'm giggling now with fuzzy-headed abandon.

I must have said something uproariously funny as everyone's in hysterics including me, until the implication of their drugged-up laughter tears across my brain like a white light. I experience an electric shock and my eyes cross.

"Groovy," Joel yips. "Didn't I tell you guys this cupcake was groovy?"

In a minute my celebrity status is begging for nickels. It seems I've been delivering dope in all its multifarious forms—marijuana, hashish, LSD, mescaline, angel dust, anything you can fly on. Five Gs' worth in every package. "Don't worry about it, baby." Joel laughs, throwing his arm around my shoulder.

"But I *do* worry about it. I'll never be able to be bonded or bred with a politician's son. I'll spend the rest of my life making license plates for out-of-province cars, like Trudeau's limousine service."

Speedballed into a go-go gadfly, he continues the superhype. "Hey, you're an ace pigeon, baby. The best runner we've ever had. The pigs would never suspect anyone as innocent-looking as you. Just do as you're told and things will be cooooool."

Thanks very much but I can already feel the cool, the chill of a jail cell—without a toilet. All wobbly-kneed and as crushed as any hop can get in a foreign distillery, I blunder to my feet ready to deliver a dissertation on the hazards of sitting on public toilet seats. "I can't work for you anymore, guys. I'm logbacked or is it backlogged—anyway, I've got a lot of double full-time coming up at my overtime job."

Springing from his chair, Joel grabs my arms and we tussle. He shoves me up against the wall. I knee him in the nuts. On his way into a screaming crouch he backhands me one across the face. I land in a heap in the corner, my brain reeling all the way to the end of the panic tape. Holding his groin with one hand, he uses the other one to pull a heater out of his jeans. "Try walking out on me and I'll burn yeh! Got it, baby?"

"Yeh, I got it. I got burned, baby."

I can only wonder where Fate got the right to cliché an old Jimmy Cagney movie.

Joel hands me another brown paper package. "Hold onto this one until tomorrow," he spits, shoving me toward the door. "Wait at the telephone booth at two. I'll call yeh with instructions. Don't fuck up and don't try nothing smart like ratting to the pigs. Remember, baby, you're in this up to your cunt hairs."

The twitchy-tendoned Tricks drives me back to the motel without a word of comfort. After a quick bath to get rid of that terminally trucky smell of bad news, I hit the streets to recharge. I can't think when I'm cooped up. Joel's right though. I sure can't go to the cop shop. But I can't keep running dope either. For a good hour I walk the streets and then mosey into the local tavern, Nick's Place, having already decided to blow this town tomorrow.

The bruiser at the door is over six feet and pushing forty in a Fiero. The bum asks to see my ID. Convinced that I'm old enough to drown myself in oblivion, I throw a constitutional hairy. "Anarchist!" I'm getting to be a real whizz at left-handed diplomacy.

But the leathery-faced armadillo won't budge. He crosses his arms in front of him like a cigar-store Indian in midlife crisis and browbeats me until I fish Sherry's driver's license out of my handbag.

"Funny, you don't look like a Cherry," he gruffs, giving it a humphing second appraisal. He's got the personality of a stump pissed on by every dog in the neighborhood. And the Stump's pronunciation of the mother tongue is almost as bad as his sense of humor.

"My cherry is my business, not yours!" I fly at him, enraged, and he grunts grudgingly as any stump must do in the way of progress and takes his arm away before I bite it.

To celebrate my defeat and demoralization at the age of sixteen, I take a corner table and order two beers in glorious self-indulgence. The room is 80 percent full and 100 percent lively and full of willing victims for any oven that will bake them into any shape their imaginations fancy. On the stage a band of Mississippi Muds with studded cowboy hats are caterwauling "Don't Roller-skate in a Buffalo Herd" which sounds more like "Let My People Go."

My part in a drug operation crystallizes into a single nugget at the bottom of my first glass of suds. *Courier.* But what am I gonna do with the stash under my handbag? I could either stick it in the postbox down the street for the government to handle or leave it on the seat for some other sap to deal with.

A mouthy slick grunt salesman in a cute three-piece suit, napkined with a paisley tie, cruises over and makes an excuse to sit down beside me. He's the size of an underwatered bean sprout and keeps me tap-dancing all over the ceiling because he never stops talking. He must be a Gemini or an Aquarius on speed. He buys me three more beers and gives me the lowdown on the state of the textile industry by comparing the polyester in my dress to the silk in his tie. I dance a couple of jigs with him to satisfy that ten-carat glint in his eye and that icky itch I can't get to right now without getting arrested. But when I reach for Mr. Silk and miss and pull the microphone stand from the stage and the Mississippi Muds become inaudible and I'm boogying inside of a wire on the floor, Mr. Silk decides we should sit this one out. Then he gets overzealous and makes a cathedral of our hands to prove his fealty. I know all about feel-tee. It starts with bubble gum exchanged orally in a phone booth and ends in a men's washroom posing as a divorce court in Tijuana. To cool him off, I excuse myself from the table and go to the can. I'm so hammered I mistake *hommes* for *home* and saunter right in and say hello boys to two guys at the urinals. They wheel around and piss themselves. Then the Stump tramps in and grabs me and throws me out of the pissoir, implying that I'm not old enough to read the French fog light on the door. I never did have a thing for *dames*.

Back at the table, Mr. Silk wants me to go back to his motel room for a neurotic nightcap. I keep giggling at him, hoping he'll melt away before last call. I'm not into silk. I'm into heavy denim with exaggerated hems and deep pockets. Another round of brew and he gets downright handzy, analyzing the texture of my Monday-to-Sunday monogrammed underwear. Feeling a draft, I realize his hand has already hit Friday night's fishnet in satin. I push him away but his hand stays and I keep praying for the end of the week.

Then the Stump shows up, hauls Silk right out of the chair, and steers him toward the door, and in a drunken stupor I follow with the billfold which has slipped from his pocket. Outside, I blast the Stump. "Why'd you do that? He wasn't doing nothing but talking to me."

"Uh huh. He must talk with his hands. Your dress is unzipped in the back. Do it up."

"How can I? I'm not double-jointed."

Propping Mr. Silk up on the curb, he sticks the billfold into his pocket and zips me up. "I can handle a shrimp like him anytime," I rally between hiccups.

"Yeah, just like the seven beers yeh polished off," he grunts, stepping into the street and flagging down a cab to bury Silk. "Why not go back in and polish off another seven?"

To bug his ass I decide to do just that. But before I've proven anything more, the bar closes down. I manage a shuttleweave path to the door and then grab for the next double-visioned landmark in sight. For Chrissake, it's the Stump again! But there are five of them. One grabs me with two paws and sets me outside on the sidewalk, a bag of garbage waiting for an early morning pickup, and thrusts a package into my hands. Shit, I almost forgot I had it.

"You shouldn't be out walking at this hour—alone," he reprimands dryly, propping me on the curb like a fold-out lawn chair. "Give me ten minutes to clean up inside and I'll drive yeh home." Sounds ass-saving to me. I fall asleep in the shape of a coat hanger. Next thing I know he pulls me apart and guides me, a zombie, to the parking lot. He drives a shitbox special, bald tires, a hit-and-miss paint job, and a passenger door fashionably held shut with a wire. He whacks me through the driver's side, turns the key, and asks me where I live; and getting my second wind, I refuse to tell him.

Cursing, he fumbles in my handbag for that phony driver's license of Sherry's. I laugh when he finds a North Bay address on it, a mere two hundred miles away. Shifting the shitbox into drive, he pulls out onto the main drag with "You can count yourself lucky. If you weren't a girl I'd have left your sweet ass at the curb."

If I weren't a girl, I wouldn't have had a sweet ass. Anyhow, I'm thrilled he's an ace at biology. My chauffeur has muddy eyes, gray-flecked hair over the ears, a nose that says he's had more enemies than friends, and no charm whatsoever. I'm just counting the minutes before we drive off the end of the earth and discover Atlantis.

Then he uses the original conversation opener, "What were you doing in a joint like that anyway?"

"You'd never believe it if I told you. I am, I must be the most unbelieved and misunderstood person in the world."

"Isn't everybody?"

"Just drop me off downtown somewhere. I'll chugalug it from there."

"Bullshit on that idea," he snaps. "I don't drop kids off on street corners in the middle of the night. I'll keep driving until your address changes from North Bay to the Falls."

I'd rather wait for him to run out of gas on a lonely stretch of road and get picked up by a UFO. In the meantime I let him know how I feel about armadillos and stumps in general. "I don't usually talk to hunks I don't like, yeh know. But tonight I'm doing the government a favor. If it wasn't for me, Social Services would have to create a whole new department just to handle you for the night."

"What the Christ do you know about guys like me?" he flares up, lighting a cigarette.

"I know you'd rather drive a tin can than have a credit rating."

"Don't like me, huh?"

"No, you're ugly and beat up on little guys who didn't do nothing wrong in life except go into the arse end of the fabric industry. So let me out or I'll scream."

He calls my bluff by screeching up to the curb, reaching in front of me, and unwiring the door handle. "Now that I know you've got a fast mouth, let's see how fast yeh are with your feet!"

I jump out, completely lost, and stumble across a patch of grass to another curb. The Stump pulls up again. "Forget something?" he bites, holding my package out the window.

Struck dumb, I can't move. "What do people say when they can't think of anything to say?"

"They keep their mouth shut and play it safe." He groans, gets out, and reaches for my hand. "C'mon. I'll take you anywhere you want to go." I let him put me back in the shitbox.

Now, something I've been getting periodically since my early teens—weird head space-warps that sneak up on me unannounced and, like a vise, clamp all consciousness out of me. It begins with a knot of pain tightening the nerve ends at the base of my skull. My vocal cords cramp, I experience dizziness, physical paralysis, double vision, and a mental blank for a period of seconds. I can't remember who I am or where I am. Sometimes I even pass out. This explains my aversion to crowds.

I'm on the climb to a doozy now. My vision is blurry, my speech is slurred, the motor in my brain is winding down to 20 percent capacity. I have lost control of my weak, numbed, lifeless body falling, falling over in the seat.

By the time we reach his place I'm unconscious.

Half an hour later I wake up delirious and dizzy on a couch in a well-furnished bed-sitter. It takes me a few minutes to gather the threads of time back together again. "How do you feel?" the Stump asks, prodding coffee into my hand. "I was gonna take you to the hospital if you didn't wake up soon."

"Thanks for kidnapping me. You have a nice place," I confess, still dream-dozed.

"I can't complain. It does—as good as does can do on minimum wage."

"That's wonderful—not what you said but how you said it. You should be composing bumper stickers for a living."

"You're drunk and shouldn't be here."

"I'm high but I'm not drunk. And I'm eighteen and can consent to anything worth consenting to."

"You're fifteen if you're a day," he insists. "And I hope you don't always talk like that."

"Like what?"

"Twisted—like it was better if you'd kept your mouth shut. Someday it'll put you in a real jam."

"I know, I know, I know, I know." I yawn with boredom.

"Yeh know, do yeh?" he harangues, raising his voice and beefing up in the face. "Yeah, I'll just bet yeh do. Do yeh know, too, that there's times when that sharp little mouth of yours isn't gonna get yeh anywhere? Yeh could meet some meatball in a bar one night. He could treat yeh like grade A meat and then kill yeh just because he didn't like the color of your eyes. What would yeh do then, huh?"

"Nothing—I mean . . . I don't know. Hey, are you crazy?"

"No, but I think you are," he grunts, releasing me. "Trusting in any asshole who comes along."

"Are you an asshole?"

"That's right. That's what I am. Another transient truckload you don't know balls about. And don't you forget it."

"So why should I pay attention to an asshole like you anyway?"

He wheels around and clamps my wrist. "Because this's my place and what I say goes and what I say is, You may as well listen to an asshole that knows he's an asshole than to the asshole in yourself who not only bullshits like an asshole but talks like a smart ass."

In an almighty huff I blast from the room. I run a bath, pin up my hair, and leave the light off and the door open so I can see to reach my toes. Like my grandma Gerty, who spent at least an hour of every day in suds. Bathing is a stimulating release of stress, an ecstatic rejuvenation of the spirit and body physical.

The Stump's not fooling anybody. I've got his act down pat. He's a misogynist who actually fears women more than he hates them.

He's damn lucky that I'm a misologist with an aversion to logic and formal beauty and a healthy affinity for ugly underdogs. Together we're a safe proposition: no rings on our fingers, no bells on our toes.

When I emerge, wrinkly, pink, and smelling of Ivory soap, the couch has been made into a pullout bed. He's polishing off a bottle of beer and watching TV, ignoring me entirely. Too tired to engage in active combat, I crawl under the covers and sink into a heavy sleep.

I wake up in the morning curled up inside the cave of his body so safe and warm I don't want to get up, wondering why she didn't make a play for him when she had a chance last night. But the wheels in my head start grinding. I pull myself out of bed and get dressed. Before leaving, I lipstick a message on the mirror of the dresser. "Thanks for the free ride and the boring conversation, asshole."

Then, a cab to the motel. Instead of waiting for that call from Joel, I shower, change my clothes, call in sick at the bakery, wait at Rollo's for the sky to fall in—and it doesn't take long.

Stewy gives me a punch in the arm and slides into the booth, fingering the earring in his left ear. "Where's the goddamn goods, baby? You didn't make the delivery."

"The pigs got it. Ask them."

"What the fuck are you talking about?"

"They raided my pad and swiped it. I got away out the window. They're still looking for me."

"You're lying, sister."

"I don't care whether you believe me or not. If you keep bugging me, I'll turn you over to them, too. So screw off!" I only hope I sound tough enough to be convincing.

"Nobody walks out on us, sister. Wait till Joel gets wind of this. You're fucking dead."

Hell, I'm not spooked. As soon as I get my act into drive, I'm splitting town. Tonight. I bomb it back to the motel to pack my duds. The Stump has left a raunchy message on the door. "Get your smart ass down to Nick's Place on the double!" I can't say I didn't expect it.

Quickly I jump on Boris and head out. It's practically dark now and the traffic is easing off. On Front Street I get a thirty-second spine tickle when a car creeps up on me from behind. Its headlights kiss my back fender, and Joel hollers out the front window, "Pull over, baby!"

"Go to hell!"

I pedal faster and faster but they put the squeeze on me and I lose control of Boris altogether, bump up over the curb, crash into garbage pails, and go over in a scraping skid across the pavement. Clumsily, I pick myself up out of the wreckage of twisted metal and bloody knees and elbows and hobble about in a stunny rage.

Joel's car screeches up to the curb down the street and rubber-burns a tire spin in reverse. Tricks and Stewy hop out of the backseat and someone yells "Get her!"

I make a crazy run for it into an alley and blunt up against an eight-foot fence with a soul-saving THINGS GO BETTER WITH COKE sign plastered on its face. I'm halfway up the bottle when they haul me down. I sink my teeth into Stewy's hand. Tricks prods the back of my neck with the cold nozzle of a .38. I give up with the nickname I gave the Stump last night forming on my lips . . . Crunch!

They hustle me to the car, where Joel is in the front seat with the driver, ordering them to move it. I'm thrown to the floor in the back between Stewy and Tricks and told to keep my head down and my mouth shut. My hands are tied behind my back with a rope. Stewy undoes the buttons on the front of my dress. Totally neutralized, I feel like pissing and throwing up at the same time.

My optimism peters out with the diminishing streetlights. We're heading for the bugaboo boonies, the unmapped pasture of no return. I'm shaking so bad I have a wrenching pain in my lungs. My bruised knees have given out altogether. Stewy is squeezing my left tit and pinching the stub at the end of it.

Tricks puts a .38 to my left ear. The *click, click, click* drives me into a hysterical crying jag. I spew and sputter and wiggle about to a steady incantation of "I'll do anything, anything you want if you don't *kill* me. Jesus everloving Christ don't fucking kill me!"

Joel reaches over the front seat and jerks me up by the hair until my scalp is coming away from my skull. "Shut up or I'll burn yeh right here. Now where the fuck is my dope?"

I keep telling him the pigs have it. He keeps telling me to spill it and he won't believe me. I won't believe that Stewy is sucking my tits. Tricks is rasping in my ear, urging them to burn me. I'm bad news. I know too much. I cry out that I'm only a girl and if God in His infinite wisdom has never expected girls to know anything about anything just what gives him the right to think I should know anything about their goddamn drug operation? Joel hollers for everyone to shut up so he can think. Tricks clicks the .38 again in my ear. I piss in my pants and start screaming all over again. Joel tells me to shut up. I yell back, "Vito will get you for this!" and suddenly Stewy stops sucking, Tricks stops clicking, and Joel lets go of my hair with "Who the fuck is this Vito?"

"You know—he owns the Rendezvous," Stewy offers, sticking his hand between my legs.

"You don't mean Vittroni—Vito Vittroni?" he yelps.

"Yeh, that's the dude."

"You two fucking assholes, I *told* you to check up on her!"

"Big shit deal," Tricks whines. "He's only a stinking Wop."

"Mob is what he is, fuckhead. I'll bet little Miss Mushy has already given him the goods on us. Haven't yeh, yeh two-bit slut?"

Drunk on dying, I nod like crazy. It's better than anything I could have invented.

"So what?" Tricks despairs in a squeaky voice. "She's still a nobody and nobodies go out clean. Yeh don't even need a shovelful of dirt to put them away."

"Vittroni is known for taking care of his own. She's not worth the grief. Let her out."

"Ah, c'mon. Let me put a few cigarette burns on her so she won't forget me?"

"Yeah," Stewy echoes. "Let me fuck her first?"

"Let her out!" Joel shrieks.

The car screeches to a sudden stop on the gravel shoulder. A knife slices the rope binding my wrists. My shoulder bag is thrust in my hands, and Joel gives me a parting piece of advice. "Better hitch it to Windsor, baby. You're dead meat in the Falls." The door cranks open and I'm pitched out helter-skelter. I roll right down a sharp incline into a bed of sweet-smelling grass and lie there numb, motionless, every bone in my body aching, my dress ripped and rumpled and wet with sweat, without underwear, socks, or shoes, waiting for the sound of the car engine to become a bad memory. For minutes I lie shaking and crying, my brain refusing to function.

Suddenly realizing that the bastards might reconsider and double back, I jump to my feet. After rubbing some feeling into my legs I hobble toward the Falls in a stupor, singing everything from "I got plenty of nothing and nothing's plenty for me" to "Officer Krupke" to keep my spirits up.

Still, I have to hit the dirt every time a car passes until the sun approaches the top of the trees. I flag down a milk truck.

The driver's an overweight rosy-cheeked Bible thumper listening to the morning's "Oral Roberts Gospel Hour" on the radio. "I went to a revival meeting and got saved but missed my ride home," I say with a painted-on smile.

What else could I say? Thanks loads, you Sunday sucker, for aiding and abetting a girl who runs drugs.

don't even consider going back to the motel in case Joel and his goonies are waiting for me. I'm too scared. Instead, I sit outside the back door of the Rendezvous, sucking the blood out of the gashes on my knees and waiting for Vito to show up.

Giorgio, the head cook, throws bread crumbs out for the pigeons and discovers a bigger bird than he expected to find. "Mamma mia!" he chants excitedly. Helping me inside, he deposits me on a big table, pours out a glass of wine, and encourages it, sip by sip, down my throat. Then he leaves to make a telephone call with the promise to return.

The effect of the wine is soothing and heady but the pressure cooker is going in my head again, and before my reflexes stop altogether I bed down on the table and slip into oblivion.

Later in the morning I wake up in Vito's office on a leather couch covered in a blanket. Vito sweeps around the mahogany desk, sits down beside me, and takes my hand. "Like ice." He smiles. "How do you feel, little one?"

"Dirty, real dirty," I croak with embarrassment. "Can I get cleaned up?"

"Yes. Then we must eat and talk, eh?"

He buzzes Angie in the lounge. She's in charge of the day staff. In short order she sees to it that I'm showered and lends me a fresh set of duds.

Smelling of sandalwood with my damp hair snagged to the shoulder, I'm suddenly seated in the lounge opposite Vito, shrinking a little in his presence. He's the epitome of regularity and formula, an artistic impression that no banal human expression could touch or destroy. Stumped for words, I wonder if I can pick a grape off the tree of an institution without insulting the whole vine. He lets me order a meal from the menu and pours me out a glass of wine. "You can tell me about it," he assures me as if reading my thoughts. "I am a very good listener when I'm with a very good talker."

When my lobster arrives, the whole story with a few choice pieces left out comes tumbling out of me in gushes. Throughout, his eyes twinkle with mischief and merriment while the expression on his face is stern and quiet. I finish off by confessing that I planted the stash in a pig's cruiser.

"How old are you?" he asks, pouring out more wine. "And please tell me no tales."

"Seventeen almost."

He ponders a moment, fingers the corner of his mouth, and I almost swallow my napkin in anticipation.

"At sixteen everything you experience is important. But wisdom must be gained from it. You're old enough to have enemies. This is good. They make you use your brains. They make you strong. Enemies create you, not friends. You think too much about friends and not enough about enemies. At six years old I knew both the minute I left my front door. Why you English make such a complicated business out of such a simple fact of life is a great mystery to me."

"But I'm not English. My ancestors come from Europe somewhere and someday I'm going back to the promised land."

"Don't you know that the old Rome is dead and that the new Rome is here to be cried and fought over? For the present, we're in control of it and you can only make the best of it," he says, dabbing at his mouth with a napkin. "Life will become a simple affair when you're married. Everything will fall into its proper place."

"Seeing how I'm out of the order that isn't, I don't think so."

"You have friends, little one. *I* am your friend. Will you accept this?"

"Yes, if you tell me the price I have to pay for it."

"You made the price, not I. Tell me the names of these hooligans who attacked you."

After I cough up the data, he pats my hand, then snaps his fingers, and the bartender brings a red telephone to the table. "Sit tight, little one. Vito will take care of it."

"But they didn't really hurt me. It's nothing . . . really."

"They're a bunch of cheap punks who must be disciplined."

Over espresso coffee he changes the subject. "I want you here where I can protect you. How would you like a new job?"

"Fine, as long as it comes with a makeup treatment."

"Good girl." He pulls out a wallet and slips a fifty-dollar bill in my hand. "Go out and have a good time this weekend. Report for work here at five o'clock Monday afternoon. Angie will take care of you. In the meantime remember one thing—creating worthy enemies requires the same care as cultivating friends."

Sergio, one of his muscles, drives me back to the motel. My brain's a miasma of confusion, fatigue, good booze, and well-cooked fishie food. Vito's my guardian angel and everybody else doesn't exist.

As soon as I enter the darkness of my shuttered motel room, I breathe easy and then nearly jump out of my underwear. A humped shadow is silhouetted in the light near the slats of the venetian blind. Stump the Crunch gets to his feet and I'm in big trouble again. "How'd you get in?" I croak, trying to sound indignant.

He ignores the question and a plastic bag whizzes through the air and drops at my feet.

"What's this?"

"Stop playacting!" he grunts, taking a step toward me. "Why'd you stick five pounds of dope up my tail pipe?"

"I don't know anything about it. Honest."

"The fuck you don't. I found the brown paper bag in my garbage this morning. Answer me and don't bother lying."

"I didn't know where else to stash it and you seemed to have all the answers. How'd yeh find it anyway?"

"It found *me* before I left the parking lot."

"I thought you'd take care of it for me."

"In hell I would've looked after it for you. Do you know what the pigs would have done if they'd found it at a spot check?"

I'm getting real scared for him as well as myself. "But I didn't think you would—they would."

"That's right, you didn't *think*!" Now he's shaking me, uncontrollably.

"Stop it! I'm only seventeen!"

"So?"

"So you're older than I am. You're supposed to do the thinking for me."

"When are yeh gonna do your own thinking—when you're my age?"

"If I look like you when I reach it, I may as well let somebody else do it for me now. Why would the pigs pin you for that dope anyway? All you'd have to do is explain it to them."

"I'm an ex-con. They wouldn't bother to ask questions. Who does it belong to?"

I make a run for the door. He lunges for me. I throw a lamp at him. He catches it. I beat it into the bathroom and try to hold the door shut. In one body thrust he knocks me flying into the bathtub. Pulling a jackknife from his pocket, he reaches for me. Expecting to be cut up and swallowed, I go absolutely bonkers.

"Calm down!" He turns me around and cuts a hole in the back of Angie's dress. Then, with a great heave, he hangs me up on the hook on the back of the door. It's as solid as the stone age it came out of. "Whenever you're ready to talk, let me know," he grunts. "Don't bother screaming or I'll come back in and make you even more uncomfortable."

He leaves me there sizzling while he helps himself to my beer and flicks on my TV. Unable to get my arms around to pull myself off, this bagged chicken can do nothing but pray for a goddamned earthquake!

Finally I give in. He unhinges me. I fall to the floor in a tangle of recriminations. Then I run a bath and when I'm up to the neck in bubbles I call him back in and tell him everything.

"Vito must have been pleased," he returns cynically. "He's been trying to dry up that supply line for six months now. He must have been a little sick, too—finding out it was under his nose all the time."

"Then you're not mad at me anymore?"

"No, rabbit. I'm more angry at myself for not beating the tar out of you. Right now we're getting rid of this stuff." With his jackknife he cuts up the remaining plastic packets and flushes the contents down the toilet.

Now it's time for me to get some answers. "How long were you in the joint?"

"Eight years."

Crunch is something straight out of the *Iliad*, powerful, mysterious, and full of dark forces. I want him, sober, and without a blown-out fuse in my head if I can manage it.

"The son of a bitch took my woman," he confesses suddenly without emotion. "So I killed him."

"Just like that?" I hazard, a thrill passing right through me.

"Yeah—just like that, rabbit. She'd been seeing him on the sly for months. If the pigs hadn't locked me up when they did, I would have killed her, too. All along I thought I knew her."

"You can't know things you can't be expected to know."

"Balls. You're born knowing everything—you just have to listen to the voice of instinct."

"What do you want me to say? That it's okay—that it's not okay? Hell, I don't know nothing. Figure it out for yourself."

"I've already spent eight years figuring it out. I guess I should be leaving now," he says uncertainly, getting to his feet.

"Why?" I announce trippingly, so wiped out I'm ready to keel over, yet so hip on staying awake I'm wingy.

He sits down again. I climb into his lap and pretend to read the fortune on his palm. I'm actually reading the mislaid fortune in his face. The lines there seem to have grown deeper since I first met him. He has a raised consciousness. I'm not entirely sure what that means. I only know that all pagan saints come with it.

Guarded and wary, he watches me undo the top button on his shirt, refusing to move a muscle. When I kiss him he lets me for a full second. Just as I figure I've beat the cook into the pantry, the bastard dumps me onto the bed and pins me down. "Does nothing get through that thick skull of yours? A fifteen-year-old kid is trouble I don't need."

I can't stand prejudice, either by the cup or by the bucket. Miffed, I snatch my shoulder bag from the floor and toss him my birth certificate. "A year makes one hell of a lot of difference to the size of the cradle, doesn't it?" he quips icily, throwing it back.

"About the same difference as the size of a jail cell."

"Smart ass. Do yeh think I don't know why you stashed that dope in my car? You wanted to get to me and couldn't think of any way to do it honestly. I don't think you know what the fuck you're doing."

"Right now I'm getting to you."

"Why? What do you want from me now, rabbit?"

"Everything that's inside of you, stupid."

"You wouldn't know what to do with it."

"Sure I would. I'd use it as bait to catch a bigger fish."

"Cockteasers like you wind up on the bottom of rivers face up."

I cool off instantly. This isn't the way the scene's supposed to be played. Ignoring me, he undresses, switches off the lamp, and gets into bed. Suddenly shivering with cold, I crawl in beside him, shut off from the reality of him, not wanting to have to *do* anything, content to let him *do* everything. But he won't *do* anything. And the more I work at denying him the more I slave at turning myself on and he slaves at letting me by pretending to be asleep. So I pretend to be asleep. Backing my thigh up against the front of his bare bulky torso in one monumental dreamsigh, I close up into a fetuslock which he encloses in a fetushold. We warm, and wallow in warm, and wait for the healing heat. Then we stop pretending, together, and come apart, together, in a perfectly synchronized freestyle foreplay. He tastes like burnt iron in the form of melting chains, chains he hasn't been able to remove from himself, and I can feel that razor-edged rage, that dark unfathomable force from the other side, turn me inside out as it holds me in bondage, swallowing me up from the cunt and I'm whining, and I'm wantonly content letting him do me and me be and won't stop and keeps—stretching . . . the moment . . . the . . .

Years later when I've been cut down from the rack, I find myself transported back to daylight saving time with one thought: the vaginal orgasm isn't a myth. It's the last Book of Revelation nicely hidden away in Proverbs. With the proverbial cigarette after sex comes the proverbial glance into the rearview mirror.

Crunch's problems all started in an orphanage operated by the Roman Catholic Church, and later, a string of correctional centers operated by the provincial government. He tells me about the brutality dished out by the priests in the orphanage as disciplinary measures— the bizarre beatings and the sodomized torture sessions. Regularly he and the other boys were herded naked outside in subzero temperatures and made to stand for an hour praying. One boy caught pneumonia and died and there was no investigation of any kind. God won't tolerate anything but totalitarian rule in His house. Crunch kept running away until he was sent to correctional centers where jailbait was kept tender for the big house. He ran away from them, too. Finally he made it out on his own at sixteen. In Toronto he was picked up by an over-the-hill boxing promoter, who took him under his crooked wing and put him on the small-time circuit. In that small cage with the big swing he won some, he lost some, and after expenses wound up with small change in a little tin cup to show for it. When he decked an opponent and almost killed him, he threw down his gloves for good and buzzed off to work on the Seaway when I was still in training panties, trying to get old shoes to float in mud puddles. From there it was all forge in, fall back, and fall out.

"Wouldn't you ever want to find your parents?" I ask, wondering if I'd want to know the name of the boat that set me adrift.

"Fuck them—they fucked me," he growls, his eyes lidded and leaden.

Leaving him with his brewing thoughts, I groove on his staying power in the sack. I usually pay for a one-way ticket and either lose it down a sewer grate or get billed again at the other end by a bum named Inflation. This time I lost the ticket, but took the trip and got sent home—free. How come I still feel robbed?

What do you know? Sex isn't only the progenitor of the impulsive, the indulgent, the proud, and the profane, it can also be the harbinger, the mentor, and the scornful supplicant of the jubilant confessor. And it makes meat and potatoes a banquet.

Before I go to sleep, I have to ask him why he keeps calling me rabbit.

"Because that's what you are. 'Mushy' is a come-on and if you had any sense you'd drop it."

herry can't stand the sight of Crunch. "He's so ugly . . . he gives me the creeps. How could you?"

As other people's opinions have never cut the mustard with me, Crunch and I shack up together in a one-bedroom apartment. Though I'm constantly booby-trapping paradise by playing the most atrocious pranks on my live-in guru, I have to admit that men are the easiest creatures to live with. You start with jungle mouth, laundry piled in the hamper, cookie crumbs in the bed, and dirty dishes in the sink, and work backward toward more cultural pursuits like flying spaghetti, pornography in the red, and the good life.

Against Crunch's wishes I begin work at the Rendezvous in a black miniskirt and a sheer red silk blouse. I save my misbehaving for home where it belongs, with a disarray of bedclothes and yesterday's newspaper.

I meet a leggy brunette stripper from the Dirty Duck Tavern who just blew into town on a firecracker from Stateside. Jackie drops into the Rendezvous every afternoon for a quick bite before her nightly gig. There's something pathetic about her luminous blue eyes, freckled paleness, and hard sleazy front she projects to hide her bra size. By the nature of her work, she's a loner burying herself in anonymity and self-scorn, a born runner just like me. She smokes pot, will screw anything with a third leg and a touch-and-go track record, and she's as readable as a layman's libido on a Friday night. While she lends me her hard-core streetwise wit, I lend her my put-your-best-finger-forward brand of optimism. Together we're an encounter group.

She's fascination-plus in other areas, too. She pumps her tits up with silicone and her stripping costume is a Calamity Jane cowgirl costume, Las Vegas style, complete with a set of jeweled six-guns, a studded western hat, and spurred leather boots.

Crunch isn't thrilled about our freemasonry, afraid she'll rub off on me and I'll start to copy and cuss. But we continue to hang out together, take in the odd movie, and go shopping for exotic additions to her glitzy wardrobe.

One night she flies into the Rendezvous, breathless and shit-scared, her mascara running, her spiky fake lashes falling off, a cloak over her costume, and pushes me into the washroom. "Can you put me up for a few days, honey? I've got to get my stuff out of my hotel—now! I'm in a fuck of a mess!"

Angie gives me the green light to split early. Jackie suddenly grabs my arm and pulls me behind a wooden partitioned planter, drawing my attention to two heavy-duty versions of the Hungarian gigolo, two dark suits who just blew in the door with such hostile overbearance I'm sure they're looking for a place to have a leak. "Those are the guys who're after me!" Jackie bursts, wide-eyed and wingy.

We flash through the kitchen, out the back door, and crouch down behind the garbage bin. She lights up a cigarette. "I saw them waste the guy I worked for," she confesses, holding the smoke in her lungs for a minute. "I thought I lost the fuckers in Chicago."

The blood drains right from my body as I pass her the butt. She stamps it under her boot heel. "Let's get us some wheels, honey," she announces, dodging toward the parking lot. I follow her from one aisle to another, checking for locked doors and open windows, realizing that the game has changed the rules. After recognizing Vito's silver Jaguar, Angie's green MGB and Sergio's red Mustang in the lineup, I notice a spanking white Oldsmobile. What kind of a nutball leaves the windows rolled down and the keys in the ignition? Who the fuck cares? Jackie jumps in and slides across to the passenger side. We take off.

"Why am I driving?" I ask, clutching the steering wheel with blind fear.

"I don't have a Canadian driver's license."

"Does it matter when somebody else owns the car?"

"When you can't drive, it does. I never learned. I never had to."

"As soon as we pick up your stuff we'll ditch these wheels. Then Crunch'll help you get out of the city."

On Canal Street Jackie gets a brainstorm. "All I've got is twenty-five bucks, honey. How far do yeh think I'm gonna get on that? Say, I know this guy who comes into the Dirty Duck every Friday night. He deals in anything hot. Let's sell the wheels to Clive."

Half an hour later we pull into a wrecking yard across town. There's a shack at the back disguised as an upgraded chicken coop with a TV aerial. Clive, a black Mario Andretti in a batik shirt and faded jeans, meets us out front. "Whooee," he whistles, sliding his hand lovingly along the fender. "How much for your big white bird?"

"A G-note," Jackie says flatly.

"C'mon, baby. Clive almost got burned touching her."

"Okay, eight hundred."

"Five—and I won't feel any pain."

"Six."

"Done—and make it quick. I want to dress her up and give her some class."

He whips a roll out of his pocket and peels off twelve fifties.

We grab a cab to Jackie's seedy room in the run-down Ambassador House Hotel. Jackie locks the door and pulls two beat-up suitcases out from under the bed. While she pulls clothes off the hangers in the closet, I empty the drawers of the single dresser held up by three legs and a telephone book.

We're almost finished packing when there's a knuckle-burning, shoe-slamming thunder at the door. Thankfully it's only in the movies that doors are made of particleboard and held together with staples. Jackie and I fly squealing for the window only to discover that fire escapes, too, are products of the movies. I've never been so gut-scared in my life—well, almost never.

Unable to will the door down with a volley of curses and shoulder heaves, the dynamic duo from Budapest pick the lock while Jackie and I are yelping hysterically and in danger of hugging each other to death. The door suddenly jerks open but jams tight on the chain lock. When one hairy paw gropes inside, we scream in unison. Throwing our bodies against the door, we catch the animal with the ten-dollar jeweled gold watch in a tight squeeze. For one brief second we're simply pitting our strength against theirs. Then I sink my teeth into the hand with canine relish and the Hungarian howler is forced to pull it free. But we're not safe for long. In one powerful thrust they storm in, pulling the chain lock right out of the wall and knocking us to the floor.

These creepoids are a plastic surgeon's pet fantasy. Ragoul is a tall, flat-assed Limburger cheese with an aproned chin and a self-peeling moustache falling off his face. Squib, his sidekick, is a short overgrown cherub with colorless smudge eyes and the stubby constitution of a Tanzanian blowfish.

Roughly they haul us to our feet. I meet them with one of Jackie's six-guns. "Put that plastic piece away!" Ragoul bellows, slapping it out of my hand. "What the fuck do yeh think I am—illiterate?" Then he pulls the real McCoy out of his coat and my stomach starts to empty. "Now which one of you sluts bit me?"

Jackie pipes up with "She did!" I couldn't be more shocked by the tattling bitch.

Ragoul gives me the evil eye but it's Squib who speaks. "Getting cozy with Hotpants was real stupid, Blondie. But convenient. Now there's one for each of us to pork before we put yeh down."

With heaters under their suit coats they escort us downstairs. The eggheaded doze on the desk, who's obviously been paid off, doesn't even raise his head from the magazine he's pretending to read when we pass through the shabby lobby.

Outside we're pitched into the backseat of a brand-new Plymouth with Squib. Ragoul takes the wheel as if he means to eat it. Crying fitfully, Jackie keeps begging them to let her go. I'm in an electrified state of shock, sweating and shaking so bad I can hear my tonsils rattle against my backbone.

We're taken to an abandoned warehouse, a red brick edifice with soot-covered walls, two freight bays, and grating and bars across the windows—a dandy spot for a remake of *The Day the Earth Stood*

Still. Ragoul slips a key out of his pocket, opens the heavy iron padlock on the big wooden door, and Squib prods us inside the musty ballpark interior with a flashlight. Our footsteps echo on the concrete floor, creepy-looking mechanical reptiles covered in sheets of dust and cobwebs hunch nearby, ready to spring, the brooding silence broken only by the flutter of bats and the muffled sound track of Jackie's sobs. I expect God to speak at any minute.

But he doesn't. Instead, I'm tied up and Jackie's ordered to undress on a dirty mattress in the middle of the room. Ragoul unzips his fly, pulls out his dong, and climbs on her from behind, and rooting like a pig, rides her doggie-style. Jackie's whimpering and he's howling and I'm wringing my bound hands. Then Squib's burning the soles of her feet with a cigarette for Chrissakes. Jackie screams and Ragoul keeps fucking her and then he's finished and Jackie's still screeching and jerking. He turns her over on her back and holds her arms and Squib shoves a long-necked bottle up her cunt as far as it'll go. Then he slams his body weight on her pelvis and something crunches and Jackie's screaming blind and I'm screaming "They're gonna kill us!"

Ragoul sends Squib out to the trunk of the car for a blanket. Jackie's still screaming up a storm when they wrap her bloody cunt in her own clothes and wind her writhing body in the blanket. Ragoul carries her out to the car and shoves her in the backseat with me. After untying me, he and Squib get in the front seat and pull out in a tire-spinning frenzy. Jackie's lying in my lap hemorrhaging all over the place. I've never seen so much blood and she's moaning deliriously and I can't stop her blood from becoming my blood and then there's a set of headlights behind us and then they disappear and suddenly there's an ear-shattering roar ahead, a river named Niagara, and we stop and I feel dead already. They're going to dump us over the Falls!

Jackie's pulled from the bloody backseat and I'm dragged out after her, clawing at the lapels of their coats and the vegetation in an effort to slow down the pace of this nightmare so I can grab hold of reality—for just a second—and maybe survive it. Then I hear a voice that is part of the whooshing washing sound and yet outside of it. "Move away from them, chickenshit!"

Squib releases his pinching fingers from my arms, Ragoul dumps

Jackie at my feet, and they attempt to pull the heaters from inside their jackets. But they're too late. Mario, Sergio, and two other muscles from the Rendezvous with .38's in their hands home in on all of us. Raising his hands in mock surrender, Ragoul makes his bidding pitch. "Ease off, Vittroni. This isn't your business."

"You've got one of my girls. That makes it family business."

"That's too bad. One broad with a mouth and a friend makes two dead broads. Can't yeh count, fuckhead?"

"Don't know the meaning of *respect*, do you, boys? You've got no clout this side of the border."

"Who the fuck cares? I'm no goddamn Canuck!"

"If my father picks up the phone and dials New York, you'll care."

"One of the boys in Chicago ordered the hit on Hotpants."

"Tell the *boy* to call my father if he's got trouble reading road signs."

Now it's down to territorial imperatives and Ragoul and Squib squirm for half a minute before getting back in their Plymouth and buzzing off. Jackie's practically unconscious, her pulse rate faint and labored, and her blanket blood-soaked. I try to tend her by swabbing the blood from her legs but beyond this I don't know what else I can do to help her. Mario orders Sergio and the boys to take her to the hospital in their car. Then he puts me in the passenger side of his Stingray.

"Cool it, Mushy," Mario soothes me, gearing up the engine while The Guess Who are belting out "No Time" from the radio. "It's all over. We've been watching them all night. But the bastards gave us the slip for an hour or so."

When he pulls into the police station parking lot, I get anxious. "You're not gonna tell *them* about it, are yeh?"

"No." He grins, amused at my naïveté. "I want to see if the cops have any leads yet. Some idiot had the nerve to swipe my father's Olds tonight."

My digestive system backs up and my bowels move into my rib cage. "I thought Vito owned the Jaguar!" I squeak thinly.

"Oh, he does—for buzzing around town. But the Olds is his pride and joy."

Mario leaves me with that one neatly phrased spellbinder—*pride
and joy*. I'll never know either again. A terrible image blots up in my
mind's eye. Vito's white Olds floating down Canal Street—repainted
fire-engine red, with dice hanging from the mirror, fake leopard-skin
seat covers, four bucks with their feet up on the dash grooving to
Motown rock blaring from the radio, and the crusher—four pompons
fluting from the radio antenna. Ohhhh, the sacrilege!

Luckily Mario has no encouraging news from the pigs so he drives
me back to the Rendezvous. Vito wants to see me and I can't say I'm
not on pins the size of lightning rods. The club has closed down for
the night and the interior is black except for the dining area near the
bar in the rear, ready for an impromptu funeral. Mine. Imagine my
surprise when I discover Crunch sitting with Vito at a table surrounded
by three muscle boys. They monitor my approach with calculated
hostility. It's clear that nobody is eager to deliver a eulogy on my
behalf. Emotionally drained from the events of the night and worried
about Jackie, I feel my head whirling. By the time I reach their table
I'm light-headed and vocally off-key. Vito asks me how I am. "I towed
your rolls!"

"What?"

"I mean—I—I stole your Olds. But I can pay you for it."

"When?" he asks stiffly, drumming the table with a forefinger.

"In small weekly allotments, maybe by 1986."

"Where is it now?"

"You don't want to know," I reply deadpan, sure I'm about to be
shot. "Maybe I can get it back if—"

"Tell him!" Crunch insists, fury tattooed into his features.

So in fits and starts I tell him everything and finish with "Maybe I
can get it back for you."

"No, *I'll* get it back, little one," Vito says sharply. "Along with the
six hundred dollars you owe me."

"But I don't have it."

"Just as I thought," he concludes with a sigh. "Didn't I tell you
that you think too much about friends?"

Crunch offers to make it up with the petty-cash roll in his wallet.

Vito waves him away and flicks a finger at me. "*You* will pay me the money, *you*." Then he dismisses me. "Go home and sleep on it and stay away from Jackie."

Outside, I breathe a sigh of relief. But not for long. Just when I need distraction the most, Crunch snaps off the radio. Then he refuses to speak all the way home. His silence frightens me all the more. Now I know I'm in trouble.

At the apartment I call the hospital's emergency ward. Jackie's still on the critical list. I pull a beer out of the fridge. But even before I get it up to my mouth, Crunch whips it from my hand and puts back a swallow himself before lighting into me. "Do you know what you put me through tonight? When I met you, you were running drugs. Now you're stealing cars from kingpins in the mafia. What the fuck is next?"

"I had to help Jackie—she needed me."

"Screw Jackie—she screwed you when she got you into this."

"What are you coming down on me for? I'm the one who almost got wasted tonight."

"When I'm finished with you, you'll wish you had been!" he thunders, lunging toward me and taking me in hand. I've never experienced such a thrashing in my life and my humiliation is total. The bum wouldn't even take a rain check so I'd be prepared for it. Later, after hiding in the bathroom for an hour, crying and feeling sorry for myself, I emerge and crawl into bed. He ignores me. In the morning when he leaves the apartment ignoring me I know that it's over. I'll never be able to live with him again or get rid of this guilt I'm feeling. So I drop an IOU off in the mail to Vito for the six hundred dollars, pack my bags, and grab a cab for the bus depot. I'm checking out.

PART II
GOING
WITH IT

9

he minute The Guess Who's bus rider rolls into Toronto, the bad, the magnitude of this metropolis shatters my sense of security—for about five minutes. Once again I've "jumped my genes" and let blind emotion take over. But I've got something in my favor: my mistakes are getting bigger. That must mean I'm progressing in life.

For decent grub you always follow the line of eighteen-wheelers at a trucker's stop. For a decent place to crash you ask the stoned cabbie who picks you up at the bus depot. Then you let him take you on the scenic route to your destination to pay for the hot tip. The oofless hack drops me off at a downtown women's hostel. St. Trinians by the Strip was originally constructed to receive immigrants from the potato famine in Ireland. It hasn't lost any of its nineteenth-century appeal—varnished mahogany everywhere, including the toilet seats. Though staffed by peahens from the Boer War, it's a pubescent potboiler of refugees, rejects, and innocents, where the resident bulldykes will sell you their protection after they've sold you their wrath on a ten-inch dildo and tried to use your cunt for a fingerbowl. My roommate, Julie, turns me on to this "scam on the slam." The can of Mace she lends me does wonders for my peace of mind in the bath when confronted with two butches on the hustle. After booby-trapping our room against sleepwalking daughters of Lesbos in chain mail, Julie and I spend the night on the streets.

If you wanna get lost from other people, go to Tibet on an out-of-body experience. But if you want to get lost from yourself, summer in the city in downtown Toronto will do just fine. No need to feel guilty about partaking. Now, it's showtime!—bought and paid for in that black-and-white war of 1939–45 by 45 million hopefuls who never got a chance to attend this gala performance—or even cash in their tickets. Utopia when off the beach is the street, a big displaced-persons camp and a cornucopia for the senses, full of new, tall sky-scrapers, new money, new blood, and new recipes for happiness sold on the hoof. Neither people nor graffiti are allowed to age. The password to this Shangri-La is *youth*. Souls come here not to get saved but to get freed and dressed up in a Saturday-night sports coat. For me it's like being a dime on a dice roll in Deathwish Alley. Everything's wide open for the pillage, including myself. Because I'm always look-ing up, I always seem to be walking in the shadow of the two tallest monoliths on the city skyline, the head offices of the nation's banking industry. Then there's City Hall, that Finnish tea service that never got airborne.

St. Trinians is located right at the heart of the Yonge Street Strip. It's a catwalk along a vaporous vista through neons of blue lightning, sewer steam, swooshing subway air vents, meteor dust, and mirrored images from store windows projecting the altered states of man as he progressed from Darwinian monkey to the Simpson Store mannequin without hair or teeth. On tap there's a panoply of head shops, gay bars, dirty bookshops, and porno movie houses where Ilsa, the She-Wolf of the SS, snaps her bullwhip at you from the billboard. The street is peopled with ragamuffined hippies hawking social revolution on antiwar placards, mortgaged-up-to-the-asshole monkey-suited cadres from the Bay Street Gleek Set, marketing their politically *right* social bias as a laundry soap called free enterprise, Jesus Freaks pushing fanaticism as the ultimate cop-out, Hare Krishna selling burial plots on a mountain in India, dashiki-shirted Blacks addressing their blackly beautiful roots with honky limericks and jungle drumbeats, Jordache jocks in muscle cars on the cruise, advertising steroids and a gravy-stained bravado, panhandlers using animal need to rope the guilt complex from human greed, hustlers hustling human weakness on the installment plan, pimps and prostitutes selling social disease by the payload, and those escapees from urban blight—those thrill-seeking suburbanites out to sight-see and reassure themselves that their credit rating matches their sociological development. They're all here sticker-priced and marked REDUCED TO SELL. They come to this flea market from every other planet in the universe to shoot crap and soul-shop. Distraction is the formula for mind control. It's the media's meal ticket and the government's meat market. And you can nod your way through this pick-your-senses-clean shakedown bought and paid for in the baby-booming cradle with total immunity—for this's *free-doom*, kid. Or *freedom* if you can't spell. So collect your dues and give yourself a bow, kid!

Doom might be free but everything else in the city costs, so I go job-hunting without a hawker's license. Since I don't have the Barbie Doll wardrobe or the Little Miss Priss presence for the nine-to-five office grind and the waitressing junket pays peanuts and wears down the Achilles heel, I nose around for something gamer with a little panache.

Noticing a GIRLS WANTED sign in the window of Club Morocco on the Strip, I give my neophobia a tickle by walking right in to apply. Doobie-Doo, the queer three-hundred-pound queen bee inside the door, pats down his bleached-out brush cut and leaves his post as bouncer to usher me to the bar where the wanted girls are having a glee-club session. Before I can get comfortable, Skinner the manager shows up. The Fruit of the Loom edition of Al Capone with his secondhand imitation Yves Saint Laurent biking suit fitted over a snowman's paunch and a black shiny stuck-on-his-head mail-order toupee whisks me away for a cozy chat-up at a private table. His one-liners smell of camphor and barley water—just like his aftershave. "Hey, baby," he says to open, "where you been hiding all my life?"

"In an incubator waiting for you." I grin, ready to tie his balls together into a bow tie. Five minutes later and I'm still waiting for him to talk shop. So far all I've learned is the name of his tailor, a Portuguese upholsterer from the garment district on Spadina Avenue.

Then, without even giving me an IQ test or asking my telephone number, he hires me on the spot. The girls from the glee club back at the bar buy me a drink and fill me in on the job, which consists of eight half-hour sets a night, wiggling your G-string-covered ass and juggling your bare tits inside of a neoned cage, five nights a hundred-dollar week—and no union dues. Skinner's got the reputation of being the biggest turkey who ever had the luck of being blown out of an April Fool's bullhorn. Since he refuses to call a plumber, the toilets in the ladies' room have to be flushed by pulling on wires connected to the boxes. Also, the staff has been ordered to retrieve half-finished drinks so the bartender can pour them back in the bottles. Who cares if they're stale or mixed? This's just the beginning of the complaints against him. He's so goddamned tight with the buck that when he dies they'll put him into the ground with a corkscrew and five gallons of mineral oil to ensure he'll make Nepal on a one-way ticket, where he'll be taken for a god and melted down for his tie clip.

My first night getting ready to go boobie-dancing in spangly shoe-laces in a cage is a fusion of the twin scourges—hair-raising fright and go-go-get-'em might. I keep playing Russian roulette in my head, waiting for another part of my brain to take over, knowing I'll never have the guts to go onstage. But I surprise even myself. Rocky around the edges, I enter the stage from the wings, trying to find a prop to hide behind and ready to panic or piss. As an initiation rite, Doobie-Doo blows me a kiss and then throws a small pail of cold water on me to set me in motion. Now I'm in a rage, shuffling sideways in a shiver. Once I'm in the cage, he locks it and I'm photographed, numbered, and framed by a waiting audience now hotly hooting their approval. When the tweeters, woofers, and boom-boom boxes burst like water pipes in a frost and the psychedelic lights explode to the steady flub-a-dub-dub of Creedence Clearwater's "Up Around the Bend," it's like being wired into a high-voltage box. My hair stands on end, my adrenaline speeds up, and I'm hoofing it up like canned meat in a heat for a bunch of peeping sleazeballs and hootenanny yahoos with a barnyard sense of humor. Am I animal, vegetable, or mineral? Who even cares?

The routine sets in fast. Finally I'm back in a comfy groove, a slot, a pigeonhole where I can roost—or be picked clean. I pay a girl down the hall at the hostel two dollars a night to keep her window unlocked so I can climb up the fire escape and crawl in, as the front door is locked at eleven o'clock sharp.

In the weeks ahead I find that boobie-dancing pays well—especially in tips that come raining into my cage. There's no power hype quite like it. This's where the action is, so I'm told by Doobie-Doo, who usually has a cigarette with me in the cool alley out back on my breaks. He slips me cold beers from the bar. I tweeze the beetles from his eyebrow line in the change room after work. So I decide to stick with being a dancing golden calf, letting horny males rub and shine my image with their eyeballs until they go blind in the glare.

One afternoon I'm waiting in the hall outside my room at the hostel to make a telephone call to Vito in the Falls. This East Indian holy roller in 1950 threads slams down the pay phone, disappears into her room, and emerges a minute later swinging a goddamn butcher knife.

"You were listening in on my call, I know you were," she shrills at me. "This morning at breakfast I looked at you across the table and saw the Antichrist! Now I must save everyone from you!"

I bug out of her way fast. It's like the wail of a wacked-out Baba Jaga voiced over "The Flight of the Bumblebee" coming after me. She chases me down the hall. En route I pull the fire alarm. Girls start pouring out the rooms in a frenzy. We collect a rip-roaring following down all four flights of stairs right into the swimming pool on the bottom floor, where I take a swan dive into the deep end. She comes in and thrashes toward me. Another drum-drumming starts up in my head. I see white and I clutch at her arm. We struggle in spirals. I give her arm a twist and she drops the hardware to the bottom of the pool. Then I squeeze my hands around her neck, push the bitch under and can't-won't let go. No way, José, she almost killed me. The white squeezing rage in my hands won't release her until a volley of hands beat on my back, an arm encloses and pulls on my neck, and I'm forced to let go and suddenly black out.

I'm dragged from the pool and dumped on the concrete floor, where I slip back into consciousness and cough up a lungful of water. My eyes focus on a spectacled septic tank standing over me, tapping her squeaky oxford. "What've you got to say for yourself, young lady?"

"I've got nothing to say for myself," I sputter, "but I sure as hell got lots to say about the goddamn lunatic asylum you're running here."

One of the dippy but lovable drones on the front desk comes to my rescue by explaining that this is a repeat performance for Battling Betsey, the hostel's official avenging angel. The holy roller is then promptly locked in her room and given a sedative until her psychiatrist is called. Our pool party breaks up.

Later in the evening I sit in my room at the window, smoking and watching a dope deal go down in the alley across the street.

Julie gets up to have a smoke. She can't sleep either. The heat is unbearable. The incident this afternoon really hit a nerve end in me somewhere. I'm not sure if I was accused of necromancy or antifeminism or what.

"I wonder if it's possible to have a normal relationship," Julie reflects, thoughtfully blowing rings at the ceiling, her voice a low resonating melody.

"Don't ask me. I'll never have one in my entire life. I wouldn't know what to do with the animal anyway."

Sensing my lack of enthusiasm, she grows quiet. She's down in the dumps, too. Her attempts to secure a job in broadcasting have drawn a blank. With her baritone voice, natural warmth, and brains she should have been a cinch.

She hands me a book of poetry by Sappho. After leafing through it briefly for dirty pictures, I hand it back. "Sorry, I only read Russian poetry and never anything about or by women."

"Why not?" she asks with alarm.

"I can't take them seriously. They're weak, archaic, stupid, and live for romance, third-rate soap operas, and door-to-door salesmen. Don't they realize it's all only a myth? I hate them, and if they were put in charge of the world tomorrow, the working-class grease monkey and the artsy Bohemian would wind up in the same concentration camp. I'd have to commit suicide or check out to Uranus."

"You don't mean that."

"I mean that more than I mean that."

"How odd. Usually we take all our frustrations out on men."

"Think again. I won't even work for a woman. Wanna know why? If they got on my case I couldn't just up and kick them in the nuts like a man. I'd be arrested for assault. They can't even fight fair. They're the enemy, not men."

"A lack of compassion for your own sex is unfortunate."

"When they start showing compassion for each other and get off the Christianity martyr trip, I'll give them an E for effort. When they cease to be controlled by their menstrual cycle, I'll give them a D for development. But as far as competing with the first sex, I'll never give them anything more than F—for futile. Men have given me the breaks in life, not women."

"Don't you ever want to be taken seriously as a woman?"

"I don't think so. I don't want to think about it. I'll leave it to men to figure out. They're smarter than I am—and stronger. If men were to take me seriously, they might just figure out how dangerous I really am and have me committed or rubbed out."

"But women aren't depending on men anymore."

"Oh, Jesus! Are you telling me I'm in trouble?"

"You could be. Maybe you should reevaluate your self-image."

"Why bother? It's in every man's pocket anyway. Why not stay a mud guppy and keep the buggers thinking they're chasing *my* tail when they're really chasing their *own*?"

This rap session fails to change my mind on anything. Or hers.

Two nights later Julie crawls into bed with me, puts her arms around my midriff, and explains that she's coming out as a lesbian. I explain that I swing so far the opposite way I can dress myself backward. She cooes and strokes my breast, stirring up a potent potpourri in Madame's labia minora. I stop her, afraid I'll submit. She says she understands and hugs me and we snuggle and talk until almost dawn.

Then one Saturday Julie takes me to a feminist meeting to suds up my brain cells. Just to gross out the witches' brood, I show up dressed as a five-dollar tart in a short tight blood-red dress, black fishnet nylons, three-inch spiked heels, hair teased to a frenzy. Julie is a little startled at my theatrics but laughs it off with "Every do-gooder in the place will be trying to get you off the street."

Women in a herd terrify me. Instantly I see class prejudice and smell hypocrisy. As a bobby-soxer I was ridiculed and alienated by society's troll set because my mother had the brass to get an education and later a divorce.

As soon as we're inside the crowded lecture hall, dozens of septic tanks and emotionally illiterate menfuckers come traipsing by in crew cuts, army boots, and parachute pants. Then from the university campuses come those who're dead from the neck down, the intellectual paper tigresses wearing polyester practicals and sensible geriatric shoes. This's going to be a definite alien encounter.

Speaker after squeaky-voiced pussywhipper take the podium to deliver yet another swan song. I tremble in my skin at the prospects they present. They know only how to play by the rules. How can they possibly survive in a world where men never admit there are any? Pretty soon everything goes in one ear and out the bottom of my stilt heels. I begin to itch in all the wrong places.

According to these stagestruck standard-bearers, I should find myself. But where do I start looking for the animal that spat instead of saying thank you? Maybe I should start growing a moustache and be done with it.

"Don't you want to be free?" they, the most class-conscious of the sexes, chant. No—I want to cost the world an arm and a leg for dragging my ass into it just to spread prejudice and folklore. "Don't you feel guilty?" they ask. You bet—for allowing myself to be so easily intimidated by the Daughters of Dogma who know no spiritual freedom themselves and must reduce man's universality to an aberration.

The only thing this revival meeting revives in me is my displaced sense of self and my gut anger. To show my allegiance to boobs-that-hang-to-the-knees, I'm supposed to throw my bra on a bonfire at Queen's Park. There's only one way of beating a man and that fortunately is in the bedroom. If another more effective weapon comes along, it'll probably be in the form of a pill. And I won't swallow it. If I do I'll be like the dodo bird, extinct. According to Genesis, the missing link in man's evolution is not woman, it's an entirely new third sex that was lost in an ecological burial ground: pity.

These explorations into the female psyche leave everything to be desired—mainly a man. If you're anywhere from normal to Scorpio rising, you have to leave so horny you're ready to ride a screw nail to Mother Earth.

Back at the hostel, Julie pours me out a glass of wine. She's always trying to get me to quit my job. "Don't you realize that you're being exploited?" she scolds playfully, pushing the same harangue she's been hanging on me for weeks.

"I know. I like being exploited. It's patriotic. It's the 'in' way to be. It's worth more points than working for United Fruit International." I don't believe I just said that but that is the honest truth. I try again. "Look, I like what I do. At least I'm being exploited by the mass public. I could be a civil servant and be exploited by the government. You're wasting your time trying to convert me back to the Order of G. In my books *goodness* spells *grief*."

"Goodness hasn't got a damn thing to do with it, as something, Mae West, I think, said. You know that," she snaps, making a face. "I'm thinking of your self-image. How you see yourself."

"I see myself just fine. It's other people who need the kick in the ass for not seeing me like I do."

"How about a change in environment—a move?"

"Sorry, but I'm too comfortable, too cheap, and definitely too lazy. Besides, I like having a live-in baby-sitter like you. Who'd look after me if I left?"

"Maybe it's time you learned how to look after yourself."

"What? And deprive you of the privilege of saving me? Never."

"Quit bluffing." She chortles with disbelief. "It's just another tight-assed gimmick of yours, pretending to be a pushover."

It only takes a week for Julie's advice to hit home. I've made enough bread boobie-dancing to move out of St. Trinians by the Strip and into a room on the top floor of an old Victorian house in the noisy transient area downtown.

My room's an eggshell-colored Cracker Jack box, cut in half by the slant in the roof. I have a deep repugnance for anything new from architecture to furniture. *New* is soulless, doesn't speak, and just sits there waiting for pigeon shit or a stitch-in-time to dress it up. People buy *new* to kid themselves, to keep in step with a "life-style" that rejects history as something to be mistrusted and feared. It carries the taint of memories that didn't make it to utopia, and germs that did make it all the way to the Holocaust.

As my search for roots in a specimen bottle is top priority, and as I always reach for *David Copperfield* when I'm in Blues City, I tack a sign on my door that reads THE BOTTLE FACTORY.

It never takes me long to make myself available. When the Newfoundlander kids on the bottom floor spy me hauling my two fully laden suitcases up the stairs with groans, suspended curses, and a rope, they offer to lend a hand.

The next day I hit the funky Queen Street shops and pick up two mini-dressers which I paint Chinese red, two low black tables, a mattress with an Iranian throw, and from the ceiling I hang two dragoned umbrellas upside down with colored lights inside of them. I set it all off with a Venus flytrap which I intend to train to eat religious fanatics, comic-strip politicians, and vacuum cleaner salesmen with even teeth. Then I spend two hours wading through the treasures in a used bookshop trying to put together a respectable library so I can educate myself and commence working on my family tree. The proprietor soon loses count of my acquisitions and decides to charge me by the pound. For a chaser to my shopping spree, I poke around Chinatown for accessories in the form of fans and a fat porcelain Buddha, called Wang. I use him to keep the door open when I need ventilation or as an excuse to invite in stray animals, lost Gogolian souls, or soddy street creatures.

A flea-bitten dog of no fixed pedigree sniffs out every room on my floor looking for a handout, and after getting into somebody's stash of pot, he pitters into my room, absolutely stoned, and sits at my knee smiling and rolling his eyes. He's the funniest contraption I've ever seen.

Since he's such a gentleman about being on the make, I decide to keep him and knight him Topper with the bathroom plunger. I water and feed him, then entice him into the bath with a trail of Oreo cookies, where I attack him with soap and a brush. When I open the door he shakes and tears through the house, howling like a Baskervillian reject. Later, he returns the gesture by bringing me in a mole for supper.

The house reeks of marijuana, patchouli oil, and the joss sticks that I burn in defiance of the rest. The interior is a picture gallery of pet phobias and range in style from black-light scratch pad kink to political top guns on a whistle-stop through enemy territory. I have breakfast with Mao Tse-tung and Che Guevara, bathe with a meditating Maharishi, and when I come home at night I'm greeted by a Rebel flag strung from the ceiling over the stairs.

The spaced-out Lotus-eaters are responsible for all the pot in the house and often leave trails of blood and human feces in the halls and bathrooms where their experiments with drugs misfire. They're always mincing through the halls like zombies in their Oriental kimonos, Indian caftans, batik shirts, and Mexican ponchos toking, toking, toking, yogasizing their brain cells, praising the good earth and the New Testament by *National Lampoon,* and praying to be delivered from the lemmings that they believe will eventually overrun the world. I wish to Christ they'd hurry up!

The Lotus-eaters and I have a love-and-ignore relationship. They represent the standard-bearer and I, the stretcher-bearer. They're coming up for air. I'm going down for the light. Sometimes we meet on the stairs. I invite them over for chili and then try to sign them up at the international headquarters of Revolutionaries Anonymous. On my birthday they throw me a party. Then after checking the calendar, they put Abbie Hoffman's name on the cake instead. I wonder if he ever received it.

There's always a congregation of kids from Newfoundland on the front steps or in Alec and Marsha's room on the bottom floor. Alec's a tall, dark, slender poet who strums a guitar and appears sucker-straight with his short hair and groomed moustache. Sensitive and good-natured, he proves a friend to all. Marsha's a bouncy high-strung brunette who talks at a hundred miles an hour and would eclipse Alec altogether if he wasn't so eclipsed himself.

I fall into the habit of dropping in after work for a midnight rap over a beer or a shot of rusty-looking 100-proof alcohol called Newfie Screech. If you don't blow the smoke off the top first, your shoes will melt and your nose will drop off in your hand.

One night I fly in from Club Morocco at two o'clock in the morning, zonked and rangy after a loaded evening. Before my shift I got swept up in a particularly violent antiwar demonstration en route to burn down the American Embassy. After nearly being trampled to death by an army of yippies gone mad and nearly being ridden down by cops on horses, I got shoved into what was left of a store window and spent two hours in an emergency ward getting my cuts patched up.

Alec is plink-plunking his guitar to a Gordon Lightfoot folkstrot, and Marsha is chatterboxing. Then this guy Vincent, a boarder I've seen on my floor, drifts in. He has straight blond hair to the shoulder, the chipped features of a Viking in season, moves his six-foot muscular frame as soundlessly as a cat, and has eyes blue and cold enough to freeze ice cubes in. They stare right through you, saying, Keep off. With the Apache headband and earring in his left ear, I take him for a druggie-pervert-weirdo. He's Alec's trusty buddy so nobody bothers with him.

Marsha's not hampered by his aloofness at all. She's constantly teasing him about his sexual ambivalence, trying to set him up with her friends so she can rate his brand of toothpaste.

I like to rib Alec and Marsha about their Newfie accents because to me they're an ocean apart from Canada. After they toss me a beer, I sit down on the floor. "C'mon, do you have a Frog, a Hun, or an eighteenth-century Limey buried down your throat?" I tease.

"None," Alec confesses with a grin. "How about a Spanish gypsy?"

"What have *you* got buried down your throat?" Vincent interjects, watching me stiffly.

"I dunno. Wanna have a look?"

"No, thanks. I might be tempted to stick something in it. You're so rich, why don't yeh stuff it yourself?"

"I got a pot to piss in and a window to fire it through, that's how rich I am, asshole. The pot *you* piss in is the same one you eat out of."

"Shove it, sister," he sizzles, and leaves, plunging through the door, totally pissed off.

"He needs a good fuck." Marsha giggles.

"I think he figures you come from money because of your style," Alec proposes, grinning to himself. "But don't pay any attention to Vincent. He's only back from Viet Nam a few months. He's still trying to sort himself out."

"I should have taken him for a Yank first off."

"Hell, no, he's a down-home boy, girl. He moved Stateside and joined the Marines at seventeen. He's been over there for eight years."

So maybe that's what makes me a little more interested in the bastard. Funny thing.

One evening after coming down from a set at Club Morocco, I get hit with a real shocker. Crunch's waiting for me at the bar. I don't even have brewing time to plan a strategic withdrawal or set up defenses, when he suddenly confronts me with a burnt-boot expression on his face. Though I'm clad up top, he's reading my party costume with disgust. I'm embarrassed, and what's worse, he knows and loves it. I let the bum speak first.

"Okay, smart ass. Buy me the drink you owe me and tell me what I'm doing here."

Stunned and shaky, I hail the bartender. "You're here on a mission."

"Wrong. I'm here to pick up the apartment key you took when you left."

"Forget it. I won't go back and rip you off. Don't you trust me?"

"I'd have to be twice dead and three times married to trust anyone. Now where's the key?"

"I threw it away," I hazard, knowing the key is a ploy and I'm the pigeon. "I'll pay to have another one cut for you."

"That you will, rabbit. And I'm sticking around until you do."

I was right all the time. He *is* here on a mission and I can't say I'm not secretly pleased to see him.

A few days ago I sent Vito a hundred dollars on the six I owe him and mentioned the name of the club I was working in. He must've told Crunch. Just as I knew he would.

Now that he's back I'm not sure how to handle him so I let him pick up where we left off and improvise. He decides to stay until the end of my shift and drive me home. Since he's clearly in charge of the situation I let him make me feel so uncomfortable throughout my remaining sets that my body moves like a broken marionette. Later, back at The Bottle Factory, he's not at all impressed with the noise and bedlam in the house. He doesn't understand that twenty-four-hour partying is a fulfillment of the national dream. Ten minutes in my room sipping a beer and he blows a fuse. "If yeh like abstracts so much, yeh shoulda moved into a cracker factory." The idea of so much flower power floating around irritates him, too, especially when he finds young marijuana plants growing in my window box. When I explain that I'm only baby-sitting them until their daddy, a kid on the next floor, gets out of jail, he grips my arm and makes me promise to pawn them off on somebody else tomorrow.

Then it's back to that damn key I took and threw away. Even a full confession of why I left in the first place isn't good enough for him. The bastard wants the duplicate made. Since I can't get to a locksmith until the morning, he's naturally obliged to stay the night as an excuse to bitch at me for dancing topless for a living.

Playing it cool, I pull a sleeping bag out of the closet and shake it out on the floor beside Topper for him. Ignoring it, he laughs at me and crashes out on my bed. When I order him out of it, he orders me into it, and fighting my feelings all the way, I give in. Then he puts out and I'm back in the passion pit in cement shoes wondering how I could ever have walked out on an armadillo.

* * *

We can't seem to ride the horse called Foreplay right through to the finish gate. Somebody's always turning up the stereo up full volume, or burning down the kitchen while doing hot knives over the stove, or doing war dances in the halls, or banging on my door for this, that, and the name of a reliable swami. Naturally it's my fault if someone needs a light for a toke or a book to find an astrological bed partner. "What the hell are you running here, a drop-in center for heads?" Crunch curses and pitches my alarm clock out the open window in a wild rage.

At the next intrusion Crunch jumps up without even dressing and whips the door open with murder in his eyes. It's Timmy, the bozo from downstairs in purple shades and an orange afro, now holding two soybean pancakes on a napkin—and he's completely wired. "Hey, man, can I see your daughter, man? She's the only one in the house with a tub of organic honey."

It's all I can do to stop Crunch from throwing him down the stairs. His verbal volley sends Timmy running for cover while I scream over his shoulder, "It's on the shelf over the sink!"

Crunch orders me back to bed, grabs a Magic Marker and paper from my orange-crate desk, and covers THE BOTTLE FACTORY with CLOSED FOR FUCKING BUSINESS. FUCK OFF!

Soon we're back at square one again and I decide it's time to give him a crash course on the sometimes erroneous state of my erogenous zones. "I don't feel a hell of a lot in the Sunday position," I confess.

"What the hell," he growls, pouring himself out another beer. "Aren't I big enough for yeh or do yeh have *another* hang-up I don't know about?"

"No, but my clitoris is too far up and my uterus is too far down on a tilt. One percent of girl babies are born that way."

"Jesus, I knew you were one percent of something," he says with the ghost of a grin.

"I'm serious."

"Okay—okay. So what do I do, rabbit? Try to push it back into place or screw with a complex?"

"Neither. Just pretend you're Neanderthal and haven't been Christianized yet."

He does.

The next morning I have a duplicate key made to his apartment in the Falls and Crunch makes me keep it. "Now I'll know it's safe and you'll know where to find me if you need me."

Something else I'm not supposed to lose. I'm not sure if I want the responsibility or not. Before climbing into his shitbox, Crunch says he'll be back as soon as he's over his parole in the Falls, which should take about two months. Then, if I'm still game, we'll take another apartment together. In the meantime, I'm on my promiscuous own. He leaves me on the sidewalk in front of the house with a tender morsel of advice: "If I ever find out you've been doing dope, I'll kill yeh with these two hands. Then I'll go after the fuckers who gave it to yeh."

And that's all there is to solving certain algebraic equations. Stick them in somebody else's mail slot!

To make extra bread to help pay back Vito, I sign up for moonlighting duty on weekends at The Slush Pit, a sleazy movie house on the Strip. Sometimes I play cashier in the glassed-in hut out front. Whores in mascara masks and hotpants knock on the window for a light. The bums bum a dollar to keep their amoeba status, floating face down in the grimy waters of social regress. Sometimes I make popcorn behind the candy counter and help fill the cup of the national budget with the sales tax, only to see that cup empty, as it headlines as the national deficit on the eleven o'clock news. Occasionally I fill in on chore-girl duty when the cleaning staff have their day off. Scrubbing down urinals, sanitizing toilets, and cleaning up after society's Monday-to-Saturday footrace seems the most appropriate way of spending Sunday.

The clientele of The Slush Pit are graduates of the city's jails, soup kitchens, and asylums. Sowhounds and stumblebums sneak in the back door and spend the day curled up in the seats, sucking on wine bottles like babies on the tit; crazies and perverts in baseball caps and jeans flex their brain cells and sex organs over porn, corn, and gummy old skin magazines; undercover narks in Serpico drag, complete with natty beards, shades, and brand-new runners, pop peanuts and nose out scuffs on the Ten Most Wanted List; shabby hustlers hang around the candy bar flashing jewelry stores from under their coats; and sugar-daddy pimps in white zoot suits, Panamas, fur coats, and alligator platform heels show off their stables of pitiful boppers. For a really nasty twist, now and then cripples and mental retards are stretched and gang-raped by rough-trade jaded queers in the men's washroom, a scuzzbowl that doubles as a fondling forum, cockadoodle glory holes and all.

The B-budget flicks range from horror heart-stoppers and kung fu acrobatics to porno prick-pumpers and spaghetti westerns. They come with garbled sound tracks and chewed-up celluloid that often hurls the victim from the hero's penthouse into the villain's torture chamber. The sex scenes come with bandaged perinea and the climaxes are announced with a pant and an "Again, Maximilian, please!" Then comes the beep, when the film snarls and a riot ensues with the audience ready to hang the projectionist up by the balls. As any filmgoer knows, a blooper as well as an obscenity is owned along with your hormones by the Ontario Censors Board; you have to go to Geneva for an official translation.

My comrades are a regular string of dingdongs. One space cadet is so zonked out she falls arse first in the garbage pail one night and repeats the performance two nights later. Wanda Weird shows us all her wedding ring, which she wears through her pierced pudendum. For contrast, Jigsaw Joan has a butterfly tattooed on the right cheek of her ass. Moccasin Mollie sells marijuana in the theater on her breaks, while Nancy Nipples balances popcorn boxes on her jugs and lines up Johns for the night. In the interests of sanity I take my breaks in the storage room cupboard in the basement. Every time one of the managers opens the door for supplies, I fall out with the toilet rolls, a flashlight, and a copy of Aristophanes in my hand.

The managers are only a little less nutty than the staff. Bobby's the dissident on the Karl Marx bandwagon, a freckle-faced, pumpkin-haired Archie with The Boy Next Door to the Armament Factory complex. He combs his hair with a waffle iron and walks like a constipated cat with a Homeric hangover—but he works cheap.

A week later two rival Chinese street gangs have a Bruce Lee rumble on the pavement outside the theater. One of them is pitched right through the glass of my cashier's cage and lands on top of me, breaking my nose. Bobby writes me off work because of the bandage across my face. Not caring what anybody thinks, I write myself back into a miracle play.

The next night a bum staggers up to the hut window, squishes his purple nose flat to the glass, cocks his head, and makes a face. "Whazzaadat?" he croaks, pointing a shaking finger at my nose.

I bend my head to parallel his. "Whazzaawhat? Whatdoyehmean—whazzaadat?"

"Whazzaadat ting?"

"Whatdoyehmean—whazzaadat ting?"

"Whazzaadat ting dere?" he croaks insistently.

I confess, "This's my whazzawhatwhazzadatingdere beak!"

Now the bugger wants me to pay him for the fractured grammar lesson. By rights he should be paying *me* but I fish out a deuce and shove it through the hole anyway.

Then I see the poor bastard get rolled by a pimply-faced punk. Before I can get out to him a Sally Ann patrol comes to the rescue and shoulders him off to the House for Sailors so he won't freeze off his whazzadats for the night.

Despite Crunch's leftover sign, my pad continues to be an on-call haven for slumming termites and rolling stones on the Mother Earth breadline. Somebody is always crashing on the floor in a sleeping bag for the night and eating into my weekly entertainment budget.

On Bloor Street one afternoon I pick up a ragged nineteen-year-old, six-foot freak from British Columbia. He's been burnt out by heavy drugs, the kinds that leave deep footprints across your brain cells. His vocabulary consists of about ten words, his speech is garbled, and he's able to think only in sudden unconnected clips of abstraction activated by an on–off switch in his head. I take the poor soul home, give him a meal, and let him sleep with me. He's as harmless as a baby.

For the next few days Robert follows me around like a lost puppy. Topper takes care of him while I'm out. But the pooch is unable to stop him from ripping off the rest of the house for food and radios to get money for drugs. In short order I'm up to my eyeballs in chili sauce. But I can't bring myself to turn him out onto the street. The only one who doesn't raise a stink is Vincent. He's got three big locks on his door. I keep wondering what the hell the bastard's hiding in there.

One night I come home racked out and peeved. Robert swiped twenty bucks from my wallet this morning, wiping out my weekly food kitty. Now he's curled up in a fetal position on the bed, facing the wall. He looks cold so I pull on an extra blanket and crawl in beside him.

The next day I rush off early, and when I return late that evening Robert's still asleep. Rolling him over, I give him a nudge but he won't wake up. His face is chalky and he smells.

In a panic I hit the hall and start banging on doors. Vincent's the only one home. He's out on the upper back veranda, stripped to the waist, practicing *savate*.

"Hey, something's the matter with Robert!" I scream.

Without a word he blots his face with a towel, flips it over his shoulder, and follows me inside. Calmly, he places a finger on Robert's throat, checks his eyes, and turns his arms over. "He's OD'd, baby. Probably last night," he concludes unemotionally, flicks his towel, and walks out. Just like that. Just like it's every day that somebody up and bites the dust in my bed.

A few minutes later Vincent reappears with a bottle of whiskey and a glass and pours me out a double shot. "Down." I'm in a state of shock.

Then the buzzed-out Lotus-eaters trudge up the stairs, their arms loaded with soybeans, crunchy granola, and organic rabbit food, their eyes glazed with happy dust. They straggle into the room and stand by the bed like a coven of Druids, come to deliver a eulogy over this human sacrifice with their goddamn oooing and ahahahing and gaad!

When I ask one of them if I can use his phone to call the police, he pulls a hairy. "Are you *nuts?* The pigs'll check out everybody in the house."

"So, I'm clean, fatso."

"Well, we're not. You won't be either when the pigs plant an ounce under your mattress. Why not stick him out in the alley behind the house?"

"I can't do that."

"Look, you brought him in here in the first place. So you get rid of him," Vincent says, leaving the room.

For the remainder of the evening I move about like a disembodied spirit caught up in a hysterical crying jag. Then, for therapy, I wash the kitchen floor twice. I bathe twice, burn a stick of joss, have two glasses of Chianti, and go through Robert's pockets. A dollar and twenty-three cents. All that's left of my twenty. He probably used it for his final hit. Apart from that there's no ID of any kind on him. So I scribble a note and pin it to his shirt pocket. "My name is Robert. I'm 19, Catholic, from New Westminster, British Columbia. Please find out who I am and send me home."

After the eleven o'clock news I grab Robert under the arms and drag his stiffening body, foot by grueling foot, along the hallway and out the back door. It's a hard move. I'm halfway down the back stairs when a clip from a horror film jumps into my head . . . didn't Peter Lorre and Vincent Price make a fortune in the undertaking business by killing-for-clients and using the same coffin for twenty years? I get so damn giddy I start laughing hysterically and nearly tumble down the stairs.

Suddenly Vincent opens the veranda door above and hollers down. "What the hell's the matter? Jesus, you're dumb—hey, hang onto that fucking corpse, baby! Christ, you've got the strangest goddamn reaction to death I've ever seen."

At this I howl even louder. He appears.

"I'll take him the rest of the way," Vincent allows, heaving Robert over his shoulder.

"Are we gonna leave him in the alley?" I ask.

"No. It's too close to the house."

Five houses down the back laneway, he deposits Robert on a bed of old rotting leaves and slips a lockpick from his pocket. Then he opens the door of a blue GTO parked beside a garage and hauls Robert into the driver's seat. To hold him in, I strap the seat belt around him, tilt the seat back so his head won't drop forward, and place his hands on the wheel. For a finishing touch, I take a pair of shades from the sun visor and set them on his nose.

"Aren't you overdoing it?" Vincent observes.

"I overdo everything."

Poor Robert isn't a person anymore. He was a statistic when I met him.

"He never asked for it, you know," I say quietly.

"Nobody ever the fuck does."

10

Life somersaults on and I'm back at Club Morocco boobie-dancing to the beat of the here and now, just another moving illusion in the fabric of reality.

After my last set of the night, I usually have a few cold ones for the road at the bar with the resident parasites and wait to get hustled. I love watching the bastards strike out.

This one night I'm chatted up by one of the sleazeball pimps I've taken care to avoid till now, a real Mr. Kool on the drool, on a punky-porno-power trip. Mr. Take-a-Piece Washington. He's a righteous pain in the ass. A Yankee dissident from The Big Apple and a first-class pimple on the Anglo-Saxon backside. This kinky-haired mulatto is in full Prince regalia—white derby, white three-piece suit draped with a fox fur coat, gold-sprayed Cuban heels, baubles on every finger, and a vinyl tongue he oils at all the girls in the joint. To set it off, he's wearing a gold Star of David around his neck which he didn't earn at Yeshiva. For some reason it hits me like a cross to a vampire. Who the Christ is this hypocrite trying to kid?

"Hey, baby. What's happening?" he shit-shoots, sidling on his hips in a slouch, drumming his manicured fingers on the barstool.

"What's happening is *you*, baby." I grin through cut glass, knowing he's out to press-gang dumb pussy for his stable, reputed to be the largest on the Strip.

He offers me a cigarette from a gold case and hails the bartender. Since middle-class morality is paying the tab, I order a double Bloody Mary on the rocks. To grease his ego ask him how he got his name.

"That motherfucking Nixon sent me a draft notice. So I sent it back with a photo of my bare ass and 'Take-a-Piece Washington' written across both cheeks."

"What'd you do then?"

"Fuck, baby. I grabbed the first bus out. And here I am, a business dude with a future."

"C'mon—you're just a third-rate pimp with a fourth-rate line."

"Hey, baby. I'm the Man and the Man is the most important social worker in the city. I keep the girls employed and the perverts out of Rosedale."

"Yeah, wonder boy. How far is Goshen, Israel, from Harlem, anyway, yeh fruitbowl?"

"What're ya telling me, girl? Ya don't like the color of my skin or my religion?" Now that he's got one foot in the stirrup, he's found a horse to ride.

"Both," I sauce back, wanting to crucify the peasant prince before he becomes a king. "What's it to you anyway?"

" 'Cause I don't like people hitting on my color or my religion, girl. I hurt and I get mean when I hurt."

"So you're a minority, big deal, big steal. You enjoy advertising it. Have you ever tried Islam on for size?"

"Did yeh hear what she's saying about the Man?" Take-a-Piece yips, raising his voice so everyone can hear him. "She hates Blacks and Jews and probably Micks and Chinks, too. Hey, this joint hires racists. Where the fuck's Skinner?"

The bartender asks Take-a-Piece to cool down and me to back off. But it's too late to parley. I'm halfway off my stool when Take-a-Piece seizes my wrist and salutes the room with "Can yeh dig that, folks? I just asked the lady here out for dinner. But she don't like nobody who ain't a white Anglo-Saxon Protestant. What do yeh think of this Waspy chick, brothers?"

He gets the snarling yells, the catcalls, the whistles, the table-thumping ovation he wanted. Before I can get away, Skinner sails up on the parade patrol, cuddles his puffy arm around me, and whispers, "That little shit drops a lot of change in here, fluff. Get him to hell out of here before he starts a bang-up. I can't afford the loss in glassware. Go to dinner with him or you're *fired*."

I hate being rousted and roasted by a back-street union man. But I play the game. I need the job. So Take-a-Piece drags me off to Lily Chong's in Chinatown. From the rock-hard egg rolls to the Mongolian grill, he tries to cozy up, by bragging on everything from how many times a night he can get his third leg to do the Russian saber dance to the hot jewelry exchange he runs part-time, from how many girls he has working for him on the street to his muckamuck connections, which must include the pope and the governor of Swaziland. I'm pissed off at this baked buttinsky but go along with the bull and keep hoping he'll drown in it. All it takes is a can of gold paint to make a brass monkey speak.

After dinner he insists I go back to visit his stable in an apartment on Jarvis, near Allen Gardens. I keep my thoughts focused on research in the raw and pray for fair seas.

His one-bedroomed crash pad is a sparsely furnished sandbox with Grand Funk Railroad and *Easy Rider* posters on the walls, and a floor model color TV in one corner. A gaggle of half-naked and strung out fourteen- to seventeen-year-old boppers are curled up on sleeping bags and blankets all over mattresses on the floor. There are butts, bottles, papers, empty cardboard takeout food containers, and garbage everywhere; the place's the bottom of a birdcage.

The bare-skinned boppers scurry up to their returned messiah, hugging his knees, whimpering and groveling for booze, drugs, and the chance to be his favored fuck for the night.

He quiets them down like a soapbox minister ready to lay his healing hands on the face of a leper. Then he starts collecting the nightly tricktake from each one. Sally's a hundred dollars short of the quota, so he slaps her across the face a few times. She thanks him for being so charitable, begs him not to throw her out, and crouches on her knees to kiss his hand. I'm sorely in need of a saw to remove the heels of his Cubans.

Take-a-Piece's plan is to tattoo a piece of my ass and lasso me into his corral but the cockeyed cowboy gets taken to bed himself by a bottle of Captain Morgan rum, which once sank the Spanish Armada, and he's soon fast asleep with five nude bodies, numbed by booze and grass, draped over and around him like a litter of newborn puppies.

A little after three o'clock in the morning I figure it's safe to split and slip quietly out the door into the street.

To dry out, I decide to hit an integrated nudist's sauna. It's empty at this fool's early hour with the exception of a Magooish yippie on the tier above, playing a Jew's harp. Wearing my towel as a turban, I lie down on my back trying to fry the fudge out of my system and ruminate life back into my limbs. After a moment the door to the sauna opens. A tall handsome Beau Brummel blows in with a black big-titted Queen of Patagonia, gold eyetooth, gold arm and ankle bracelets and all, her entire head a mass of tightly woven braids decorated with brightly colored beads and feathers. They've obviously just been to a native-style memorial bash for Captain Cook, and they're drunker than I look.

Beau Brummel crashes out on the floor and his queen, still in a standing position ready to sacrifice herself to the River Styx, straddles his waist. They clasp hands tightly. Placing his feet on her stomach, he propels her up into the air until she's horizontal. Then, regulating his breath and counting to himself in a series of wild aboriginal war cries, he does his push-ups facing godhead.

"What are you two doing?" the yippie asks in a troubled voice.

"I thought you'd never ask," Beau muses, a touch of tartness in the English accent. "It's an ancient rite practiced by the Aztecs to exorcize demons from the sweat glands."

"I think you both belong in a cage," the yippie announces with buzzed-out eyes.

"Well, as long as it's not in the same one as you, I think we'll survive and the human race will multiply."

The yippie goes back to his harp. For a grand finale Beau Brummel balances his queen up in the air a solid three minutes, using just one leg, before they both expire in a puddle on the floor.

Beau notices me watching so he introduces himself to me as Simon. "Are you trying out or trying on?" he asks with a mischievous twinkle in his eye, wondering if I'm really game or merely lame with a game complex.

"I'm in no condition to do either. I'm just trying to get a close fit," I say, trying to be precise about being untried and untrue.

"Touché, darling," he quips with a grin. "Only mad dogs and Englishmen go out in the dawn's early blight."

He drags his queen and me into the showers and we wash each other down. Then, wrapped in towels, we gambol out onto the roof to watch the sun come over Neill-Wycik College. Simon pulls a bottle of Lafite Rothschild 1953 out of a tote bag along with three glasses wrapped in tissue paper, a package of stale crackers, and a jar of Russian caviar, and we have an early breakfast.

This gifted Romeo posing as a mad dog turns out to be the real live blueblood from Limeyland, the Earl of W. He's moved to the sister-land to work on his anthropology doctorate with an anthropomorphizing twist at the University of Toronto, and to study colonial culture with a K.

He invites me over Saturday morning for brunch. His downtown pad is a real class act: rooms blocked off with ricepaper screens, ethereal watercolors on the walls, a futon, exotic plants in the corners, Union Jacks draping all the windows, and Queen Elizabeth viewing everything with a benevolent nod of approval. I'm fascinated.

"It's not where or how you dine, darling," he insists. "It's the eloquent state of mind you dine in." He presides Henry VIII style, over an 1825 silver tea service from his throne aboard a Louis XIV chamber pot. On the floor at his feet, I pay lip service to the lord of the manor and watch him smoke a cigarette through a silver holder without inhaling. "Always buy silver, darling, never gold. Gold is gaudy, gauche, and carries the stench of the marketplace." He's right. Ever since Moses, gold has been a beggar's booty, a trinket to self-make the selfless. My brain's in a whirl. For once I've been intellectually subdued and realize how much I'm intellectually starved. I love it.

Our friendship develops. Simon and I share the same ribald sense of humor and outrageous delivery. He's a Renaissance rake, a connoisseur of art and fine living, educated in private schools in England,

Switzerland, and Japan. I'm the wet-behind-the-ears peasant who's always up to her ass in hot water. The bridge that connects our grossly opposite backgrounds is a respect for diversity without pretentiousness—except in jest—and exchanging identities. He's witty, unpredictable, and rambunctious and I laugh at practically everything he throws at me. Over the next few weeks I fall in with every crazy thing he wants to do. He's the new light in my life.

Simon's tutoring is unparalleled. He says that I'm a barefooted barbarian but if I'm good he'll assist in filing down the barbs. I tell him he's a finger-up-your-nose snob but if he's bad I'll expose him to my Book on the Ploughman's Plunder and Everyman's Complaint. For a chaser he tells me that I walk like a trucker, that my bras remind him of Dixie cups and my briefs are early Puritan pull-ons right off the boat.

So in short order I'm introduced to a rich cultural canvas of opera, Tolstoy, the Russian ballet, Racine, Tennessee Williams, and Bach concerts. I'm also taught the difference between Waterford and Wedgwood. Actually there is no difference. They both hold water and lettuce juice and can be smashed with the same frivolity in the same fireplace.

Simon sneaks into my room one morning and wakes me up by blasting Beethoven's Fifth at top volume. Like a shot I fall out of bed and land at his feet in a tangle. "Good morning, darling. What a lovely day for a visit to the shops," he says, opening the curtains, handing me a cup of Earl Grey tea, and perching his buns on his shooting stick.

"You're a bloody sadist!"

"I know." He chuckles evenly. "Isn't it thought-provoking?"

We head downtown and enter a naughty-but-nice shop of women's lingerie, strictly haute couture. Start from the bottom up, that's Simon. He's adamant about changing my image from a fraught flower child to a judged Jezebel. He introduces himself to the troll on duty as M. Plentafook, my pimp, explaining that he's making seasonal alterations in accordance with the impending recession. "Could I see the fall line, please?"

The dingbat buzzard watches us with hostility, humphing, hawing, and pulling hairs out of her nose. Ignoring her, Simon wades through racks of frillies, lacies, and transparents, and fires his selections over his shoulder into my arms. Then he accompanies me right into the change room while Boxcar Bertha prowls to and fro outside. Simon gives her a malicious grin and coos at me, "Looks great in the crotch, baby," whisking the curtain closed in her peeping pugface.

My beastie-meanie friend then makes me struggle in and out of underwear I sometimes put on backward, corsets I can't get out of at all, negligees that cling to every pore of my skin, and bras that look like chastity belts, Siamese-style. "But ribbons come off in the wash and lace itches," my practical self complains.

"Nonsense, darling," Simon scolds. "Vanity is washless and ouchless. Suffer and love it."

Simon suggests I regard him merely as my patron. I prefer to regard him as my patron saint, a tab he admits finding "blushingly bearable." He becomes the platonic playboy brother substitute I've been waiting for.

In the meantime, Take-a-Piece keeps dogging my ass, trying to cozy into my confidence as well as my pants so he can stick me on his scuzzy payroll. He's always hanging around Club Morocco and The Slush Pit, hassling me and trying to get me fired. Word on the Strip is that he's put out a body contract on me. A hundred bucks to anybody who manages to get a heroin needle into my arm and delivers me to his apartment in a gunny-bag.

I decide to rap with a friend of mine to ask her advice. Sugar Allways is a black prostitute working the Strip. I met her at the snack bar in the back of the Strip's twenty-four-hour pharmacy where the street scrubbers meet at about five o'clock in the morning. At the moment she's parked at her usual spot on the street wearing her standard pukka shells, junky earrings, satin hotpants, and knee-length snakeskin boots. I hand her a bag of freshly roasted chestnuts and get to the point. "That hairpin is still giving me the gears. How do I shed him?"

"Why, girl, don't you know?" She laughs loudly, mocking me.

"Give the prick what he wants. Slip him a Mickey Finn and give his handle a kiss. He'll think he made you, come all over himself, and blow away like rain."

"But what if he doesn't come and I get a dose?"

"That's the breaks, girl."

Conflict within the house often comes from outside. It's well after midnight when a speedball with a frizzy hairdo turns up in the kitchen to raid our refrigerator and wakes up everybody on the floor when he can't find a stash of pot by cursing Canada, Henry Kissinger, and somebody called Monty Hall in a Brooklyn accent. Then hard-boiled Vincent appears at the door before any real damage is done.

"Are you a Yank, too?" screams the druggie.

"No, I'm a homegrown horseradish," Vincent growls in a mood to kick butt. "I've got a Maple Leaf tattooed on my ass. Wanna see it?"

Blindly the speedball goes for his throat. Vincent brings his leg up and bounces his chin off the top of his head. It's done so expertly that we're speechless. The Lotus-eaters, however, aren't amused and begin chanting in unison, "Don't be violent—there's no need to be violent. Peace, brother."

"Go fuck yourself, androids!" Vincent barks back, dragging the speedball to the back stairs outside and kicking him down head-first.

When the air clears, I make a dash for the back stairs. The speedball is crumpled in a heap at the bottom. I'm halfway down when Vincent sticks his head out of the window. "If you touch that son of a bitch I'll come down and lick you good. Get your ass to bed!"

"Mind your own business."

"Try me."

"I was just gonna see if he's all right."

"You don't pick people up off the street like stray animals. You've already got one fool in your bed to play house with. Why play for two? Get back to your room."

"Babykiller!" I shout, hightailing it through the kitchen toward my room. He grabs me just before I reach the door, whirls me around, thrusts me up against the wall, and squeezes my arm purple.

"Talking without a brain is dangerous."

"It's more dangerous not to talk at all."

11

Marsha invites me to a barnstormin' be-in two streets over. I trade shifts with another girl so I can take the night off and catch up on future shock.

The house is easy to find. It's on the eve of destruction. There's an acid rocking amplifier for a front door and an APOCALYPSE IMPENDING sign instead of a welcome mat. A party in this neighborhood isn't a gathering of eagles. It's a happening. Not only does it cut clean across all social classes, but it's a communal effort to levitate the world's consciousness with the power of brain waves. And it isn't a single-pad event. It's a territorial crossover with evolutional possibilities on the downhill slalom. It started in an apartment in the storm cellar and has now worked its way up to the widow's walk on the top floor where a Vietcong flag is flying at half-mast.

The dark, congested, smoky storm cellar has all the charm of a dungeon for killer gnomes on an exchange program with guerrilla theater: lighting by candle and entertainment by Nazareth, overamping. To keep psychologically paranoid, I keep following the neoned tokes and stokers until I blunt up against an alterpiece draped with a Judas Priest T-shirt and framed with candles: a blow-up of fifty million counterculture flies making love to a single pile of shit.

All the wingy wacked-out Lotus eaters from my house are here mixing with heavy metal bikers and student yippies from the Woodstock field trip that turned into a rally for media junkies. The command center is the floating bar operated by an iron butterfly handing out high-test orange sunshine, red hearts, cloverleafs, blue speck, emerald sky, strawberry alarm and white, pink and purple blotters. This's the magic carpet ride to free booze, free drugs, and free sex for anyone with three stomachs to consume it. I feel a fig overdressed in a pleasantly peasant potato sack and sandals because this's where the world's Levis come to die.

I go cruising to see if I can't find something that comes with a label saying DON'T TOUCH ME and a set of instructions. I whirl and run smack into Vincent. Nature Boy looks like he just tumbled out of the Mekong Delta, with his headband, green army fatigues, open flak jacket over a naked torso, and biker boots. Marsha gyrates up, throws an arm around my shoulder, and eyes Vincent. "What's happening, Mushy?"

"Nothing this side of something. Where's Alec?"

"Damned if I know." She laughs, unconcerned. "We're splitting up and I'm moving into my own pad next week."

"That's too bad. . . . I'm sorry."

"Don't be. It's been coming. All he wants to do is sit around in the dark playing his guitar, trying to tune in to the universe. Shit. I wanna turn on, not tune out. I wanna have fun." She takes Vincent's arm and wheels him away.

Marsha and Alec's breakup is just what the doctor ordered. I've had designs on Alec since I moved in. I love his shy sensitivity and am intrigued by signs of artistic temperament.

I find Alec in the middle of a group of bikers sitting in a circle and doing something profound with a giant-sized wine decanter and yards of rubber tubing. They look as if they're going to use him as bait to catch a duck-billed dinosaur in Toronto Harbor. He exudes that kind of innocence on the run. I nurse my drink in the wings, waiting to make my play, and get that hook out of his mouth. Earl, a dark dude from my house, handsome, tall, and doomed, comes up for a rap. He's heading for Bolivia in a couple of days to buy some prime dope. "For Chrissake don't get caught," I warn him. "Better yet, don't even go. Those bastards killed Che Guevara."

"I've been down there before. I know the ropes and I'm not a Communist. You?"

"No. I'm a Corinthian."

Hell, it isn't my fault. Simon said I must use this tag with Revenue Canada or Everyman on the street. It's certainly more divine than describing myself truthfully as an agnostic boobie dancer and part-time political aerialist.

I give Earl my best wishes and instantly forget him. Two weeks later I will hear that he's languishing in a Bolivian jail and his girlfriend has flown down and been unsuccessful in buying his release. He might still be there.

Doubling back to find Alec and caught in a squeeze of hot, sweaty bodies, I stumble into Vincent and spill my drink on him. Stiffly, he stares down at me and I feel like a child caught shoplifting. I apologize and am about to bugger off when he grabs my arm. "Having a good time?"

"My pupils were dilated when I came in."

"So I noticed. Forget Alec. He's not for rent or for sale and definitely not for you. He's so far out you'd never find him. If you did, you'd soon know it was a wasted trip."

My embarrassment is so acute, I forget that I'm angry. He pulls me into the middle of the floor where two other couples are having intercourse in a snake dance position. I've never seen him so ooolay exuberant and loose. He pulls me close through "Who'll Stop the Rain" and I'm suddenly intoxicated by his physical presence—the sweat matting his blond hair to his forehead, the patchouli oil and body musk emanating from his neck, and the strength of his thigh pressed against my own. Now I know what turned me off about him in the first place—the fact that he turned me on.

While the night is busy undressing my senses, Vincent is busy stripping me down to my vulnerability. After a few more beers and three rounds of making love in pantomime, I've regressed to the point that I'm ready to sprout fins and balance a red ball on my nose. Before I have a chance to fully disgrace myself, Vincent takes my arm. "C'mon. We're packing it in."

"But I didn't even get what I came for," I whine, balmy.

"Don't kid yourself. You probably got more than you bargained for."

He steers me outside to his bike parked in the alley behind the house.

"What's this?"

"A Harley 1200 Dresser."

"No. I mean what's its name?"

"I don't give inanimate objects names. I'm not a child anymore."

"How about a brain bucket—you know, a helmet?"

"We're only going for a spin. You don't need one. Get on and shut up."

He turns the key, jumps on the throttle, and we're off. Block after block, the lights keep blurring into swiveling strobes until I'm sure I'm riding a meteor through the Milky Way. The constant gearing up and down keeps me sober but wet in the saddle and full of teen worship. Thankfully, he pulls into a garage on Bloor Street for a fill-up. I complain about being cold. Vincent whips a black leather jacket from the carrier and I shuffle into it. There's an inscription on the back. WHEN I DIE I KNOW I'M GOING TO HEAVEN BECAUSE I'VE ALREADY BEEN IN HELL. NAM 1963–1971.

Farther on, Vincent gets miffed. "Stop blowing in my ear."

"I'm concentrating on not falling off."

We make for Yorkville, where the beatniks once grew beards to hem their life-style and later the hippies grew hair to give their life-style a new hemline. Now it's a free-loving, freeloading hot zone of selflessness, peasant-style; a home to thousands of castaways casting off their chains. Every yippie sitting on the sidewalk sharing a toke with his dog has got squatters rights and the market cornered on venereal disease, dope, and revolution. Only the pigeons have no status. I guess it's only normal to be neurotic, plastic, kinky, kool, oversexed, and a Big Pink Deadhead. Criminals, monks, lunatics, and rejects from the Church of Scientology have all the luck in the world.

Vincent follows the jam-up of tourist traffic past the Mina Bird, The Riverboat, and the groupie hangouts and head shops. Then he pulls into a no-parking area beside a convoy of mechanical chariots owned by bikers. "C'mon, baby, let's go and look at the fruits and the freaks."

The street sizzles with sweating denim, Rasta colors, and melting grass roots. The hype of flower power reeks from every tableload of earth beads, leather belts, head pipes, and East Indian cotton. We take sanctuary in a coffeehouse. While Vincent shoots the shit with a trio of scary-looking acidheads plucking the strings from a guitar, I fight my anthophobia by sitting down at a table with a swami and let him read my palm. According to him, my life's work will be found as either a farmer or a terrorist. Over a cup of espresso, I try to find the parallel between the plants in my window and the military books piled in my closet.

Then we leave and go on to High Park. We follow the pavement all the way to what I call Dead Man's Pond because it looks like a dandy spot to commit subliminal suicide. I sit down on the edge of the pond, remove my sandals, and dangle my feet in the water, waiting for the slime to coat my toes. "Why in hell did you turn up at that freak show?" I have to ask.

"What did you go there for?"

"Something to do."

"Liar. You went for the same reason I did—to get laid, without complications."

"If you're so afraid of complications, why not just stay at home and do it in the closet with a six-foot-tall mail-order bride. All you have to do is blow her up."

"Sorry, I'm not into plastics."

"You should have picked up Marsha instead. She's easy, uncomplicated, and she's nuts over you."

"She's a hell of a lot more complicated than you think and I don't like her style. She's got too much brain to her cunt and too big of a mouth in her head."

"Is that all?"

"No. She wears her jeans like a butch broad. I like my women the same way I like my meat—even if tender cuts tend to be stupid."

"Boy, did you make a mistake. Not only am I tougher than Marsha, I'm not nearly as stupid."

"Like I said—they tend to be stupid." He laughs so sarcastically I decide to change the subject.

"What are the women in Saigon like?"

The smile fades from his face. He lights an Export A in the cave of his hand, then releases a jet of smoke from his nostrils. "You want to know, don't you? That's the tragedy—you really want to know."

"What's the matter with that? I like to know about things."

"There's some things you're better off not knowing. Got me?"

"No, I don't 'got' you at all."

"Aren't you glad you can be controlled with a swat in the head?"

"Thanks a hell of a lot."

"Baby, I've watched you operate. You play at life from the sidelines, getting your ass wet, that's all."

"That's not true!"

He flashes me a cold stiff look and gets to his feet. "I'm not gonna argue the point. If you're smart, you won't make me. C'mon, let's go."

The ride back to the house is a hydraulic thrill. To keep awake I ruminate on my reputation. Maybe I've screwed myself onto a board I'll never be able to unscrew myself off of.

We take a brief detour to Rochdale, the Toronto headquarters of The World Liberation Front which hides behind "Head Hostelry International" for cover. They must have amplifiers at every window and turned up to the highest volume to create such a stentoraphonic nightmare. Now I know how they plan to take over the world—with a Led Zeppelin Mach wave.

While Vincent drops off a small package to one of the many floors above, I wait downstairs in the lobby, listening to a motor moron with a three-string guitar translate George Orwell's *Animal Farm* into conversational Hindi.

Eventually, Vincent and I are back at the boardinghouse. He invites me into his top-floor bunker for a nightcap, and intrigued that he would ask, I accept. After opening the three locks, he ushers me into his den of inhibition. There I experience a sudden chill. What a surprise—his shoebox is the epitome of surgical neatness: not one picture on the wall, a futon on the floor, an expensive Telefunken stereo setup, two fire-engine red double-decker tool chests—with locks—on casters made of heavy-duty steel, a three-foot replica of a

Cambodian dragon, and a table stacked with books. Everything has
a place except me. I should be hanging from the ceiling by my neck
like a deposed kitchen witch.

Without switching on the light, he pours a glass of wine. The room's
partially washed in a hoary glow fed by the light outside on the veranda.
Pulling a roll of bills out of his pocket, he peels off two and hands
them to me.

"What's this for?"

"A fuck. What else?"

I throw the drink in his face and he backhands me a good one
across the mouth that sends me reeling back into the wall, where I
hit my head so badly I whirl uncontrollably into the corner and then
cower there on my knees, holding my cut lip, tasting my own blood,
and buzzing in the brain.

"Don't ever do that again!" he says coldly, finally, furiously, moving
a step toward me. "I won't take it from you or any other woman!"

"Piss off, Babykiller!" I say, scrambling toward the door, but he
slams his body against me from behind, crushing me, knocking the
wind out of me, and putting on a full nelson, his fingers locked into
a fist behind my neck and his hip dug into the small of my back. I'm
rendered helpless, unable even to scream.

"I'm glad you can handle the truth, baby," he hisses, nipping my
ear. "Not many whores can."

In one practiced movement, he unzips the fly on my jeans and
slips his hand inside my bikini briefs and when he reaches the wetness
between my legs I suck wind for a minute. He moans satirically,
taunting, "Tell me that babykillers don't turn you on, baby. Go on,
tell me."

I'm breathing too heavily to answer and I'm too angry with my *noli
me tangere* to want to. He isn't a fiddler, a petter, or a pawer—he's
a button man, boorish and jingoish enough to be strictly army surplus.
The grand manipulator moves his middle finger up inside me. I jump
spasmodically and he hisses, "Stop faking it!" and returns to the button
and I hiss, "Stop fighting it!" and return to breathing heavily, ready
to lay an egg or deliver an oracle.

We end up on the bed by mutual consent and still he orders me to undress. Military men want their women gift-wrapped. Their women want *them hors de combat.* I resist.

"What gives?" He grins, yet irritably. "You don't mind showing your ass six nights a week to the freak majority. What have they got that I haven't? Or better yet, what have I got that they don't?"

"A conscious conscience."

Quickly, I tear off my T-shirt and jeans and he pulls me on top of him and kisses me, oddly, lingeringly, his tongue searching the vagina of my mouth as if for another little button to push. Not letting my lips leave his body once, I lick the anchor and chain tattooed on his arm, unzip his fly, and take his fatigues with me as I tongue the streak of lightning tattoo down his thigh to the miniature butterfly on the instep of his left foot. (He had them done, I will learn, in a drunken stupor on furlough in Saigon.)

Tossing his threads on the floor, I slide back up the bed sheet until I reach the Tropic of Cancer. "Is it all right?"

"Yes—all right," he articulates, barely, spacy and subdued.

Now it's revenge on the rebound and I'm in the driver's seat—I think. Though his military training has closed him like an orchid at midnight, just below the skin he's raging. Opening my mouth further, I accept what nature delivers, intent on draining from him the parts of himself he's been unable to commit, as if to waste, and nature proves not only generous but more than ready to rise to the occasion.

He plays with the strands of my hair falling across his stomach while shuddering in tiny intakes of breath and I wallow in the heat of his life source, trying to control the contractions that are turning his sex into knots of throbbing nerve tissue.

He's working against the tugging, pulling, pumping manipulations of my mouth, by deliberately holding back and extending and heightening every minute on the clock until it can be measured only in heartbeats. Frantically, I increase my rhythm and stride until he spends himself and somehow I spend myself and he's free and I'm free having watched him. He's almost as good as Crunch—almost.

We fall asleep, and about an hour later Vincent wakes, turns me over onto my stomach, rests his chin on my shoulder, and enters me from the Northwest Passage until I nearly bite the pillow to pieces, waiting for him to climax in my mind's eye so I can climax in the body physical. Then I discover he's playing at the same game, so we play it together until there's one eye and one body between us to beat the devil's tattoo all the way to second heaven. Still, he has Crunch's rage but not his depth or breadth. And it's not his fault that he can't match up. It's mine.

About five in the morning, I wake up to visit the Kitty Litter. Afterward, Vincent sleeping soundly, I decide to go investigating. I've got a nose for trouble, especially other people's. What's he hiding in this room?

Since the one metal tool chest is locked, I check the other one, which isn't, drawer by drawer. Nothing, but tools of every description and an alligator travel case. Miffed, I crawl over the boots in the closet and flick my lighter. The flame stands tall and licks greedily at a crack in the wall. My brain does a quick chemistry printout. What ignites? Paint ignites, glue ignites, sulfur ignites. I let the flame eat away at the crack and follow it down and across the wall until a square is created. The "wood" inside the square isn't wood at all but a plastic dummy door. Taking a jackknife off my key chain, I pry the door out of the wall. Since this entire floor was at one time an attic, I'm now right under the eaves of the roof. I flick my lighter again, and after probing farther, discover an arsenal. Handguns; pineapples; knives; nunchuks, the chains with balls on their ends; deathstars, those blade-pointed, kung fu throwing objects; and a steel box. It's not locked. I'm not surprised. Why lock a box that any expert could open if he was smart enough to find it? Inside, there's a number of credit cards and passports, some in languages I don't recognize. Finally, I come on an identification pass from the Department of National Defence, including a picture of Vincent, short-haired and in military uniform, along with a white plastic card with a green dot in the corner. It's quite possible that I'm in love with a fantasy figure from my childhood. But who? James Bond or John Dillinger?

"How do I look?" Vincent's voice is a rasp from the door. I jump to my feet, his flashlight blinding me.

"What's this for?" I mumble.

"In my business you live by insurance and favors owed, whether it's by the mob or the Feds. If anyone comes down on me I've got something to negotiate with."

"So this's Vincent's contingency fund?"

"That's it. If you open your mouth, you'll be dead within twenty-four hours. Guaranteed. I have favors I can call in, too."

"You'd really kill me?"

"If you come between me and a jail cell, you betcha. I'm not goin' down."

12

allout Friday night again and a foul-up on the subway line has me boogying into the job an hour late. A whistle-stop for the Ploughman's Plunder and Everyman's Complaint, the club's noisy, smoky, and prick-thick with the after-work rumba crowd. Noticing Skinner at his favorite table staged ringside, I beat it into the change room but a second later the hot tamale storms in after me, his toupee riding his bald spot sidesaddle. "What do you think I'm running here, a drop-in center for cheap meat? Yeh can roll in any fucking time yeh like? Get your ass out there and sell it!"

Ignoring him, I slip into my party tutu, throw on a sweater overtop, and scramble out to have a cold one while waiting for fill-in Wendy to finish her set.

My eyes do an instant double-take. Crunch and Take-a-Piece are rapping at the bar. I didn't even expect Crunch this weekend. Already I can sense overloaded circuits and smell smoke. Spotting me, Take-a-Piece gives me a kiss on the wind and says something to Crunch. Then my eyes cross and my vision goes haywire altogether.

Crunch's arm has busted loose from his body and Take-a-Piece's hat is flying and he's wheeling and doing a backflip right over a lounge table and taking the occupants with him. Before he can scrabble out of the confusion, Crunch hauls him up by the hair of the head and is batting his head against the bar when Doobie-Doo and another heavyweight leap on his back. I've never seen Crunch out of control and I'm petrified—of him and for him. Releasing Take-a-Piece, he kicks the heavyweight patron in the nuts and delivers a knockout blow before throwing him over the bar. Then he grabs Doobie-Doo in a bear hug and they go crashing through the crowd, upsetting tables and people and booze, and through the uproar I can hear, "He's the sucker who decked the Man! Get him!" and "The bastards got him outnumbered! Help him!"

The hammer's been tripped. All remaining hell breaks loose.

In seconds everyone seems to have muscled his way into the free-for-the-breakup. Hysterical by this time, I'm stumbling through the obstacle course trying to get to both Take-a-Piece and Crunch. Tables are going over and bodies under them, beer glasses are on the roll everywhere, and people are slipping, sliding and skating in the suds and going down under the volley of fists. A fat businessman is dancing in a pool of beer, holding his cocktail glass above his head. Someone knocks him and he goes down, taking three yahoos with him. Mini, the transvestite, is riding around on the back of a bullish Spartan, who's doing mad blind spirals trying to dump her while she's pulling his ears and beating him about the head with her patent leather purse. A cowboy snatches the Rita Hayworth cold wave from her head and it's flicked about the room like a dead rat carrying a disease. Finally it lands in the lap of a drunked-up monkey suit on the floor crying in the corner who uses it to wipe the cigarettes from his eyes. One man is being choked by his own tie and another by his beard and still another is down on all fours, puking, while his bloody hands are being stomped on. Finally I manage to tag Crunch's arm just as he's about to tackle another spar mate. Paying no attention to me whatever, he picks me up bodily and sends me skidding across the wet floor on my bottom. I only stop when I hit the bar. Now I'm holding Take-a-Piece's unconscious head in my lap, trying to control the blood draining into his ears and mouth by swabbing it with the sleeve of my sweater. Nearby, Skinner is using his overturned table as a shield until a body tackles it and he's buried underneath. And Wendy is still boogying in her cage, oblivious to her surroundings.

At the first scream of a siren, the war immediately shifts from man against man to the people versus the motherfucking constabulary; and they the people, now dubbed the rabble, heap tables and chairs into a barricade and when the goon squad from 52 Division storms in, their arrival is hailed with bottles, ashtrays, glasses, and corks released from champagne bottles.

When this light artillery is used up, the rabble, now those Commie Criminal Types, start throwing the tables and chairs and then themselves at the M.F. Constabulary, now those Fruity Fascist Finks, who move in with their clubs swinging, beating on heads and faces while the sound system's pumping out the Beatles' "Let It Be."

Crunch is now on the other side of the bar wrestling with his own image—beyond my help. Terrified of being jailed, I leave Take-a-Piece and manage to slip out the door with the other girls before the cops tighten the net. Then I hole up at The Slush Pit for an hour before calling Skinner to get the news. Crunch is in jail along with forty-four others and Take-a-Piece's on the critical list at Toronto General. The creep had tried to sell me as a trick to Crunch, not knowing that he was my pagan saint.

Shaking badly, I rip the bloody sleeves off my sweater and grab a cab after lighting a cigarette, not even stopping to consider that there might be such an institution as visiting hours. I'm turned away at the door.

The next afternoon I show up at the Don Jail, that soot-covered Frankensteinian boot factory standing on a barren hill right in the heart of the city on the putrid banks of that open sewer known as the Mighty Don River.

Apparently conditions in this pisshole haven't changed since the days of the Boyd Gang and my uncle Teddy. Water still seeps through the unpainted stone walls, floods the cells, and mildews the bedding. The lighting hasn't been improved since Edison and is so poor that *everything* the inmates read is considered yellow journalism. You can't have a shit without expecting a rat to climb the plumbing and take a chunk out of your ass. The cells are so overcrowded you go to sleep sucking somebody's big toe and the heating system is used solely to warm Twinkies for the staff. The damp, ominous cold creeps into my bones like necrophobia.

I'm early, so naturally I'm reduced to pacing, smoking, and ruminating on a plan to break Crunch out of this criminal hatchery. I despise waiting. Impatience is my worst failing. I can't deal with the animal at all unless I've been bound, gagged, and locked in a shipping crate with a Bombay address.

The redneck guards are withered bucks in damp, crumpled uniforms. If they hadn't roped these glory jobs out of thin air and deep water, they'd be pushing a broom on the poop deck of a scow in the harbor or emptying slop pails after chimpanzees at the zoo. Not one of them has a brain bigger than a mouse dropping. But then there are only two prerequisites for the job. They have to be able to fit into King Kong's jockstrap and bark on cue.

They do their bullying best to intimidate me by puffing themselves up into gaseous doughballs that no doubt deflate when exposed to toxic street air. The bums quickly succeed in driving me into tears by telling me that Crunch is a bad onion who's destined to go up for life.

"Go suck eggs!" I finally burst out, turning into a bad onion myself.

"Now we know what end of town you're from, don't we?" hoots one heavily jowled Judas.

"Yeah, just two doors up from you."

I even packed Crunch a whole bag of goodies, from dirty girlie magazines to the hot side of a razor, but the bucks won't let him have them and suggest I leave everything behind.

"Go ahead and take them!" I concede huffily. "You look like you'd need help jacking off anyway."

They exchange empty grimaces and the Judas says smugly, "How did such a sweet-looking kid get such a dirty mouth?"

"From getting screwed up the ass by Neanderthals like you."

Presently Crunch is brought into the booth. There's an impoverished cast to his eyes. I long to put my feet through the glass and hug him but instead I have to talk to him through a glassed-in cubicle with phones. He shifts uneasily in his chair, starts, and shoots straight from the gut. I'm not supposed to say anything I don't want repeated on the six o'clock news. The lines are bugged and every word taped and used to entertain the pigs at their weekly underground bat-a-ball banquets in a bungalow in North York.

"I knew you'd turn up sooner or later," Crunch says on the crisp. He's not even shocked to see me. Somehow, I figured he would be— I know I was.

"You've gotta tell them what really happened," I argue.

"I have nothing to say, rabbit. And neither do you."

"But it's my fault. That prick should have been wearing his balls for a cap weeks ago."

"What are you trying to do—give me a complex?" he fires off, angry. "Rabbit, I told you before—I'm raked over coals. Any way you want to look at it, I couldn't stop myself and they're gonna send me up. I'm not dragging you into it, too. The publicity would ruin everything between us. You'd change—I don't want you to change, rabbit."

He's grabbing at these very slimy stone walls that surround him, trying to find a ledge dry, wide, and sturdy enough to support him, so he can spring up and over the top. He not only wants to see daylight, but wants to lose himself in its void, its unfathomable nothingness, and find himself reborn.

Now he's going up on an attempted murder rap that his lawyer is trying to get reduced to aggravated assault. He could get anywhere from three to seven years, depending on how the hapless Take-a-Piece does in the hospital. The corker: it took five pigs to get him into the cruiser when he was arrested and he broke one of their noses, so a minor charge of assaulting a police officer's pending as well.

Before I leave, I promise to have a chat with his lawyer and come back tomorrow. The whole thing is so senseless and ridiculous and it's my fault crime pays.

I grab a cab downtown to see Crunch's court-appointed flunky. Mr. Summers has a tacky little office on Parliament Street. The coatrack in the corner is the only comprehensible prop I can appreciate. After a five-second rap with his secretary and her bleached-out brain and Max Factor smile, I long to stick a hat on the rack and dance the bastard out the door and under a streetcar.

"If you're not testifying in this case and not related to the defendant I can't see why you wish to see Mr. Summers," she whines in her nail polish.

How beautifully candid I could be at this moment. I settle for being crudely creative—when candy won't work, try beef jerky. "Look, the mug raped me a month ago. I'm pressing charges against your boss for helping him get a parole and allowing such a monster out on the street."

Like a shot I'm in to see Summers, a dumpy spectacled blimp with the teeth of a shark. A lawyer doesn't have to worry about being bugged by his client if he's in the lockup. But if he has friends on the street—beware!

"I'd love to put you on the stand," he confesses. "But Crunch is my client and according to him you don't exist—and my client's word is gospel. You should be relieved that everyone at the club covered for you."

"What do you think I am—stupid? They were saving their own asses on orders of the manager. He doesn't want it on the record that the club is an on-call meat and drug market. Is there nothing I can do?"

"I've got a witness who can't be a witness because the defendant refuses to defend himself and I've got the testimony of a banged-up three-cent pimp that Crunch attacked him for no reason. What do you want from me, sweetheart?"

"When Take-a-Piece recovers, I'll go to see him. Maybe I can get him to change his mind."

"That's the worst possible thing to do," he insists brusquely. "It'll only aggravate the situation. Stay away from the shit—do a disappearing act until this thing's over." Then, noticing my frown, he changes. "Hey, I'll get him off. That damn pimp has got a record a mile long. I'll see if I can't dig up some more dirt on him. Maybe I'll get lucky and one of the girls in his stable will talk." He hesitates to give the information time to sink in. "Say, what're you doing after work tonight?"

"I'm breaking into a florist's shop," I bite back. "I intend to steal a thousand pink carnations and have them sent to the Toronto General with your name on them."

He smiles thinly, too stupid to see the metaphorical equation, too smart to want to. When I leave the office minus the coatrack and my sense of humor, there's a funereal smell in the air.

Crunch's trial date is pushed ahead all winter and the day finally arrives in early spring, a perfect day for a hanging. Courtroom No. 21 in the Old City Hall is an airy, antiquated edifice with highly polished marble floors and varnished banisters. I have a sudden rush of panic. Courtrooms are at the bottom of the pit called hell. I keep having nightmares about being put on trial in a dark temple on the banks of the River of Forgetfulness.

This is the operating room for muckraking mortals, where injustice is cut out of a man with a double-edged knife, the pieces nailed up on the wall under a Greek-motifed sarcophagus, and the man's wound plugged with newsprint and regret.

I take a seat in the cheering section. Mr. Summers comes over to console me and himself. "Don't worry, kid," he whispers reassuringly in my ear.

Why's he so damn fidgety then?

Crunch is brought into the prisoner's box and I start shuffling in my seat. Crunch sits down quietly and dumbly, his back right against the bench. He doesn't even glance my way.

A tin soldier announces, "All rise."

I'm waiting for the ceiling to descend, the overweight magistrate sails in, the eternal bat in the rafters. Watching him grunt himself onto his heavenly throne, I remember that even Ulysses wasn't conceived by the human imagination to be judged by mortals.

Two witnesses from Club Morocco start the cradle rocking by spilling their guts on what went on at the club that night. They're grilled in exhaustive detail but their dental records aren't even mentioned.

Mr. Lyons, a spectacled potatohead, is put on the stand. He's a psychologist on the prosecutor's payroll. He testifies that Crunch has definite antisocial tendencies and is unable to function on the street. Mr. Summers gives me a practiced smile, manufactured in the Law Society of Upper Canada's theater arts program. I long to fire my handbag at his head.

There's no one at all to intercede on Crunch's behalf. It wouldn't do his case any good even if he did agree to let me testify. I'm that skidkid who hangs out with trolls, gnomes, piggies, and other disgracefuls. If the buggers started sticking pins in me on the stand, I'd cut loose and make an ass out of myself and put him further in the soup.

Into the limelight steps the prosecutor, a tall, gangly broccoli with permed hair and horn-rims. He wakes the magistrate by ah-hemming and clearing his throat in stereo, which is the signal for everyone to stop breathing. Take-a-Piece Washington is trundled into the courtroom in a wheelchair, which is unfortunately not connected to a high-voltage box with a switch. His head is in a cast and he's doing his pimply best to play humiliated victim. When he places his hand on the Bible I expect it to melt. His testimony is a sugary piece of handcrafted fiction. Mr. Summers's cross-examination turns into a slanderer's snub, frequently attacked by the prosecutor and seconded by the magistrate. The court makes it clear: the banks are closed and the churches are open and this's Take-a-Piece Washington Day.

The pig who Crunch assaulted takes the stand and gives the court his perdurable penny's worth using a Detective Friday voice box.

After an hour's recess the actors in this dream play are brought together once again. Crunch is told to stand while the sentence is passed down. The magistrate spiels off a weary, pumped-up tirade, dragging through an oyster bed, about how Crunch is still unable to cope in society. Unable to cope myself, I'm shaking with rage and alarm. Crunch's eyes sweep through the spectator's section and fasten onto me. I can barely breathe. I'm weaving in my seat. I think I'm gonna be sick.

Thirty months.

Crunch is taken out and I'm still standing in the aisle, shell-shocked, ready to make out my last will and testament. Instead I pen a message, rolled up in a fin, and pass it to a Sally Ann corporal, choking up a little. "You don't have to pay us for this service, miss," he says in a kind voice.

"Fine, accept it as a donation then."

Rubber from the neck down, I gulp a coffee and three Anacin in the hall outside. I'm shaking bad, my vision is blurring, and I'm on the climb to a blowout. The corporal returns with a note written with a dull pencil on a brown paper bag. "Please see me back at the Don today. Sorry. C."

When I see Crunch at the clink in the early evening, my inner wires are tremulous and taut, ready to snap altogether. I've prepared a tidy little list of things to say—otherwise I'll draw a mental blank. There he is, sitting on the other side of the glass, waiting for me to pick up the phone. Squeezing the note into a ball in my hand, I put on a smile. "Hi—how're you doing?" It's so corny I kick myself.

Crunch is the one who clams up. He doesn't seem to mind if I beef up the conversation with sugar or horseshit as long as I keep it going. There's no way I can reach him. His world is becoming smaller, and without him mine is getting bigger.

Awkwardly, we play out this highly charged soap without script, director, or key grip. I don't want to mess him up, pressure him into making decisions he doesn't really want or need. His intentions are the same as mine. What do I know about responsibility or relationships anyway? The chasm between us is mammoth, held together by a single unspoken word. Since I'm the one on the street, the onus is on me. All he wants is my promise to write him once a week, keep away from perverts and drugs, and not take a hike to the altar. Though I chuckle at the prospect, he's as serious as salt on an open wound. So I agree. It's a toss-up if we'll ever get the kinks worked out of this mother lode or even if it's worth saving at all. I don't even know if we're a twosome or an and-then-some because we don't really *know* each other. All I know is that all we've got is each other and I guess that's enough to make it matter.

For a lyrical spin-off, I make monkeys out of all the guards, giving them ludicrous nursery rhyme names, imitate them in caricature, and attribute to them far-out social diseases that they've already attributed to the inmates. Crunch laughs hollowly and keeps wiping grimaces from his face. When the guard appears and announces visiting hours are over, the reality is crushing. He's being pulled away from me and it hits me full in the gut and nearly throws me into a fit.

I've just lost the only insurance policy I've ever had against getting involved. Crunch gave me an excuse to say no to the marriage broker and yes to a wild night on the town. Now on my sweet own.

The street outside is an extension of my emptiness. I try to put a world back together again. Crunch will be okay. He's an Aries, the strongest male in the zodiac. I only got that gem out of him by using bedroom blackmail one night. He wouldn't tell me before, the slob, figuring I'd dump him if he was born in the wrong month. Had he been one of those sleepy Cancers or strung-out Fishies, I damn well would have, too.

13

And so every week I religiously scratch out funny newsletters to
Crunch, including cartoons, and ongoing bulletins on the nonsense that regularly goes on in my life. For all my secret babbling
I skip the prison censorship by writing Jo metaphorically that my letters
can only be understood by an expert. These letters become a work of
art for me and a migraine for Crunch. I think about them for hours,
drafting them at work or in The Bottle Factory. For the next couple
of years I curse and love him in livid code. He says that he spends
hours before lights out, penning epistles of his own. That's quite a
leap for him. He could neither read nor write when he went up for
his last stretch.

I visit him twice in Kingston before he tells me to come only every
couple of months and to write longer letters. He's the one on the
inside and I'm the one who turns hostile. I want to bite all the guards
and leave a bag of dynamite at the front gate along with a lit fuse. I
talk like a sailor and begin thinking like Ma Barker the minute I'm
in the door. I don't understand this world of walls and locked doors
any more than I understand the prison I'm currently living in, inside
myself.

My relationship with Vincent works because it isn't bred of need.
We have a comfortable arrangement, comfortable because I don't have
any mental or emotional battles to fight. I know what's expected of
me and let him do all the legwork. I'm available only when he wants
me. I work and sometimes exercise my hormones between the bed
sheets. Since I hardly ever see him, when he does come knocking on

my door after midnight, it's a worthwhile wingding. I would never have the brass to knock on his door. Unless a bee stung me. It's not only plausible and pathetic but a fact of life that I do pick up a number of bites.

Vincent has his quirks, too. He deplores the chic and the made and according to him the two greatest evils in the world are hypocrisy and pseudo-intellectuals. I learn to adapt to his moodiness, tendency to nit-pick, droll cutting remarks, and the condescending smirk that haunts his every expression.

To celebrate the official coming of spring, the Lotus-eaters build a shrine to Dionysus in the backyard with Popsicle sticks, dress their hair with potted mums and lettuce leaves, set fire to their income tax forms and a copy of *The Guinness Book of World Records*, and then dance around it holding hands and chanting that old top-of-the-chart hit from the bubonic plague, "Ring around the Rosy!" in Latin.

To convert me into their coven, they spike my homemade rhubarb sauce with marijuana while I'm out on the back veranda watching Vincent and a Korean boy practice *savate*.

I've always been terrified of dope, knowing that my voltage level is too high to handle it. A buzzing starts up in my polychromed head, complete with a foggy set of values. In no time I'm spinning like a top. Having just read *The Seven Pillars of Wisdom*, I crawl into the sink to bathe, believing I'll be reborn, and to exhibit my telekinetic powers by making the table rise and Topper's tail drop off. Then, to test the immortality of Isadora Duncan, I try to glide off the back veranda on a stray air pocket. Vincent grabs me at the railing before I make the fatal plunge and is forced to smack me out.

When I wake up in his bed, he's sitting cross-legged on the floor, talking in subdued tones with a buddy of his, Tommy Running Deer, an Indian boy he met in British Columbia after he left the service. They spent all last summer touring the west coast on Vincent's Harley before cruising east to Teronna. Tall, lean-hard and reed-slim, Tommy's, a Micmac from eastern Canada with straight shiny shoulder-length hair, a leather headband, and a bear's tooth around his neck. Not only does he speak his own language and Algonquin fluently but he's a skilled canoeist, trapper, fisherman, sculptor of stone statues, and has his bachelor of sciences degree. Presently he's winging it, trying to fit comfortably into the white man's lie, while at the same time taking a pilgrimage through his heritage.

His tribe, numbering about four thousand throughout the Maritimes, has adapted to the modern world surprisingly well but Tommy still suffers from two maladies, *badtreaties* and *reservationdoom*, invented by the great white hunter to make him feel guilty for bowing down to the good god Manitou instead of a John A. Macdonald Moosehead.

Vincent and Tommy are planning to nip up north for a few days on business. The warm weather has made my genes anxious for some kind of action so I pester Vincent to take me along. Observing me thoughtfully for a few minutes, he strokes his inscrutable lower lip with his thumbnail and that contagiously controlled expression I will never know how to take. Then he exchanges a sly glance with Tommy, voracious with nuance. "You just go down asking for it, don't you, baby?" he chides accusingly. "Okay—just this once. But don't dare ask me again. As a rule I don't mix business with pleasure."

"Neither do I."

"You can't help it, baby."

Saturday afternoon I shove some clothes into a rucksack and wait out on the front steps. The Newfies have offered to dog-sit Topper while I'm away.

Vincent told me to dress like a groupie on the Lawrence Welk circuit in a cotton sundress, not very practical for land cruising but coolly comfortable for the heat that's hit the city.

In short order he pulls up on his Harley and Tommy swoops in at his side on a blue Norton Commando. I climb on behind Vincent and we're off.

I haven't got a beggar's clue about our destination and refuse to take a swat in the head by giving in to that demon curiosity. Vincent isn't partial to twenty questions.

Tommy winks at me, teasingly, a secret code between us meaning,

Stay cool, everything's fine. It's hard to keep my eyes off him. He's
wearing nothing but sun-bleached blue jeans and worn moccasins and
should be riding with Geronimo or leading a rebellion at Wounded
Knee.

After three exhausting hours we pull into a big dirty yard that I
wouldn't put a pig in to wallow. The house was once a bungalow in
a rural setting with a barn and outbuildings. Now it's a bungheap
sitting splat in a communal dumping ground of old engines and car
and cycle parts. A row of big heavy choppers glint menacingly in the
setting sun. Vincent doesn't give me a chance to ask him why he
booked me into the brain cell of a night crawler instead of the Hilton.
Quickly he hustles me across the courtyard.

Inside, skunk-breathed men, or chimeras, depending on the cave
of light they emerge from, lounge around in denim and leather,
shades, junk jewelry in Teutonic knight tradition, flashing tattoos at
one another. They're excessively hairy and dirty. Across the room are
three little mothers in Medusa Girl drag, two bleached-out blondes
and an orange-haired frizzball with Andy Warhol face masks, wearing
tight popped-out T-shirts, beaded phosphorescent vests which are
probably radioactive, skin-tight black leather pants, and purple nail
polish to match their lips. It's a toss-up which one rides bulls and
which one wrestles tigers in their boudoir rodeo. Clearly, they eat
nails for breakfast and wash it down with tar or turpentine. For lunch,
I figure, they take bites out of the furniture and for supper they eat
each other. Jesus, what a mob of cannibals we got here!

The living room is done in wormy, sloughing couches and chairs.
Its linoleum floor is worn through to the pitch and littered with scraps
of remnant carpeting and food. Particleboard–covered tables are laden
with beer bottles, nuclear meltdown in ashtrays, and magazines. Garbage is piled up in the corners. The room smells of rotten meat,
decaying brain cells, unwashed flesh, sour booze, and urinated clothing. Everything left living here must have a healthy dose of the itch
and no medical insurance; even the rats have packed their bags and
moved on. The background music, provided by an expensive stereo
system in the corner, booms out frontline Black Sabbath at top volume.

The roaches are dancing on the floors, the flies are unable to light on the shaking walls, and the hops in the beer bottles are hysterical, begging for release. The exciting news is that this shrine to copping out would be a cinch to clean. All you'd need is a match and a can of gasoline.

Vincent did this to gross me out. I feign indifference with lightning-struck calm. The bastard doesn't know that Vicki and I used to thumb rides back from town when we were only fourteen and the only ones who often picked us up were bikers who dropped us off later with everything intact except for numbed nostrils.

Suddenly the door blows open and this big motherfucker stomps in. That's the only suitable way to describe this fat fish that broke the line, sank the boat, and drained the bay. He's red-haired and bearded with craggy brow bristles, an eye patch, a buckskin jacket, and a missing arm. The shark who took it probably choked to death. He is addressed by the others as Bear. It takes no brains to figure out that he's the chief of this tribe of Cro-Magnons. A mean-looking black German shepherd trots faithfully at his heels, waiting for another human leg to be thrown his way.

Heartily, Bear slaps Vincent on the back and grasps Tommy's hand like a lifeline. An animated conversation ensues, too garbled and distant to interpret. A few minutes later they glance in my direction and Bear rubs his beard speculatively, as if wondering where to lay the odds next.

He's interrupted at the salt lick. A perpendicular wooden box is then trundled into the house and an assortment of handguns and shotguns are distributed to the fellowship. This must mean they're going fox hunting, Bronx-style.

Vincent tags my arm on the way out. "I'll be back before morning. Don't sweat it." He leaves me like a sacrificial lamb at a tribal meeting place. Everyone buggers off, including the three not-so-Supremes. I'm left with Bear and Snake, a stringbean who's an interbred cross between Rasputin and Tiny Tim. Given the amount of grease running down into his catty eyebrows, he's not going because he'd slide off the seat of his bike.

Dumbly, I stand at the window watching the convoy zoom out of the yard. After which Bear opens up in a woolly voice from his armchair throne in the middle of the room. "Sit down!"

I obey and slip Buddha-style to the floor. Snake lops the caps off some beer bottles, five in a row. "Can't yeh do that with your teeth?" I tease, trying to be friendly. "In the movies they always do it with their teeth."

He tosses Bear and me a beer and then takes a slug of his own. "Who does? Who the fuck, who?"

"Amos Magilicutty."

"Never heard of him. Hey, Bear, you ever heard of the fucker?"

Bear burps from the gut, draws a fleshy hand across his mouth, and rolls his eyes. "She's making fun out of yeh—can't yeh see that?"

Snake sneers and sucks in his cheeks until they're part of his eyeballs. "If she is, I'll pulverize her."

"No, I'm not," I argue frantically. "I'm making fun out of movies and bottle cap companies. Both should come with instructions, don't you think so?"

They exchange empty shrugs. Then Bear watches me critically, his lips twisted with sour amusement, while Snake eyes me with black suspicion. They're both trying to frighten me. What they fail to understand is that I was born phobic.

"Want another beer?" Bear suddenly roars at me.

"Uh, okay . . . I mean, thank you."

"I haven't even given you anything yet. So what are yeh fucking thanking me for?" He gulps and fixes his iron eye on me.

"For nothing . . . I'm thanking you for being a sweetheart and giving me something not to thank you for."

"Christ, she talks funny," Snake brays. "Can I pulverize her now?"

"No, she's mine to pulverize. Where in fuck did you learn a word like that anyway, off the cornflake box?"

I'm dying to ask Snake who stretched his neck and fertilized his eyebrows.

"Up to a little fun?" Bear asks.

"Sure," I affect stupidly. "If you have a deck of cards and some bubble gum handy."

"I'm talking about some *fucking* fun."

"I'll think about it," I hazard, getting to my feet. "First I have to go to the bathroom. . . ."

He makes a jerky movement as if to grab me and roars with laughter as I shriek and run toward an acrid smell of urine and moldy clothes that must signal a bathroom and it does thank God and after locking myself in their sewer I can hear the cretins still buckling with laughter outside.

I've got to get the hell out of here. Fast. Unscrewing the screen with my nail file, I crawl out of the pint-sized window and fall onto a heap of dusty old tires.

In a half crouch I head straight for the cover of the trees nearby. I'll hole up in the bushes near the road and wait for Vincent. It's twilight already and the crickets and frogs are going full steam in the swamp. Then a dog starts barking too close for comfort so I go up the branches of a large oak tree.

Killer, the German shepherd, tears out of the yard and barks frantically at the base of my tree. Bear blots into focus, his meat hooks wrapped around a twelve-gauge. "C'mon down out of there!" he hollers.

I hold onto the branch tight, praying he and his shotgun will give up, go away, and hold up a bank instead.

"I'll shoot you out of the fucking tree if I have to!"

"Don't be silly," I quail. "I'm not bothering you any. You're nothing but a bully. Go and eat a truck for excitement, why dontcha."

Kaboom!

The blast nearly takes my ear off and wipes out a clutch of branches above my head. I'm going to faint. I know I'm going to faint. But first I'm going to piss in my pants.

"The next one is really gonna tickle your fancy!" he thunders. "I'll shoot to maim!"

I've already got enough parts that don't work right so I just give up. Shaking so bad on my way down, I miss the last branch and end up ass-over-kettle at his feet, whimpering like an idiot. The slob doesn't even offer me a helping hand. But Killer licks my nose like an appetizer and I'm suddenly giggling hysterically.

"Think it's funny, do you?" Bear asks, prodding my shoulder with the barrel of the shotgun.

"You're not supposed to hurt me," I rage, jumping to my feet. "I'm a guest here and you don't shoot your guests." I make a grin for Killer. "You don't eat them either."

"Who the fuck said that?"

"I dunno."

"Well, it sure as fuck wasn't me and since this's my show, my word is law. Got it? And I don't have to hurt you just to have a little fucking fun."

Where the hell is Vincent anyway? Goddamn it, he's gotta be back soon—he has to be.

I'm dragged back to the house, and Bear leaves Killer outside to patrol in case I try crawling out the plumbing again.

"You shouldn't have treated me like that, Blondie," Bear snarls.

"How would you like to have *you* for a baby-sitter? Wouldn't you take a hike, too?"

He puts a bottle of beer to his lips. "I'm responsible for your ass to your old man."

"He's not my old man."

Playfully rumpling my hair, he orders me to sit down and pours out a glass of firewater. I decline. "No, thanks."

"Drink up!" he barks. "Or do you want Snake to open your mouth and pour it down?"

Grudgingly I oblige. There's rust floating on top and I expect to see a human finger surface any minute. It sears me all the way down to my toes, a sign that it's home brew. To be sociable, and kill time, I drink some more. Bear and Snake do, too. Soon, giggling to myself, I roll up a *Playboy* magazine and start flicking live June bugs out the door—so they won't get stepped on. Then Bear flourishes his arm with an order. "You—sit down and take off your clothes."

"Only if you take off your eye patch first." I gulp, trying to buy time.

He slips it over his head, revealing an empty eye socket. "Like it Turns you on, huh?"

"Sure—I've always been partial to Cyclops." I drink again to calm myself. "You don't need it anyway. One is as good as two. So how did you lose it?"

"The same way I lost my arm. Got shot off my chopper."

I'm not myself anymore. The whiskey has done its magic. Part of me has transformed itself into that hairy monster under the cushion of the chair. I can feel myself growing thirty-two sets of legs.

"It's your turn, Blondie," Bear bellows. "Take off your clothes."

"Did losing your eye make you a bigger son of a bitch than you already were?" I ask, still stalling.

Bear gets to his feet, grabs a bottle by the neck with one hand and me with the other. "You asked me a question, Blondie. So, I'm gonna give you an answer."

Sometimes I wish I wasn't so inquisitive.

Minutes later, he has hauled me over his shoulder through the yard and into the barn, and after dumping me on the floor, lights a lantern and shows me his prize chopper, a real nightmare of shiny chrome and black metal. Someday, he says, he plans to be buried with it.

"Will you be buried pushing it, riding it, or standing alongside it, like you're posing for a picture?"

"Shit, nobody ever asked me that before," he admits, rubbing his beard for a minute. "Fucking riding it, I guess."

Wow. I can just see the expression on Saint Peter's face when Bear goes gunning through those pearly gates.

"How're you going out, Blondie?"

"In the hole upside down so I can dive straight into the deep end of hell and leave the world kissing my ass."

"Now that's fucking different. You always talk like that?"

"No—sometimes I sit on my knees with my hands behind my back and eat birdseed out of the hands of priests."

Away from that slimy lizard Snake, he's not half bad. He doesn't have to put on the Bear thing. Soon I'm not afraid of him at all. Vincent will come and save me. . . .

Bear pushes me up the ladder to the mow, shakes a musty blanket out on the straw, and stands with his hand on his hip and a cocky

expression on his face. Shivering with cold, I don't even resist when
he pulls me down on the blanket, rides a fleshy hand up my leg, pulls
the elasticized top of my sundress down to my midriff, and then whisks
it right off my body entirely. Hunching over me, he moves his mouth
down my naked body as if paying homage to a prize ham, licks and
pulls at the nipples on my breasts until they harden in his mouth.
Slowly he moves south of the equator to more torrid zones and I try
to stop him. But he pushes me down again and his tongue keeps
tenderizing and suddenly I'm falling, giving in completely, now wet,
wanting him. So he stops, poised in a smirk above my crotch.

"I'm going now, Blondie." He grins. "You can stay here until your
old man comes back."

For revenge. The bastard is teasing me—the way I teased him all
evening.

"Don't go," I plead, a mink in heat, trying to drag him back into
the underworld.

"You asked me how big a son of a bitch I am, Blondie." He grunts.
"Now I guess you know."

For a minute I see nothing but white. I jump up and slap his face
as hard as I can. He just laughs and laughs, pushes me down again,
kneels, and returns to the spice lick. Gently, surprisingly, and slowly,
he eases my trembling knees apart, places one hand on each leg, holds
me firmly down and spread wide open, leans forward with his devilish
darting stroking tongue, stretching me splayed and probing, has me
wiggling like a worm on a hook, molding his lips around my pleasure
dome and sucking it to ecstasy and I'm howling, trying to hold myself
back and can't-won't-will give in, feeling as if a bullet is firing electrodes through my body and I lose count of the times I self-destruct
and finally I'm inflating and deflating and jerking with contractions
and it's over.

"Did yeh like that, Blondie?" Bear says, wiping his mouth as he
comes out of hibernation to peer out the loft window.

I nod numbly. But in a minute I shout at him. "How come you
didn't screw me?"

"Eating babycunt is rare delicacy. Vincent owed me a favor. Now it's paid. You tell him that when you see him."

"Thanks," I mutter, as stunned as always.

"There you go again," he grunts quietly. "Fucking thanking me for something I didn't do."

Suddenly an ear-shattering buzz of hollow aerodynamic thunder transcends the sound barrier of my thoughts. The barn door below bangs shut and Snake appears at the top of the ladder. Before I can say a word, he's straddling my waist, one hand diving between my legs and the other clapped over my mouth. "Clam up, little mama," he rasps in my ear.

The thunder from outside is enough to shake us out of the mow. Bear hunkers down on his haunches beside us, explaining that the Vipers, an enemy tribe, are here to do dirt.

"Fuck her later if yeh like but let's get her to fuck out of here first." He trains his twelve-gauge out a crack in the partially opened shutter. "Motherfuckers!"

There's a helluva commotion in the yard outside, growling engines and the yipping war cry of the Vipers circling the clubhouse. They obviously think everyone's gone.

Prompted by the angry whispers of Bear and Snake, I put myself together fast. My dress goes on inside out and backward to boot. I can't locate my underwear at all. Snake probably ate them.

We climb down the ladder to the floor below. Bear grabs his wolfskin jacket off a hook and inches open the barn's back door. Snake unlocks the wheels of Bear's chopper and climbs on, hugging the winged handlebars. Bear picks me up and puts me on behind Snake, then climbs on himself. Though the bike will accommodate two lard-arses, it's still more than a tight squeeze. I'm jammed between them, grasping Snake in . . . well, a bear hug. Then Snake jumps on the starter, revs the bike up, the sound screened by the rumbling engines and whooping Vipers outside, and in one galvanic jerk forward we burst out the back door of the barn, the headlight opening up the weed-infested dirt path ahead. Glancing over my shoulder, I see the club-house behind being swallowed in flames.

It takes us seconds to cross the broad empty expanse of field. But the Vipers have seen us and a string of headlights are edging out from behind the burning clubhouse.

We pull out onto the paved main road where we can make some time. Now maybe we can lose them.

The cool wind tearing at my face dumbs my senses. The countryside is a black overcoat unraveling into the gray sky and I can't tell where one ends and the other starts. The morning sun is just dawning, a faint furry orange glow to the east. It's like penetrating the void of space. Somewhere in my head I'm with Wagner and the flight of the Valkyries, riding a pale horse.

The Vipers are veering down on us from behind. In no time they'll overtake us and we'll be run off the road or worse. Why the hell aren't we going faster?

Confused and panicky, I have a momentary weak spell and mental sway from side to side unsteadily, sure I'm gonna fall off. Bear digs his fingers into my waist and keeps me in the saddle. "Don't worry, Blondie," he whispers in my ear. "They'll never catch us. We've got the magic machine."

Snake shifts into a secret gear that power-boosts us forward at a frightening clip, zooming like a rocket, as if a LSD pellet has been dropped in the gas tank. Soon we've got a big lead on the Vipers.

Minutes later Snake cuts his speed and veers off onto a side road, negotiating the turn so sharply that for a second the bike seems to be lying on its side and I can almost feel my knees scraping the road.

Eventually we take yet another side road and roll out onto the high cliffs of an abandoned gravel pit, the battlefield where, according to Bear, the main body of the Vipers and his Cuntlickers have already tangled. The choppers are arranged in a circle near the edge of the cliffs and the encampment is in a state of carnage, from broken tail pipes to broken, bloody heads and limbs wrapped in homemade bandages. I can't see Vincent anywhere.

Bear jumps off the bike and immediately starts firing orders, preparing for another attack. "The fucking Vipers burnt the clubhouse! They're on my tail! Pull the wasted meat into the center of the choppers! Put that goddamn fire out! Get out the fucking hardware and load up!"

I think he'd gladly make a run for it if there was time to get the wounded out successfully. I'd gladly make a run for it if I could find somewhere to run. Without a word of consolation Vincent appears at my side and roughly pulls me down behind his Harley. "Tommy's gonna look after you. Do what the fuck he tells you and keep your fool head down!" They're both dog-tired, their faces caked with dirt, beaded with sweat, and creased with a hormone giddap.

Then comes the unearthly round of thunder and a small convoy of headlights throb against the horizon as the Vipers swoop up into a line of offense at the perimeter of Bear's acknowledged piece of hard-won turf, choppers idling in park, pursue and breathing heavy.

Shutdown.

Their leader steps forward to meet Bear halfway. He's a long-haired bearded roadhog, wearing a black combat helmet, army fatigues, an open flak jacket, boots to the knee, a snakeskin coat over his shoulders, and weighed down with a heavy-looking iron swastika lying on his chest on a chain like a shackle. "No firepower, fuckhead!" he announces to Bear from the bowels. "Or do you fuckheads need it to win a second bout?"

"I don't need no fucking fire to send you back to hell!" Bear belches.

For a solid minute they face each other down, snarling and ogling with hatred. Just when I expect them to bite chunks, Bear spits and turns back. The challenge's been accepted.

Vincent and Tommy take a pull at a canteen, offer me some, and then crush the butts of their cigarettes underfoot.

Showdown.

The Vipers rev up and move out, heading straight for us, our backs to the edge of the cliff, in spearhead formation to split our ranks. Then their flanks fan out to the left and right with the intention of enclosing us in a noose. As they circle in, some are clubbed from their choppers at point-blank range and the steering columns go jack-knifing into the dust sideways, while two or three are sent zooming off the cliff into the pit below. Soon Tommy is hunched protectively over my body inside the circle of bikes and I'm clinging to the arm of a wounded biker lying on his back at my feet. He's in pain and delirious, his teeth clamped down on a branch to keep from biting off his tongue. A section of his cheek has been opened up and is hanging off his blood-soaked face like a clamshell.

In the hand-to-hand, a gloved hand clutches a gurgling throat, a chain zings against a tire iron, one club knocks against another one, a knife sticks a bloated gut, a boot slams into a man's balls, a tire iron zaps a knife out of a tattooed hand, a club crunches against a face turning it into a mask of raw meat, and mouths curse and howl and spit blood and dirt.

I spot Vincent dancing a two-ton Viper around in a circle, the Viper snapping his chain off the ground until he accidentally catches it on a chopper brake. Vincent moves in with his feet, thumping the air out of the biker's rib cage.

The Vipers have broken into our circle, and one of them lumbers toward Tommy, swinging a club at his head, and like lightning Tommy slips a bowie knife out of the sheath on his belt and shouts at me to make a run for the woods. Then he wheels to confront the mad dogs swarming through the choppers.

Dodging the swinging, cutting, kicking knots of violence, I manage to break through to the safety of the woods. Once in the trees I'm so freaked out I've gotta take a piss. I dive behind a bush, drop down on my haunches, and feel blissful relief. Suddenly, a pair of hands grasp me from behind and I'm hurled forward in a slide onto my stomach. Then I'm flipped over onto my back, pinned to the ground, fighting nauseous waves of urine and sweat from my attacker while hands are ripping at my clothes and a hard prick is throbbing against my leg. Then, out of nowhere, a knife appears at the Viper's neck and a finger presses a magic button, immobilizing him completely. His deadweight slumps forward. When he's rolled off of me, I find myself gazing up into the face of Vincent. "Don't you know better than to drop your pants in front of a biker?" he chaws, snapping the hem of the dress down past my midriff and hauling me to my feet.

"I wanna go home," I whimper, swooning on his shoulder.

"It's okay, baby," he soothes, panned out himself. "I'm a son of a bitch, you're a whore, the battle's over, and now it's time to eat dust."

14

B y now the sky has opened up, and by some curious unspoken agreement the battle *for* blood has turned into a Red Cross effort to *stop* blood. Everything has wound down to a draw. The mopping-up operation has begun. The wasted meat is being patched up and lashed onto what's left of the road chariots. The war-weary warriors seem keen on making a fast but functionable getaway. Bear orders Vincent, Tommy, and me to ship out, too. There are no Hallmark card good-byes, only grappling handshakes and blasphemous "Hallelujah, brother!" salutes.

I should be furious at Vincent for orchestrating this Night of the Fire-eaters. But I'm too fagged and numb to respond to anything, let alone the sacking of Rome, and my priorities too blurred to hurl stones. I can only collect them for future use. Once on the Harley behind Vincent, I'm so weak it's a major effort to hold onto him. Eager to vacate the area as soon as possible, we're on the road for close to an hour before pulling into a truck stop to gas up, anthropomorphize in the washroom, and breakfast on the $1.99 lumberjack special.

Afterward, Tommy leaves us to visit friends at a nearby reserve and we pull into a motel with a half-moon neon snoozing on a fence out front. As soon as we book into a room, Vincent strips down and slips into the bath. I follow him and sit down on the edge of the tub, watching him scrape a bar of soap against his head and ignore me. In no time my second wind transmits a wake-up call to my brain and I'm cooking. I keep telling myself that the true test of a ball is in its bounce—not its roll. "Aren't you gonna apologize for what you did to me?" I challenge.

"Why the hell should I? It was only a test and *you* bunged it up good, baby."

"Thanks for setting me up, you prick."

"Aah—come off it, I didn't leave you with a monster."

"No, you left me with myself—that's almost as bad."

"Jesus, why don't you drop your goddamn, mushy, come-on crap? Always pretending to be stupid, gearing yourself up to be taken advantage of. You know you're just fucking tragic. Anyway, since you're blonde and childish, you fit Bear's bill to a tee—so I thought I'd shake you up a bit."

"I hope you fry in hell, you bastard! I'm leaving!" I say, getting to my feet.

"Always want to leave, don't you?" He pulls me down. "Always packing and unpacking, climbing in and out of windows in the middle of the night. Can't face anything, can you?"

"I rode with bikers when I was a kid so I know what they're about. You don't know balls about me."

"I know your type—the eternal victim."

"You sound better when your mouth's shut."

He grabs my wrist and twists it until I yelp. "Right now I'll pretend you're teasing," he says icily. "But when you get mouthy again, I'll smack you in the head. Then I'll use my imagination. Remember that."

Releasing me, he lays the washcloth over his face for a minute. I cross my arms on the edge of the tub, wondering what to say next. Suddenly he sparks again. "While you were playing footsies with Bear, I was out working. Check the bayonet on my belt. Go ahead—check it."

I bring it to him. There are traces of blood on the blade. He washes it off in the bathwater. "And that, sweetheart, is what I do. I kill people who are crying for it. This motherfucker deserved to buy it under the table. He dumped a girl's dead body on her parents' doorstep after shooting her up with heroin."

"What's his name?"

"C'mon—would I tell you his name when I wouldn't even tell you my own?"

Since the beginning it has been an understood conclusion between us that he's an anonymous screwball. However, I have learned that Vincent's beginnings are as obscure as mine. It's typical of castaways who've divorced themselves from the umbilical cord of place and name, for reasons that are at once simple and complicated. Vincent's been playing at the Order of D even longer than I have.

Now comes the lecture I'll hear time and time again and still refuse to accept. "What you've got to remember, baby, is that people are basically maggots. Out for what they can get—and that, unfortunately, is always your ass. The dog-eat-dog credo is the only reality because it's the final one. Take those middle-class assholes who own this joint, the third-degree treatment they gave us when we registered. Figure they've got the world by the balls because they own this trap. Never been nowhere, never done nothing they'd have to stand behind with their lives. They want to play it safe. That's why they can shoot off their mouths. Their credit with the bank is gonna protect them against everything—except us."

Without warning, he hauls me into the bath and undresses me while I try to inflate his fake rubber dinghy. Then with an elastic grin on his face he begins soaping me down. "Talking to you is like walking through a revolving door," I confess mulishly. "Haven't got a good word to say about anyone."

"Don't be cute. Name one person who doesn't deserve to be called a son of a bitch and I'll show you a hypocrite."

To stop me from contradicting him, he twists on the shower full blast and laves up my hair with shampoo until I can only see, smell, and taste soap and steam and feel his hard hands sliding all over me like a wet massage. It's time to put the dinghy out to sea.

What do I see in him? Vincent's my pragmatic saint. There's nothing in him that reeks of the ass-grabbing assembly-line petty bourgeois. Singularly or together, we're going nowhere—we share the same penny delusions.

But in my head I keep hearing, You have to get away from him—he's lethal—he's an unbeliever.

*　　*　　*

With the onslaught of an early spring, Vincent cruises down to New York City for a week on what he calls business. I call it a bad feeling in my gut.

When he returns I manage to elude him for an entire day. He finally comes knocking on my door, his eyes glazed, full of charismatic renewal. "Whenever you're finished being a child, I want to talk to you," he says levelly with a hint of excitement in his voice.

"Okay, I'll put my dolls away. Shoot."

"I'm leaving tomorrow for Africa. Will you take care of a few things for me while I'm gone?"

"Sure, as long as it has nothing to do with the ammunition dump behind your closet. Where in Africa?"

"I can't tell you. Get dressed and we'll go out to celebrate."

We wind up at a schmaltzy Chinese restaurant downtown. He orders two Peking ducks and a bottle of Dom Pérignon. I open the menu and come on with all the questions. "Will you be able to write?"

"I'll send messages back if I can. Keep your answering service—just in case. If you don't hear from me within the year, you'll know I bought it."

His voice is Sensurround in the surreal and mine's flat and stilted. He's stranger-than-tabloid fiction and I'm as wishy-washy as yesterday's hangover. I realize this is the way it has always been with us and I'm still in his power.

"What do you see in me?" I ask curiously.

"I keep you around to amuse me. Every so often I need a laugh to stay sane. The chance of coming across a nutball like you again without having to advertise is dicey."

I give him a saccharine smile and he smirks coldly over his glass.

"You need somebody around, baby. The truth is you can't look after yourself. You attract every fly in the shitpile."

The ultimate putdown I can't dispute. I wouldn't even want to try. Besides, I'm in a welter of conflicting emotions about him leaving.

"Stay close to that Simon character, too. He knows life," he continues, lighting up a cigarette.

"I didn't know you'd met Simon."

"He dropped around one day when you were out. We had a hell of a rap. We think you're a perfect example of a working-class guilt complex in action. But it's not your fault. The system's programmed you for it since birth. Simon can pull you through class intimidation but self-intimidation is your baby."

Then the food arrives and I've already lost my appetite. Vincent digs in like mad. I've never seen him consume so much at one sitting. For once he's even making an effort not to be distant or abrupt. "Are you gonna be all right?" he asks after watching me daydream with an egg roll in my hand for five minutes.

"Yes, I think so. I mean no, I don't think so. Oh, hell—I don't know what I mean."

Back at his room the banter continues in bed. There's a bizarre excitement in him tonight. It burns up, dims, then burns up again. "Are you afraid of me?" he asks bluntly.

"Of course not," I confess easily.

"Why not?"

"Because it's too easy for me to be afraid of you."

Quickly he butts his cigarette and puts back a swallow of Scotch. "Maybe I can change your mind on that score. Make love to me and I'll tell you a secret."

He might be an ace at bedroom politics but I'm a whiz at bedroom blackmail. "I have to get something from my room," I say, climbing out of bed.

I return with an empty peanut butter jar. "What's that for?" he asks suspiciously.

"I'm starting a sperm bank. You're the first to donate. Congratulations."

"Like hell I am!" He laughs in spite of himself.

But I'm not laughing at all. Secretly, I'm wishing I could link myself to him—biologically. And pregnancy would be just the ticket. What a beautiful child Vincent could make me. And I'd never really lose him. And that's what is really frightening me—losing someone else. Suddenly, I remember that I will probably never see him again, that I must work to make tonight memorable so I'll never forget it. Maybe

Vincent's right. Maybe I am carrying around a lot of loose change upstairs. Maybe I should just live for the moment and forget everything else. Regaining my playful mood, I throw a ball back. "It's your own fault. I'm not allowed to take a picture of you and you even insist on taking your toothbrush tomorrow. Can't you leave me anything? What's the problem?"

"You—you're the goddamn problem," he says, pulling me on top of him. "You're fucking crazy."

And "fucking crazy" just about sums up our last supper. Vincent's as close as I'll ever get to the nerve center of the sixties. He's so clued-in he's been able to make the decision to turn off. Me—I'm at the center of sensation, solitary, fixed, without an orbit of my own. Vincent's so connected to the sociological grassroots of what's happening, it's like going to bed with 1968 and wondering how it can feel so great to feel so undeserving.

Next morning when I awaken, my road warrior is gone and I think it significant that I should discover Vincent's one weakness is one I share: he hates good-byes, too. I've always loved being around men who were more clever than I was, convinced that they could teach me something. I hesitate to consider what Vincent has taught me. I've made up my mind to be very philosophical this morning in order to mask the emotional panic and void I'm feeling. Meanwhile, Topper is sitting by the bed, wagging his tail with a mouse in his mouth. The bum has been out all night and turned *tomcat* on me. I accept the gift as a tribute to his nocturnal prowess, also because he's one of the truest friends I have left. Blankly, I stare at the ceiling trying to put the day, the month, and the year on the calendar.

I found out a couple of things last night. Since his return from Nam, Vincent has found a career. He's a professional assassin for hire. But he loved the smell of guerrilla warfare too much to stay away from the real action for long. I also found out where he was going.

The closet door yawns emptily with the exception of the box of the goodies I'm supposed to keep for him and which Topper is nosing through with interest. The fifty bucks on the table is a crude joke of his: to pay me for the night's services rendered. The six cans of dog food and brand-new collar underneath is for Topper, whom he was very fond of. The rosebud in a silver vase is for levity and the half bottle of Bollinger for medicinal purposes—or to salute his passing. I'll use the deathstar as a paperweight and the nunchuk as a flower hanger. His bayonet is for protection and laying a landmark.

Shit, I think, the bastard has just left this sinking ship for higher ground and taught me the eleventh deadly sin—noncommitment. I could just spit.

In the afternoon I assault the information desk of the local library. "What have you got on a place called Angola?"

PART III

GETTING INTO IT

15

W hile Vincent's educating himself in Angola and Crunch is in the jug sorting out his priorities, I'm back on the Strip making a few changes in my life in the raw. The Newfies adopt Topper and I move The Bottle Factory to a flat in the attic in Simon's house in the snobby, quiet, tree-smothered area of Deer Park at Yonge Street and St. Clair. Now my patron saint is right across the hall and we can brunch on my balcony over the garden. And for purely aesthetic reasons there's even another coven of Lotus-eaters to keep my nightmares company on the bottom floor.

Having finally paid Vito back, I can my jobs at The Slush Pit and Club Morocco and look around for something different. I catch an ad in the newspaper, make an appointment, and find myself at a massage parlor hidden away on the second floor of a renovated old office building near the Times Square of Toronto—Yonge and Dundas. While the Kabuki Club has borrowed its name from the Japanese, the decor reeks of middle-class crass in the fast lane. Smoked-glass tables dot the lounge, and deceptively comfy sofas in gold velvet line the walls. It's high-gloss schmaltz supported by music to melt by, to keep the loafers from loafing and the insistent, insisting for pleasure— and in a state of high anxiety.

I arrive expecting a bare-breasted tribe of hungry Amazons and instead find a bunny patch of bored fluffs lounging around in bikinis, hotpants, baby dolls, and negligees. I'm introduced to Sometimes Sheila, Debbie Tongueheavy, Catch-me Candice, and Rah-Rah Ronda.

When my name's called, I slip a humbug candy under my tongue to keep the Scrooge in my nature resilient and follow a leggy brunette down a corridor washed in an eternal sunset. The moment I enter the office I know I've stumbled on the official meeting place of the Hole-in-the-Wall Gang. The graffiti on the walls include dirty limericks, work schedules, fingerprints, and a gallery of girlies' pinups who've popped their seams, all over the place.

The manager behind the desk jives to his feet and introduces himself with a hand dressed with baubles and a body itching with reggae. He's the smallest black man I've ever seen not stretched by the wonders of Cinemascope. Three other black buddies of his have dropped in for a chat and are lounging in calypso hats and candy-stripe suits opposite.

Jonathan outlines the job in detail, using a vocabulary that is both colorful and overloaded, with three adjectives for every noun. The girls are supposed to dress up in sexy outfits and hit up the clientele in the lounge with a cute come-on line and the club membership spiel, which includes a dissertation on the rates for half-hour and hour sessions and baths. The girls are paid strictly on a commission basis. They're supposed to wait until they have the sucker in the massage room before telling him the bad news—No Extras. Then Jonathan explains the hazards of working under-the-counter, or skin-fluting without a music degree—instant dismissal and maybe jail if an undercover dick nails your ass first. To reassure me about security precautions, he shows me a big club the size of his ego that he uses to scare troublesome hairpins who threaten to eat him. I call it a St. Mary's Persuader after a company of the same name which used to market black hickory hardball bats. Jonathan doesn't mind flexing his jaw muscles on anyone who crosses him. I'll sure as hell never be that white and unlucky.

Then he gets to the punch line: the girls do the massages in private rooms in the nude. My walls of vulnerability start to close in.

"Take off your coat," he orders suddenly.

I shuffle out of my short lambskin creases. He inspects the insides of my arms and I apologize for the lack of tattoos, knowing he's looking for track marks.

Even before I've had time to consider the maybe-huhs, he says I can start in five minutes.

How about five minutes to consider the five minutes?

He thinks I'm joshing because I've got a grin on my face. The erotic overtones of this job that promises top billing attract the flirt in my female psyche for *safe* tease and sleaze and at the same time prod the gung-ho gambler in my nature to try something different. Besides, the pay is great. So I give in. The basic decisions in my life always seem to be made by other people. "Congratulations," I assure him. "You just bought yourself a thirty-two-dollar-an-hour egg roll."

Besides Jonathan, there are two other partners in the business who help manage the place—Sonny, and a certain Mr. Big who slips in from time to time to go over the books. Jonathan introduces me to Sonny, who has just rambled into the office. He's a sleepy, swarthy slob, the white Mutt to Jonathan's black Jeff, with the paunch of a football player who's deteriorated and who owns an eternal hangover. He's got the saddest moustache I've ever seen. I have to ask if he bought the animal wholesale from an unemployed wine sniffer.

"That's real funny, kid." He yawns with an expressionless face. "Glad to have you aboard. I could use a few laughs."

He could also use a kick in the arse to put him in second gear.

I'm taken to a room the size of a jail cell, filled with a cold bluish light which, as I will learn, throws an unnatural silver cast over the raw pink color of human flesh. "Okay." Sonny groans, uninspired. "Strip down and get on the table."

I can't bear being touched unless in a heat of passion. "How about if *you* get on the table and I'll take notes," I suggest.

He's dozy enough to take the wisecrack as bait and in short order I have the recipe for cooking these turkeys. Stick in shower, then wrap in towel. Put bag over head if ugly and paper slippers on feet. Then if he doesn't want to be basted in bath, take to the massage room. Uncover and lay out on the table, faceup. If turkey tries to eat the cook, beat at high speed with wet towel for thirty seconds or add dash of alcohol to family jewels.

Tenderize with baby oil or powder.

Then massage meat, starting from middle of body to spread warmth and work out tightness in digestive system. Use long circular strokes, increasing movements in preference to adding pressure, in flowing rhythms. Allowing little finger accidentally to brush family jewels during process is optional.

Flip over with kind word, pinch, or king-sized spatula.

Repeat process.

Wipe powder or oil off with alcohol-soaked towel.

Shuck turkey into sauna and bake for ten minutes until red.

Put in shower with washcloth to chew on until water runs clean and turkey comes out of shock.

"Got it, kid?" Sonny asks an hour later.

"Yes-no-maybe-huh?"

My first customer is a regular, a young blond construction worker with a smart mouth who puts every new girl through her paces. First he lies on his back, trying to flatter by complimenting my body physical.

Someone in the office shoves the tape of Carole King's "Tapestry" in the sound system and while I'm massaging oil into his chest from the top of the table, he keeps pretending he's going to finger-flick the nipples of my tits and bends his head back as far as he can and tries to lick my cunt hairs. I reprimand him. "Keep doing that you'll turn into a Push-me Pull-you."

"What's that?" he says, straightening out.

"An animal with a head at both ends of his body."

"I already got a head at both ends." He grins mischievously. "Or haven't you noticed?"

Touché. How could I miss the bullhorn he's rubbing with both hands, trying to make it stand up and take a bow? I look. I *do* notice. Soon, the goddamn thing is hypnotizing me. Funny—the worst thing I expected was getting mauled or propositioned, not getting turned on.

Every man's winning card must ultimately be his sexual performance. Jack Be Nimble is treating his prick with a longing not unlike cult worship. "It's a big one, isn't it?" he asks, excitedly hopeful, pumping with one hand, eyes big as plates.

Ignoring him, I nod blindly, trying to be philosophical. "I heard once that foresters can tell the age of a tree by counting the rings on the trunk."

Whoops.

"Go ahead—count them, baby," he says, encouraging me with a catch in his voice. "I'll let you guess how old I am."

"Can't count," I quip, noticing that he's sprung a small leak. "I'm just a dumb blonde."

Now that I'm working on his thighs, he takes his hand away from the Frankenstein monster he's created, struggles up on his elbows, and with fascination watches it dribble, stutter, and salute as if it's a separate entity with a mind of its own. Suddenly he grabs it again. "P-l-e-a-s-e jigger it!" he cries pathetically. "I'll give you twenty-five bucks! It's in the pocket of my robe behind the door!"

Christ—I'm wet, too, damn it, and I'm almost tempted. The question is squeezing my clitoris like a clothespin. But I keep massaging slowly in a trance, more afraid of Jonathan than myself, willing myself to hold back when the monster simply self-destructs. The session is over.

Quietly embarrassed, I follow him out the door, and Jonathan and Sonny tag Nimble Jack in the hallway. "Well, what happened?" Jonathan asks sharply. "Did she come across?"

"No."

"Did she take money from you?"

"No."

"Well, that's all the fuck I wanted to know. The kid's in."

Seeing my crimson face, all three burst into gales of laughter. "C'mon, kid," Sonny encourages with a pat on the ass. "We have to check the girls out. If we didn't, we could be closed down tomorrow. Don't worry about getting horny or embarrassed, that's par for the course, baby. It happens all the time to the experienced girls."

I give in again. He's right.

And so I progress from boobie dancer to sex therapist and part-time aerialist. I'm in a higher tax bracket, which is comforting because in a couple of years I'll be over the hill and twenty.

For solace I hold vespers with Simon at an all-night bistro up the Strip. Over a bottle of Moët and a pizza, we discuss the ramifications of my complete entrance into the world of cheap-jack. I can't find anything wrong in taking off my clothing. Simon can't either. We decide that the experience is a necessary hazard in the course of my somewhat unorthodox education. So we clink glasses over it and Simon leaves me with one reassuring thought—I'm the sacrificial lamb used to appease the Philistines.

To sweeten the pot in my favor I pay a visit to the shops in Chinatown to buy a horny-looking tip box, a pink hippopotamus with purple spots on his back and a slit in his bum. I call him Hoppy. For all those regulars of mine who don't speak through marbles or cut glass and leave fat tips, I add a few sticks of joss, sandalwood soap, oil of spearmint, and basil juice to my shopping basket as well.

The mob always sends in a representative at least twice monthly to try to add us to their payroll. There is always the spiffy dude in an imitation Gucci suit with the black attaché case chained to his wrist and his wooden-faced bodyguard who stands just inside the door of the massage room with a .38 under his coat. But as long as you can spell linguini backward, you're safe.

Mr. Big finally comes in to go over the books and check any new girls out for traces of active immorality. If she comes across, Big lets her and then gives her the boot.

Though most of the clubs are owned by the mob in New York, word has it that there is also some heavy money from City Hall backing some of the clubs on the Strip. I'm not even surprised.

The next day a scarecrow cruises in with eyes squeezed into a beanbag face, a tricked-out cowboy hat, preshrunk Levis riding halfway up his calves, and a little beaded denim coat, two sizes too small for him. Harry's the club gopher who peddles flyers up and down the Strip and pesters the girls to go out with him after work in a whiny singsong which grates on everyone's nerves. To stifle his pleas, I accept a date with him for the next night.

Then Jonathan blunders in and rants at him, "Get the fuck out of here!"

Harry cowers and sidles to the door. He has a faint limp, which makes him appear lopsided when he walks.

"How could you?" I pipe up angrily.

"The little fucker won't work unless I kick ass!"

Reality—that fly in the ointment called *love*. Someday I'll learn to deal with it when I don't have four coffees in my hand, a stack of towels over my arm, and one bum cooking in the sauna.

Before I know it, Harry drags me down to street level to view his new two-sided wooden signboard for his job. He hefts the board over his shoulders like a life preserver. Now he's a three-dimensional conversation piece, open to the ridicule of the masses throwing pop cans and food at him. Who else but Harry would be cracked enough to swap all sense of autonomy for a two-cent-an-hour raise?

A vet from Dieppe is taken onto the payroll to run flyers with Harry. He's a legless creature who lives aboard a four-wheeled cart. His dirty mouth, the slash marks covering his bald head, and passion for knives inspire me into dubbing him the Barber. Jonathan won't allow him inside the club in case he scares the customers. Sometimes he sells pencils in a can on the Strip and has some choice fights with other hustlers and panhandlers over territorial imperatives.

Jonathan's a nervously excitable, always bombastic burnt peanut who throws underground porno magazines at me in the lounge. I merely pretend that they're printed upside down and are incomprehensible. He tries to prove that Blacks invented sex. I tell him that all they invented was suntans, minorities, and horny music.

Whenever he tries to bully me, I call him a Jamaican racist. Then he calls me poor white trash in a leaky bucket. I remind him that the only difference between poor white trash and a nigger is the color of his blues (as in the roots of jazz).

As promised, I have coffee with Harry at four in the morning at the grease stop known as Joey's on the corner, a twenty-four-hour jobbie with mirrored walls and a street-surfing clientele, rarely able to ride the economic wave off of it on a twenty-five-cent coffee in a Styrofoam cup that can buy you an excuse to keep warm.

My confederates at work are a curious lot, strange to some but totally unlike the phony, puritanical, socially and sexually repressed, pussy-whipping femmes fatales in the white-collar arena. Some are straight street material while others are students, unskilled single mothers trying to survive on their own while educating themselves at night, or, like me, simple researchers in the raw trying to connect to the essence of life without resorting to such cop-outs as diets, drugs, or organized education or religion. One girl actually left her job in a swanky Bay Street law office just to see the netherworld as she has leukemia and six months to live. We're so exposed to each other and so dependent on each other for survival, we share an earthy, almost spiritual camaraderie. We're not part of society anymore, merely painted on its pastel background in charcoal, all because of an ounce of hot flesh, which is essentially, physically ours and emotionally, ultimately theirs because they want to claim it as their own, which will all end up in the same cemetery anyway. Survival depends on our own gut-grounded instincts. Forgetting to frisk a customer before he leaves the change room can be hazardous. The bastards have a nasty habit of trying to sneak in everything outside of wallets, everything from axes up the pant leg to knives, with the intention of cutting us down in one blow. I have to admit that I'm one of society's laziest laywomen. I love reading road signs neoned in the dark. Imagine trying to detect a lie on the tongue of a doctor, lawyer, politician, or other policy monger—out there in the real world!

But in here the game is all stagecraft and the knack to staying alive is to keep the front lines for show but depend on the rear guard for go.

I'm constantly improving my education. Conversations at the club can be edifying—with all kinds of flotsam and jetsam on the rebound from Alice's Restaurant. We talk about ethnic talk. Yanks will run on about anything and everything they know everything and nothing about. The French will talk about everything that nobody else is currently talking about so that they can be heard by everybody and understood by nobody. The Brits will talk about something they know everything about and something about everything they know nothing about to the point you're sure that they are lethargic about literacy itself and have cornered the market on inanity. Canadians will talk about what everybody else is talking about, whether they understand it or not, and wind up agreeing with everybody and nobody. The

Germans won't talk about anything but the failures of everybody else so they can be heard and hated by everybody. The Russians will talk a lot about nothing and say very little about something while listening to everything and nothing from the mouths of the literate dead. Then they'll go back to Moscow and make decadent notes.

Canucks can't decide whether to jump into bed with the Yanks or the Brits so they're happy to suck up twilight from the one and the comedy of manners from the other, as little brother in this ménage à trois, not only pinching their elders' candy but tying their shoelaces together under the diplomatic table as well.

All Johns come in fifty-seven varieties and none of these, fortunately, is acknowledged in the *Encyclopaedia Britannica*, though they have been known to receive honorable mention in *The Guinness Book of World Records* and *Field and Stream*. The dreariest and dirtiest of the crop are white-collar workers with their flowered ties, fruity designer underwear, permed hair, monogrammed smiles, and musky stale perfume. They stand in the showers as if they're being baptized into the Brotherhood of Everlasting Stodge, letting the water rain on their faces, afraid of touching the soap, which could completely destroy their identity. Later in the room, when you're taking off the oil, the alcohol-soaked towel always comes up with a week's supply of dry rot. Men from the working class know they're dirty; these deskbound fools won't believe that sweating is nature's equation for purification.

I never knew there were so many ways to amuse yourself in the bath. The Portuguese fisherman says his prayers and places a cross of the Madonna around my neck. Archie, the bald-headed bartender, juggles five pieces of soap at once without a tall mix glass. Alfie, the actor from Stratford, recites from Shakespeare but steals from Tennessee Williams. Topo, the Maple Leaf Gardens wrestler, slips down below the waterline like a human torpedo and produces a convoy of Evinrude motors. Sadsack, the jockey, gets the second toe of his right foot stuck in the faucet and can't explain what the bugger was doing out of the stirrup in the first place. Jamie, the cartoonist, makes effigies of rabbits and extinct dinosaurs with his hands on the walls and I give them tongues and make them speak. Bart, the burglar, hides the soap in a nasty place and I'm forced to probe the corruptible depths for buried treasure without a map. Kurt, the sorcerer's apprentice, leaves Beauty in peace to smoke a cigarette and read a book while he manipulates the Beast into subjection and resurrects like Lazarus. Shyster, the middle-aged Machiavellian barrister-at-law, tries to subpoena this citizen's body physical with such eloquent jurisprudence she is forced to appeal to the Court of Common Pleas. Beau, the bountiful telephone company linesman, pulls me into the bath for a brief skin-diving lesson and gets shipwrecked on the Galápagos for his trouble.

In our spare time we girls put together a rhyme: *John, John, the Piper's son/Lives to lead, not to be led/Give him a ladder and he'll give you a bed.*

he opera season I've enjoyed so much with Simon is now over and I'm down in the dumps—but not for long. Even Massage Mollies must have a treat of the week to keep going. So every Thursday night after we close down, the booze is pulled out, food ordered in, and a troop of soldiers from Fort York climb up the fire escape in full regimentals and stamp into the club and we party, sauna, shower, massage, fornicate, and play bawdy war games, a weekly orgy fondly known as Babylonian Box and Cox.

To liven things up, one night Jonathan takes me over to the Muumuu Club, another massage parlor down the Strip owned by the New York mob, to meet the girls, and while we're there the pigs run a raid. In a flash someone pulls the fire alarm and it's instant pandemonium, naked men and girls flying out of the rooms, colliding with each other in the Waikiki-postered halls, and converging on the locker room for their clothes, pushing and shoving at the window, and clambering onto the fire escape while the vicers are hacking down the front door.

I jump into a large laundry basket to hide and Jonathan immediately yanks me out by my hair and in minutes I'm in the office going through a trapdoor hidden above the tiles in the ceiling and then walking on the roof while the fire engines and police cruisers are queuing at the curb below and the paddy wagons are being loaded with hysterical girls and Johns with a sudden need to wear Hawaiian grass skirts over their heads like an overturned plate of rotini.

Close call.

And the incident isn't lost on me either. I've learned my lesson, which is how to sniff out undercover dicks from the vice squad.

Whether by accident or design they all seem to visit the same barber, shoemaker, shrink, and wash in the same aftershave.

A new girl is a perfect mark for these crackerjacks. They only have to arrest one girl for soliciting to close down the club.

So as soon as I see Mr. Dick in the lounge, holding a lungful of Export A for a full three seconds in his lungs, along with his scalloped hairline and squeaky leather shoes, I know he's trouble in an Old Spice bottle. The other girls immediately invent handy excuses to exit stage left. So Jonathan backs *me* into a wall with a big evil grin, and after haggling it out, finally works a deal with me if I'll take on the vicer. Tomorrow I only have to work one shift instead of two.

In the locker room Mr. Dick keeps sweeping his eyes around the walls, searching for bugs with legs or Mickey Mouse cameras. To complicate matters he refuses to remove his towel, afraid I'll mistake his childish water pistol for a bazooka. "Give me the works!" he announces as soon as he lies on his back on the table awaiting last rites. "Do what I tell you. I'm the boss!"

Right on, Mr. Major Monster, sir. Living is the vice he'd like to wipe forever off the rearview mirror of his soul if it didn't give him such an erection. A pig has his criminal tendencies inverted. Like all boss men, who wear their wallets in their mouths, their intellects up their arseholes, and their opinions up their noses.

I whip back a nonchalant "Thanks—but no pranks." My anger has surfaced in the tips of my fingers, creating pressure points destined to cripple his shoulder muscles.

When he opens his mouth next, a chorus line of sewer rats Charleston out of it, followed by three blind mice in trench coats. "C'mon, you fucking slut!" he bellows, his BB gun dancing under his towel.

Again I refuse. Now nothing but an object of power and animal gratification like any other sod on the street, he leaps off the table. Before I can get a knee into him, he smacks me across the face, rams me up against the wall, stops my uncivilized shout with his mouth, and upending me, jams his swollen prick into my cunt and starts banging me as if his balls are on fire. Shout or no shout, they must be able to hear the racket outside on Yonge Street.

Jonathan pounces in like gangbusters, his St. Mary's Persuader arched for battle, and gives Mr. Dick a good clip on the shoulder. The cop in turn gives me a few more hefty pumps before pulling out and spurting off over both of us.

Dazed and sore, I crumble to the floor, groping for a towel to dab my bloody nose, while Jonathan and Mr. Dick face each other like two bulls in the ring, yelling up a storm of obscenities.

Later, Dumb Dick is thrown out of the club and I'm thrown out of the office so Jonathan can make a blustery call to the big shot down at 52 Division, giving him shit for the strong-arm tactics of his undercover vicers.

Sonny passes me in the hall, touches my breast, and tells me to go take a shower and play it cool. So, yeah. That's what I do every time it happens with Mr. Dicks or Everyman Sams. But I always find a place to stash Vincent's bayonet in case I run up against an armed handful. These thumps, crashes, and bangings against the walls always bring in either Jonathan or Sonny. If they're not available, we girls whirl in on the unlucky offender in attack formation.

I haven't heard a word from Vincent. I wonder if he's still alive. News from my soldier of fortune on this continent is virtually nonstop. The latest heart-throbber from Crunch asks, "Why not start a letter-writing service called Terror By Mail?" He's made the mistake of reading sections of my letters to his fellow inmates and now they want a serialized rag sheet every week.

It's hard not to analyze my feelings for either Vincent or Crunch. Both are filled to the brim with the one quality that attracts me to a man—*guts*. One is doomed to prowl a cage inside of himself in Africa, the other in a cage outside of himself in Canada. The one that Apollo sends back to me, his soul impaled on a thunderbolt, is probably the one I'll end up with.

For my birthday Simon buys me a white duck and I call him Piddles because that's the first thing he does when I pick him up. Then we dig up an antique bathtub and build a platform around it so Piddles can get in and out by himself.

My relationship with Sonny the doze happens quickly and stupidly, which just goes to show that I'm more of a doze than he is. After the club closes around four in the morning, we sometimes have a party of our own in the lounge and include any regulars who're still kicking around. Surprisingly enough, Sonny is in his element and after midnight wakes up and becomes the instigator of these foregather frolics. Sometimes he even flies two girls and me down to Disneyland for the weekend. His twin-engined Cessna's the only toy he brought with him when he moved from Miami to Toronto. His life Stateside is strictly top secret and he won't tell us a thing about it.

One night we take our party out to Bedlam's Beach and while the Johns and girls are playing touch tag in the sand, I'm with a soused-up Sonny in his yellow Firebird being attacked by a gearshift. How the hell did he get that far anyway without hitting a land mine?

At the end he's so polluted I take the wheel back to his apartment. All of a sudden he's adamant about flying down to Miami within the hour. Cool idea. In his shape he'd get sucked up the exhaust of a 747 before we even left the runway. To discourage this, I drop his plane key to the bottom of his beloved aquarium and bewilder his fat tiger oscar fish, Flynn.

In the morning I discover that Flynn has a realistic approach to anything bewildering—he simply eats it. Sonny's furious and chases me around the living room in my underwear with the omelet pan. Then I'm forced to dissect Flynn to recover the keys because Sonny hasn't got the stomach for it. As compensation I buy him a Jack Dempsey fish the same day.

This explains how my relationships usually take off—default and defect, followed by a coroner's report.

Sonny is the perfect partner for someone like me who doesn't want commitments or his and her towels in the bathroom. He's a bit of a lush, a bit of an ass, his lovemaking is not vigorous or imaginative enough to cause lust or obsession, he's lax and funny enough to keep my high voltage diffused, and he drops heavy tips in restaurants. In a word, he's safe.

*   *   *

Jonathan opens up the club one morning a few months later and gets a nasty reception. The office has been ransacked, papers strewn everywhere. Someone has thrown quite a bash, but who sent out the invitations? Jonathan's sure it was mob-sent. Worked up to a frenzy, he throws me out of the office and makes a string of phone calls. For the remainder of the afternoon he chews us all out.

As soon as Sonny waltzes in after the dinner hour, Jonathan buttonholes him and they have a shouting match in the office. The soap opera continues all day because Mr. Big shows up to add more fuel to the battle. As for me, I'm too smart to take sides.

I suppress my curiosity and refuse to question Sonny later. But a few days down the road, we're three quarters of the way through a lobster dinner at the Holiday Inn when he sheds his Good-time Charlie rubber suit and broaches the subject himself. "I have to sell out my share in the operation," he suddenly confesses, plucking nervously at his tie. "I've got me some enemies, kid, and they've tracked my ass up from the States. The bastards are out to get me. They're probably watching me right now."

"Jesus, thanks a million for putting me in the line of fire," I fly back, noticing that he's the one closest to the wall and can scan the room at a glance.

"What can I tell ya, kid? What can I tell ya?" He sighs blankly. "Self-preservation is a self-made condition. Just cool it. They won't try nothing here."

A consoling thought surely. "Who's *they*?"

The truth, like rusty tap water, comes out in one gush. Sonny had owned a string of clubs, Stateside, across the country from Los Angeles to New York. When he refused to sell his operation to the mob or pay protection, they burnt him out systematically club by club. The last fire put him out of business entirely—but not out of danger. He was forced to pull up stakes and disappear underground. After paying a plastic surgeon to alter his features, he gained fifty pounds and slipped across the border to Canada. I suspect there's more to the story than that. Sonny must have done something far-out to the mob Stateside to elicit such attention up here. But he's not talking. And I don't press him.

"So what are we gonna do?" I hazard, watching him put back another Jack Daniel's.

He shrugs emptily and clasps his hands in front of him into a worry knot. His only remedy is no remedy.

I keep wondering why Canada attracts so many runners from Stateside and, worse, why I seem to attract so many runners. Unless it's because I'm a runner myself.

Sonny is finally pushed out of the club operation altogether. He's not even allowed on the premises. Everyone's terrified of the mob. Whenever I mention Sonny, Jonathan blows a fuse. He knows I'm still seeing him.

Can't say I blame him. Sonny and I are tailed everywhere we go. Just for practice, we're run right off the road near Cherry Beach.

One night at his apartment, I'm sprawled out on the floor at his feet, watching the tube and eating pizza, when an explosion blows a section of the picture window right into the room in a sucking vacuum of cold air and broken glass. Terrified, I stay on the floor with my hands over my head and scuttle behind the couch, expecting a second barrage. When it doesn't come, Sonny pulls me out.

The window has a hole in it the size of a football. I'm hysterical and Sonny's shellshocked. He pours us out a glass of Canadian Club, shakes me back to sanity, and feeds me sips of the whiskey. "It's okay, kid. They're only trying to scare me." With me, they've succeeded.

Then he plops into an armchair in a stupor. "Know what, kid?" he ponders, up in his cups and down in his glory. "I've had everything. Two beach-front homes with swimming pools. Coupla planes, a small cruiser, charge accounts, trips to Europe, two big-titted blond wives, four kids—the works. Now all I've got left is a fucking fish tank, minus one tiger."

"And me," I remind him. "You've got me."

"No, I don't, kid. You stay with me I'll have you on the street tomorrow, hooking for me—guaranteed. See, kid, I'd have to." He puts back another hefty swallow and gets to his feet to pour himself another. "Everything I say probably sounds like Greek to you now," he continues, in the low monotone of a confessional. "But maybe someday you'll find out what being desperate is all about."

"Maybe," I say. Then:

"What about your plane?" I pipe up optimistically. "Can't you sell it?"

"Didn't I tell you? It conveniently caught fire last week. Even if the insurance wasn't under a phony name, they'd still figure I started it myself."

"The Jack Dempsey is alive and growing. That's a good omen."

He laughs hollowly. "The eternal optimist. I like that in ya, kid. I always did. I've got to get the fuck out of here. Go underground until things cool off. Maybe I'll set up in another part of the city." Springing to his feet, he prowls the room in a nervous lather of excitement. "I've got a few favors owing," he suddenly admits prophetically. Then he shoves me into the bedroom and makes another string of calls Stateside.

So Vincent was right. A man doesn't live by the money he's got in his pocket but by the favors owed him.

Half an hour later Sonny calls me from the bedroom and yanks the telephone cord right out of the wall. "Wouldn't anybody help you?" I ask timidly.

"When ya got balls for collateral, all you've got's balls, kid. But I managed to have a few bucks wired up from Miami. Better than nothing, I guess."

"Can't anybody *do* anything about these guys?"

He laughs caustically. "What can I tell ya? America isn't controlled by Washington—it's controlled by the mob. Look, I'm leaving this joint tomorrow with nothing but my clothes."

"And me?"

"I know where to find ya."

"What about the furniture?"

"I'll sell it."

"But it's rented."

"All the better." He grins. "The son of a bitch who's buying it won't know the difference."

Against all the laws of leavened logic, he gets strangely giggly, kisses me hungrily with his tongue, and hauls me aboard the conscience couch. "Tonight we'll forget the whole goddamn mess and party, yeah?"

I've never heard a better excuse for reading the Book of Ecclesiastes than a sudden clitoral eclipse.

We get it on awkwardly and hurriedly. Sonny's so physically detached from himself, he's loose, and when I straddle him it's like making love to the Goodyear blimp. That's okay. I'm so psychologically detached from reality I'm flying in some terrestrial Twilight Zone, trying to find a human meteor.

Later, when he's comfortably snoring on key, I crawl out from under him, quietly dress, and go to the phone booth down the street. I call Vito in the Falls. He answers my heady pleas on Sonny's behalf with a promise to call me back after he's done some checking. I have a coffee at the Harvey's next door and am back in the booth half an hour later. Vito opens up with one hell of a dynamic dictum.

"Your Sonny isn't just a loser," he says, "he's a dead man."

I listen in silence.

"Get away from him, little one."

Suddenly it's winter again and I'm riding the Christmas-to-Easter ho-hum depressies by working double shifts seven days a week. Just when fatigue has caught me by the cerebral cortex and my metabolism has begun to throw sparks of hysteria, Simon shows up at my door one morning. Just arrived back from a dig in Tanzania. My eccentric crony insists that I take a three-day break from my hectic schedule. Toronto is buried under a staggering snowfall and there's another blizzard warning out on the airwaves. But according to Simon, "It's a lovely day for a picnic, darling."

Giving in, I call up Jonathan and plead another Hong Kong flu epidemic. After lunch, Simon and I pick up twenty-dollar raccoon coats and woolen toques, mitts, and scarves, and thus outfitted in the latest Salvation Army, head out, pulling a little red sleigh loaded with two big sheepskins, a picnic basket, lantern, Coleman stove, blankets, and all the necessities for a camper's night out. At the bottom of Yonge Street we haul the sleigh aboard the ferry and twenty minutes later step onto Toronto Island. While I throw a sheepskin rug over a picnic table and use another one to carpet the inside of our tent, Simon surreptitiously scours the Toronto horizon with a set of binoculars, searching for Mongol horsemen and runaway convicts from Siberian salt mines. He hesitates a moment to read the label on the bottle of wine I brought. Then he affects a pained expression. "Let's put it in a glass, shall we, darling. I'm dying to know if it'll evaporate or simply devour the crystal."

Funny, very funny. It's society's fault that I'm still judging labels by the size of the bottles.

Throughout the oncoming zephyr, which lasts all night, we lie warm and snug wrapped in sheepskin, drinking iced vodka and vinegary wine, eating caviar on wheat crisps, listening to Tchaikovsky on my tape deck, and toasting our toes by the stove.

"It's time to own up, darling," Simon says suddenly. "What is bugging you?"

When I tell him about Sonny, he wails, "Oh, Lord, how the world loves a goose! Why do you always end up with reprobates?"

"Sonny isn't a reprobate."

"Anyone running from the mob would be lucky to be called a reprobate, darling. I suppose in the end I'll have to sell you to an Arabian sheikh to keep you out of trouble."

"I might even go willingly. I'm getting sick of being a sucker, too."

"Why not go professional, darling? Hang out a shingle and go into the business of being made and laid? You could make a bundle."

I give him a startled look and he groans melodramatically. "I can see I've still got a lot of work to do on you to make you totally incorruptible."

We awaken in the morning to frozen muffins and hot Spanish coffee. As an encore to our fool's night out, I take pictures of Simon against the Toronto skyline, sitting in a snowbank on the lunch basket, wearing his tails, a top hat, and a truss, pouring out a glass of champagne with white gloves and making one of his classic toasts, "Here's to Eve, who gave the apple back to the snake. And to Adam, who stuck an olive branch in his navel and went chasing butterflies."

Back at the club there's a new face on the scene. Dave is a burly, fun draft dodger from the States who's added to the payroll to share Harry's shift handing out flyers. He's presently being terrorized with death threats and back-alley beatings from a bunch of vengeful ex-marine Yankee hawks, up here systematically tracking down draft dodgers from Stateside. One night he rushes up to the lounge, his face beet-red with embarrassment. "Two pigs from Fifty-two Division just grabbed Harry," he says, out of breath. "They dragged him down to the cellar."

"Why in hell didn't you do something?" the girls say.

"I'm in the country illegally," he pleads. "How could I?"

Enraged, I grab the elevator down to the lower level. Harry's pockets have been turned out and he's being held by one pig while the other one is applying muscle to his face and torso. I scream blue murder and my throaty pagan war cry works its magic. Harry is instantly released and crumples to the stone floor in a daze. I run to help him up. "Is this how you get your jollies?" I fly, tearing into the pigs.

"Shut up or we'll take you in!" one of them lips.

"Oh, yeah—on what charge?"

"Soliciting. It's your word against ours—and yours isn't worth this little shit, sister."

Then Jonathan blunders off the elevator shouting a storm and the pigs immediately clam up. Jonathan lights into them with a vengeance. They have little to say in response. Jonathan grabs Harry, drags him upstairs, and unceremoniously dumps him into a chair in the office. I try to clean up his face with a Kleenex while Jonathan sits on the edge of the desk, slapping his club into the cave of his hand. "Now what the fuck happened?"

Shaking in his pants, Harry cringes and searches the floor for a toadstool to hide under. "I didn't do nothing," he mutters thinly. "No, I surely didn't."

Jonathan runs his hand erratically through his tight mat of hair, a clear indication he's about to blow a fuse. Anxiously, I tag Harry's arm and kneel beside him. "C'mon. What did the shits want you for, sweetheart?"

"They took my measly seven dollars," he whines in a small voice. "Called it their supper money. But I was saving it for something special. I was gonna buy this real neat wallet with colored cowboys on both sides so I could keep funny money in it so if anybody ripped me off all they'd get is—is—"

Jonathan leans toward him. "Your wallet, asshole!"

Harry nearly jumps out of his socks. Now I know why he's afraid to carry anything bigger than a fin unless it's Monopoly money: he'd be rolled or shaken down by either a pimply-faced sweathog or a pig.

"Do you want a drink?" I ask him softly.

"Thank yeh kindly, Mushy. But I never touch the stuff when I'm on the job because I forget I'm drinking when I'm on the job and then I forget I have a job until I've lost it and then all I know is that I'm drinking to forget and can't figure out why I'm drinking at all."

"Give him a goddamn drink and maybe he'll make some sense!" Jonathan pulls a bottle of Scotch out of the drawer of the desk. I pour some into a Dixie cup and hand it to Harry.

Getting more literate by the second, Harry finally after another cup of whiskey spills his guts. "Do yeh know Roxanne? Well, she works up the street as a stripper at the Escapade and sometimes I get her little things like those green candies that melt fast on your tongue—and she said she loves me. She truly did. And I can prove she truly does."

Jonathan starts to laugh but Harry continues anyway. "Well, it's true—she loves me and she gave me this real expensive ring to prove it. I always wore it around my neck on a chain so I'd remember she loved me. And those pigs took it. They said I must have stole it from somebody. But I didn't. I surely didn't and—"

"Both of you get out of here before I fire you!"

Harry is half-pissed and can't possibly resume his beat on the Strip so I stick him under the table in my room to sleep it off and cover him with sheets.

When my next John, an ex-biker from Detroit, arrives and Harry starts snoring, I invent a shaggy-dog story to cover up. "Well, it sure snores kinda funny for a dog," he drawls skeptically.

"German shepherds are born with a blockage in the nasal passages," I scramble.

"Uh-huh. That's exciting news, baby. I've had one for ten years and never noticed." Getting off the table and looking under it, he pulls the sheets off Harry.

I'm forced to throw the long bomb. "Oh, well, you may not believe this but the magician who was in here before you said he could change my dog into a man. Of course, I thought he was full of shit."

"Somebody's full of shit, baby," he says, hoisting himself back onto the table again. "By the size of him, I'd say there's only half a man down there. Where the hell is the rest of him?"

"Out for repairs."

With a grunt he sticks a twenty-dollar bill in Hoppy's bum, my unique tip box. "This's the looniest conversation I've had in months and you're the looniest broad I ever talked to. Let's go for another hour and see where we end up."

Later on, I'm pulling towels out of the hall cupboard when I feel someone's heavy breath on the back of my neck. I whirl around and Jonathan is grinning evilly at me, rolling his eyes like a set of loaded dice. "What's the matter with you?" I say nervously. "Too many hot peppers in your pizza?" He follows me right down the hall without a word. "Okay, what did I do now?"

He backs me into the office and slams the door. "First I hear you've got a dog in your room. Then I hear it's a dead body. Now one of the Johns has called the cops."

"Some people take everything literally," I return weakly.

"Two shits from Fifty-two Division are here to investigate a possible homicide. If I set sight on you again tonight, it might just be one— yours. You're goddamn crazy, you know that? Now get your ass out of here!"

The next afternoon I pay a backstage call on Titian-haired Roxanne in her poor excuse for a dressing room at the Escapade. When I tell her what went down with Harry, she throws her pasties at the mirror. "Those assholes. Why aren't they pulling in pushers or murderers instead of beating up on him? Sure, I gave the little guy the ring. A five-and-dime special. Harry does little errands for me so I figured it would keep him happy and square with me, yeh know? I'll drop down to the drugstore after the next set."

Roxanne keeps her word and by suppertime Harry's wearing another fake rhinestone around his neck on a shoelace. He's as pleased as punch.

My *mal d'amour* continues . . . from a carefree rodeo broncobuster from Wyoming, in town for the stampede at the Canadian National Exhibition, to a conscience-burdened Métis journalist who writes for a leading national Indian newspaper.

Then comes Derrick, a dark-haired, blue-eyed American from Texas who enjoys dancing, soft conversation, stimulations, and owns a construction company up here. He's in town on business and I see him on and off for two full weeks. He's all spit and polish in designer duds, his blue eyes snapping with goodwill and mischief. Derrick is an excellent way to take my mind off the men *not* in my life.

One night at his motel we're nicely into a round of lovemaking, the pump well primed for the eventual damburst, when there's a mad thumping at the door. We try to ignore it but when it keeps up, Derrick curses, slides into his pants, unlocks the door, and slips into the hall. I can hear a woman's hysterical voice outside. "Who've you got in there with you? I want to know who the hell she is. Don't fucking tell me to go home! Let me goddamn in!"

Derrick returns and reaches for his shirt and he doesn't look too happy. "My ex-wife," he explains heatedly. "I don't know how the hell she found me. Just give me five minutes to get rid of her, baby." Then he disappears into the hall and the door locks behind him. But he forgot his key on the dresser.

I start to relax back against a bank of pillows and reach for my wineglass when, stupefied, I see this classy blonde push open the other sliding glass door at the opposite end of the room which leads to the lawn outside and lunge toward me with a broken beer bottle in her hand. For a split second I can't move—I can't believe that she's for real. But the bottle is.

"You little slut!" she's crying hysterically. "I'll cut you up so bad no man will ever want you again!"

I snap out of freeze-frame and scramble naked off the bed. Cagily, she edges around it. In a panic I try to reach the door. But she lunges at me with the bottle and we do a cat dance on the carpet while I twist and jump away from her erratic thrusts. Somehow I grab her arms and we're on the floor thrashing, and she's grabbing a fistful of my hair and bending my head back and I'm squeezing her neck and trying to bite her arm. Now new arms are grabbing and pulling us apart.

In a daze I see some other dude, an overstuffed drubbie in an overcoat with dented features and a cigar in his mouth. He grabs me by the back of the neck with one hand and sharply brings me to my knees. "I wonder who the fuck attacked who?" he spouts gruffly to Derrick as I struggle and curse. He hauls me to my feet and gives me a hard slap on the ass. "Knock it off—or I'll give you something to fucking holler about."

So there I am in my birthday suit with half the occupants of the floor here for the party, leering at me from the doorway. I'm also bleeding profusely from a deep gash at the top of my right leg. By nature I'm a born kicker. The witch is being restrained by Derrick. She has a bruise on the side of the head and a bloody nose—I've also got a talent for hitting with a closed fist. I limp over to the bed and take a dive under the covers.

While the drubbie puts an armlock on the witch, Derrick comes over and pulls the sheet from my face. "Sorry, baby. She's crazy—always was. This fella here is gonna get you to a hospital. I've got to quiet Beth down and get her back to her hotel. I'll call you tomorrow. Okay, baby?"

Dopey as hell, I hold my throbbing leg and nod numbly. He kisses me and leaves with his witch. I'm left with this down dude. He puts a light to the cigar hanging out of his mouth and looks at me with a tight grin, proving to be as disagreeable as he looked at first. "You look like somebody pulled you through a knot backward, Blondie," he says. Ignoring him, I guzzle a glass of Derrick's left-behind Dom Pérignon and he rips two bandages out of the bed sheets and disappears into the bathroom. I pull the covers up around my throat, waiting for him to make the next move. He emerges with a crooked smile splitting his ugly face, sits on the side of the bed, and zips the sheets from my body. "Now don't go and pretend to be modest, Shortcake. That would make us both look like jerks."

I turn my head to the wall and let him bandage my bloody leg. He swabs the wound with one wet sheet and binds it with a dry one. Now my leg is throbbing even louder and it's only a question of time before I pass out. He zips my clothing from the back of the chair, tries to fit my bra over my shoulder around my tits, and roughly pulls my head forward into his lap while he curses and fiddles with the back clasps. "Don't worry. I've seen everything you've got—in bigger weights and measures, too."

I'm in no state to argue. He slips my underwear up my legs, yanks my dress over my head, straps my feet into my spiked heels, and props my twenty-dollar raccoon coat around my shoulders. Then he picks me up and carries me out the sliding door to the parking lot.

It takes him an eternity to clean the newspapers, candy wrappers, and clothing out of the passenger side of his beat-up cream-colored Oldsmobile so I can get in. Then he pulls out of the parking lot as if late for the Daytona 500 and flicks on the squealer under the dash to listen to the police calls, pure rapture on his face. At the report of a burglary on the Queensway, he gets all excited. "Wanna have a drink with an over-the-hill dick, Shortcake? You look like you could use one. There's cups and a bottle in the glove compartment."

I light up a cigarette and pour us each a cup of Scotch and hand him one, along with a four-star question. "What the hell were you doing here tonight?"

"I was paid to follow you and Muscle Boy by his old lady," he confesses lightly. "I've been on your sweet tails for the past week. And in case you wanna know, it's been no goddamn picnic."

"You could have stayed in the car and played with yourself."

"And frost my balls off in the process? And watch your tongue. Another crack like that and I'll add it to your tab and take it out of your hide."

"I don't owe you nothing!"

"You owe me more than you know you owe me. I could have

tipped off Muscle Boy's old lady three days ago. But I figured since she could afford to fly up here from Miami she could afford to pay me for five days as well as two."

"I think I'm gonna be sick," I confess, rocking from side to side to keep down the pain in my leg and the fizz in my head.

"We'll be at the hospital in a few minutes. Hold on."

"Forget it," I mutter with my head back against the seat. "I'm going home. I want to die. Also, I hate dicks."

"I like that," he says cheerily. "I like a chick who's honest. Even if it isn't gonna do her a goddamn bit of good. By the way, I'm Biscuit."

"Biscuit?"

"When I walked the beat I always chewed on those Sweet Marie chocolate bars. They say you are what you eat."

"So you were a pig, eh?"

"Yup. Traded in the flat feet for a flat ass. Now my rearview mirror sees more of my puss than my old lady ever did. That's why she split. I wish to hell she had split sooner. Who knows—maybe I would have had money in the bank and a decent sex life to boot. But let me tell you, when I met that Beth broad at the airport this morning, I knew she was bonkers. She hired me by phone from Miami. I got a nose for trouble—you can't be a smart dog without one. But I figured I'd tag along behind her and get in on the action. I don't see much of it these days except at the movies. I wanted to see how you'd stack up, too. For your size you didn't do too bad, Shortcake."

Then he swings into the emergency entrance of the Toronto General.

"I'm not going in. I also hate doctors."

"Is there anybody you do like?" he bursts out, cutting engine. Despite my protests, he hauls me out of the passenger side and whispers in my ear. "I'm your uncle Arnold and you fell on a broken beer bottle."

"Why Arnold?"

"I had a dog once and his name was Arnold. Used to fall for every slutty bitch in the neighborhood. One day he took off and I never saw him again. Probably turned queer on me, the bastard."

Inside he pulls a detective badge at the desk and gets us through Admitting super quick. I'm practically numb by the time the doctor on call sits me on a table and probes my leg. Biscuit sticks around holding my hand while I'm stitched up.

In the car on the way home, the son of a bitch gets even more perverse. "Say, how much did you charge Muscle Boy for a piece of tail?"

"I'm not a whore!" I flash, high on pain-killers and fatigue. "I like him, that's all."

"Okay, okay," he soothes gruffly. "So have another drink and don't bite my head off. I know where you work and I figured you were in on the game."

"That's okay," I reply dully. "I'm not into *selling* my ass."

"Good. I like a woman who's easy to get along with. But how much would you charge if you were in on the game?"

"I dunno . . . hey, are you hustling me?"

"Yup, I guess that's what I'm doing. So what do you want me to tell you, Shortcake? That a guy doesn't live to score? Sorry, but it's not true."

This conversation is getting so garbled I wish to hell I'd pass out. "But I can hardly walk," I argue illogically.

"That's okay." He grins, slipping the end of his cigar out the window. "I'm not looking for a female jock. A crippled runner will do me just fine."

"You're obscene."

"Look, I'm not so bad. I figure I treat broads damn good considering what they're usually worth—which is balls. I wine and dine them. I hold doors open for them. And I never touch them without first washing my hands. How do yeh like that for a male chauvinist pig?"

His homegrown philosophy of table manners is so ridiculous I break out into a delirious giggle.

"C'mon," he continues seriously. "Muscles was madder than hell because he missed last call. Why waste an already fucked-up evening? Just because you started off with a clean nail don't mean yeh can't finish it off with a rusty screw."

By the time we get to my place I'm in a puddle of puzzlement. Blitzed out by pain, drugs, and the evening in general, I can't think of any way to veto his advances.

Now he can't find a parking space on the street, so the bastard creates one by simply punting another car forward into a tow-away zone.

"You better hit it again—it's still kicking."

"Those fucking foreign rustbuckets shouldn't be allowed in the country," he says to himself in a lather. "They take jobs away from guys that need it."

I let him carry me inside. The Lotus-eaters are having a love-in with the cosmos in the foyer and on the stairs, riding high on blotters of LSD and hits of MDA. Quickly, he gives them the boot by going bulldog. "Take a hike, kiddies, and I'll pretend this isn't a police raid."

Then in my flat he filches a beer from the fridge and a can of soup from the cupboard and sets it on the stove to boil.

"What makes you think I want that?"

"*Want* never has anything to do with what's good for you. That's why God created sons of bitches like me. Somebody has got to dish out the burnt soup."

Later he makes me choke down a pain-killer and carefully undresses me and puts me to bed. Then he invites himself for the night. I watch him strip down and hang his shoulder holster on the back of a chair. "You're licensed," I observe groggily from under the sheets.

"That's right, Shortcake," he growls, switching off the lamp and crawling in beside me. "I've got the legal clout to deal with anybody who doesn't like my politics. Every son of a bitch who's worthy of the shitpile he was born in has his own personal edition of the Bible. Now it's time for me to find out how you like being a crippled runner."

Though half-zonked, I'm totally embarrassed by having this ex-pig pin me to the bed and begin slowly kissing and fondling me with such a gentle finesse that I'm suddenly carried away.

And so begins my damnably durable relationship with Biscuit, the rusty screw. Despite the fact that he turns out to be a running dialogue of acid abuse on everything from the economy to politics, I find his rough manners and warm heart delicious.

There's a phenomenon at the club called the Tender Trap. It can put you into an entirely new tax bracket. It starts when a John says a girl is the cutest piece of fluff he's ever seen. To keep him talking, she either screws him or blows him, trying to force another compliment out of him, which usually comes with two tenners and another appointment. The graffiti on the back of her brain and the money in her hand are an instant high—and it was so easy. It isn't putting out that makes you a pro. The minute a girl hooks onto a John's bull and takes her first dollar for the compliment, she's hooked. She discovers that her fingernails can be lengthened and polished, her hair curled and bleached, her eyelashes darkened and thickened, her tits siliconed, and her wardrobe expanded. Her lack of self-esteem has been suddenly shoved into reverse overdrive. To accommodate this ego-builder, she can do nothing but strive to service the market of supply and demand. You can improve on the female condition by dressing it up with all the trimmings and selling it at cost.

Two of my comrades, Sally and Sabrina, quit and take an apartment together. They hang out a shingle and start business with Johns from the club. Now they've asked me if I want in on the enterprise. Sorry, but I'm not ready to plunge into murkier waters yet. I'm not desperate for the extra cash and I know that prostitution won't give me the ultimate high. Also, my ego couldn't be that easily shortchanged. I'm quite happy just swimming around in the tank with the other fish. There's no exchange rate on sex or promises.

17

Other offers come in. Now that Sonny is desperate, dogged by the mob, and gone underground, he's turned into an ace skuzzball with credentials. From time to time he surfaces and skulks around on the street outside of the club, trying to rope my cashiered comrades into working for him. When he asks me to make bootleg porno flicks, my sensibilities order out for a Bloody Jesus—on the rocks. "No way, José!"

Eventually I feel sorry for him more than anything and agree to meet him for a tête-à-tête before work one afternoon. After falling into a chair at a nearby restaurant, I decide that I'm beginning to become much like the chameleon who's constantly rearranging her spots to suit the snake in the grass.

"I need a favor from you, kid," he pleads right up front.

When I refuse to answer he continues. "C'mon—we had a lot of laughs together, didn't we? I wouldn't pull a fast one on you."

I have to agree or go away feeling guilty all day.

He wants me to go out with a business partner of his, a recent widower. Just to take in a show and have dinner, no hanky-panky unless our chemistry happens to touch off a tropical heat wave. "Pretend you're going out on a blind date and give him a tour of the city," he concludes. "And don't mention his wife, he's still strung out on her."

So I meet Ron for cocktails at the Hyatt Regency on Friday evening. At first glance he seems like any other dark-haired spectacled dip in a monkey suit. But he's well educated, his manners so polished and his repartee so stimulating and sweet, I can't fathom where somebody like Sonny ever met somebody like him.

After taking in the road-show *Fiddler on the Roof*, we cruise around the city in his Mustang and then to a room at the Sutton Place Hotel, where Sonny has arranged a midnight dinner for us. The stage setting seems a bit odd but since Ron makes no comment about it, I don't either. I can only speculate that taking a massage-parlor chippy to his home would be distasteful.

Ron's sense of humor and knowledge of the arts are so appealing that I figure I just might want to see him again—if given the chance. Then Sonny arrives with a bottle of champagne and pours us out two glasses to celebrate a secret business deal he's made with Ron. My curiosity strains at the leash but I keep my mouth shut and, faking indifference, sip at the bubbly. A minute later there's a knock at the door and the catering service wheels in the surf and turf. Sonny gives us a conspiratorial wink and a whistle and disappears, with Rimsky-Korsakov's *Scheherazade* playing on the stereo.

Ron and I do our level best to combine an economy of time with the modulating mellow of good drink, good food, and stimulating conversation. Then suddenly over a lobster claw something goes wrong. The room turns sideways and I'm speeding toward Pluto on three-dimensional wheels while Ron's face across the candlelight takes on a radium-induced glow. To my star-studded eyes he's become not just nice but paradise embodied, in human form, and I'm so horny I can't stand it. I can actually feel my clitoris pulsating like an amplified heartbeat and my brain is hot and flying in agonizing slow motion toward Ron and I'm crashing through windows in space, unable to stop. The table goes over and Ron falls under it, fighting his way out from under an oyster bed. I can't dig him out fast enough to suit the stamping of my cloven foot or the shaking of my hands and the buzzing in my ears. He reaches toward me, his face suffused with fire and his head sprouting horns until he's the reincarnation of Mephistopheles. I take the horn in my teeth and then our bodies are caught up in spasmodic contractions, part of a satanic ritual, and we're writhing with a pile of lobster heads, tearing at each other's clothes and fucking and screaming and reproducing our way to immortality.

Infinity finally knocks twice at the back door of my brain and the memory reel in my head slips from fast-forward into play though my body is still locked into eject. My head is being held over a toilet and my fingers are groping the depths of my throat and I'm crying for death and throwing up devils from a single Christianized brain cell dated to the Dark Ages. I can't stop.

From somewhere in this nightmare the voices of priests flute in and out. "What can I tell ya, Joe? What can I tell ya? You measured wrong and gave them too much, you fucking asshole!"

Centuries later I wake up in my own bed, nude, sweaty, smelly, and thirsty. Sonny swabs my head with a towel and puts a glass of water to my lips. "You're here," I observe dully.

"Somebody had to be. I owed ya that, kid."

"What happened?"

"You can't handle your liquor, kid. It's that simple."

Happy only to have survived, I try to put the nightmare out of my head altogether. Being totally out of control is nothing one wants to remember. Sonny calls Jonathan and tells him that I have the flu and then carries me into the bath because I'm too weak to walk. He stays with me for three days, nursing me back to the land of the living. Then I'm back at work, groggy but sane.

One afternoon Ron phones me at work. "I have to see you," he says bluntly with starch in his voice. "It's urgent."

I agree to meet him for a quiet drink at the Holiday Inn. When I arrive, he's at a corner table, coddling a Black Russian. Uncomfortably I approach him, not sure what line of dialogue the scene calls for.

The minute we face each other, the memory reel in my head locks into rewind and waves of embarrassment creep over me. I'm not the only one. Ron looks just as pained. Why would he want to see me again?

Getting to his feet, he waits until I'm seated before speaking. "What will you have to drink?"

"A Bloody Mary. Thanks."

He tags a passing cocktail waitress and then, toying again with his drink on the table, gets down to business. "I would have liked us to meet again under different circumstances," he confesses awkwardly, sliding a brown envelope across the table. "You'd better take a look at these."

He removes his glasses and rubs his eyes while I flip through the six eight-by-ten color glossies of two naked bodies fornicating in flight, giving each other oral massages, and more. What's left of my self-respect drains away altogether and I start to tremble. Carefully I replace the glossies in the envelope and hand it back to him. "That's not you and me, is it?" I ask stupidly.

"No. That's you, me, and Spanish fly. We were set up."

My Bloody Mary arrives just in time for me to order another one. Stiffly, Ron offers a cigarette from a silver case, takes one himself, and snaps a light to both.

"I don't understand. Sonny told me you were in business together."

"Oh, he's in business all right," he says scathingly, flicking ash over the tablecloth. "It's called Blackmail, Inc. You see, I bought a couple of flicks from him for a friend's stag. Then another friend of mine asked me to buy a couple for him. That's how I got mixed up with the bastard. Last week he must have found out that I come from money and decided to make a haul. He asked me to do him a favor and take you out for a night on the town. I was more or less obligated, you understand."

"Then you're not a lonely widower?"

"No more than you're his baby sister dying of cancer."

"The slimebag!" I light up another cigarette. "Both of us could have overdosed on that shit. How in hell did you find me?"

"It wasn't easy. I had one hell of a time. Thank God you were as open with me as you were. All I remembered was your nickname and that you worked at a massage parlor downtown. I hired a detective to do the rest and track you down." Then he toys with the envelope on the table. "This isn't all. There's an uncensored film to go along with it. Both were delivered to my father's office on Bay Street three days ago."

"Have you seen it?"

"My father thought it best I didn't."

"I guess we're in a bind, huh?"

"Not you—me. My father's in the Ontario Government. This kind of dirt could wreck his career—and mine."

"How much does Sonny want?"

"Fifty thousand dollars."

"Whew—is your father gonna pay it?"

"He doesn't have much choice. But the thing about blackmail—it never stops. There are no guarantees Sonny doesn't have ten duplicates of everything stashed away. He could bleed us dry."

"Is there anything I can do?"

"No, I'm afraid there isn't. But it would help if I knew where to find the bastard."

"Well, he sometimes hangs around the club where I work. But after all this he probably won't show up there again. At the moment I don't know where he shacks up. But I can sure find out. I'll get the sleaze to give everything back."

He looks at me quizzically. "Do you really think you can?"

"I can try," I say almost smugly, for Ron's sake, exhibiting more optimism than I feel. Yet I smell a challenge in the air. "But I want something from you in return."

"Something like fifty thousand dollars, I suppose."

"No." I laugh. "How about a private showing of that film?"

"What a masochist," he remarks, relieved. "Look, if you can trip up that bastard, I'll arrange it."

To find out Sonny's whereabouts I contact one of the ex-club girls who now works at his underground Paramount. For backup I call Biscuit.

When I tell him about Sonny's scam, he's not thrilled about my plan of action. "Don't go off half-cocked, you stupid broad," he curses thickly.

Since I have no intention of fighting with him or being talked out of anything, I tap the dial tone a couple of times. "Sorry, I have to go now—termites on the line." I hang up and grab a cab.

That cashewed Caliban is shacked up in a little disaster on the top floor of a house near Coxwell and Dundas in the east end. It's already mid-evening when I arrive. For five minutes I bang at the door downstairs, demanding entry. A curtain moves in the window upstairs but there is no response. "I'll get you, you son of a buggered blackguard!" I curse to myself.

Sprinting into the backyard, I see a ladder. Slanting it up to the window, I start climbing. At the top I tumble through the window right on top of a naked French flesh layer-cake. Each layer shrieks and I eeek back. A lamp is knocked to the floor and somebody hollers, "Fuck off, Valentino!" Then I'm attacked by a coven of screaming banshees, slapping, smothering, kicking, scratching, and using me as a punching bag and I'm trying to fight my way out of a tent of covers and a quagmire of thrashing limbs. I bite a foot and get booted right onto the floor.

When the lights finally go up in this bedlam's bakehouse, I find Sonny in the sack with two blond busty bollocks playing three-card Monte. "What the hell are you doing here?" he bellows over the side of the bed, too dumbfounded to be angry.

Jumping to my feet, I slap his face, and enraged to the point where I'm three feet off the floor, I stumble into the kitchen, where I pull open the cupboards looking for the contraband photos and film, and when Sonny and his bimbos make an attempt to stop me, I begin pelting them with pots and pans and foodstuffs—anything that'll fly, yelling at the top of my lungs, "How could you do such a rotten thing to me? I trusted you!"

Finally I run out of ammunition and Sonny lunges at me. He grabs my wrists, spins me around, lashes his arms around my middle, and wheels my feet right off the floor. "I needed the dough, kid! I had to do it! I didn't mean to hurt ya!"

Totally out of control, I try to kick myself out of his grasp while he continues to play smoothie-kiss-it-all-better. "Cool down, cool down, kid. Let's talk this out."

Amid all this uproar, nobody hears the banging on the door downstairs or the lock being picked. Everyone jumps smartly to attention when Biscuit appears at the top of the stairs and flashes a fake police badge. "Everyone present and accounted for?" he roars with a lethal penetrating stare.

No one says boo.

"Good," he barks. "All I came for was the goddamn broad. And while I'm here I'll take all the copies of the film and the pictures the goddamn broad came for. And I better have all of it or I'll be back."

Sonny lets me go and I kick him in the shins. He limps into the bedroom and returns a few minutes later with a brown paper bag.

"Now you can all go back to your fucking party," Biscuit bites, taking the bag from Sonny. While everyone just stands there sucking air, he hauls me down the stairs at a frantic pace. Now I'll have no bargaining chip at all in dealing with him. "Fucking termites, huh?" he growls under his breath. "I'll show you one that comes with more than teeth!"

Refusing to hand over the contraband, he takes me back to my pad, where he treats me to a tongue-lashing on the hazards of being a prime pawn.

The next afternoon I call Ron. When I tell him the good news, that Biscuit that morning gave me the prints and the reel, he's ecstatic. He picks me up after work and whisks us off to his home in Rosedale. After dinner Ron sets up the projector and screen in the library while I nervously sip at a glass of La Tache 1953 and chain-smoke. Then he switches the lamp off, clicks the projector on, sits down, and reaches for my hand.

The theater of degradation has never produced a better Cine City porn commercial. Ron and I are devastated. He keeps taking off his glasses to rub his eyes and I can't stop shaking. Now I wish I hadn't insisted on screening it. I had no idea that such madness was possible in a human being—on or off hallucinogenic drugs. Worst of all, that madness is plainly in me, along with the devil. Watching those two pathetic animals writhing painfully on top of each other is finally too much for me. Hysterically I burst into tears. Ron snaps off the projector and takes me in his arms. He's shaking, too. For minutes we just hold each other in the dark, saying nothing.

Two hours later he turns the lamp back on and opens another bottle of wine and we clink glasses over the death of the world as we know it.

Crunch is hinged on the notion that we'll get together again once he's out of the slammer. I put off making a firm decision. I've never been good at cornering the animal.

Thoughtfully, I sit at my desk and gnaw at the end of my pen. I've always been a sucker for cons. When I was fourteen I wrote a letter to a guy on death row in the States. There was an article on him in *Life* magazine. I often wondered whether he had time to read all twenty pages before they pulled the switch on him.

See, I've always figured that cons have one extra layer of intelligence more than the normal Everyman Sam on the street. But what to do with Crunch? The way I see it, he's got four things going for him. First, he's older than I am, so he's smarter. He's industrious and tragically honest. That adds up to three. And, yes, he can control me.

He wants to leave society in the lap of moral decay and move north into the barrens. An interesting notion and a frightening proposition, and first I only think about it a little. Then, when I'm fighting it out with another idiot on the floor under my massage table, I think about it a lot.

One day at work I'm approached in the lounge by a tall, blond, muscular man around thirty in a gray tweed overcoat with a scar stitched into his suntanned cheek. His penetrating brown eyes cut right through me. "Are you free?" he asks in a thick French-Canadian accent.

How odd—he didn't even give the other four girls an eye. Nor did he wait for me to deliver the standard come-on line, which goes something like "Have you been suckered here before or is this your first time window-shopping?"

Pascal, as it turns out, is not smart-mouthed or aggressive so I drop my defenses a bit and try to be my own lighthearted self. After the first hour waltzing around the mulberry bush, he pays for three more sessions and I'm happy to let him take the lead. I must be doing something right. Instead of having me work, he asks me to light up a cigarette and sit down beside him. He tells me a lot about Montreal, including how he came from a poor area of the city. Then he asks if he can see me tonight after work. I almost say yes. But I reconsider and decline the offer, pleading fatigue. Owing to my recent brushes with misadventure, little warning bells have been going off in my head at the mere mention of any kind of involvement—especially with someone I don't know.

He shrugs tightly. "Fine—I'll be back tomorrow then."

Sure, I think. Tomorrow—the day after yesterday.

After he leaves, it finally occurs to me what it was about him that bugged me. He didn't smile. Not once.

The next day Jonathan has all the symptoms of a bad cold mixed with a basically grumpy Virgo constitution. I mix him up a couple of hot-tea-and-vodka fireballs to sweat the John Knox out of him.

Pascal shows up again in the afternoon and books me until well after midnight. Again the same proposition. Again I refuse to give in. There's something creepy about him, a dark force trembling just under the surface of his skin—and it frightens me.

For the next five days it's the same ritual. He strolls in the club around two in the afternoon and buys my time straight through to midnight. He feeds my tip box and invites me out and I refuse each time. But the persistent Gemini won't take no for an answer. After the fifth night Jonathan pulls me into the office. "Get rid of that guy!" he says. "Something's wrong. I don't like it."

"Why?" I say, feigning ignorance.

"I don't know—just call it a gut feeling. A bad fucking feeling. That guy is trouble."

"He pays in cash, doesn't he?"

"Look, anybody who throws around that much cash in less than a week on one girl is out for more than that girl's ass."

"Worried about having to pry your teeth out of the woodwork?" I tease. "I'll gladly hold them for you. If you don't want him here, you throw him out."

He shakes his head. I suddenly realize that Jonathan's afraid of the dude, too.

The next afternoon Pascal shows up right on schedule. I'm so embarrassed by the attention I want to crawl into a hole. I try to elude him by hiding out in the office. But after he's been in the lounge for a full hour asking for me and refusing to leave, Jonathan sends me in, afraid of trouble.

Why have I been singled out?

Jonathan's got a cheap answer to the question. "You're blonde. Not only do you look easy, you are. A guy like him goes for that."

His response is so reasonable I can only reply, "Kiss my ass, you crumb."

During the massage Pascal makes a confession to me which changes things considerably. He pulls a photograph of his wife out of his wallet and tells me she died a year before of leukemia. I feel an odd, prickly sensation, no pun. She has a startling resemblance to me. Now that I've got an honest excuse to explain his attentions, I don't see anything wrong with going out with him for a meal. After all, what the hell could happen in a public restaurant? Besides, I find his hot hypnotic eyes exciting, like aromatic heat released from the sweat glands. Gentle or not, he might prove to be more macho than Vincent and Crunch.

For the remainder of the evening I rush around like crazy and finally finish my stint shortly after two in the morning. As Harry has the tendency to wait for the girls downstairs and report to Jonathan as to who picks them up, I climb out the back window to the alley, zip down the fire escape, and meet Pascal in front of the Brown Derby.

A cold snap has snorted in. The night air is bracing and blustery. I love it. Winter is my favorite season of the year. With the exception of a few stray taxis, skidding across an iced-over yellow line, the streets are practically deserted.

As nothing is open on the Strip except the drugstore and Joey's, the hamburger joint, we chugalug over to Chinatown. I start shivering inside of my flimsy synthetic shawl and skip over the sheets of ice and snow in three-inch heels, clutching Pascal's arm.

Chong's Restaurant is practically empty and there are only two waiters to serve the tables. The owner minces over in soundless slippers with a smile big enough to skywrite on. He makes a small bow and shakes Pascal's hand graciously. It's obvious that they're old friends. He takes Pascal's overcoat and ushers us to a table in the middle of the room. Pascal explains that corner tables make him feel like a trapped animal. He orders us a round of drinks and the owner hands me a menu.

Our conversation shifts from Toronto to Montreal, and I suddenly remember a fragment of time, and I'm eight years old with my auntie Jane and her Chinese boyfriend, visiting Montreal's Chinatown for the weekend, dancing with a bunch of kids behind a crazy dragon and throwing firecrackers across the pavement under the feet of startled pedestrians. . . .

Pascal toys with his glass for a minute and then breaks my train of thought by lighting up another cigarette. "How about returning to Montreal—permanently?"

"I don't know French."

"You don't have to. But if you want to learn, I'll teach you."

"How'd you learn English?"

"I paid an English boy to teach me."

He offers me instant employment as his housekeeper. I toy with the chopsticks, waiting for his sun in Gemini to convince my sun in Sagittarius. His face and cool delivery produce an exotic mirage which gets brighter and brighter on the horizon of blah. A spacious modern home in north Montreal with park-sized grounds and all the conveniences—all at my disposal when he's away on business. Why the hell should I spend the rest of my life massaging hot human flesh when I can sell my independence and live like a normal person? I can't really afford to miss this opportunity. But what about my relationship with Crunch? Well, I'll worry about that later. Right now I'm gonna think about myself first.

"Can I leave anytime I like?"

"Of course," he says, reaching for my hand. "But because of the nature of my work, I must take precautions."

"Work?" I echo.

"Security for the government."

When I ask him about it, he blows his cover by hastily lighting a cigarette and keeping his eyes averted.

"You're an agent!" I gasp in spite of myself.

"Sort of," he confesses with nervous restraint. Then he waves his arm and orders another round. "Now you see why I must have you cleared with security before I can employ you. It won't take long. Then in the morning we'll fly to Montreal."

In a daze of booze, fatigue, and irresistible excitement and intrigue, I give in completely. I'm still letting other people make my decisions.

Pascal doesn't even pay for the meal—it's on the house. Clutching my arm, he maneuvers me outside to a waiting taxi and into the Stardust Motel. At the end of the line I'm stuck with the taxi tab. He has nothing on him but a wallet full of R.C.M.P. goodwill and credit cards.

He scrounges a bottle of expensive Bordeaux in an ice bucket and two glasses from the desk clerk, who seems to know him on a first-name basis. It appears as if Pascal's connections are endless. In the room he locks the door, corkscrews the bottle open, and pours us out a glass. "Sit down and relax," he commands, pushing me down on the blue-flowered bedcover. Is it my imagination or is he the one who needs to relax?

"Is anything wrong?" he asks suddenly.

"Of course not," I lie.

"Good." He picks up the telephone, dials a number, talks with someone for a minute, and then hands me the receiver.

"I'm not sure if I want to now."

"You're not obligated," he insists, lighting up a cigarette. "If you want to pull out tomorrow, you can."

The cop or government agent or whoever he is on the other end of the line identifies himself as Ed. He sounds impersonal but at the same time friendly, and instantly puts me at ease by explaining what Pascal already told me—that for security reasons they need the dope on me. It's all on the level and I'd have to go through the same screening procedure if I applied for a job with the Department of Defense. So I allow myself to be interrogated in detail for half an hour or more and am asked very personal questions about my family and work history. But I'm especially careful about editing my friends out of my life entirely.

Pascal is becoming more nervous and remote, pacing a path between the door and the bed, firing up one cigarette after another with the wineglass trembling in his hand. A darkness passes over his face when he glances my way, as if he's not seeing me at all but someone else.

I wish to hell I had my tarot cards with me so I could do a reading but maybe my intuition is just as good. Meanwhile, I cling to the receiver as if it's my only lifeline to security. I'm beginning to feel like a caged animal myself.

When the government man hangs up, Pascal takes the receiver from my hand. Even before he has it cradled, I'm edging across the room in full retreat. Then I bolt for the door. Pascal springs toward me like a cat, throws his full weight against me while I'm trying to unjam the lock, and seizes my wrist and twists it until I let go. "What's your hurry?" he rasps unnaturally, his face tight with fury and shiny with sweat and inner heat. "You don't want to leave yet—stay for a while." His complete transformation from Jekyll to Hyde and the cold delivery scares the shit out of me. This is like a really bad C film.

"I've watched you at work," he scoffs, pulling me back to the bed. "You act like you love everybody—everybody but me and I pay the most money." Unloosening his collar, he lights another cigarette. "You don't love me, do you?"

"Love you? I don't even know you."

"Oh, I think you do, English."

"I've talked to you for hours but I still don't know what to expect from you," I confess, hoping I can talk the demon out of him before it's too late.

He fluffs up a pillow and stretches out on the bed with a cigarette and his wine. "Come here, *tout de suite!*"

Afraid of angering him again, I sit down on the bed. He fondles my face for a moment and then slides his forefinger into my mouth sideways. "Bite it."

I don't exert enough pressure to suit him. "Harder!" he shouts, and keeps shouting and breathing in gasps until my teeth break the skin and blood is drawn. Gingerly, he glosses my lips with it and pulls me over and under him with rough practicality and his voice turns scath- ing. "I want you to be natural, happy, and funny—like you are at the club. If you do everything I tell you to do I won't hurt you."

Numbly I nod and let him pull my dress over my head and remove my undies. The sight of my naked body seems to have no effect on him at all. Before things get totally out of control I make an excuse to empty my bladder. After locking myself in the washroom, I take a glance in the mirror and scare myself. The enormity of this warped situation hits me in nauseous waves. There's not even a window to climb out of. Christ, am I cooked!

He bangs on the door and over the whirr of the fan I can hear him shouting. "There's no way out, English. Go ahead and yell all night. The staff won't come—they know me!"

I sit hunched up on the floor, and suddenly it hits me like a sledgehammer: this motel is known as the unofficial Toronto hangout for mobsters from Montreal's French underworld. So is Pascal a gangster, too? And if he is, what is he doing with R.C.M.P. intelligence? For minutes I remain in a crouch and wallow in self-pity. I already flubbed puberty—now this.

"I'll shoot the fucking lock off!" Pascal screams.

Great—he's got a heater and I don't even have a shoelace for a slingshot. Out of stark fear I give up, unlock the door, and step out. He's waiting for me with a .38 in his hand, naked. All night I've been more or less tinkering with the panic button in my head. The minute he dumps the heater on the dresser, I fly at him with both fists. He whirls around and slaps me a strapping stunner that lands my body on the bed in a fit of hysterics. He dives on me and keeps slapping until I scream for mercy. "Is this what you'll do for me in Montreal?"

"Never give me a reason to be bored," he says coldly. "And you'll never find out. Deny me nothing and you'll have nothing to regret."

The blood on my lips turns him on. Again he finger-paints my face with it and then grasps his huge hard prick like a battering ram and tries to jam it between my legs. The madness in his twisted face throws me into another spasm of biting, kicking, and screaming. His body turns rigid on top of me. He clamps his long muscular fingers tightly across my mouth and they transform into a hangman's noose, enclosing my throat and squeezing. Helplessly, I clutch at his wrists, choking on time, his voice a spearheading sound track in my head.

"You're gonna end up like the others, English!" he rasps in my ear, his face as frenetic as the distended purple between his legs.

Suddenly I'm six years old and falling from the top of a snowbank into the road. My arms are going like windmills and my lungs are collapsing and I can't breathe. . . .

So this's what it's like to die!

18

At the back of my brain a solitary thought penetrates my senses and I know it's my last. I hear a steady "Play dead! Play dead!" Releasing myself to the blackness that is swallowing me, I let my body fall limp. It seems to detach itself from my being and slip away into oblivion. Immediately, Pascal's hands loosen and through a hazy spray of eyelashes I watch him sit back on his haunches, breathing heavily.

In one gush, I gag and take a gulp of air. My body joins my brain and I come to, groggily, weakly, feeling as if I've just blacked out for minutes. Without a word, Pascal plunges inside me, imbued with an unnatural strength from some unnatural source, as if he's punishing the wanton womb of a poxed whore. The initial thrust sends me into a twisting howl of pain and I bite the nipple on his chest. That only seems to excite him and he pounds away at the raw dry walls of my vagina until he comes and his sperm slithers down the inside of my thighs like paradise's snakes rejected.

In a minute he relaxes back against the wooden headboard and lights a cigarette, as if we just met over tea and crumpets, for godsakes. He's drained, debauched, and detached. I'm confused and mummified in numbness. I struggle hard to console and control my sanity and try to deny that he just tried to strangle me and poured all his hatred and aggression into me. The survival game isn't over yet. The Hyde syndrome could strike again. Like a zombie I stroke his forehead, more to comfort myself, and murmur at him with feigned motherly softness. "You almost killed me—do you realize that?"

Blankly he stares at the wall and addresses the room unemotionally. "I didn't—so it doesn't matter."

This Pascal character is no more a Pascal than I'm a Mushy. We're merely playing sociological roles at a biological level. The greatest curse in my life has been my five planets in Libra, full of suck-ass servitude and stall. But on further reflection, maybe they've been less of a curse and more of a charm.

Suddenly he snaps out of his stupor and grasps my arm like a starving dog begging for a bone and makes a confession. He tells me that his violent blowup tonight wasn't in his plans, that it just happened. He also implies that it is all my fault for playing hard to get for the past week. Then he makes his pitch. "You haven't changed your mind about Montreal, have you? Tell me you're still coming with me!"

"I'm still coming with you," I echo in a singsong, still afraid of him.

Mechanically, he kisses my forehead, rolls over, and falls to sleep, not realizing that in *my* head I'm probably more lethal than *he* was half an hour ago. I'm getting stronger by the minute. What would Crunch say if he knew? Knowing him, he'd say little—it's what he'd do to me.

The others. Pascal said that. So I'm not the first? Did they survive or are their bodies now rotting in this dump's dump, their souls freed forever?

Once more my emotions and reactions are confused. To me Pascal's not only the Antichrist who held my life between his trembling fingers and judged this Roman thumbs down, giving me a death sentence, he's also the vindicating messiah who saved me before I mounted the scaffold. Both of us seem to be stereotyped victims. All he wants in life is a synthetic cunt and all I seem to want is a rubber cock.

For an hour I cuddle myself under the covers, hugging the silence, savoring what is left of security. Then I creep out of bed on my hands and knees into the cold blackness of the room. My clothing's scattered all over the floor. Shaking with nervousness, I dress quickly. While fastening a garter strap, I notice the glinting steel of Pascal's .38 on top of the dresser. Fascinated, I reach for it and check the magazine— the bugger is loaded. A frenetic heat gospels in my sexpit and I have a wild urge to shoot Pascal. How sweet to squeeze the revenger's rod, O what exquisite delivery! I've never felt such near rapture. But something stops me, and trembling, I place the .38 on the carpet and finish dressing. Pascal's snoring soundly so I start moving across the room in a crouch. I'm shaking so badly I'm afraid he'll hear the thrusts of my heartbeat or the rattling of my limbs.

I can't hazard tripping out the lobby. The night clerk would grab me for sure. Expecting Pascal to wake up at any moment, I disappear behind the curtain, unlock the sliding glass door to the outside, and with hollow dread step into a snowdrift right up to my knees and start running like a jackrabbit. It takes me a whole half hour to flag down a goddamn cab. I'm shaking something fierce from the cold. I ask the cabbie to drop me downtown.

For an hour I walk the streets in a daze, blocking out the dread memory. Finally I wander into Duffy's Open Kitchen on Dundas Street for a coffee to keep me warm. The swillhole is full of the usual dregs—purple-faced Indian alcoholics, tattered welfare bums, emaciated heroin addicts, and all kinds of transient truck with tattoos and jumpy nerves. Duffy the owner is standing at the counter, peeling potatoes with his fly open. The place is crawling with lowlife and cockroaches. When one of the resident pushers puts the move on me at the counter, I give him the finger. "Sit on it and rotate, you crock!"

This whole scene is so depressing and downwind of hell I make a major life decision on the spot: I've gotta get out of this racket for good.

Pascal will go back to the club to get me. I know it.

Then I realize I'm not only angry, I'm hungry, too. That means my brain is still functioning and my body isn't dead. If I'm alive, I don't need this bullshit anymore. So what do I do now? I can't risk going home. Pascal knows where I live.

Unable to decide what to do next, I just crash on the curb at Yonge and Dundas. Right away I get into a rapabutt with a frosty-tongued cop over whether I've got the right to put my feet in the gutter. Shit, the gutter belongs to the damned who roll there, not to the powers who piss there. Then the asshole wants to take me in for vagrancy.

Mercifully, the legless Barber from the club wheels it on up the street and scoots his cart between us. As soon as he finds out what's going down, he shoves a can of pencils in my hand and tells the cop that I've been waiting to help him collect money for Saint Peter's Church. So the cop saunters off and I zip into a hamburger joint and return with two coffees and two honey buns and the Barber and I breakfast while he sends his squinty eyes up and down the Strip, searching for human pigeons. Suddenly he finds a mark and gives my knee a slap. "Wanna see something sweet, Big Eyes? Watch what I do to those fuckers over there!" He grins, whipping the can of pencils out of my hand.

Those fuckers turn out to be a very hip business couple dressed to the nines, probably on their way to Howard Johnson's for a breakfast of eggs Benedict. They stop to buy a paper.

The Barber gears up his cart. With his small pudgy hands spinning the wheels, he plows straight for them at top speed and skids into their ankles. The woman tumbles arse first into two inches of slush at the curb and the man is thrown off balance into the newsstand at the corner. Robbie, the crippled-up midget who runs the newsstand, has a conniption fit over the couple's roughhousing and the man is forced to fork out enough to cover twenty copies of *The Toronto Star* that just slopped into the street to avoid being bitten. I can't stop giggling.

Meanwhile, putting on a gargoylean face of rapt remorse, the Barber helps the woman to her feet, making sure he gets a good peek up her legs. Red-faced and muttering apologies, she winds up not only gathering his pencils and handing them back to him, but slips him a fin before fleeing in an emotional dither.

"Say," the Barber banters, wiping saliva from the corner of his mouth and watching her body totter across the street. "Her cunt's Sunday is sure something. I wonder how it would go with my cock's Saturday night." With a raucous laugh he rolls off down the Strip in search of a dime to roll.

In short order I spy Billboard Harry seesawing it down the street. Figuring I've got nowhere to go and nothing to lose, I quickly latch onto him. "I'm in a jam, Harry. I need a place to crash for a couple of days. Can you help me out?"

Beside himself with concern, his eyes light up like bottle caps. "You can stay with me as long as you like. Yes, you surely can."

I hail us a cab and we're off to Harry's one-roomed catastrophe on the bottom floor of a dilapidated four-story Victorian house in Cabbagetown. A single light bulb hangs forlornly from the ceiling, a dirty mattress covered with blankets languishes on the floor, along with a table and chair beside the window. "Make yourself at home," Harry crows, as if he's just given me the keys to Camelot.

When he leaves for work, I run down to the telephone booth at the corner. What day of the week is it anyway? Shivering and fumbling with change in my hand, I place two calls, the first to Simon, asking him to look after Piddles. The second one is to Biscuit. I don't give him the scoop, just a sizzling headliner—I'm in a pickle, as usual, and need his advice on preserving one hothouse tomato. I ask him to pick me up a case of twelve with a promise to pay him when he delivers.

"You're goddamn right you'll pay me, Shortcake," he shouts. "One way or the other, you'll pay."

I grab cigarettes and bathing aids at the Chinese grocery on Dundas and dash back to the room for a bath. The rust-stained vessel hasn't been used since the Boer War. When I'm up to the neck in hot suds, I open a paperback novel and release my pores to bubbles and bliss.

The outer door bangs shut, the floorboards creak in the other room, and before I have time to gauge my fear, the Barber wheels in right up to the edge of the tub. He must be a part-time squatter here, too, crashing with Harry when it's too cold to seek shelter under cardboard in an alleyway. He still has his can of pencils, only Saint Peter is now twenty-five dollars richer than he was when I left him thumbing humanity on the Strip.

I refuse to appear embarrassed. With lust in his eyes he watches me run in more fresh water, soap myself down, and the nipples on my tits harden. To return the favor of the free show he shows me the stash of knives he has hidden in a secret shelf on the underside of his cart. Then he picks up my underwear and I let him. Since he lost his legs to a German tank at Dieppe, it's the patriotic thing to do. Horned up to a frenzy, he pulls out his wiener and masturbates. "Do you know what I'd do to you if I had legs, Big Eyes? I'd make the devil blush."

In the late afternoon Biscuit shows up with a case of beer, a bucket of chicken, and a dandy dose of five o'clock malaise. I answer the door in a towel, clutching a fistful of dollars. Roughly, he waves the money away with "Why pay me? I'm not your pimp!" Then he breaks into the dimness of the room and completes the standard dick's twenty-second appraisal. "What're you doing in this dump? I thought for a minute it was one of your— Who pounded the piss out of you?"

Surprised, I pass a frantic hand over my face and dash into the bathroom to check myself out in the cracked dirty mirror over the sink. I have a black eye, a puffed upper lip, and purple marks on my neck. I was so fried this morning I didn't notice. Padding back to the room, I open Biscuit a beer and explain.

"Those fuckin' Frogs," he curses, pulling a chicken leg out of the bucket. "I wouldn't trust one of the fuckers."

"His religion's got nothing to do with it. What should I do now?"

"Get dressed and have something to eat. For Chrissake, you're always waltzing around half-naked. Don't you own clothes or do you just like screwing up an old man's lunch hour?"

"I'm not hungry just yet."

"I am," he roars indignantly, tearing a chicken breast to pieces. "That's just like your generation. You don't give a fuck if anybody eats but yourself."

"Do you think Pascal will come back?"

"This's the way I see it. He won't want to cause any more bad vibes right now. If he said he was leaving town today, he probably will. Besides, he doesn't want to put his job with the R.C.M.P. in jeopardy. But he'll try to pick up your trail again. Not because he wants you, of course. Because you got the goods on him and got away. You're a loose end, Shortcake. A fucker like him don't like broads giving him the slip. You're gonna come and stay with me for a couple of days. I don't haul beer all over the goddamn city and give advice for nothing. Now get your things together and we'll get the fuck out of this dive."

"How about tomorrow? I promised Harry I'd stay the night."

"Tough shit for him."

"I gave him my word," I insist. "I'll go tomorrow."

He drains the beer bottle in his hand and throws the bucket of chicken on the table. "Okay, Shortcake. I'll pick you up in the morning. For fuck's sake be ready—your tab's running up. You'll be going out the door the same way you answer it. Have you got enough bread?"

"Sure—I'm loaded."

"You're fucking loaded, all right," he curses, stomping out and slamming the door.

That night I sleep on the dirty mattress on the floor, swamped with blankets. I'm jolted awake at about two o'clock in the morning when something tickles my arm. Jumping up, I switch on the light. The mattress is covered with cockroaches. Screaming, I do an Indian war dance on the kitchen table.

I'm still cowering there, hugging a blanket around me, when Harry blows in. Seeing me upset, he becomes upset himself. "Don't be afraid—no, surely don't. I'll run you a bath. You'll like that, huh?"

"As long as cockroaches can't swim, I'm game."

Afterward, he pulls a chair into the bathroom and we have a talk. When I tell him everything about last night, he points to his twisted nose. "I got that trying to forget. Every time I got hit, I forgot a little more."

In the morning I plan to sneak out to call Jonathan but before I can, he's beating down Harry's door and he's in a real dither. I've never heard him so abusive and foul—well, almost never.

"What the fuck is the matter with you? Leaving me in the lurch and saying balls about it!" he thunders, his eyes rolling crazily.

"Let me explain."

"You don't have to. It was that French dude, wasn't it? I told you he was bad news, didn't I? But no—you know everything—trust everybody."

"How'd you find me?"

"Harry told me. All I had to do was shake him. Everything came out, including his false teeth." He grabs my dress from the chair. "Get dressed and I'll take you home. Don't worry, the prick hasn't been back."

Then a minute later Biscuit bursts in without knocking. I don't have to introduce them to each other—they share the same stretch of Yonge Street turf. Biscuit shakes his hand with the usual guffaw. "Don't tell me you're here for a piece of ass, too? Well, you're too late, bub. She's gonna service me for a couple of days. I haven't had a cleaning lady in for months." Then he glances at me and scowls. "Still not dressed, eh? Just as I figured." Cursing to himself, he removes his coat and throws it around my shoulders. I barely have time to snatch up my clothes before he whisks me out the door.

I stay with Biscuit for a week. After sanitizing his sty from top to bottom I draw up an itemized bill and at supper serve it to him with dessert. He puts a match to it, then bulls me into the bedroom and pays me back in flesh.

Having decided to get out of this racket altogether, I phone Jonathan up the very next day and quit. He calls me back the same afternoon to tell me he's glad that I did. The R.C.M.P. called, asking for me. Apparently I'm wanted for questioning, but they refuse to say for what.

Now I know I've got to go underground and I'm sick about it. Despite the on-the-job hazards, I've been happy at the club and warmed myself in its glitzy illusion. I've felt secure in the company of my oddball cronies and enjoyed the hype of living close to the wire. Now the merry-go-round has stopped and I don't want to get off the dancing horse. How unadaptable and soft I've become.

Late one night Biscuit arranges for a friend of his to collect all my belongings from Simon's house and he sets me up in a bed-sitter in Little Italy.

After I'm nicely settled in, I hit the Strip, looking for an underground job and my old friend Sugar-Allways, the black prostitute, turns me on to the perfect gig. The next afternoon I'm thoroughly screened by an Italian in a slick three-piece suit at Howard Johnson's. The following evening a black Cadillac picks me and four other girls up in front of a designated restaurant and we're whisked off to an abandoned warehouse.

I step into an old elevator that takes me topside to a surprise, a posh phantasmagoria. The rooms are decorated in rich autumnal shades with wood paneling, leather and mahogany chairs, green baize tables, roulette wheels, and fans going quietly in the ceiling. The stakes are high and the clientele game, claustrophobic, and thirsty.

All we do is parade around like fluorescent flamingos in pink cantilevered corsets and garters, flesh-colored stockings, dainty open-backed stilt heels with pink feathers on the toes, and matching pink fans in our hair, serving watered-down drinks, lighting cigarettes, and replacing ashtrays. Meanwhile we watch the cards go down and blood pressures go up. On hand there are the tuxedoed croupiers with toy spatulas and the stone-faced condottieri policing the scene. Then there are the typical gambling groupies who follow the action anywhere from Vegas to Monte Carlo plus the Bay Street Bad Boys and transient big shots who splurge, hoping to bulldoze the corporations who own them.

Later, when I'm dropped off at my door, I'm three hundred dollars richer. Not bad for five hours' work. I decide to hang onto *this* three-nights-a-week gig.

For a change of scenery Biscuit often takes me on boring stakeouts where we watch rejected husbands make it with rejected wives in a hotel room rejected by the Department of Tourism. Sometimes he drops me off at his dinkhole office on King Street and I spend the day answering the phone and arranging his files in alphabetical order. Soon he blows a fuse because he can't find John Doe's settlement under yesterday's half-eaten corned-beef sandwich.

Then we get word that two men showed up at Simon's house looking for me and I'm ready to pack up and leave town. Biscuit's advice is anything but comforting: "Get in any more trouble and I'll beat you to a pulp!"

Biscuit has always been jealous at not getting top billing in my life. "Middlemen," I tease. "Always the pulp at the bottom of the glass. Can never let the world forget they got left behind."

Cut off from the hectic mainstream and forced to retire in the sidelines away from my old haunts, I fall in and out of black depressions. It's only natural that when my practically nonexistent social life has a night out, it should steer toward the offbeat and be an all-the-way proposition.

To cheer me up, Simon's got a funny idea for our next caper. He plans to smuggle me into a top homosexual club along the Strip and enter me in the talent show at midnight. A female crashing this all-male fraternity is strictly taboo.

It takes us an entire afternoon to put the masquerade on the drawing board and pick up the costumes and accessories at Malabar's. I wiggle into the Georgian tuxedo he's rented for me but the tricky part comes when I try to attach the blond moustache above my upper lip. The bugger won't stick too well at first. With it finally in place, I tuck my hair up inside a boy's wig that matches my moustache, apply the top hat to my head, and we're off. Simon is wearing an Eric Ross and Carrolls Company brown funeral suit and swings his shooting stick by his side.

The Rhapsody Club on Yonge Street is a modest little place that boasts red silk walls bordered with dark wooden paneling, licorice all-sorts carpeting, a black ceiling with circling strobe lights, candle lamps on red-clothed tables, a gilt-framed bar backed with mirrors and lit up like a marquee, and a small stage with a proscenium that laps into the audience like a lewd tongue. This interstellar watering hole is only missing a punkah and a snake charmer from Marrakesh.

The clientele is a menagerie of expression in the extreme—chic-stuffed snuffs from the Bay Street Stock Exchange in their Gucci suit rentals with Dash Hammett moustaches and army haircuts, damp gaudy starboys in baggy plus-four suspendered trousers and circus T-shirts flashing glitter on their eyelids and metallic paint on their fingernails, and the strutting six-foot Aphrodites with their Louis XIV wigs, Marcel Marceau makeup, and plastic tits, wearing tight polka-dotted prick teasers. The rumpus room is jammed and Elton John is belting out crocodile rock from the sound system. The educational value of this theater of the absurd is not to be missed. I'm all ears and eyes.

Simon gets us a drink at the bar and we find ourselves a table near the stage. We're no sooner seated when an obstreperous young nightflyer with a flaming red Harpo Marx hairdo in a gold lamé jumpsuit has the effrontery to insinuate that my moustache is a shade darker than my hair.

Before I can open my mouth, Simon intervenes. "You should see the color of the hair on the rest of his body."

"I'd like to—sometime," he croons silkily.

I nearly choke on my drink and Simon suppresses a grin.

The nightflyer continues courting. "How about tomorrow? My place—say eleven. I'm a *genius* with quiche."

He's also a genius winker, blinker, and blow kisser. Despite everything, his pursing pouting lips are having a strange hypnotic effect on my sexpit. Knowing that his quiche would melt on my palate like a grilled fig, I look to Simon for inspiration or a bag to crawl into. "What a shame," he confesses coolly. "Otley's got an electrolysis treatment tomorrow at ten. That prickly needle puts the poor kid out of whack all day."

The nightflyer wiggles and buzzes out for a moment, thinking on the prickly needle, but comes back, promptly. "Otley? How oddly awe-ful." Then he turns to Simon. "And are you his bedfellow or his guidance counselor?"

"Neither," Simon says, patting my head like a cocker spaniel. "I'm his patron agent. The boy is going into show business."

"Ohhhhh—just an apple a day." The nightflyer's gurgling. "I'd love to see the sweetie perform sometime."

"Then stick around for the talent contest." Simon prods me toward the bar.

The nightflyer blows me a kiss and waggles a finger wave. "My name is Fred. See you later, sweetcheeks."

Women worldwide will be thrilled to know that chivalry is not dead. He just changed his name to Frederica!

Simon is getting one hell of a charge out of the masquerade but I'm not so sure about sweet Otley: his bladder is filling fast, his ass is picking up pinches by the bucket, his top hat has fallen off twice so now he's carrying it like a chamber pot in his darling little hand, and the sweat on his face is loosening his silly moustache.

I'm so busy on the way to the bar that I trip over a pair of outstretched feet in the aisle. An Afro-haired poofball in circus-tent originals comes to my aid and helps me up—crotch first. For a second we look at each other horror-stricken. "Why, I think you're putting me on, dear," he sums up in a whine, flashing his spiky eyelashes.

"I hid it down my pant leg to fool you," I say, leading with a grin.

"How terribly exciting. Which one?"

Simon comes to my aid again by patting me on the head. "Poor boy—he's just had—ah hum—the operation. Still experiences elements of guilt and hysteria about revealing himself."

"Maybe I can help," the poofball offers. "Anatomy is my major at the University of Toronto."

"I'm sure it is," Simon remarks. "Whenever I have a spare cadaver on hand, I'll give you a ring."

A three-hundred-pound Albatross sitting nearby, who's been listening, takes instant pity and pulls me onto his knee. I'm starting to get giddier than hell. Mimicking irritation, I swat Simon and the poofball with my coattail. "Go away, you brutes you!"

"Ahhhhh, don't worry," the Albatross says. "I'll protect you, little fella."

I start to giggle so that my moustache falls right off in his drink and I have to gulp down his entire Black Russian to fish it out. "See what those beastly shock treatments did?" I wail pathetically.

The Albatross slides his hand up my pant leg and I slap his hand. "Well, they certainly did a good job on you!" he moans in heat. When he discovers that the doctors in Switzerland gave me tits, too, he nearly passes out on my shoulder in ecstasy.

This fat fellow's lap is like sinking into a live bowl of Jell-O. Frantically I look around for Simon. Maybe he can throw a bucket of cold water on our budding romance. I catch sight of him at the bar, trying to get our order past the Conklin Shows chorus line. To get free I'm forced into tickling the Albatross under the arm. His reaction is spontaneous and wild. Howling with laughter, he knocks me onto the floor. Before he can get his hands on me again, I'm striking off for the washroom. Sneaking by the lineup at the urinals, I slip into a cubicle and lock myself in. No sooner am I emptying my bloated bladder when a bushy, red-haired version of Robin Hood's Little John leers at me over the partition. "Ohhhh—a squatter! C'mon over, little honey, and big brother will show you how it's done. I'll even hold it for you."

"Go look for a textbook peacock and don't bother me!" I quickly pull up my trousers. How in hell could I have forgotten to wear the most important prop in the masquerade—a tie-on dandy dildo?

Outside, the waiters have transformed themselves into belly dancers and are now shimmying amid the tables with jeweled trinkets in their navels, doing a wild cushion dance while announcing the forthcoming drag show. Then, one by one, the female impersonators in the molds of Danny LaRue, Craig Russell, and a South American Carmen Miranda with a fruit basket on her head take the spotlight. Soon they are tripping down the ramp in slinky gowns and wingy wigs, imitating everyone from Barbra Streisand to Mae West. Expertly. They're so good I experience an identity crisis.

An hour before the talent show, Fred the nightflyer suddenly grabs me off the dance floor and whisks me away to one of the cubbyhole dressing rooms at the rear of the stage, where Simon joins us with my bag of accessories, two glasses of wine, and a good-luck kiss. It turns out that a secret deal has been struck: Fred and I are to go onstage as lesbians. "I thought you could do with a partner," Simon briefly explains with a grin, closing the curtained door in my face. Then it hits me.

"You knew all the time that I wasn't a real fruit," I fly off at Fred.

He/she hoists me up onto the counter under the mirror. "I admit I'm a rather colorful queer," he confesses. "But I'm not a stupid one. I love a daring imaginative cunt even more than a wet one. So make yourself useful, sweetcheeks, help me with my bra. Then let's talk choreography."

The show begins when balloons are released into the spectators from a net in the ceiling. After the drumroll, the masked MC, in drag as Harlequin in the knavish originals, comes onstage and announces the talent contest with campy slapstick buffoonery. One by one the

performers take the spotlight and disgrace their way into Hermaphrodite's good books.

Then it's our turn. Fred and I are introduced as the French maids
Monique and Gisèle. We're turned out in short side-slitted black
dresses with white ruffles on the cuffs of the sleeves and at the neckline,
white organdy aprons, black garter belts, black-seamed stockings, and
black high heels. I'm supposed to carry a tray of buns and they're
neither iced nor hot. Fred gets an ewer of milk.

At the whispered panting echoes of "Money, Money," we start a
duet from *Cabaret* and the honky-tonk strikes up. Fred grandly trots
me in a circuit to show everyone exactly what makes the world go
'round. Then at the shake of the maracas, the tinkle of the triangles,
and the clang of a cowbell, we drop our maidenly manners along with
the buns and the ewer into the audience. Fred grabs my thighs from
behind, then rides me across the stage like a donkey. Then he rat-a-
tat-tats on my buttocks and to the delight of the audience pulls an
inflatable dildo out of the apron and proceeds to blow it up. When
in pumping pantomime he starts to screw me from behind, the audience is on its feet, laughing and hollering.

The kick is over. We didn't win a prize but we did lay an egg. Now
Bacchus has rolled up the burlesque tent and carried it away on his
back. Simon and I resume our identities as furies of the night.

Thus begins my fling with the Boys in G Company. Their private
fraternity offers the perfect sanctuary and the perfect diversion while
I'm temporarily shelved on the layaway plan. When not working I
hang out and on at the Matador, a posh bar on Yonge Street where
the mailroom commando and the Bohemian pop artist come for kind
hearts and coronets and a little battledore and shuttlecock.

Sometimes we clubhop and sometimes at midnight they drag me
off to a tidy little war zone tucked away in a ravined park, city stage
center, where I set up Camp X by spreading out a blanket on the grass
and removing the wine and appetizers from a picnic basket. When
the boys have gone their merry way, I switch on CHUM and plug in
the earphones to drown out the blitzkreig of snapping belt buckles
and the sneakered footfalls and the caterwauling sirens caught in the

Give Me No Mercy maelstrom where pain meets pleasure, and pleasure meets the Holy Ghost at high noon. And periodically, the boys make fleeting visits to my faghag free clinic combination drop-in center for faith, hope, charity, sustenance, Vaseline, and Kleenex tissues. And it all works out—just as long as Sister Courage thinks she's in charge of the kitchen when she's really in charge of the pantry.

For me, emotionally, the gay scene offers a comfortable trade-off of affections. I play the sister they always wanted to tease and sometimes be, and they play the brothers I always wanted to please and sometimes hold. They air their guilt with the outrageous and the intellectually stifling and I air my lack of it by simply doing what I do best—being available. We share pillow talk, Ivory soap, nail polish, and *The New Yorker*, and always we share the freedom of having no morning-after sex stain on the bedding to launder.

n the meantime I'm hidden away in Little Italy, working on my family tree for recreation, deprived of most of my old cronies, nervous, overly cautious, and as inflammable as ever.

Only three people know my whereabouts—Simon, Biscuit, and Sugar-All-ways—and Sonny puts the squeeze on her in order to find me.

He pounds at my door in the middle of the night and he's in a terrible state, fatigued, unshaven, and jumpy. I refuse to let him in but he puts his foot in the door and presses the issue with his 250 pounds of *sauve qui peut*. "C'mon, kid—I've got nowhere left to go!"

I direct him to the Scott Mission or to Amnesty International but he hangs on with his teeth and we thrash it out in the doorway. Seeing honest desperation in his face and not wanting to cause more of a scene, I let him in and give him a double shot of Canadian Club.

Plopping down on my sofa bed, he hunches over his drink like a doomed man. "My porno operation's been scrubbed, kid," he says bitterly. "One of my girls squealed. I've been on the run for two days. The pigs have got a cross-Canada warrant out on me and the mob, a contract. It's official now. They just wanted to be sure they had the right dude before."

Great—here we are, two fugitives waiting like pigeons for the ax.

"I've got a passport and twenty grand stashed," he continues, taking my hand. "All I need is a place to crash until I've got everything fixed. Then I'm taking off for Brazil."

I fold his shaking hand in my own and trace the roughness on his fingers where he had his prints burned off. He's waiting for an invitation. I've never seen him so hyped up and shit-scared.

"Okay—you can stay. You've gotta know though that I work at a gambling operation owned by the mob. But that shouldn't be a hassle. What will be is that this's Little Italy. You're grounded until we change your appearance. No way am I having your post-mortem on my conscience."

Sighing with relief, he passes me a .32 snub with a handful of shells and I turn absolutely green. "I don't want it."

"I know, kid. But take it anyway—for insurance."

After hiding it in the top drawer under my underwear, I push its existence to the back of my mind. Why should I worry when Sonny sleeps with a .45 under his pillow?

I spend the next morning cutting his hair and dyeing it gray along with his eyebrows. Then I shave off his moustache and sideburns. Add a pair of thick horn-rims and—*voilà*!

We take a cab to the Toronto Dominion Bank in the east end and retrieve Sonny's passport and money from his safe-deposit box. Then I spend the afternoon shopping for his new conservative wardrobe. It's like turning Fred Flintstone into the Man From Glad.

Later, back at the room, I get Sonny to model a herringbone suit. The slob stands before the full-length mirror on the back of my door and he nearly bursts into tears. "What've ya done to me, kid? I'll never get a young piece of ass again. I look like an over-the-hill stockbroker ready for a pension and a crematorium!"

"You'll *be* in a crematorium if the mob catches you. Besides, girls will take money over age any day."

He completes a few turns in the mirror, utters a few lowly harrumphs, and throws his hands up in despair. "What can I tell ya, kid? What can I tell ya? You're a witch!"

Without a drop of collateral Sonny asks another favor. On Friday night I boogie down to a tavern on Bloor Street and contact a guy who'll apply and stamp Sonny's new photo onto his passport—for a grand. The following Monday I pick up the doctored passport at a bistro on College and book Sonny a flight to Rio de Janeiro.

A few days later there's a knock at the door one morning. I wake Sonny, pull his groggy, cursing, half-naked body out of bed, and prod him into the closet.

An elderly man in a brown tan suit stands in the doorway, jingling change in his pocket. I'm expecting him to pull out a heater and blow me away when he smiles and reaches for my hand. "Don't recognize me, do you?"

He's familiar to me, but not immediately familiar. "No, I don't."

"That's a relief, mate."

My memory reel locks into rewind for a minute.

"Uncle Teddy!" I cry, kissing and hugging a ghost from the past. "How on earth did you find me?"

"I went to your last address. A guy called Simon told me where I could find you. He wouldn't have told me if I hadn't conned him with that old death-in-the-family line."

Uncle Teddy's now gray-haired and much thinner than I remember him. I pull Sonny out of the closet, take the .45 out of his hand, and put the coffee pot on to perk. I introduce Sonny as my boyfriend, who's wanted by the cops and staying with me for a while until he can get out of the country. Teddy shakes his hand, remarking, "You must play with the same set of odds I do, mate."

Later he invites me out for the day and while I dress, he and Sonny rehash the gambling action in Miami. Then we drive to Woodbine Racetrack in a freshly stolen car and he chains an impressive-looking alligator-skinned attaché case to his wrist in the parking lot. Inside the gate his gambling fever takes over. With trembling hands he scans the racing form and lights one cigarette after another. After placing bets, we move through the crowd, assessing the sucker action. He can't stand still for a moment. His eyes are always roaming, furtive and restless.

Over the course of the race he presses binoculars to his eyes and strikes up a conversation with a red-faced businessman beside us, introducing me as his daughter. With easygoing candor, Teddy pursues a line of dialogue that's delivered with so much speed and with so many twists I get lost in the snakes-and-ladder logistics.

The crunch comes when he directs Mr. Smith's attention to this nondescript guy nearby. "See that man over there . . . he's Samuel Bronfman's younger brother, Reuben. Doesn't look the part, does he? Eccentric as hell. Always travels incognito. I would, too, if I had his money."

Fifteen minutes of working on the Bronfman name and Teddy pulls a business card out of his pocket. "I'm a financial consultant at Molsen's. That's why I can afford to play the track in the middle of the day." He chuckles easily.

Mr. Smith isn't long in making subtle inquiries about what companies would prove a lucrative investment at the moment. Teddy's there with all the facts and figures and gives him five good reasons, including Gulf and Shell Canada, why the stock of Henderson Mines is going to skyrocket within the week. Mr. Smith nervously blots his face with a handkerchief and responds with twenty questions. Taffy answers him by flicking his briefcase open and pulling out a number of documents with a loud letterhead. "I can sell you some shares today. But of course I need Reuben's signature first. I don't like to bother him on his day off but . . ."

Now Mr. Smith is hooked.

Teddy gives him an indulgent smile and walks right over to the nondescript, shakes his hand, pulls a paper out of his briefcase, and does business. When he returns, Mr. Smith writes him out a check for five thousand shares of Henderson Mine stock and Teddy hands him the certificates and a receipt.

Then he excuses our hasty exit with "I'd better go and pick up my winnings before the government finds a reason to tax it."

Uncle Teddy has no intention of using the same stolen car twice. In the parking lot he pulls a lockpick, about the size of a bobby pin with a file on the side, from his pocket and I cover him while he opens the door of a red Corvette. "This's just the car to celebrate a sting, mate."

On the way downtown I'm still afraid *for* him and in awe *of* him. "What the hell did you say to that guy?"

"Which one?"

"The nuclear scientist on the dole."

"Oh, him. I asked him if he could change a twenty for a ten. Then I asked him to sign a petition to save trees in downtown Toronto. Told him I was a horticulturalist with the city. I hope we make the bank. It's already after two o'clock."

I don't bother asking him any more questions. I'd never get a straight answer out of him. As luck would have it, we get stuck in a pileup traffic jam on Queen Street. So Teddy leaves the keys in the ignition, wipes the wheel, and we ditch the car right there in the middle of the street, causing a honking traffic pileup of our own. It's just like old times, running the quarter mile in a flash, and when we reach the bank, we're breathless. While Teddy is inside, I wait next door, holding his bunco bag, feeling very much like the wheelman in a holdup.

To celebrate the victory of blood over white-collar morons from Bay Street, we dine on prime rib with the appetite of Caligula.

Uncle Teddy leaves me at my door with a hundred dollars, a kiss, and a grin, as always playing with the change in his pocket. I beg him to stick around another day but he's as itchy-footed as ever, eager to pull a few more stings before leaving the city so he can gamble in the Bahamas and play the greyhounds in Miami. In parting he gives me some of his homegrown advice. "Even at eleven years old, I could see you were a match for your auntie Jane. Just remember—you can't make a full house come together unless you're playing with a full deck. Stay away from buggers like me, and only buy one house when you can afford two."

It continues to be good-bye and good-advice time. The day of Sonny's flight out of Canada, we have a few drinks before his departure in the Toronto airport lounge. At the gate he reacts to my schoolgirl tears with some counsel. "Get out of this racket, kid. You don't belong in it—you never did." Then he kisses me like a big brother and grasps his flight bag. "I'll write you."

"No, you won't," I fling back, knowing him for what he is, but liking him despite it. "You know you won't, you big slob."

Throwing his arms up in a surrender, he sighs. "What can I tell ya, kid? What can I tell ya? You're learning."

Since I left sanctum sanctorum I've managed to keep in touch with my family by telephone, and whenever I could, paid them a brief visit on holiday weekends. I have even managed to invent respectable secretarial jobs to cover my free-spirit life-style. Having a sudden urge to tug a neglected apron string, I call up my dad and get shaken right out of my socks. The R.C.M.P., or someone using their ID card, has been on the blower to him and other family members, inventing atrocious lies in order to scare them into revealing my address. Thankfully I had the foresight never to give it to them. My family are small-minded provincials who believe in the pooped-up propaganda they were breast-fed. To them there is only one god and one law—the divine right of the constabulary. Actually this latter attitude is inspired more by fear than patriotism. Bucking the system would put their entire existence in question.

The powers that be are better at fiction than they are at fact. Apparently I'm wanted for stealing stocks and bonds from a brokerage firm in Toronto. Also, I'm wanted for questioning in connection with a homicide. And the kicker is that some guy with a French accent phoned up and said that I'd just won fifty thousand dollars in a lottery and he wanted to know where I could be reached so it could be given to me personally. Pascal.

The real shocker is that I'm still on a hit list and my family has become involved. I've taken pains to keep my two worlds separate. Now they've collided. I appease my dad by telling him that there has been a simple mistake of identity which I have already straightened out. But after hanging up, I realize that the mistake was mine—to have been so stupid as to create a file on myself for Pascal.

When I was four years old, my mother gave me a brown hard-covered book from the library. Inside, the writing sat big, bold, and black on the page; and a colored picture of two lost babes in the woods took my fancy. I probably saw myself as one of the babes. After cutting it out with plastic scissors I hid it under my pillow and my mother conveniently found it one day when making my bed. "The police will come and take you to jail! You'll be locked in a small dark room and given nothing but bread and water!" she threatened day after day.

So at every knock at the door I crawled behind the couch or dived under the rubbers at the back of the closet. At Christmas I went hysterical until the fat man in the red suit with the black bag left the house.

Yeah, I know all about fear—it starts with Santa Claus and ends with a police siren. And this cricket in the woodwork isn't taking any chances, not with that maniac Pascal on my tail.

For the first time in my life I'm not able to advertise for help. Within two days I'm ready to blow town. I've quit my job, drained my bank account, my belongings are in storage, my telephone answering service is paid up to the end of the year, Piddles is temporarily nesting at Simon's roost, and my knapsack is packed and standing in the corner of my room.

The night before I hit the pavement with my thumb turned back, I have dinner with Biscuit and as always his parting shot has all the subtlety of an electric enema. "Got poked up the ass again, huh, Shortcake? Well, go ahead and blow the head off it. I'll keep your bed warm. Just don't go and blow your goddamn cover too. That *would* be a fuckup!"

Biscuit isn't sold on the poor little blind girl waiting for Father Great Leap Forward to take her to dinner. Why can't he accept the fact that the poor little blind girl has already taken Father Great Leap Forward to lunch by not becoming a government statistic in the great come-on?

20

t takes me almost five days to hitch it across country to the East Coast.

For three days I traipse around the city looking for a place to crash, hopscotching from one cheap flophouse to another, some too small to be called a dive, others a mere misconception. Needing a bad angel to help me survive this end of town, I buy a four-foot stuffed Muppet man dressed as Captain Highliner, king of the frozen-fish counter at the supermarket. I strap him to my back and dub him Mr. Blighty. Madness is the one disease people don't like to mess with. Then I stand on the wharf and wave to the sailors aboard a Russian freighter moored in the harbor, wishing I could smuggle myself in the hold and sail away. . . .

Almost flat broke, Mr. Blighty and I crawl into a waterfront warehouse for the night but we're quickly driven out by the squeal of rats. We wind up in the Dirty Sea Dog, the raunchiest tavern in town, where there's a head-breaking fight on the hour to scare the cockroaches into submission. I allow myself to get picked up by an aloof, shifty-eyed streetwise freebooter in jeans and cowboy boots, who I instantly sum up as an undercover Serpico type. I've already guessed he's married to a secret cause that doesn't have political affiliations. Mark offers me a place to crash until I'm on my feet.

He lives in a crash house on Fletcher Street called Timmy's Hideaway, a firetrap complete with its own ghastly charm. I discover that Mark and I have something in common—a healthy dislike for the powers that be. He's wanted by the R.C.M.P. but he won't elaborate on the reason. He drinks wine only occasionally, doesn't smoke or take drugs, has a 1,200-page file with Interpol, and works out daily in the martial arts. As a quirky distraction that I find admirable, he writes poetry. All this only adds to the healthy animal appeal under that two-bit bum facade. As a lover he's not as lethal as Vincent or as possessive as Crunch. He likes to experiment with an Eastern flair. Having a live-in guinea pig to practice on, he lets me seduce him as a stimulant to my ego, not realizing that I appreciate his expert handling the more. He shows me a new position, a kind of hamstringing leg spring done in a face-to-face squat against the wall, in which I become a highly literate slide ruler while he's merely the measuring case. Hence, I learn how to use mechanics to turn on. He doesn't have to teach me how to turn off.

Within the next few days I take a job at a greasy spoon nearby. When I'm not rubbing plastic flowers from the tablecloths, taking orders in pig Latin, counting flies on the yellow sticker streamers above the grill, folding napkins into Shriner hats, or eluding the hairy paws of the owner, I'm usually hanging out in the Dirty Sea Dog, recuperating.

Mark lends me enough bread for a week's rent. Timmy, the Hideaway's five-foot proprietor, who smokes so much dope he's permanently popeyed, decides to put me in the glorified bread box under the stairs on the ground floor. It used to be a pantry until a single bed was squeezed in, with a shelf overhead, and a handful of clothing hooks screwed into the walls in knit-one-purl-two formation. Timmy tries to charge the pants off me, knowing they're in the wash. So we haggle over a set of loaded dice which I throw across a chewed-up stretch of linoleum in the hall. Taking 25 percent off the suggested price, he has the nerve to write out a receipt with a crayon on a piece of toilet paper.

After only a week on the job, the owner comes on to me in the stock room between the rows of canned tomatoes and peaches. All because I failed to match the alphabet noodles left at the bottom of a customer's soup bowl into three words, *Fork out, baby*. And because I refuse to fork out, baby, to this Scrabble-board shark as well, I'm forced to punch the pervert in the nose. Having broken it, I'm given the sack.

Now that the money tree has shed its last leaf, I'm desperately game for whatever the dregs dig up—and for Timmy's idea of a self-help program. He suggests I clean the junk out of his basement and we sell and split the profits. I pop down to this subterranean garbage dump just to test his philosophy of hard sell. After a moment's appraisal I can see nothing worth a capitalist's sweat. Then, among the litter of broken furniture, bric-a-brac, and rusty tools with teeth, I discover the room that Timmy built without the approval of the city housing inspector or the Humane Society. The plywood wigwamlike cubicle in the corner is so small that the squatter who rents it can't invite me in for tea. So I ask him out for bagels.

Benny the Shnook is a late-blooming hippie from the nineteenth century waiting to be raped by a space-age Mother Earth. He used to worship the sun until it went underground to spite him. He has a degree in theater arts and carries tradesman's papers as a pitwright. His haircut borders on three weeks' neglect and his wrinkled tweed suit reeks of Aqua Velva. But despite the fact he's traded in his love beads for an Iron Cross, poverty looks good on him.

I take him out of MacArthur Park and put him on my scavenger's payroll. Half an hour later we find what could be a gold mine—at least a hundred cases of beer bottles. We spend the better part of an afternoon loading them into a friend's pickup. Then we take them to the Liquor Control Board. Benny buzzes inside for a shopping buggy and buzzes back out in a fever. "They won't take them here!"

"Where can we redeem them then?"

"Try Amsterdam. You know, Holland. Nobody takes Heineken bottles."

The man at the beer store threatens to call the police if we leave the bottles behind. We're forced into driving around the city for two hours after dark, searching for a suitable drop-off site before finally dumping them off behind a City Works Department office, a remedy which lives up to the promise of government policy: pass the buck.

Back at the house, Benny climbs aboard Timmy and threatens to strangle him for not telling us about the no-return payload. Timmy's only crying line of defense is "Look—if you want to make an asshole of yourself, why should I stand in your way? Nobody ever stood in mine. It's a free country."

It's a broke country.

The next day Benny gets lucky job hunting and comes back in a joyful mood. After he dances me down the hall, we go out for burgers and shakes to celebrate. We start working tomorrow morning but he won't tell me where.

Come 8:30 A.M., there we are. Benny in his jeans and me in a railroad cap with my hair tucked underneath, and a pair of farmer-almanac overalls, standing with shovels in a *cemetery*. Twenty-five bucks a grave, plus all the worms, slugs, and pet rocks you can gather, eat, or see. The boss has a strict policy about not hiring girls so Benny told him I was his young brother Charlie. Only twice does the boss show up while we're on the job. Benny rambles off to chat with him at the fence. Charlie keeps on digging . . . and cursing . . . and digging.

We work as gravediggers for three weeks, jumping from one molehill to another.

We decide to have a party at our last work address, an unkempt graveyard back in the sticks. We invite everyone from the Hideaway and as they drag along their friends, we gather three pickup loads of social goulash, from college students to yippies, whores, sailors, and dope dealers.

We build a bonfire behind the crypt and I open and operate a bar from the back of the pickup, which is loaded with cases of Molson Export contributed by everyone from the Hideaway. Someone passes around a toke. When one of the girls sees Diefenbaker's ghost, a game of hide-and-seek looking for our one-time prime minister takes off around the tombstones. Meanwhile, around the fire more tokes are passed around and more beer is opened. Mark and a gang of five, myself included, have a blistery banter over the correct way to hit a Brink's truck, using bazooka rockets, laser ray guns, and laughing-gas pellets.

A highlight of the evening occurs when Benny makes his debut in the twentieth century and starts to dance on the wooden platform above the crypt. Suddenly, there's a crunching sound and a crash as Benny disappears from sight. We scramble toward the hole. Benny's pirouetting on the stone floor below, calling for the ghosts of the living dead to join him. The kids produce a rope and toss it down. But he won't come up.

Three whores from the Hideaway lie on their stomachs and reach for him, chanting like a Greek chorus on Valium. "C'mon up, Benny. C'mon up. Don't you know how much we love you?"

Since he still refuses to ascend, the others lower me down. Benny catches me in a tumble that throws us both to the stone floor. I light a candle and demand that he grab the rope before I kick his ass.

"Isn't this spooky?" he cries in a dream, a lopsided grin on his boyish face. "All those dead sons of bitches watching us and laughing. Can't yeh hear them, baby?"

"Every time I put my head to the pillow."

"Hey, did yeh ever do it in a crypt before?"

"Not lately."

"Let's give them a thrill. Do it with me and I'll be a good boy and come up."

I snuff the candle with a wet finger. To make sure the ghosts of hell get their money's worth, Benny vocalizes. He fucks loudly with the velocity of a disc jockey on speed, grunting, panting in stereo. The whorish chorus in the belfry pick up his lyrics and vamp a chant that reeks of a pagan fertility rite. Meanwhile, down in the black hole of Calcutta, it's like being humped by Bowzer, the RCA bull terrier.

Ten minutes later we clamber up to ground level. By now everyone, with the exception of Mark, is pretty well hammered and paired off into all sorts of kinky equations. Benny disappears with the whores for a game of cup-and-ball in the honeysuckle and I go back on bar duty convinced that everyone loves his bartender and will end up there for a midnight confessional. Not long after, Mark slips in behind me and slides his hand up my leg. It's time to close shop and leave the Eros worshipers on their own doorstep.

Seeing the bonfire and hearing the action and music, a passing farmer calls the R.C.M.P. The sound of approaching sirens propels us into immediate hysteria. Benny tears out of the woods with the whores, all four of them in or out of their underwear. The rest of us are in no better shape, pulling clothes on as we leap into the back of the pickups. The first one is already pulling out in a squeal of burning rubber when Mark climbs into the cab of the second and puts the gas pedal to the floor. Benny, the whores, and I barely have time to jump in on top of the beer cases. Bouncing in and around the trees, we follow the first pickup down a rough rocky lane in the woods into a tunnel of darkness. Suddenly, two pig cruisers are speeding up behind us. Frantically, we start flinging beer bottles at their hoods to slow them down while Benny is hollering incentives and the girls are yipping with glee. The defensive ploy turns into a full-scale offensive. By the time the cops are forced to pull over, with cracked windshields and such, we've already gone through five cases of two-four and the lane behind us has been turned into an obstacle course of broken glass. Benny gives a big whoopee and a few miles farther on we stop, figuring we'll have another party on the beer that's still left.

In the morning we wake up in an open field and we're surrounded—but by bulls of another kind. A herd of angry-looking Aberdeen Angus.

Benny moves out of the Hideaway, and I miss him horribly—for five minutes. As I orbit at the outer radius of society, I naturally rotate toward the whores, Beth, Sharon, and Jackie—Clitty's Chorus—my fellow roomers at Timmy's Hideaway. Every morning we meet in the communal kitchen for rapabutts (coffee, conversation, and cigarettes) and to bum each other's shampoo. For economic reasons I offer to prepare our meals before they go out for their evening pavement prowl.

They turn me on to a job at the Elitist's Club, one of two massage parlors in the city. It's once removed from a whorehouse. You're supposed to ripen the Johns' hormones for abuse, then wait for an offer of sexual provender and steer the traffic back to your place later. I steer mine instead toward Clitty's Chorus and the deal works to everybody's satisfaction.

Lovey, Timmy's lard-arsed girlfriend from Sackville, is due in town for a two-week visit—and she wants private quarters. Pleading on his knees, Timmy asks me to vacate my pantry until further notice. Happy at not having to pay any rent, I agree and crash on my sleeping bag in the Rumpus Room on the second floor. It's a recreational à la carte with its two ratty couches, a TV set, and two card tables: a makeshift bar, game room, off-hours whorehouse—a congenial hot spot where everyone's got a bottle in his coat, a bag of marijuana in her pocket, and a dose of social paralysis which they carry instead of a credit card.

I take up a position at the card table in the corner, put Mr. Blighty in the opposite chair, and try to compose another masterpiece to Crunch, trying once more to explain the inexplicable: where I am, why I'm here, and how I paid an arthritic Egyptian scribe to pen this letter. Stuck for strategy and unable to concentrate, I buzz off to get a six-pack and a bullheaded bottle opener. When I get back, another lodger is sitting in my chair hiding behind thick horn-rims and the book *The History of Medieval Europe*. This is the lodger reputed to be the Marquis of T., a British blue blood with a divine eccentricity, the one commodity that can't be bought. Sandy-haired and young, tall and skinny with the features of a defeated hound dog, he's clearly one more vulnerable intellectual to have on your side at an international fencing contest sponsored by *Debrett's Peerage*. He's wearing lime-green socks and white boots sneakers and his Marks and Spencers hand-me-downs have enough creases to support a three-day rain. This signifies he's a diehard conservative with an artist's bank account—or vice versa, since the two seem to go together anyway.

When the pump of human virility runs dry and the ships are all to see if they can score elsewhere, brains have a tendency to attract, biologically. The members of Clitty's Chorus and I have developed a fawning interest in this peevish pedagogue who's always got his head stuck in a book.

He slips his horn-rims down on his Norman nose and extends a long hand toward me. "I'm Lester. The seating arrangements were unsuitable so I changed them."

"I'm Mushy and I liked them just fine."

"Are you the sensualist who fornicates in crypts?"

"No, I'm a Bolshevik from the battleship *Potemkin*."

"Oh—you're one of those," he says, prodding his high forehead.

So, Lester likes to play verbal tennis. The challenge is to keep the bogus ball going between courtesy courts. I'll have to learn how to cheat fast. I'm used to whipping balls out of the court into the spectator's section.

"You're a Gemini—I can tell," I say, batting a foul.

"Tsk, tsk, tsk. Not into that nonsense, too, are you?"

"What do you do besides blink and swallow air?"

"Sparkle," he says, to corrode my confidence. "How about a game of chess?"

At five o'clock in the morning he's still sparkling. Meanwhile, two wine bottles have died on the floor and are rolling beneath the feet of the hangers-on and Beth and a drunken sailor are fornicating on the floor under our table. "You can stay in my room tonight," Lester offers dryly.

Contrary to anything I normally attract, or look for in a man, he's a safe prospect—so I accept. We go to his room to endure the reparations of war. Whether the damnation is in me for producing the impetus, or in him for producing the props, it boils down to an innocent question on my part. "Which side do you want me to sleep on?"

"Wherever you feel comfortable. But the springs are popping out on your side."

I love to make a decision without having to consider anything as gauche as an alternative. It makes me feel like a real first-class citizen.

To repay him for explaining the Magna Carta, I switch off the light and swan-dive into the bed and it falls down on my side. I roll down the incline onto the floor and Lester drops like a feed bag on top of me. "What kind of a maniac are you?" he questions, groping for his horn-rims.

"The curious kind. Not only do you have popping springs but you've got termites, too."

"Funny, I didn't have them this morning. You must have brought them in."

To test his schoolboy shyness, and try first things first, I pull his head down. Score. He has the pucker of an electric eel and the tongue of a cleaner fish. But abruptly he pulls himself away. "Let's put the bed right. I despise fornicating at the base of a landslide."

I have only one comment to make on shy Lester's sexual manners— he has too much staying power. I fell asleep when he was still inside me.

I wake around noon the next day and have a marvelous conversation with a pair of brown scuffed oxfords by the bed—until I find that Lester has walked right out of them and left the house. He refuses to tell me what he does for a living besides sparkle, but he does mention an estate in England and a bottomless trust fund. During the next few weeks I arrive home from work at about two o'clock in the morning to an empty room. Lester doesn't crawl into the sack until dawn. I don't ask questions. Vincent taught me that.

His room is a solid-gold interpretation of Murphy's Law. The chain on the lamp is for show. The floor is lopsided so the door won't stay shut. Every time I kick it, the light flickers, the curtain falls down, and the doorknob drops off and rolls under the dresser.

One day when we're at the supermarket, Lester gives me an insight into his consumer talents. He wears a rangy trench coat with more pockets on the inside than creases on the outside. A quick tour down each aisle and we're lined up at the check-out. The bugger pays for a single loaf of bread and we're out the door with enough goodies to last a week. Then he hops on his red scooter with the blue carrying case and I'm soon chasing him down the white line, collecting the booty bouncing from his fifty pockets.

The only trouble with my moody bedfellow is his periodic sorties into intellectual terrestrials, when he paces the room in long strides, his hands behind his back, bitching to himself about the fly on the ceiling and the sparrow on the window ledge. His own imperfection is one second compared to the world's.

But I can only stand polemics, platitudes, and latitudes as long as there is an anteater around the house to help consume it. Then one night I fly off the handle. Lester suggests *I* have a serious vitamin deficiency. *I* suggest that *he* join a local order of Augustine monks and slam the door nearly off its hinges, leaving him to meditate with the lights off and the drapes dropped. In a blind rage I take Mr. Blighty down to the Dirty Sea Dog for a few drinks.

21

One afternoon I'm sitting around the room in a towel doing my nails for work when Sharon bangs at the door in a panic. "Mushy, the R.C.M.P. is searching the house! Get rid of your dope!"

As usual, my blood is high on sugar. I jump up and down for a minute and then realize we don't have any dope. But thrown into a razzle anyway, I fly around the room searching for the fake ID I always carry on me. Lester's sole line of rhetoric is a hackneyed "For Chrissake, compose yourself." Then he fills his pipe and puts a match to it.

Out in the hall I can hear a thumping on the stairs, rounds of muscled artillery at the doors, and a volley of screams and shouts. I try to crawl under the bed and discover five boxes of books holding it up. No room. Then I scramble in the closet and an empty suitcase falls on my head. Finally I spy Lester's battered-up seaman's trunk in the corner. "What's in there?" I cry.

"Ohhhh—trinkets for bartering with the natives," he says calmly, put-putting on his pipe and watching me.

Not waiting for him to elucidate, I grab my cigarettes and my handbag, open the lid, and hop in.

Lester answers the door at the third knock. "Come in, come in, gentlemen. What can I do for you?"

It's obvious by the familiarity of the conversation that the police have been introduced to Lester on a previous raid on the house and have already summed him up as a harmless eccentric. But I'm still cursing him to hell and gone. It's a turn-of-the-screw proposition for me. Why doesn't he just offer them tea and cakes and be done with it? What a cool piece of soft-soaping Lester does on them. The pigs don't even search the room and apologize profusely for bothering him in the first place.

Now that we're out of immediate danger, I can examine my body physical, stuck inside the big box. A sharp metal object is pinching my thigh. I light a match and pick up a silver goblet. A pearl necklace drops out of it. And there's more of the same—including diamond earrings, bracelets, and brooches, opal and sapphire rings, gold watches, and an antique tea urn the size of a flowerpot in the corner, filled with gold and silver cigarette and cosmetic cases. Having a sudden sucker's manic urge to laugh, I slip a cigarette nervously into my mouth.

As soon as I hear the bedroom door close, I throw open the lid, wearing the urn on my head and ropes of pearls around my neck.

"Don't you feel a little ridiculous for jumping the gun?" He removes my newfound treasures. "Knowing the female's fondness for snooping, I'm surprised you didn't find my little cache before this."

"I don't snoop in other people's stuff. It's one of my male idiosyncrasies. I suppose it's all paste?"

"Tsk, tsk, tsk, you stupid girl."

"Where did it all come from?"

"Contributions," he confesses, floating around the room on a cushion of guile.

"From who?"

"An eager and willing majority—my eternal trust fund."

"You're a bloody thief!"

"Bite your tongue. You're in the presence of a genius. I'm no common run-of-the-mill thief or cat burglar. At my best I keep the iceman hopping. You might say that I serve society's greed."

"Oh, I see—people really want to be robbed and you're just doing them a heap big favor?"

"Quite. You see, people have an inborn desire to be fleeced and fucked. Then they can do the same without feeling guilty. It paves the way to a clean conscience. That's why it was dastardly easy for me to seduce you the night I met you."

"Hey, *I* seduced you." I'm ego-stricken.

"Yes, that's another way of explaining the inevitable."

"Did you really swipe all this stuff?"

"I'm currently on holiday from Monte Carlo and it helps to keep in practice—even if it is chicken feed. One must make a living—unfortunately." He shudders in disgust. "By trade I'm a professional trader in jewels, other people's. I'm not messy. I never experience pangs of guilt. And most important of all, I never get caught."

"Why live in this flea trap then?"

"Firstly, I can keep close to the criminal elements. Secondly, it's a rather fun deception and an excellent way to fight boredom. I meet the oddest assortment of people. Thirdly, I can move at will without drawing attention to myself. Until I'm in my South American villa in the jungle, this life will do just fine."

"Why tell me? I could turn you in."

"I doubt it, my dear girl. There are only two things you appreciate—guts and brains in the abstract." He disappears into the kitchen and returns with two jars of Russian caviar, a box of English crackers, and a chilled bottle of Roederer Brut. Then he fills two silver goblets from the trunk and makes a toast. "Let's celebrate man's greatest virtue—his corruptibility."

Often he has a meeting-of-the-minds session in his room with Fingers, a seedy Jiminy Cricket character, just back from doing a dime stretch at Dorchester Jail. He's a permanent fixture down at the Dirty Sea Dog. Lester and Fingers discuss the contradictory nuances of safecracking and handling sophisticated burglar alarm systems and explosives.

According to Lester, the high point in his life will be in knocking off the Diamond Exchange in London with two cronies of his who're currently on the Monte Carlo circuit. He's already single-handedly done a bank but he won't tell me where. Lester is the greatest living proof that the blue bloods of Europe are not an extinct species, as is the popular notion. While the commoners' wheels spin on, an ingenious handful of aristocrats are quietly and expertly ripping off the socialist establishment that ripped them off in the first place.

One evening I call in sick at work and crash with Mark for a few hours. After dark I slip out the back door of the Hideaway in a pair of jeans and a T-shirt and hide behind a snowball bush down the street. When Lester leaves the house, I tail him. It's all I can do to keep up—he moves so quickly. Six blocks later, we're in the ritzy end of town. Neatly, he disappears through a hedge and like Clark Kent emerges in the garden in a hooded black outfit and soft-toed foot-huggers. I follow on a merry chase through backyards and over fences, obstacled with swimming pools, swing sets, and rock gardens. Finally we hit the back of a house that exudes French Provincial and Lester hesitates. I sneak up on him from behind, and whirling, he throws me up against the side of the house, claps a hand across my mouth, and drags me into the bushes. Then he looks. "What the goddamn Jesus hell are you doing here?" he rasps.

"Research," I croak, lamely.

"Shut up," he commands, squeezing my arm. "I'll deal with you later, you silly girl. Now do what I tell you. Wait here and keep *down*. I'm going inside to shut off the alarm system."

He climbs a tree bordering the patio and, using a rope, swings over to the roof. With an instrument from his belt, probably a nail bar, he removes the window. It takes him about five minutes from the second he climbs through the window to the moment when he zips the patio door aside to let me in. It's rare in this neck of the woods he says, later, for people to have every window in the house wired. Lester regards this gambit as one of the easiest, a cinch. He settles me in a crouch behind a winged armchair with stiff no-marching orders. "Don't move. Don't even breathe until I get back."

I nod convincingly, which means no to all the above.

Lester snaps on the flashlight and skulks toward the front of the house, obviously trying to find the safe in the study. As soon as he's gone, I take off in the opposite direction. I like to be well up on how the rich relax in their homes and hormones.

I come upon a large bedroom with a modular suite, complete with a brass bed. The closet is full of clothing belonging to a woman in her middle forties. On the vanity there are stand-up photographs of four boys. My senses tell me that the room hasn't been used in ages. I can smell death in every corner.

Off the bedroom, I discover a bath built into the floor, with gold faucets and mosaic tiles, surrounded by a jungle of tropical plants. What do you know? The rich sweat a lot and have bathrooms attached to their bedrooms where chapels once were. The Spartan setting also tells me that they're organized right down to their monogrammed tubes of toothpaste. Overwhelmed, I figure I'll give it a whirl and take a dip. It can't hurt. Nobody's home and it'll take Lester a few minutes to crack the safe.

I run the water almost to the top, strip down, pour in a liberal amount of oil from a glass ewer on the shelf, and hop in. I'm soothing my templed nihilism and watching it rise in steam from the surface of the water when a ragged voice from the doorway throws me into a fit. "Who the hell are you? And what are you doing in Marion's bath?"

Who the hell is he to be bathing in my sunshine? I blanch and throw my hands across my tits, trying to contemplate the size of the shoehorn I'll need to get out of this one. My skin has turned transparent and I'm shaking inside it.

This one's a fiftyish, physically fit, balding-fast business blunderbuss in a maroon smoking jacket, who's not used to playing tiddledywinks in the dark. Taking a wild chance, I employ my best childish voice and smile sweetly. "Surprise, surprise! Happy first day for the rest of your life! Compliments of your four favorite sons!"

"How'd you get in?"

"Now if I told you that, I'd be squealing on the hand that paid me," I quip naïvely with a foolish grin. "I've been instructed not to let the cat out of the bag."

"I'm calling the police."

"Why cause a scandal? I didn't do nothing I wasn't paid to do. How do you think I got in if one of your sons didn't provide the key?"

"Scott . . . was it Scott? I'll have that little bastard's balls for this.

Marion's not even in the grave a year when he puts a whore in her bath."

"Excuse me, sir. I'm not a whore. I'm a baby-sitter extraordinaire."

"I don't give a damn who you are! You're not supposed to be here!"

Fear drives me into an indignant snit. "Look, I could have been popping out of a cake tonight for three hundred smackers. Instead, I'm here getting bullshit for only a square two hundred. If you don't want your money's worth, just say so and I'll leave."

He looks at me quizzically and seems indecisive. I begin climbing out of the bath but he bellows at me again. "Stay where you are!"

"Why don't you get a bottle of bubbly and some glasses? Then we'll talk about it," I urge in my most suggestive voice.

"I'm not doing anything until I find out what the hell is going on!" he snorts, stomping out.

He's gone for a coon's age. I'm nearly sick with expectation. Has the bridge out been lowered or raised? Maybe I should at least don a towel in case he calls the R.C.M.P. Or should I wait and pray? What to do? Make a run for it or stay and grin along with the consequences? And what about Lester out there, crouched under a table or hiding behind a curtain? Did he find the safe?"

Suddenly Mr. Blunderbuss appears, calmed, with a bottle of Charles VII and two glasses. "I didn't find anything in the house amiss," he confesses, smoothly pouring me a glass of champagne. "For the present, I'll pretend you're on the level." Surprisingly enough, he strips down and slips into the bath with me.

I'm so relieved he hasn't called the police, my emotional self salutes the ass-saving moment by sliding into a cheerleader's miniskirt and performs "Hallelujah, Brother!" for the home team. I work to keep his glass filled and him talking, soon enough, glasses later, about his wife's death and his inability to accept it. His face reddens and he finally reaches toward me across centuries of subterfuge. We're both so tipsy and hanging onto each other so desperately, I'm afraid we'll drown in the unwritten scriptures that come after Revelation. The ritual moves continue from the steam to the cream in the bedroom, thence to sleep.

From somewhere in the netherworld, a hand pinches my ass—it's
Lester. Carefully, I crawl out from under Mr. Blunderbuss, cross-
eyed and thirsty. Lester helps me struggle into my dress and we hike
it out the patio door and back to the Hideaway before the sun comes
up.

Lester is angrier than hell at me for the screw-up, even given my
inspired solution. "I told you to stay put."

"Can I help it if I sleepwalk?"

Ignoring me, he inspects the diamond ring and necklace through
a loupe at the north window of our room just as soon as the sun comes
up, in order to get the most accurate reading. He's looking for the
four C's—clarity, color, cut, and carat weight, while searching for
carbon spots and other flaws, and waiting for the light to reflect back
in the colors of the rainbow. He gauges the loot to be worth a cool
thirty thousand dollars on the market underground.

After we hit the sack, I toss and turn in bed with recurring nightmares
about the ice. My third eye knows what I'll do even before I find
myself sneaking out of bed and recovering the ring and necklace from
the seaman's trunk. I put them inside a brown thermal envelope and
leave the house.

At a nearby coffee shop, I address the envelope and write out a
card, signing it, "Cheers, Missy," with the name I gave Mr. Blunderbuss last night at the height of certain frenzied foreplay. If it had
been anyone but him, I wouldn't give a goddamn. Yet I realize that
Lester would argue that "anyone but him" would only include Jesus
Christ and Mickey Mouse. But I also realize that all that I have and
all that I am is what I feel. And that ice was all he had left of his
wife's jewelry. Its emotional value is priceless to him.

After sending it out by registered mail at the post office, I wander
down to the wharf to forget that I just pulled the plug on Lester. How
I hate Guilt and his blood brother, Gall.

For two days I hide out with Mark. Then, unable to stand it any
longer, I materialize at Lester's door to clear the air. But he's not even
home, so I hit the bath, wrap myself in a Turkish towel, and sprawl
out on the bed to wait.

Eventually Lester strolls in and with controlled hostility removes his glasses and folds them up into a case. I sit up, expecting the Epistle to the Romans. A bad sign truly—I expect the worst. Before I have time to prepare a Socratic defense, he backhands me across the face and lights into me verbally. "That felonious highbrow knew all along I pinched the family heirloom."

"Whhaatt?"

"Quite simply, he checked the safe on the way to the bar."

"Why didn't he turn us in then?"

"He wanted a little fun with you . . . while waiting for me to vacate the premises. Too bad he played himself short by getting drunk and falling asleep."

"I don't understand. Why did he want me charged and not you?"

"You're the patsy. I had the ice and insurance's a still bigger payoff than flesh. If I was caught with the ice, he wouldn't get the insurance payoff. You should be in raptures now that he has both—all for the price of a cheap fuck."

I'm speechless. He lets me stew uncomfortably for a while before, to my complete astonishment, he goes to the trunk and takes the diamond ring and necklace I mailed three days ago out of it. "How did you get them back?" I gasp.

"While you and Mr. High Society were in the bath the other night, I used my time profitably. I discovered a second safe in his bedroom. Then, when you and the ice went missing the other day, I knew you weren't the type to sell it. Besides, Timmy saw you leave the house with an envelope. So figuring what you were up to, I went back to High Society's place last night. Knowing he wouldn't keep the ice in the safe in the study for insurance reasons, I hit the safe in the bedroom. And presto!"

Though he refuses to forgive my stupidity, the afternoon finishes the way most of our nights have begun—in an altercation that somehow crests in a lover's lock.

Lester continues his nightly escapades for the next month or so. To get back into his good graces, I allow myself to be pressed into service.

He trades in his motor scooter for a two-seater Vespa and I'm elected to use it to pick him up at predesignated points just before dawn.

A month later we part at the Halifax airport. Lester's working his way to Vancouver, via every major city en route. Next stop—Montreal. When I sling a flight bag over his arm and hug and kiss him, he's all good-bye and good riddance and good God, unhand me, please!

"I'll call you in Toronto, if you ever have the luck to reach it," he promises, pecking me on the forehead like a little boy who's leaving for private school in Switzerland. His last piece of advice is choice. "If you can't be good," he says, "be defiant."

Forlornly, I watch his plane taxi out the runway. Will I ever meet anyone like Lester again? Would I want to?

Now Mr. Blighty and I have Lester's room all to ourselves. I've managed to start a bank account and the Jell-O is beginning to set.

Then the bottom drops out of everything. One of the girls I work with at the Elitist's Club is found raped and stabbed in a rooming house downtown and her murder is said to be "drug-related." The club is temporarily closed down by the police for an R.C.M.P. investigation and I'm out of work.

When I get back to the Hideaway about eight o'clock in the morning, the R.C.M.P. are searching the house and stop me at the front door. Convinced they're here about the murder at the club, I pull out my fake ID and they ask me a slew of questions about Mark, who they say is wanted on a string of warrants from extortion to attempted murder. I attempt to act as stupid as I look. I never hear or see anything; my eyes are filled only with rising and setting suns.

Hoping that Mark will return, they leave but I know they've put the house under surveillance. I bathe, change my clothes, and slip down to the corner to call the Dirty Sea Dog. Just as I expected, Mark left a message. Making sure I'm not followed, I meet him down at the docks after lunch. He's ready to blow town immediately and me along with him. But first I have to smuggle out that suitcase he has hidden in the cellar of the Hideaway and pack up my knapsack, which contains a change of clothing, and memorabilia and monkey business from my trip to the East Coast.

The next morning I meet Mark at a motel outside the city. We manage to grab a ride out of the province in the back of a farmer's truck with real pigs and two crazy Newfie boys. Newfies are known for their down-home sense of logic, so it's not surprising that they utilize the nation's highways to transport care packages and even appliances from Newfoundland to relatives in Ontario and vice versa. On this particular trip the boys are traveling with two cardboard boxes and a Franklin stove, which contains a bag of clothing marked *Johnny's Pants from 6X to 8*. Johnny's cousin in Toronto seems to be at the receiving end of this hand-me-down pipeline. After a year's work in Toronto the boys tell me that they'll be on their way back to Newfoundland with a used fridge for their mother's birthday. I can just see them now, hitching it along the Macdonald-Cartier Freeway with a Maytag edition of R2D2.

After partying for an entire day and a half, the boys and Mark and I are ready for market and the piggies for deliverance. The jump-off point is Montreal, Quebec.

PART IV

GETTING
AWAY WITH IT

22

Mark and I crash in a small hotel near Lafontaine Park for a few days. It's a shame that the only French words I know are either chic or dirty. While Mark buzzes off to look up some friends of his in the underground, I decide to play a hunch I've had for some time.

After doing some serious shopping for clothes, I show up at the campus of the Quebec Police College, which trains cadets from all over the province. I'm carrying a French dictionary, wearing a London Fog trench coat, a brunette wig, and glasses, and swinging an impressive-looking leather attaché case. Posing as a student of criminology at the University of Toronto, writing a thesis on organized crime in Canada, I have no trouble at all gaining access to their library. The staff are only too happy to assist me with my research on Quebec underworld figures.

Since I don't know who Pascal really is, all I can do is begin leafing through any books containing mug shots. For four solid hours I skim one book after another, sure that the picture I'm looking for is only a page away.

Finally I bump on a face that sets me trembling. The eyes of this Jesus Christ Superstar are terrifyingly familiar and the side shot clinches it. I've just found the identity of Monsieur X.

Quickly I jot down his real name, trying hard to compose myself, and in minutes I have the staff going through the index cards and pulling books that have information on him.

Some of the cases in which Pascal has been implicated (and which for obvious reasons I am unable to detail here) are so gruesome that I feel queasy and hit the washroom to throw up.

A few minutes later I wander into the audiovisual department with a list of reference numbers to check out the newspaper clippings on Pascal that are on microfilm. To the astonishment of the staff, but not myself, we discover that every clipping has been meticulously removed.

I leave the college in a daze with a folder of Xeroxed material under my arm which I've labeled EXPENDABLE but not UNEXPLOITABLE.

As soon as Mark returns to the hotel, I show him what I've come up with. He gets right on the blower to an R.C.M.P. friend of his who's leaving the organization and meets him at a café down the street. The next day his friend does a computer check on Pascal.

Mark tells me that Pascal is no longer on the R.C.M.P. payroll as an informer. Having proved himself as a hundred-out-of-a-hundred shot in the field, he's now on an R.C.M.P. intelligence assignment overseas—as an *assassin*. To the programmed Joe on the street, this would be incomprehensible or bizarre and he or she would probably laugh in disbelief. Most folks see the R.C.M.P. simply as those heroes or "mounted dudes" on parade at Parliament Hill in Ottawa. But the States has the CIA, the Soviet Union has the KGB, and Britain has M16.

According to Mark and his friend, Pascal was recruited into the inner circle of R.C.M.P. intelligence from the underworld; and though he's not liked, he is needed.

The good news is that Pascal flew to Paris on assignment a month ago and now he's apparently in the Middle East. Maybe I'll have some breathing room in Toronto while figuring out what to do next.

Anxious to hit the road again, I say good-bye to Mark and hitch it to Queenston, where I intend to drop in on Crunch. I'm already shaking at the prospect. After all, he hasn't received a letter from me in weeks, only Hallmark greeting cards with my signature inside of a laughing sun at the bottom.

Our reunion is neither laughing nor sunny. Crunch refuses to speak to me at all when he's sitting on the other side of the glass and merely looks at me stiffly, shooting bullets with his eyes. I finally threaten to get up and leave the visitor's section of the prison altogether—and the slob lets me.

Crunch puts me through the wringer over the next two days until I'm allowed to see him again. It's like I've lost my only hold on life. I don't know what the hell to do—go back to see him or forget I ever knew him?

I settle for a return visit. Though Crunch tries to hide it, I can tell he's delighted I cared enough to come back, so delighted in fact that he throws the opening line. "How many men have you fucked since you left me? Or did you have time to stop and count?"

For minutes we're silent until he lifts his head and looks at me. "Thanks for giving me a reason to live, rabbit. I can hardly wait until I get out of here so I can wring your fucking neck!"

Great—now we're back to normal.

For spite I respond the very next day with a birthday card—"To a nice little boy who just turned six." Then I decide to stick around for a few weeks to tame him down, or let him tame me down. I can never figure out which one of us is the basket case.

Back in Toronto the Indifferent, I call Biscuit and Simon to say hello and whip down to the Strip to visit Jonathan and the girls. Not only does the club not exist anymore, but a lot more has gone down since I left and this is just the first in a list of shockers.

One of the shoeshine boys who used to sit in the doorway downstairs at the club was lured to an apartment above another club by three perverts, brutally tortured, and murdered. All of my whorish friends are still in a dither about it since he was a good kid and it happened on their turf.

As a consequence of the public outrage, all the clubs on the Strip have been closed down to protect the City Hall bigs who supported and sometimes owned them. In their rampage to cover up the obvious and clamp down on vice, the stupid pigs have succeeded only in virtually sending out invitations for someone else to handle it.

They have arrived. The talent has moved in from Stateside to clean up on the conscience of City Hall. The motherfucking pimps and whores from Detroit have taken over the streets and they're also into more sophisticated crimes like child pornography.

The Barber was stabbed to death in a barroom brawl and Dutchy, queen of the Yonge Street hookers, had her neck slit by her comrades for becoming an informer with the police. Harry is now running flyers for an X-rated movie house on the Strip. Jonathan is operating a massage parlor underground. Quickly, I find a room in Little Italy and reshuffle my priorities.

In Queenston I promised Crunch that I would give northern Ontario a shot on a six-month trial basis when he got out. So the motivating factor now is simply to make some fast money in Toronto so I can move there and set things up for us.

My funds are depleting fast, I've got diddley-squat to live on, so I answer an ad in the newspaper for strippers and line up an audition at a nightclub in the west end. The head honcho is a slim, studdy Greek in an Armani suit with a sapphire on his finger and a pearl-drops smile. He owns his own booking agency. Andros provides all the girls auditioning with a round of drinks to loosen our prime-time yes-no-maybe-huhs. Then he gives us pointers on how to sell flesh by the pound when you have neither a scale nor a press agent. "Fake it and bake it until it's well done or the oven blows up."

We try out. I've boobie-danced topless and massaged naked but this's different. Not only do I have to put everything on the plate, I have to sell it as the Last Supper. I'm so busy trying to hide in the wings, I feel like Shanghai Eve just released in the Street of the Thousand Assholes. Thankfully, I've thought to bring along a disguise in a brown paper bag. Styx's "White Collar Man" booms out from the amplifiers, the colored lights blink in synch with the heavy metal, and I'm chased onstage by my own shadow. Every eye in the universe is pressed to the keyhole of my bedroom door.

When I finally come down in a haze-daze, a drunked-up salesman at the bar intercedes helpfully. He suddenly hollers, "Hire her, Andros. The kid needs the money for a face job. I've never seen an uglier dog in my life. She's got more hair on her eyebrows than she does on her cunt. Hell, her tits don't even have nipples!"

I don't feel a bit embarrassed when I arrive at Andros's table. He leers at me and then proceeds to not only remove my Groucho Marx combination eyebrows-spectacle-nose shades, but zips the flesh-colored pieces of masking tape from my nipples and closely examines the black Magic-Markered eyes I've drawn around my tits, the pig nose I ballooned from my belly button, and the sunny half-mooned smile below. . . .

The son of a bitch hires me on the spot. It seems that he likes his meat fatter on the hoof so they'll bounce better on the spit, but I come with something just as marketable—kink on the slink. Now I have to put some seriously sexy costumes together. And I'm supposed to call Andros every day until he has a gig for me.

I make do with a synthetic leopardskin rag I buy off the rack from a Queen Street big-game hunter and sew a four-foot-long tail on the back of it. Then I disguise myself with an Afro wig and brown theatrical grease from head to toe. Up close I look like a breadline bush bunny.

Andros soon has me booked into a roadhouse in the city's submerged suburbs, owned by a greasy little Greek I quickly nickname Nick the Prick. With dirt under his fingernails, the zipper on his fly always riding at half-mast, he's so irascible I'm immediately jealous of the guy who must've shot the hot poker up his rectum.

My real live dynamic debut as a bare-assed stripper is a shell-shocker. To prepare myself I down four beers at the bar. Then Nick the Prick tosses me three quarters from the cash register and, iced into inebria, I feed the jukebox in the corner.

Instead of the proverbial blanket on the floor, I use straw. Bought a garbage bag full of it from an Italian kid who raises chickens for slaughter.

When Led Zeppelin's "Whole Lotta Love" hits the air, I begin the physical loco-motion with a lead-in walk on the climb to a spin, which progresses to a roll on the deck, to a twist on the roll, to a writhe inside of a writhe—which means that you split yourself wide open up the middle and pray your ethnic origin isn't showing.

I come down from the first set with a scrambled set of directives and try like hell to figure it all out over three more beers. Am I supposed to be fucking the audience or myself? Worse, are they supposed to be fucking me? Where's the focus? If I don't find it fast I'll become either a schizophrenic or a sexual cripple. So I decide to work from the-devil-may-care-but-I-care-more syndrome to the-devil-don't-care-and-neither-do-I. Why not be sanguine about the business and feed that North American brain drain called the MacDonald's Meat Market, or the Asses Culture Club, where society's shopping-center mentality levels out into a classless mass of nerds with a single phallus. I respond to the so-called primitive jungle drumbeats and the lack of classical rhythm by reacting spastically: I simply pretend that I'm being screwed by Flotsam, the national deficit, and Jetsam, the multinational charge card.

At the end of my first week, Nick the Prick refuses to pay me the whole two hundred and fifty dollars cash I was promised on the premise that the government gets 30 percent of my ass.

"I'm self-employed!" I rage, high on fatigue and worry. "You can't deduct for pension, tax, or unemployment insurance!"

"But I almost forgot the thirty percent Andros gets as your booking agent and the twenty percent stage fee you owe me," he offers by way of challenge. "I hold one week's wages back so I'll pay you your hundred and twenty-five bucks next week."

I haven't got a union card, a Bay Street lawyer, or a big brother with hatchet-boy biceps so I'm really in the soup. He quiets me down with a free beer while I wonder how I'm going to survive the next week, never mind get home. The Prick, his own sweet charity, suggests a solution. "How about twenty-five bucks for a fuckie, eh?"

I remind him that flattery will get him everywhere but that fucklore has it that either a SALT talk or a genteel war of attrition should precede an act of love. Instead of telling him he's in the wrong role at the theater, I suggest that I'm in the wrong seat. Then, realizing that I'm the one who's speaking Greek and he's the one talking logic, I give in.

Feeling as if I've just had acupuncture with a rosebush, I accompany him down into the vault of my own subconscious, an unfinished cellar consisting of piles of junk and a hodgepodge of boxes. The stripper's dressing room, which I've never used, has a white vanity and chair. Nearby, there's a small room in the corner, blocked off with a dirty blanket on a rope. Shaking from an inner chill, I slip inside and crawl onto the mattress on the floor. Nick the Prick climbs on top of me and transforms into Nick the real Prick with a fornicating right finger. It's the most humiliating experience of my life with the exception of the night with Pascal. I will never forget the moment I walked through the portals of the oldest profession. . . .

Afterward, I climb the stairs to the bar and my employer offers me another watered-down beer and pays me before I hit the road.

Great—now I can get a cab home and eat for two days. I've only begun to climb rage. I've discovered a fine white flame at the top of it and I want to walk it like Jesus over Jordan.

The next day I'm settled on a barstool when Mr. Nick invites me over to his private table and introduces me to his buddies, five Greek businessmen. They're smooth-tongued, clean-looking carrot cuts who use this pit stop to play sexual backgammon.

After half an hour's banter and free drinks, I walk back to the bar hiding a smile. Then Nick the Prick saunters over and transforms himself, again, into Nick the Pimp. "Twenty-five bucks each for all five."

Now that I've got him by the balls, I nurse my beer, grooving on this revenge at the Ritz. He sold my services without *my* permission so *I* raise the price to forty bucks a trick without asking *his*. What can he do? If he fails to come through for his buddies, he'll look like the asshole that he is.

My abacus has already done a quick tally. Two hundred bucks in neon lights. Jesus, another cab home tonight instead of a cold bus-and-subway ride. I can get a pizza on the way. And I might brunch tomorrow at the King Eddy. Better yet, I'll be able to survive until next week.

It's a grab-bag proposition for both fuckers and the fucked. What the hell, I finally announce, Tally-ho and take my beer down to the room in the cellar, and one-two-three-four-five it's touch-tackle tarantella around a mushroom bed that leaves me trembling and fighting hysterical tears. To each one I explain it's my first time and their pitying comforting caresses become sillier than my attempts to give the ball some body English by force-fed groans. Pricks are always the same size, incapable of filling the void of illusion.

My third eye throbs with a question. Is this female fungus which I suddenly hate about my body only good for wrapping around a jagged rock? Or is it that I haven't yet learned how to fuck with privilege, the luxury of having no conscience?

Deciding I've had enough of booking agents and white slavers posing as quaint tavern owners, I quit Andros's agency and strike off on my own. I land in the Pleasure Palace on Bloor Street, which provides stripping acts between porno films. I have to provide the tapes for the sound system and get paid cash for every set. The manager is young, friendly, and kosher, which makes it a congenial place to work. I shake my stuff for drunks, deadbeats, and sociology students in the afternoons, and for white-collar window washers who are very drunk and even more deadbeat in the evenings. At least with the drunks I get the odd cigarette package or small change thrown at my feet.

From there I wind up at the Bombay Express on Yonge Street. The risk of working on the Strip doesn't bother me now. Pascal is in the Middle East and my disguise is far too good for anyone to see through it.

One night, as usual, after my last set at the new stripping palace, I'm having a drink at the bar with Bennie, a pool shark who just came from Chicago looking for a private high-stakes game of eight ball, and the midget-sized swindler Manhattan Freddy, who wears a white suit with spats, a matching fedora, and mirrored shades, and travels with two four-foot Dinky Toy toads posing as bodyguards. Bennie totters to his feet, orders another round for everyone at the bar, and wades through the smoke toward the can at the rear of the room. With the noise and the music and the Bloody Mary in my hand, I'm thinking how immune I've become to sensation altogether, how nothing seems to bother me anymore—when out of the corner of my eye I notice a man slide onto the barstool beside me and touch his moustache. Out of habit I pull a cigarette out of the package on the counter and like magic the man turns toward me and snaps a lighter to it with *"Ma petite blond amie. . . ."*

   Pascal.

23

You can change the color of your hair, English—but your eyes are forever," Pascal sneers.

My deepest fear has materialized: I'm trapped. In shock, I accept the light along with another drink.

He burns his hot brown eyes on me and probes deep, deeper. "Why'd you run out on me?" he asks, walking a high wire over a tempest. Which one of us is sweating more?

I can't believe the question or supply an answer. I'm still struggling with the question of how the hell he found me. All I can do is tremble, spill my drink, and drag on my cigarette as if I'm having an attack of reefer madness while my imperative third eye frantically searches for an out. "Let's go to dinner and catch up, eh?" he seethes, turning an invitation into a command.

It's impossible to deny him. The .38 he has under his coat makes it impossible. So I hastily agree and butt my cigarette. "I have to change out of these no-clothes first—just give me ten."

Welling up with motion sickness, I slip off the stool and make for the zip-up rooms. But they're occupied so I crash into the office, my brain on fire. Newton, the manager, is behind the desk energizing over a copy of *Penthouse*. He's a spectacled blimp, *pâté en croûte* stuffed, a product of the Canadian elite—gone to the dogs. His chief enemy is boredom, a growing pain he'll never outgrow. He only hired me because I gave him ten outrageous reasons why he wouldn't. Sometimes I think we're turnips in the same vegetable patch.

When I start peeling down behind the screen in the corner, he pipes up. "Sit down, toots. Let's talk."

"Not now, Newy!" I fly off, hyped on escape. "I'm in a rush."

"Always in a goddamn rush," he says, good-naturedly. "Why are you so mean to me?"

"You're an unproductive product of an unproductive society. And I'm not mean, I'm indifferent."

"Tell me a secret, toots. What would put you in drive?"

"An American Express card with my name on it. Failing that, a night of harpsicord music from the fourteenth century performed by Edward the Confessor."

"You're mad." He chuckles. "But I knew that when I hired you. C'mon—can't we work something out?"

"Sure—but in the meantime I need a favor."

Newton immediately perks up. He loves favors on the fawn. Giving me the green light, he phones Whimpey at the bar and tells him to flick off the alarm buzzer on the exit door. On my dash out, he throws his magazine in my direction. "You owe me, toots."

Sure, I know the way it is. Everybody owes everybody in society's cosmetic cookie jar, where human emotion must be reduced to salable solubles of suet, spit, and shit. And I still refuse to believe it.

In the alley out back, I stop to catch my breath and I'm so relieved to have gotten away I'm giddy—until Pascal steps out from behind a garbage bin with a cigarette in his hand and I nearly jump out of my skin. "I know you a little better today than I did yesterday, English," he bites, clearly pleased with himself.

"Jesus!" I start to shake all over again.

He takes hold of my cold sweaty hand and grips it until I yelp. "You won't get away from me this time. If you try, I'll kill you." Isn't it the truth—that reality often sounds like old-fashioned melodrama? Numb now, I let him escort me around the corner to the Strip.

Yonge Street is hopping in an abstraction of lights, noise, and facial composites, a bowling alley of fragmented neons, all hammering away at the muted frailty in me. I feel utterly annihilated.

Quickly pushed into a cab, I'm taken to an intimate little French restaurant in a Victorian house just off Bloor Street. At the table he orders a white Beaujolais and keeps my glass filled, his eyes pulsating with a demonic passionate stare, his lips formalizing my doom with "Let's pick up where we left off." Then he snaps a light to his cigarette and I answer him with a brisk nod of the head that fools neither of us. It seems to be an eccentricity of his to lay down the ground rules with a threat in order to establish himself as the one in charge. Not only so that he can then read my compromise as self-motivated but so he can put our dumbshow on in public, the ultimate test, to assure himself that he's been accepted by the world at large. And it is this universality in his sociological makeup that must eventually work against him because he can't be a servant with two masters.

The smoked salmon arrives, and after his third glass of wine his moon lightens up a bit and he presses the issue. "I want you with me," he continues, his features strained and his voice ragged and raspy. "Why do you think I bothered to track you? I want to look after you. Don't you believe in happy endings?"

The question needed no answer. It was supposed to hang in midair like a break in a symphony. My trusty third eye keeps locking into rewind and playback, in stereo—while his ambiguous delivery slowly hooks me into dangerous distraction.

His effect on me is deadly. By the time we hit a local hot spot, he's limber and restless, and I'm wobbly and light-headed, clinging to his arm as if it's my only lease on life, playing the role that he likes so well. When he folds his arms around me on the dance floor, that dark primeval intensity in him trembles and grates me down to sand. I can feel my emotional self steering into a skid, hurtling toward an abyss. The dark force in him is too strong. I can't stop. Worse, I don't think I want to.

An hour later we take a cab back to my room in Little Italy. When he takes the key from my hand, unlocks my door, and impatiently prods me inside, I'm suddenly plunging through windows in space, lost and afraid. I don't fight taking the trip. I let him pull my legs up around his neck and when his Godrod ritualistically jabs my warm pliable cunt I don't resist and twist excitedly. It seems as if I'm standing in a lighted open doorway, being scorched by a ray gun from the darkness without, and the sounds of my heightened responses connect me to him.

When his darkness swallows me up entirely, he rolls away and quietly lights a cigarette. Suddenly reminded of time, he glances at his jeweled Seiko, pulls me up to dress, and makes a telephone call to the airport. Then he paces the room waiting for me to pack a single suitcase. I make a point of omitting anything of a sentimental nature. Mechanically I scratch out two short notes at my desk, one to Simon asking him to baby-sit Piddles for a while longer, the second to Biscuit with a check, asking him to put my personal effects in storage. Before slipping them in the envelopes, Pascal gives the notes a quick scan to make sure I'm not giving away my whereabouts. Before leaving he pours a glass of wine and insists that I put it back in one swallow.

Down the street I post the short letters in the mailbox at the corner and Pascal flags down a cab. At Toronto Airport everything is a blur. As I love flying, it's a cozy blur. It takes us an hour to get runway clearance. Meanwhile, I sit in the lounge with Pascal, zonked out on his shoulder. Finally, he helps me out into a four-seater private plane and I'm in cloud nine. When we're whirring over the lights of the city, I slowly realize that I've been drugged. The wine. I grab at Pascal's coat sleeve, wavering between hysteria and giddiness. "It's too late, isn't it?"

"For you, English, it's always been too late," he assures me with a strange compressed smile.

Around noon the next day I wake up in a strange bed in a strange room and I'm wearing a strange nightgown. The room is strictly middle-class flash-in-the-pan: pink walls, chintz bedspread and curtains, French provincial furniture and a cheery three-piece bath-combination-boudoir for teacup poodles in season. The room must be well soundproofed for it's unbelievably quiet. No beeping horns, no squealing tires, no galumphing street cars, no sirens, no wolf calls, no cat calls and no maids babbling away in Portuguese as they trundle laundry carts up the corridor. This motel must be Toronto's newest hormone hideaway because it's not on my list of the tried and trusty. I must take note of the name before I leave. I'd like to come again.

Groggy and famished I open the curtains to let some smoggy sunshine in and get my bearings. I'm expecting to find myself in the middle of a downtown parking lot. Instead, I discover I'm in a parking lot inside of a wild game preserve in the boonies. A high wire fence looms up in the distance and a middle-aged man in an overcoat is walking along its outer limits smoking a cigarette. Beyond, the trees of a park, partially buried in the snow.

Now I'm awake and ready for a marathon run all the way to Labrador. I have a terrible feeling whirring in my gut. Quickly, I scan the room again. But this time I'm more observant. No telephone. No color TV. No heavy-duty carpeting. No complimentary towels or soap in the bathroom. No neatly typed NOTICE TO GUESTS sign posted on the back of the door. And the clincher—two Wedgewood figurines on the lace-covered vanity.

My heartbeat has accelerated to the point where I'm quite possibly on fire. The heat in my head is actually making my ears ring. Little by little the jigsaw of the previous evening pierces my mind like streaks of white lightning. I remember Pascal describing his home in North Montreal . . . a twelve-foot electric fence . . . patrolled by two plainclothes security men who share a twenty-four-hour shift . . . Stop your shaking!

I'm going to panic. I know I'm going to panic. But first I have to have a cigarette so I can do it properly. After I check the closet and the dresser drawers, I really start to sweat. They're stocked with another woman's clothing. Where the hell are *my* things?

Desperately in need of a nicotine fix I assault the door I've been trying to ignore for all of three minutes. Just as I feared, it's locked, so I begin banging and kicking it to death. Then, between rally cries, footsteps and salvation—a key jiggles in the lock. Pascal, dressed in a maroon satin dressing gown, comes in as self-possessed as ever. "Did you sleep well, chérie?"

Substituting one rage for another, I jump him in a fit. "Do you realize what you did last night? You left me without cigarettes—not one. Are you trying to drive me batty?"

He suppresses a smile. "I'm sorry. I forgot."

"How could you possibly forget? And where's all my stuff? I came with more than my sense of humor."

"Later," he says, taking a pack of smokes from the pocket of his robe. I take one, and he snaps a lighter to it. While I inhale euphoria he whips a chenille robe out of the closet and I slip into it. Then he combs my bangs out of my eyes with his hands. "Come on, I'll show you around," he says tonelessly, holding the door open.

Now that I've dealt with crisis number one, I can address crisis number two—but not until I've had my morning coffee.

The large modern bungalow is laid out in the shape of a horseshoe and for the exception of my room exudes a cold bachelor air of a drop-in chophouse. Leather couches and knockabout ambivalence mixed with a smattering of fine antiques from a bankruptcy sale. On the main floor, a laundry, a kitchen, an adjoining sunroom, a dining room, a living room, a den, and four bedrooms. I'm not shown Pascal's room. According to him, it's off-limits and contains the only telephone in the house. Downstairs in the day-lit basement, a private shooting range with an arsenal-sized gun cabinet and a recreation area with a fireplace, bar, and pool table. Through the sliding glass doors at the side, a patio, a peanut-shaped swimming pool, and a quarter of an acre of what in the summer is a hedged-in garden.

The tour concludes at the dinette in the sunroom upstairs. I'm not impressed with this department-store example of new money. I've seen splashier setups in *Playboy*. The place doesn't have a drop of character. I didn't see a thing to read—anywhere. No big yeller dog snoring by the fireplace either. A trophy room of waxed human heads would have been a perfect touch.

I'm pretty well hinged on the notion that I have Pascal all to myself here when, to my surprise and disappointment, lunch is wheeled in on a cart and served up by complication number one. A short wiry Canadian Indian in a T-shirt, jeans, and Adidas, his long hair tied into a pigtail at the back of his head. He takes himself so seriously as a major domo that I can't. What the hell is he doing here? When Pascal introduces him as the housekeeper, it's all I can do to keep a straight face. Then Riel gives me a formal nod and I'm instantly sobered. The sudden rush of hate in his deep Metis eyes gives me the absolute creeps.

During the tour of the house my subconscious kept picking up weird vibrations all around, pushing me away. That's why I can't connect to anything—I'm not supposed to. I'm an unwelcome house guest. If I don't kick up some dust I'll get swept under the carpet.

The crab salad looks appetizing, but despite the rumblings of my empty stomach I'm unable to eat. I'm so high on suppressed hysteria I'm drunk. It's all I can do to remain seated. I fill up on coffee instead and nibble on a croissant for effect. And yes, as usual, my brain is speeding at a hundred miles an hour and focused on one thought only: escaping.

Pascal suddenly excuses himself and leaves the room, only to return minutes later with complication number two on a leash—a thirty-pound leopardlike cat which he identifies as Bebe, his pet ocelot.

I wish to hell men would stop trying to gross me out. I've been there already. When I fell into the light at birth I was grossed out. I've been working my way back to the darkness through cultural degeneration ever since.

"I thought only zoos were allowed to have cats like that," I remark without thinking that this *is* a zoo or remembering that two of my lovers at the club in Toronto had exotic pets—one a scorpion and the other a boa constrictor. I only found out about *them* when I got up for a pee in the middle of the night. Actually, I should consider myself lucky. Pascal could be into orangutans.

Cats have a mind of their own so I don't even try to make friends with Bebe. At the same time I'm careful not to exhibit any fear of her either or she'll play on it and make my life hell. For minutes we just stare each other down. Then she spits at me, a clear sign she doesn't like competition. Pascal quiets his furry concubine down by petting her in long rhythmical strokes and speaks to her in French until she nuzzles his arm. His effect over Bebe is as mysterious as his effect over me. I experience a twinge of jealousy and I'm unable to fight it. Maybe exotic men have exotic pets so they can only be appreciated by women with exotic phobias.

Pascal pours out more coffee for me and resumes eating. I watch the surgeonlike way he handles his fork, waiting for him to stop playing charades. I don't have long to wait. "You'll learn to like it here," he begins, laying down the ground rules in Braille.

Oh Jesus, here it comes—that bad feeling whirring in my gut again! But now it's moved up into my rib cage and I can't regulate my breathing. My heartbeats are hammering at my ears in stereo, and my hands are so cold and clammy I'm clenching them into fists in my lap to keep them from shaking. I wish to hell he'd shut up and leave bad enough alone. But he won't.

The good news is that I'm allowed to have the books in my confiscated suitcase but not the clothing. From now on I'll dress from his wife's wardrobe. I've always wanted to play Nora in A *Doll's House*. Despite his earlier promise, I won't be able to communicate with anyone either by telephone or mail. Third, I'll only be locked in my room at night—for my own protection. Doesn't it ever occur to him that he might be the one needing protection?

"But why *can't* I come and go as I please?" I ask stupidly, just to hear the sound of my own voice.

"Why would you *want* to go out at all, English?" he asks cynically. "You have everything here."

"I might *want* to start consulting a shrink," I sauce back, unable to stop myself. "I *might* have a sudden urge to take skydiving lessons. I *might*—"

Bang! His coffee cup goes over.

I'm struck dumb. He hits the table instead of me and leaps to his feet in a rage. "Shut up!"

Now he's beside my chair, blocking out the sunlight and clutching a swatch of my hair. The back of my head is being pulled so hard it hurts. All I can read is the salt-and-pepper pattern on the ceiling. "When I talk, say nothing," he commands. "When I stop talking, say nothing. Just listen. When I want *you* to talk I'll tell you. Do you understand, English?"

My subdued yes goes well with my shattered nervous system.

When he's like this it's easy to believe his criminal record and keep wondering about what has been left out.

He releases me and begins pacing. The cigarette in his hand is shaking worse than I am. He tries to pick up where he left off, but he's too agitated to do it properly. "If you need something—anything, tell Riel. He'll order it in. I want you to like it here. I want you to have fun and be yourself."

I can't believe he just said that. I don't know what mesmerizes me more—the man or the man's logic. They're both steeped in black magic.

When I was a kid I was put into a roller coaster and told, "This is fun. You'll like fun. Fun is fast and upside-down crazy. Hold on and enjoy it." After the bottom of my stomach fell through my abdominal cavity, I screamed for the big hairy dummy with the tattoos at the controls to stop it—but he didn't. So I jumped right over the side and only managed to crack my head open and break an arm. Would I be as lucky this time?

While Pascal's waiting for me to transform into the Walt Disney fairy, Riel cleans up the spilt coffee on the rug. He's smirking in my direction. The little rat looks good on his knees. Wait till he starts cleaning up my messes. I'm as clumsy as hell when I'm forced into playing blindman's buff.

Pascal takes his place again at the table with a fresh cup of coffee and indulges in that nervous habit of rubbing his left thumb and forefinger together. Knowing he won't release me until I ask, I decide to give him what he wants—chopped liver with a pickle on the side. "I'd like to go back to my room, now. How about some writing material first?"

"Why?" he asks, to see if my motor's still running.

"I want to write myself a letter from God. Don't worry. I don't plan to mail it."

Irritably he crushes his cigarette in the ashtray and releases me with a threat. "You think you're being so clever, but you're really being very stupid. Tonight I'll show you how stupid."

Riel brings the writing material I asked for to my room. I have a bath to celebrate. Giving me a pen and paper was the worst mistake he's made to date. Now I can put the emotional mishmash in my head into conversational Yinglish and some kind of order. I can set up defenses and offenses and I can plan my future. I'm armed and dangerous too.

Late in the afternoon Riel shakes me out of a sound sleep and instructs me to dress up to the nines for dinner. Exhausted by sugared brain cells, I have a thumping migraine. I pop a few Anacin and see if I can find something in the closet to accommodate my disoriented sense of self. Pascal's wife didn't buy off-the-rack crap. She just bought crap with last year's designer labels. Every outfit suits one blasé mood of the blind sophisticate on the altruistic roll call. I finally slip into a lime-green number straight out of Harlequin Romance doing Las Vegas. That's when I discover that Pascal's wife was one size larger than I am. To pick up the slack I pin up the spaghetti straps at the back so I won't be taken for an asparagus sprout on the rise.

That night Pascal and I begin playing house in Colditz at opposite ends of a long mahogany table in the dining room. The background music, compliments of Paul Mauriat and the wine and the fondue, compliments of Riel doing his man Friday routine. But I should talk. I just stepped off a two-thousand-year-old Grecian vase and don't know whether to play the clinging ingenue or the heavy vamp. Since I didn't eat lunch, I'm ravenous. Maybe I'll leave the question of which role to play a hanging one until after the chocolate mousse.

Pascal is taking pains to be congenial and twice he almost smiles. Almost. Like any born chameleon I adapt. Remembering his threat of a long time ago—*keep me from getting bored and you'll have nothing to regret*—I keep making withdrawals from that storehouse of trivia locked in my memory bank, searching for interesting conversation pieces to crack nuts over. The wine does wonders to loosen the screws that connect peculiarly resilient smells to particularly solvent time slots. I have a phenomenal memory and can even bring back the moment I took my first step. Pascal doesn't appear to have a memory at all. Like everyone I seem to meet, he landed here from Mars and the details surrounding the crash are not to be discussed.

When he's happy with me he calls me chérie. When he's not, he calls me English—for spite. He can tell by looking at me I'm poor mongrel truck with a yippie complex. Yet, he doesn't want or need to know any more and I take the precaution of not filling him in. What's it his business if I'm a homogenized Kraut with a double-barreled Yiddish connection? It's not that anything not French is automatically English, rather that anything not French is automatically Irish stew. A full-time misanthrop and part-time classicist just hates Irish stew.

He's right though about the Anglo-Saxon race being washed up because of genetic overlap and biological fallout. But he's wrong about it being their fault. He's also wrong about everything being lost in the meltdown. I'm the perfect example of hopscotching genes. The only relative I resemble is three generations removed. Isn't that scary? He seems to think so.

As the night gears up, my defenses wear down. Zero hour approaches when Pascal abruptly leaves the table in a huff and takes his Drambuie into the living room. Was it something I said?

The countdown commences when I join him. Riel fetches his dressing gown, opens another bottle of wine, and sets a log to burn in the fireplace. Pascal strips down and stretches out on the rug. Taking his lead, I straddle his waist, rub oil into his shoulders, and massage his back. Blessed be the peacemakers, he's falling asleep.

After fifteen minutes of sweet distraction, hypnotizing myself with the movements of my own hands, Pascal suddenly rolls over, upsetting me onto the rug. He reaches for his robe and a cigarette and the night is launched into the fathomless unknown.

To begin with, Riel appears like the Sorcerer's apprentice swinging a worn lady's train case at his side. With mock reverence he sets it before me on the rug, and Pascal asks me to open it. Inside, a cloth makeup bag and a fascist's idea of a night on the town. A shiny black-leather corseted cockteaser with a belt, garter belt, meshed stockings, and knee-high stormtrooper boots with three-inch heels and twelve-inch tongues. He must have been shopping for bumper stickers in Hamburg recently.

With every fiber of my being I'm fighting the gigglies. I'm hoping that *he's* not going to transform into a drag queen. My funny bone couldn't stand a workout tonight. But he quickly dispels that fear by ordering *me* to transform into the queen of spades.

There's no point arguing with the abnormally normal in a bomber jacket. While I undress to dress, I curse that frustrated artist that lives in Pascal's soul. Why doesn't he move to Paris and get a job as a waiter by day and a street painter by night? Artists were invented to wash the devil's dirty laundry. Whores were invented to hang it out to dry. Lawyers were invented to fold it, politicians to sell it, and the public to buy it. A legitimate employment for the depraved and the deprived.

Five minutes into the departure, I'm *en grande tenue* and pissed off. I've been doing everything possible to dump the Hun I found in my family tree, hoping someone would take me for a lost Polack, a forged Czech, or a White Russian instead. Now, just like that I'm a clone of Christmas past. Just like that, I'm a Third Reich kewpie doll on parade, a 1939 price tag still dangling from my tush.

"Are you drunk?" Pascal asks from miles away.

"No, I don't think so."

"Maybe it would be better if you were," he says from point-blank range, upending a glass at my lips that breathes fire in liquid form.

Then it's makeup party time, sponsored by Barnum and Bailey Street Decorators and Pascal with a sculptor's nervous hand. My eyes aren't big enough, he's got to improve on Mother Nature and create her melodramatic understudy. As the final mad touch, he messes up my hair as opposed to painting on a moustache.

Numbly I sit back on my haunches waiting for a cue card. He snaps off Paul Mauriat and switches on the Cars. Settling into a deep arm-chair with a cigarette, he watches me watch him imitate Ingmar Bergman on a shoot.

What's the turn-on? Poor, stupid, intoxicated me, I don't get it.

A glass almost too fat for my fingers to hold is molded into my hand. In almost a somnambulist's stupor, I sip, tasting nothing but sand and potash. A maelstrom of deafening echoes awaken me to a dream. I'm in the middle of a verbal cross fire without subtitles. On one side of the room, *Love*, the master, and on the other, *Blind*

Obedience, the bondsman. *They're fighting!* I gulp faster and through dazed, slanted eyes watch Pascal's scurrilous jawline as it rises up—vital, orgasmic, awful against Riel's capricious brow as it falls—shrinking, passionate, wonderful. *What are they fighting about?* Dehydrating fast, I drink until Pascal, triumphant and grotesque, walks toward me through the bottom of the glass and takes it right out of my hand on the bypass. Riel, looking like a drowned spaniel, swings by on the inside straight and folds up into a lawn chair and pushes me down onto the rug, his black eyes fixed on a pin point on my blank forehead, his arms open in a hate embrace. *They're fighting for meeee!*

Sure he plans to work me over, I jerk my knee, and he collapses on my stomach, clutching godhead between his legs, momentarily disabled.

What's this? A vibrating uvula from the polling station upwind. I've never heard Pascal laugh outloud before. I hope it's not contagious. What's he laughing at?

Now back to Riel. No, not back to Riel. Back to *They're fighting for me again!* Back to forever enigma, Pascal, reading the riot act while that French germ worships the occupation of private places in the heart, his arm a part of his hand, his hand a part of his mind's eye holding a .38 projectile.

Now back to Riel, still in the grip of that pathetic, cellophane-wrapped expression of gay, queer, faggoty morbid phallic dread in need of a priest or a talisman called Pascal, the perpetrator of *Why are they fighting for me?* when Riel pounces, agonizingly limpid, and I let his grievous mother lode grapple me under, and over, and onto my stomach on the marriage bed, stained with *They're not fighting for me! They're fighting* over *me!*

Back to Pascal's ammo dump of flesh-of-my-flesh desire, in a bigamist's binding arms, linked with the bridegroom in waiting, at the altar, on the steps of consummation, with the gifted Daedalian, for that veiled-in-saffron, plug-ugly Riel, now hunkering, hungering down, lifting by cheek-in-each-hand those rounded haunches of symmetry *Why are they fighting over me?* as I'm riding Valhalla low in the saddle, lit end up, with the dark under-skin exposed down, waiting to unleash that unflagging feebleness of the wounded persona on the maiden of Nuremberg, to release that voluptuous urgency rubbing itself on the soft-skinned impotency in his hand, as he wedges a thumb in my mouth sideways with *bite it!* familiarity, releasing a trap doored codpiece in leather in the female eunuch's tailpiece, while gasping, "Shut up and fake it or he'll kill us both!"

Back to Pascal. No, not back to Berlin. Back to Kabbalah. *They're not fighting* over *me. They're fighting* through *me!*

Back to finger-fucking Riel and that crescent-shaped sepulchre where the heart wears Cupid's bow tie.

Yecch! So this's what it's about—humiliation.

Back to Riel. No, back to Woden taking the vindicating stick from Pascal's hand, and retribution loading that weapon of retribution, and injecting the empty hybrid places, to restore the lost soul in lumber squirm-around darkness, shedding its moaning, wailing Kaddish, giving the kiss of death to Aberglaube, sodomizing the Fatherland with the purgation of Israel, and I taste blood—his, mine, ours, through his warblingly defiant falsetto, "You did this to him—you!"

Riel spends the next afternoon in my room while I try on every number in the closet so they can be sent away for professional alterations. We don't speak about last night when I was used as a pleasure factory combination whipping post, SS style, in a made-to-measure ménage à trois. I don't remember much about it myself, except waking up back in my own bed, wearing that same made-in-Italy nightgown, mascara smudging my face.

For reasons of which I'm not quite sure, I attempt to draw Riel out so I can make up whatever it is we have to make up. But he wants no part of me or my life cycle and ignores everything I say to him. On his knees, with spittle in his mouth, he curses in French under his breath, tacks up hemlines, and draws in side seams, sticking pins in me like a voodoo doll.

The following weeks take on a daily routine which I find frightening. There's no need to divide time when it's all in one ballpark called *extracurricular activities.* I should have had enough experience at this to make it easy. But it isn't.

I take long walks in the morning around the grounds and especially along the perimeter of the fence. But my efforts to elicit help from the Brothers Grimm security patrol prove fruitless. They simply ignore me and when I get too conscience close, simply wave me away and walk faster to escape me altogether.

At my request, a TV is moved into my room to keep me brain dead. But even that fails to keep me entertained so Riel orders a library for me from a bookstore in Nôtre Dame de Gras. My reading material falls under only one censorship restriction—no French dictionaries. They don't want me to get too chummy with the native tongue in case I discover what they're really saying to me behind my back is really what they're trying to say to me to my face.

Now figure that one out.

Pascal visits my room the night after my initiation rite for a chaser. His sexual episodes haven't lost any of their motel-in-Toronto tarnish. In comparison to last night, it's almost a welcome relief. But I'd still like to know if I'm supposed to be the matzoh ball or the after-dinner mint.

Pascal comes and goes, sometimes for days or weeks at a time. I'm the major bone of contention in the house no matter if he's home or not. When I crave peace, I keep as low a profile as I can. When my energy level blows a fuse, I seek out Riel. He considers the kitchen his domain and prepares all the meals. I can't even make a hamburger to go without causing a fuss. Crumbs on the toaster, dirty spoons in the sink, and water spots on the faucets drive him to distraction.

"I told you to ask for what you want," he flings in my face.

"I didn't want to bother you."

"The very sight of you bothers me—now get out!"

I'd take my case to Pascal the next time he's home, but I despise a snitch. He manages to get involved in our squabbling anyway, and I think it secretly amuses him to play us off against each other.

I've got a lot of time to think about what to think about. Crunch will think I deserted him like everyone else. Simon will think I deserted myself and be right. Biscuit will think I've been kidnapped by aliens and wait for the gods to shuffle the cards.

The nights are the worst, I'm used to being on the move till dawn.

The hysteria I've managed to beat down all day just has to pop its cork. The cage I live in suddenly closes inside of myself. I'm not even content with my books. I pace my room, chain-smoke, and flick the dials on the TV until there's nothing but a screen of phosphorescent moon dust and I imagine I'm being attacked by electrodes produced by an intelligence with a UFO charge card. For inspiration, I work on my lists of incentives until they become so sophisticated and scrambled I throw them out before I lose my marbles altogether. I need pills to help me sleep but Pascal won't allow me to have them. It's all right for me to be addicted to fear, rape, and dissipation, but drugs, depression, and suicide are no-nos.

When Pascal does arrive home, against all my powers of reasoning I can't help becoming the backstage groupie waiting for him at the door. And he plays the cat's meow like the king of hearts, presenting me with cheap department-store jewelry and perfumes he knows I wouldn't wear even if I didn't have to please him. Him and his hang-ups and me and my hang-ons.

One night after sex he pulls me on top of him in the bath and suddenly I'm full of ESP and enterprise. In a word, I get reckless.

"When are you gonna kill me? Today? Tomorrow? Next week?" I ask.

His mouth says, "Why would I do that?" but his eyes say "The only thing I like better than killing you is the rush I get wanting to."

I repeat the question and he twirls one of my hair ends into a moustache under my nose. "Why do you English ask such stupid questions?" he asks dreamily.

"Why do you Frenchies like tradition so much?"

In a sudden spurt of energy, he upsets me with a splash until he's on top. Our naked bodies squeak against the sides of the tub, and he's holding my head like a pomegranate he means to crack. "What I get from you in bed, I could get on St. Catherine's Street at half the price, English. What I want is your cunt's brain."

Think again, maestro. Mine doesn't come with a brain. It comes with teeth.

He keeps seeing me as wanton when I'm actually wantin'. He likes me undone, to see how far I'll unravel. How long can I keep tracking for mileage?

Once Bebe realizes that I'm a permanent fixture in Bleak House, her attitude toward me changes from hot dislike to a cool grumbling indifference. I start leaving my bedroom door open so she'll think I don't mind her tearing my bedding to pieces. And she takes the bait. Aiming the nozzle of a can of Lysol at her face when she gets ugly wins her respect. Stealing leftovers for her from the kitchen when Riel's not looking wins her trust, even though she's careful not to show it when Pascal is home. Eventually she becomes my only confidante, especially now that she has a fetish about sleeping on my pillow shams until I'm in a stroking mood.

My environment is starting to crush me from the outside in. Maybe I should change it from the inside out. How about having the wall-to-wall carpeting torn up and replaced with Aubussons and Axminsters? How about moving in a truckload of plants and donating his leather couches to a legal firm in Mount Royal? The complaints add up until they become a list. Then one night I present that list to Pascal at dinner, only to be told: "Why would I need an interior decorator in the house when I've already got a paper tiger?"

It isn't as if I have something to feel guilty about. It's not as if I haven't tried to escape. It's only that I tried too hard not to be caught instead of just getting on with the business of escaping.

Once, I wasted a perfectly good Italian nightgown plugging up my toilet. But when the plumber came, how was I to know I'd be locked in the spare bedroom before he even reached the front gate? Then, to get *his* attention I had to get Riel's attention, which means I not only had to start banging hysterically on the door, but I had to have a legitimate reason for banging in the first place in case the plan backfired. Which brings me to the curtains I set on fire.

Riel responded to my hysterical banging with a fire extinguisher. Pascal responded to my escape attempt by smacking me around when he next arrived home. The plumber got away with my nightgown and I got the bill. Oh, somebody please bring on the clowns!

Talking about *bugs*. That's all I do is think about what's bugging me.

Initiation night has been asked back by popular demand as a sporadic one-night stand whenever Pascal is angry with Riel and wants to make him suffer. Consequently, my ongoing war with Riel is getting out of hand. He'll win. He has to. It's his turf.

Almost six months has passed. I've gone from Congreve to Thomas Hardy and I'm still here buried alive in the garden outside, watching the daffodils come up, planting the seeds of yet another season of stir-time and lost-time up Frenchman's Creek.

spend every waking moment trying to hatch an escape plan. The first week of June I'm ready for Operation Desperation. In five days when the moon changes I'm going over the Berlin Wall in a wet suit, rubber boots, and gloves I found in the garage. I'm taking out the security man with a frying pan I filched from the kitchen. Hell, I don't even know if I'll be grounded. I'll probably be electrocuted. It's got to be the craziest idea I've ever had but it's the best one I can come up with.

As it happens, Jupiter finally comes to my rescue. Pascal does some shopping and purchases an expensive art deco couch from an antique shop in Old Montreal. The afternoon the gaudy bumholder is delivered, I'm curled up in my room trying to pick up a few pointers on Roman lechery from the pages of I, Claudius. Anxious to see any face from the outside, I creep into the kitchen in my sundress and sandals. Three working-class hunks in overalls are hauling the paisley couch in through the patio door. Minutes later, they throw a big white cloth over the old couch. Riel takes the sales receipt to the dining room table to inspect and sign, the three hunks following at his heels. Riel is so methodically mulish. As I observe their turned backs, it suddenly hits me. Freedom in all its blue-skied glory is staring me right in the face. I have only a split second to make up my mind. I'll never get another chance like this. Ripe with fear and challenge, and shaking so bad I nearly collapse, I drop to my hands and knees and scuttle forward and when I've closed the gap and can no longer be seen through the dining room door I swallow a breath and keep moving and there it is only a few feet away and here I am alongside the old couch and reaching for the edge of that white cloth and lifting it and hearing Riel's voice and footsteps getting louder and I'm slipping under—under—and my fist is in my mouth and I lie perfectly still wondering if I've made it. The voices of garbled French are right beside me and I'm under the big white creases and folds biting my fingers and sweating and praying that I'm not discovered.

Suddenly strong arms heave and I'm airborne and moving. What if the morons drop the goddamn couch or tilt the sacred goods on an angle-on-the-spill? I'll slide off like a pea off a plate and be squashed underfoot. Oh, Zeus! Hang on, don't piss in your pants, and don't breathe. Riel won't miss me until he calls supper and Pascal's in Europe so he won't miss me at all.

I hear a squealing sound and I'm being lifted higher, probably aboard a mechanical lift at the back of their truck. The door is clanged shut and a lock jammed into place. An engine sparks up and I'm riding inside its vibrations. I'm practically comatose with fear. Then we stop. It must be the front gate. Then we're moving again. When we start to pick up speed, I'm ecstatically chewing *I, Claudius* to pieces and wondering how it could have been so damn easy. Realizing that I still haven't escaped the truck and even if I manage it I don't have so much as a dime for a phone call and could still get caught, I fall back into fear and paranoia. Riel might knock on my bedroom door to see if I want anything, which he usually does before starting a major household chore so that he won't be interrupted later. Not getting any answer, he'd naturally let himself in and initiate a search of the house and grounds. It wouldn't take long for him to put two and two together. He'd either call the R.C.M.P. or the city police. It wouldn't matter which. Pascal's in bed with both of them, too.

About half an hour later, the driver wheels the truck to the right and we grind to a halt. I sit bolt upright, fling off the cover, and start kicking frantically at the door as soon as the engine dies down.

When the door is jacked open, I leap out onto the pavement and land in a somersaulting sprawl, screaming the few dirty French words I know. The hunks are so startled, they merely bleat out a few feeble *Sacré Christ*s as I scramble to my feet and they make no attempt whatsoever to stop my flight pattern.

Not knowing where to hell I am, I hoof it along the sidewalk like a fireball for at least a mile on no predetermined course and soon realize I'm still in the suburbs. Too close for comfort. I've got to get downtown. *Fast.* I put out the old thumb and before long a Frenchman in a blue Fiat picks me up. I dodge his curious questions by explaining that I'm an English major at McGill University and since St. Catherine's Street is the sole compass point in my knowledge of downtown Montreal, that's where he drops me off.

The street is crowded, noisy, and hot, a mosaic of clothing shops, banks, and sidewalk cafés. Now that I've survived the escape, I've got to survive the consequences. It's always *something.* I have to make some money double quick or, if all else fails, steal it and get the hell out of this province.

I bumble around for a good hour in a daze, drinking in the sounds and the people, and the hungrier and thirstier I get, the more determined I am to score. A swarthy middle-aged smoothie sidles up and tries to put the move on me. Since my French is strictly kindergarten cop-out, he quickly switches to English. He asks me if I'm lost, if I've been in the city before, and if I'd like to join him for a bite. I know exactly where this conversation is going. So I let him settle me down at a checker-clothed table at a street café and order a carafe of Chablis and a smoked salmon sandwich. He doesn't seem to be hungry. I don't feel much like eating myself. I'm too nervous and jittery. But I choke it all down anyway. Who knows when I'll be able to eat again?

About an hour later, when the wine and the package of cigarettes he bought me have served to calm my nerves, and the conversation has dwindled out to a dead end, he offers me thirty bucks for a fast fuck. Realizing that I've got something he needs, I try to raise him to forty and we settle at thirty-five. Impatiently, he pays my way into a movie house and escorts me into the last row, which is empty. Then, with both eyes glued to the Danish orgy on the screen, he pushes me to my knees, sits down, unzips his fly with trembling fingers, and pulls my head into his lap. Servicing him is an exercise in Gestalt therapy. I make myself believe that the pure pulp of my life is worth the sum of its seedy parts.

Back out on the street, I clutch my thirty-five bucks optimistically.

The first thing I do is buy another package of cigarettes, a six-pack of beer, and a bag of fruit and sandwiches at a delicatessen. The sun is going down and I'm suddenly chilly so I add a sweater to my purchases. Then, for hours, I wander the streets in a daze, skittishly avoiding the police and trying to lose myself in the heavy pedestrian traffic. I'm petrified that I'll be grabbed by Pascal's men if I attempt to take a bus or a train out of the city. Then, fatigued and footsore, I stop in a parkette to have a snack and ruminate. Now that it's getting dark, it's time I thought about a place to crash for the night. I wonder if a church would be a suitable sanctuary. I see a bag lady feeding the pigeons and give her a fin. In return she tells me how to get out of the city via the underground and I decide to split Montreal tonight. Her directions are about as muddled as my bearings. I get lost and start asking questions, and about nine o'clock in the evening find myself in the city freight yards.

For what seems like ages, I scout row upon row of carbon-coated boxcars, smelling of tar and gasoline, taking care to evade the railway workers. Finally I notice a whole line of boxcars linked together on one track with a caboose on the east end, which must mean it'll eventually be heading west. Now all I have to do is get aboard. Afraid of getting locked inside, I start scaling a ladder to the roof when I suddenly hear an exaggerated "Sssssssss!"

Jittery as a squirrel, I jump down, shaking with fear. What the hell is it?

"Sssssssssssss!"

I spin on the balls of my feet and notice an elderly Black man with white-tinged kinky hair sticking his head out of the car behind, motioning to me. The only thing whiter than his teeth is the mischievous glint in his eye. "Come on in here, missy!" he husks in a whisper. "It's a hell of a lot warmer."

"But we'll get locked in!" I object.

"The brakeman gave me a free pass on this car, missy. He didn't say nothing about extra baggage." He extends a hand and hauls me aboard. The inside of the car is empty. He directs me to his one suitcase in the corner where he's set up a temporary camp on his coat.

"Make yourself at home," he insists with a grand sweep of the hand.

"What do I call you?" I ask, sitting down beside him.

"Missy, you could call me a son of a bitch—and I wouldn't blame you. But Bub will do just fine. I'm a trapper."

"No kidding. What animals do you trap?"

"The only animals I trap is two-legged." He chortles, rolling his eyes. "I'm a drummer." Untying a set of bongo skins from the handle of his suitcase, he gives them a pat-a-tat-tat to the beat of a song that sounds remotely like "The Lonely Bull." Then he gives me a sermon on the proper way of traveling in the modern world. "Third-class is all in the price of the ticket," he insists, taking the cigarette and beer I offer him. "Since I don't pay for one, I don't travel any class but my own. And mine's always first-class sideways—with room to stretch. I don't have to trip over anybody's feet to get to the pisser. I can just stand at the door and let the wind have it. Being rich is all a degree of privacy. Mr. Molson don't sit with the common herd so why the hell should I? And don't worry about my morals, missy. I could wash myself twice in your sunlight and still come up black-arsed. Say— whatcha got in that bag there besides beer?"

"All kinds of first-class goodies," I assure him, handing him a turkey sandwich. He thanks me, pulls out a bottle of Guinness and a bag of chocolate bars. Then he asks me where I'm going.

"Back to Canada."

Suddenly the car jerks forward in a series of spasmodic jumps and we're rolling, slowly, until we reach the outskirts of the city. The wave of relief that sweeps over me is total. Meanwhile, Bub and I sit near the half-open doorway, watching the sun suck up the last remnants of twilight from the passing houses and trees silhouetted against the skyline.

Bub is from some ant mound in Nova Scotia called Nigger Hill but he hasn't been back there since he was fourteen years old. That's how old he was when he ran away. His forefathers crossed the border from the States after the Civil War. The biggest game in his village when he was a kid was initiated by the poor white trash nearby. The kids would blast up the road every Friday night in pickups, trying to hit one of the Blacks with a broom. The game was called broom-a-

coon. When a Whitey hit a nigger, he got a point. If the Whitey
dropped the broom or a nigger got it, he was out of the game. This's
how Bub explains it to me and also how he says he learned to get fast
with his hands. "It was good training for a trapper," he confesses
reflectively. "I wonder if it did any miracles for the Whiteys." Thoughtfully, he bites into another sandwich. "I got my first job in Montreal
selling papers to pay for lessons. Then I kinda leapfrogged it with a
number of bands doing gigs at night and on weekends until it started
to pay regular. I don't do much work nowadays. Every so often I get
the itch to come to Montreal to see my old friends. My old woman
lives in Toronto."

For the last while I've been getting sharp needles of pain in my
lower back and abdomen, not unlike menstrual cramps at their worst,
so I don't take much more notice of Bub. But by the time we reach
Jamesburg, I've started to hemorrhage, the pain is unbearable, and
I'm writhing on the floor, screaming. Poor Bub tries his best to soothe
me and talk the pain out of me. He pulls a towel out of his suitcase
and uses it to absorb the blood on my legs but soon there's so much
of it, he gives up. I think he knows what's wrong with me, but he
won't say. As soon as the train stops, Bub quickly gets me to the door,
lifts me out of the railway car, and sits me down alongside the track
while he goes back in for his suitcase. Then he beckons a brakeman
and together they help me into a cab at the station. Bub accompanies
me to the emergency entrance of the nearest hospital. I have no ID
on me of any kind so the fat orange-haired fruit cup at the desk is
something suspicious when Bub hands her *his* medical card. "I can't
believe that this girl is your grandchild," she gibes in a nasal octave.

"No more than I can believe your hair color didn't come out of a
bottle," he flings back angrily. "And I would raise sons to marry
nothing but pure white trash." When I start screaming the gods down
from Olympus, Bub whisks my delirious writhing doubled-up self right
through a set of doors, and a doctor and two nurses take over, lifting
me onto a stretcher on wheels, and on my way to the operating room
I manage to call out Biscuit's telephone number and beg Bub to call
him.

After a preliminary examination, which takes all of about five minutes, the medical staff concludes that I'm having a miscarriage. Miscarriage? "But I can't be pregnant!" I shout back, trying to squirm my way off the table. "I'm wearing an IUD, goddamn it!"

I'm right out of my mind with the pain and the shock and to quiet me they try to make me breathe into a gas cup but I keep kicking and screaming at the quacks to help me and the gas not only makes me light-headed but sick to my stomach and in one horrendous final spasm I not only throw up but abort a four-month-old fetus. . . .

Slowly, mercifully, the physical pain gradually ebbs and I'm given an injection and transferred unconscious to a private room, where I continue to bleed all night as my temperature stays at a dangerous high. I wake up and toss and turn in a delirium in and out of sleep, slipping from cold shivers to fighting for air inside of a sweat box and every half hour a nurse arrives to take my temperature and blood pressure, change the blood-soaked sheet under my thighs, and tuck my bedclothes up to my chin. I keep thanking them for the illusion of peace and asking for water. . . .

Sweet relief in the form of Biscuit shows up at my bedside late next morning with Bub. He opens up by telling me that he had to drive all night to get here and I owe him fifty bucks for gas. By his rumpled appearance and the bags under his eyes I know he's telling the truth. When he awkwardly lays a wilty-looking bunch of flowers on the sheets as if he's at a grave site, I smile inside—my first in a long time. "Thanks," I say weakly, feebly fingering the petals. A young blond nurse waddles in to take my temperature again. "Where did you buy them?" I ask in a daze with a thermometer under my tongue.

"Buy them? I fucking stole them from the tombstone of one Monsieur Ronale De Fifi buried in Mount Royal Cemetery. A guy like him don't need flowers, he needs a priest."

Horror-stricken, the nurse snaps the thermometer out of my mouth while Biscuit and Bub laugh themselves sick at the joke. The nurse gives them both a scalding glance and Biscuit's eyes follow her out of the room. "What a sweet piece of tail," he observes with a grin. "Which brings me to you, Shortcake. If you don't get fucking better

I might have to go for potluck and get stuck with a dose." Then he gives me a peck on the cheek and promises to take care of me. Knowing him, I find this encouraging news.

Before leaving, he throws an arm around Bub's shoulder, basically to keep from falling over from fatigue. "The nigger and I are going barhopping."

"Now you know that white trash has a luster all its own," Bub says, chuckling with a wink.

Watching white-mug and black-arse go out arm in arm, I can't quite figure out the camaraderie between them. Maybe it's that divine universality which binds men together and drives women apart. But to me they're a shot of sunshine. They are "good" people, the kind I never seem to meet on a day-to-day basis but yet seem to cross paths with when the chips are down. Biscuit lives up to his promises to (1) take care of me and (2) paint the town. The two days I'm recuperating in hospital, Bub and Biscuit take a motel together and every time they pop in for a visit they're both queasy, wide-eyed, and hung over.

As for myself, my thoughts are in a whirl and my emotions alter from self-pity to relief to self-questioning. I can't help but wonder what Riel would have done if I had had a miscarriage. Would he have taken a risk and called for help from the outside or would he have left me on my own? Maybe it would never have happened at all had I remained at the house. Perhaps my escape alone prompted it to happen. And what would Pascal have said and done if he knew I was pregnant? Would he have wanted either of us? Now I'll never know.

The day I'm released, Biscuit and Bub thank me for the binge they've had before depositing me in the backseat of Biscuit's post-Depression hearse. All the way home, I'm flat on my back singing tunes from Broadway musicals while Biscuit and Bub are in the front seat shooting the shit over this, that, the other, and Oscar Peterson, reliving an era I was merely shot into. Once we're in Toronto, it takes a good half hour for Biscuit to drop him off at his digs in Parkdale. I kiss Bub good-bye. They keep rehashing the good times on Bub's front step until I holler out the window and Bub's wife, a rotund knockout with a scarf tied around her head, comes out, gives me a goodwill wave, and drags Bub inside.

Biscuit gets back in the car with a heavy sigh as if he's just lost his best friend. I've already hiked it over the front seat and try to boost his spirits by cozying up to him. But he pretends not to notice.

"Aren't you gonna ask me anything?" I finally pipe up, peeved that he's so quiet.

"Not until I have you in bed back at my apartment," he says stiffly, suddenly draping a negligent arm around my neck. "It's the only place I'll ever get an honest answer out of you."

"Why are you always so belligerent?"

"Consider this, Shortcake," he continues, hugging me closer. "You up and took off and only left me a note I could hardly read, a key, and a blank check without a signature."

"Sorry, I'll pay you back. . . . Did you put my stuff into storage?"

"When did you ever have reason to doubt I'd fuck you?" he says, instead of yes.

"Why do it for me if you're mad at me?"

"I had no goddamn choice, that's why. Shortcake, you never give a man any. The only reason any John latches onto you is to find out what the hell is gonna come next. I don't know whether you're the stupidest or the smartest broad I ever met. Probably the stupidest. Five minutes after you've met any son of a bitch, you've given him ten good reasons why he should be canonized. And you do it without even trying."

"Where's the crime in that?"

"You fucking mean it—that's what's wrong."

"So what's wrong with giving?"

"Receiving—with a grin on your cunt and not a dime in your pocket. Kid, you haven't done a goddamn thing in your life that was smart. You survive on a few fuckers like me who care and on luck. Did you manage to find out who this Pascal really is?"

"Yeah, but it's not gonna do me any good now."

"If you're wise, you'll pretend you never met. And you'll keep under wraps for a long time."

"You sound like you're afraid of him."

"I'm not afraid of any motherfucker who's gotta lock broads up to get them to sweat between the legs. But he's big league, Shortcake. He's got Spy City in Ottawa in his pocket. I don't fight a motherfucker who can't fight fair."

After all that's happened, it's a major miracle that I've finally managed to put my priorities in order. I've got to get the hell out of Toronto altogether and relocate in a new area where I'm not known and begin again. In the meantime I stay with Biscuit. On his advice I sign up at an entertainment agency, with a standing request to be sent to the bugaboo boonies. After a couple of weeks I'm offered a job stripping at a hotel in northern Ontario. It sounds great to me. I'll be settling up there with Crunch when he gets out of jail and it's a great place to hide out and disappear.

Though he knows it's a wise move on my part, Biscuit's not thrilled about me leaving. The last three days I'm in town he's in a bitch of a mood. Then we have lunch with Bub over in Parkdale, and Biscuit makes his peace with me.

Because I'll be taking Piddles plus a lot of extra baggage on my trip, I have to consider alternate transportation. As it turns out, I'm getting a ride with a geologist in a van, who advertised in the newspaper for a traveling companion.

As a bon voyage treat, Simon takes me to La Scala the night before I leave for Darkest Canada and he leaves for a vacation in Japan. He makes a toast over a bottle of Moët & Chandon. "To life with Machiavelli and to death with Plato! . . ."

25

B ig Rock is lost in mile upon mile of tall timber smack dab in the middle of empty. It's a Norman Rockwell edition of Dodge City on a Friday night and comes with a population of 3,500 souls owned by the nearby mine and pulp and paper company. Both sides of the main street are lined with box-framed canister sets in brick and clapboard with gingerbreading on the eaves and coned windows. You can walk on turn-of-the-century wooden floors at Woolworth's, buy jelly beans and rock candy from a glass jar at the Food Mart, use a ladder to get to the top shelf at the hardware store, and reminisce about last year's caribou hunt with an Indian on the street corner. There are more churches than bakeries, a movie house, and a representative from the major banks in Canada, but not one tattoo parlor. The sole sinbin is the Moosehead Hotel, which boasts the area's skuzziest tavern.

I arrive in town with Piddles shortly after lunch. The hotel's Wampum Room is a glorified beer parlor, clip joint, and anything-goes after-hours speakeasy. An ossified moose head racked on the wall over the bar is dying over the centuries from a bad case of knockaboutwurst on rye.

With a napkin applied to his florid face, the potbellied manager introduces himself. Petrie's all fire and brimstone and three-quarters gas, the son of a baked apple and a pugnacious pottypoo. He drinks so much that he's incapable of lusting after anything except with his eyes.

The gig pays three hundred bucks a week plus tips for wiggling your naked fanny six times a night. In between sets you're out there in nothing but a G-string oomphing it up on the floor, serving drinks.

Eureka—looks like I just hit pay dirt.

After making a fuss about me bringing Piddles, Pottypoo calls out his gravelly-voiced spouse, a scrawny leather-skinned fiftyish tough nut who talks like Ethel Barrymore playing a hood. Norma shakes my hand so hard she nearly pumps it off. Then she studies me narrowly but not unkindly. Obviously, she's the frontline gunner. Pottypoo is the rear-line battery, who should be sleeping it off at a Red Cross unit.

Norma shows me my dinky room upstairs and gives me permission to keep Piddles. Also she gives me the lowdown on the job. Apparently, she has a real problem keeping girls. They keep running off with the clientele or their boyfriends muscle their way in during a drunken stupor and break the place up. Norma appreciates the fact that I came with nobody, belong to nobody, and like my solitude when the opportunity permits. With an emphatic grin she assures me that my ass is safe here. She keeps the peace with a shotgun named Buster.

The Wampum Room is always packed with whopping lumberjacks or yipping miners taking the high road to Elysian fields through low pastures. They get worse when they're in their cups and down in their glory. There is at least one head-crushing fight a night just to prove the infallibility of the human ego. I've never seen so much physical violence in the guise of a spaghetti western turned hillbilly family reunion. A fight is never considered to be officially finished until everyone is down or Norma fires another blast at the cowbell hanging from the ceiling over the door.

Since this is the only air-conditioned matchbox in town, they straggle in, plastered with dust and sweat, and grab you by the G-string in the middle of the cakewalk before you can dump a beer over their heads or box their ears. Every night between stripping, I light their cigarettes or run the cold side of a beer along their foreheads to wake them up or cool them off. When a fight starts, I either crawl under a table or duck behind the bar, where Pottypoo is always crouched first, sucking on a bottle of Guinness.

I've never had such a healthy yet unorthodox response to my stripping either, especially when I decide to take the show from the stage to the floor to create the illusion of intimacy between myself and the audience. Norma pretends to ignore the hands fondling my tits and pinching my thighs and only intervenes when it appears I may be eaten or drowned in a bath of beer suds. To make a fast buck in this business you've got to depend on a man's blindness. When he's fishing bills out of his pocket, the darkness of the room makes it easy for him to mistake a twenty for a one. This is in addition to the bogus bonuses you have tucked into your G-string.

I take my meals in the kitchen with Minnie the hotel cook and Larry her homely hubbynut. I don't know which one of this vaudevillian comedy team is crazier—Millie, who wears a bra over her blouse and a slip over her skirt, or Larry, who keeps losing his glass eye in the potatoes he's peeling, or down the front of my dress when he has a sudden hankering to fish out of season.

For more stimulating entertainment there are the four bums who live in the alley out back just below the window of my room. I dub them the Whoopsey Gang. Joe the Rat, who slinks around a lot, is an ex-trapper with a beard that reaches almost to his belly button. Morgan the Pirate thinks he's a WWI flying ace, wears a helmet and goggles, and travels with his cosmic cat, Cornish, who can climb ladders so well the fire department wants to put him on the payroll. Pissy McCoy has a purple nose and a kidney problem. Crazy Jack, an ex-school teacher is a jaw-jutting philosopher with a black pilgrim hat and a matching woolen suit no matter what the weather. He spouts quotations from the Bible, slips into Shakespeare, and often finds himself drowning in James Joyce. All four are confederates of Larry in the kitchen. He sneaks food out to them and keeps the cellar door open so they'll have someplace to crash on cool nights. During the winter they each have a cardboard box to sleep in behind the furnace.

I love misfits because, like the street, they're turned inside out. They wear the grit and the madness of the human soul like most people wear dinner clothes.

Now that the Whoopsey Gang know there's a sap up here in the crow's nest, they won't quiet down unless I throw down either a bottle or a fin.

Succotash!

One night at the hotel a lumberjack loses his change in the cigarette machine and becomes so upset with it that he pulls out a .38 and empties its chamber into its face. Sure that he's killed the animal, he reaches through the jagged glass and retrieves a package of Players. Then he totters back to his table, plops down, and orders another five beers. Nobody gives the incident a second thought. But when Pottypoo places an OUT OF ORDER sign on the machine, he's immediately assailed with jeers, whistles, and pelted with bottle caps and pretzels.

Then out of nowhere a hand grabs me by the G-string and a big dude with a tanned face and sky-blue eyes stuffs three bills inside it. "After work—thirty dollars," he bluntly quips in a rough voice. He's so good-looking that I nod without thinking, and mechanically transfer the bills to the deerskin pouch Larry gave me to wear around my waist. The evening tapers down with ax-grinding slowness. The problem is in myself. I still haven't learned how to add two and two and come up with an entry on my side of the ledger.

When Pinky, the hotel caretaker, is running a mop under the tables and Pottypoo is prodding the last of the besotted ballyhoos out the door, I take the blond dude up to my room and he waits for me to shower.

I'm only in the room for a few minutes when the verbal abuse from the Whoopsey Gang in the alley below becomes much too much. I pull a lawn hose out from the storage cupboard in the hall, attach it to the tap in the bathroom next door, angle the nozzle out the window, and turn it on full blast. With the exception of Pissy McCoy, who's curled up in a cardboard box sleeping it off, the others quickly disperse with animal grunts and howls while Piddles sits on the window ledge covering their retreat with a wild quacking.

I return my attention to my newfound Adonis. Says his name is Willie and he's a German bush pilot who basically lives in the skies and considers himself a hermit.

I open a beer for myself and another one for Willie. He's well on his way to getting soused. Suddenly he opens up like a black rose and totally contradicts the quiet, unassuming role he played earlier in the Wampum Room. Now I know why he sat by himself all night. His brutal tongue would keep anyone away. I'm surprised it didn't get him into a fight. He despises everyone and in turn is probably despised by everyone.

Willie confesses, after much coaxing from me, that he comes from a staunch military family in Germany. During World War II his father was a member of the SS, a sadistic demagogue who meted out cruel discipline on his children. Willie was ritualistically beaten senseless and locked in a woodshed, sometimes for days at a time without food, for the slightest infraction. In 1945 he was drummed into the Hitler Youth to help defend Berlin, crouching in trenches with other terrified young boys clutching Panzerfaust bazookas. He's lucky to be alive today. If you can call soul sick being alive.

Willie doesn't come with swastikas or dogmas. He realizes they're outdated. But he does come with racial slurs about melting Jews and gypsies into soap in his father's basement. I won't give him the satisfaction of watching me cringe. Besides, despite everything, I can tell he doesn't mean it. I just turn a deaf ear and play the wise listener.

The dream that holds Willie together is simple—he intends someday to make a million dollars prospecting in this Wilderness of Zen. He even has success worked into an equation. Most of the men up here blow their money as soon as they make it on booze and women. Not so with Willie. He only visits the hotel when he needs a quick lay. Anything that interferes with his stoic regime of practicality is subversive and counterproductive. Not only does he have a strict operational procedure on how to undress me, but also has the evening's sexual format mechanically laid out as well. It's quite possible he even has his orgasm timed. Okay, what he lacks in imagination, he makes up for in power. Yet Willie seems so cold I suspect that he was born dead and is waiting to be dug up. As we move, I have a feeling that tomorrow I'll be pigeon-toed.

His face is broken in the dusky pale light like the lining of his soul.

Though he's patient but firm, he's so wickedly deliberate about every movement that he drives me near-crazy trying to claw the moonlight from the walls. If his face is clean of expression, I can feel rage cringing behind his forehead and launching his soul like a missile toward Valhalla.

Somewhere near dawn a garbage can flips over and rolls down the alley below, creating a hell of a racket. It's probably one of the Whoopsey Gang coming back to claim his turf.

Before Willie leaves, he promises to return next month. Already I know that I must see him again. Through him maybe I'll be able to understand the damnable Germanness of my own ancestry and learn to despise it a little less. He's the *Judgment-at-Nuremberg*-meets-Mount-Mariah proposition my parents never told me about. They never said I'd have to deal with it on *this* continent because they never did their homework about *that* continent.

I stumble down to the kitchen, half dizzy. "It must have rained last night. The alley is swimming in puddles," Larry observes, deliberating over his bowl of lumpy oatmeal.

I take Piddles outside so that he can play and run smack into the Whoopsey Gang. They're none too thrilled with me for raining out their party last night. To compensate, I steal them a bottle of wine from the bar. Over breakfast I chat with Minnie about her habit of wearing her underwear over her clothes. "I don't want to get my clothes dirty, now do I?" she explains very matter-of-factly.

"Right. And who else can remove their underwear before their clothes."

"Yeah—and that, too. They're too pretty to hide."

Suddenly, Norma checks in with a pile of menus in her hand and a cigarette hanging out of the corner of her mouth. "Sweetie, I think you and me better have a talk, eh?" she snaps.

With a bad feeling whirring in my gut, I follow Tugboat Annie into the office. I should be ready for anything she dishes out, ready to pack up and split on the slightest provocation. But I'm not. I'm sinfully settled and comfortable here.

She drops into the chair behind the desk, pours herself a tumbler of Scotch, and rolls a cigarette between her orange-stained fingers. "I got used to this in the war," she begins in her usual monotone. "Can't say I like it—a damn lot of trouble. But I'm too old to change." Then she snaps a light to it and faces me square, her arm slanted across her washed-out face. "You're too young to know what change is all about, sweetie. There was a fella in your room last night."

"That's my business."

"When they pay for it, it becomes *my* business. He paid you so don't bother to deny it. Everyone in town knows that crazy Kraut only shows up here for one reason."

"He's not a crazy Kraut," I fly back, partly to defend him and partly myself.

"Sweetie, you accept too much in other people, and not enough in yourself. What did he say to you?"

"Nothing—he said nothing."

"No, he never does. Likes to get his money's worth, I guess. He's gotta be the most hated man in these parts." She takes a belt of Scotch and starts rolling another cigarette. "Let's put our cards on the table, sweetie. I like money. I like making it and I like spending it. And you like to fuck. I'll work it the way I always do with my girls."

"It was an . . . isolated incident," I stammer awkwardly. "I won't take a dime for it the next time."

"C'mon," she admonishes dryly. "You're brighter than you look. But not all that tuned in. Why in hell would you give it for free, when you could get paid for it? I've been around the block, sweetie. Men expect you to charge them. It's a privilege they want to pay for. The exchange of money eases their conscience and makes them feel all clean and churchgoing afterward. No loose ends or obligations. And once you start giving it to them, you don't stop. I've been watching you out on the floor—you like men too much to be able to stop. And if you're smart, you don't have to."

"I'll think about it." I squirm in my chair.

Norma continues to work on my five planets in Libra and my moon in Capricorn until they're transiting Venus backward. "My cut is sixty percent," she says in conclusion.

"But I'm the one doing the work," I argue. "Thirty percent or forget it."

I'm expecting to hear some cliché like "Accept it or you'll never fuck in this town again." Instead she comes back with "I'm the one providing the overhead and the business. Fifty percent and I'll throw in your room for nothing. And have it redecorated for you."

"Okay—but what about protection?"

Her eyebrows arch significantly and she suppresses a grin. "Can't you look after yourself? Most girls up here can. They have to. For your size you do all right for yourself. But I'll tell you what—I know most of the fellas roundabouts. So if someone blows in that I don't like the look of, I'll wait outside your door." She pulls the twelve-gauge out from under the desk. "Nobody likes having words with Buster."

There is one final condition to the arrangement and I have to bring it up. "I don't go with anybody I don't like."

She shrugs emptily. "What the hell is to like? You don't even know what you're selling."

Norma is an absolute witch. Men and women alike are terrified of her. But she's true to her word. She has my room painted a soft pink, adds a flowered comforter to the bed as well as a new mattress, puts fresh cotton curtains on the window, along with two hanging ferns. To reinforce her shrewd business sense, she informs me that the "Kraut" was on the house. To reinforce my own business sense, I keep a notebook and do my own bookkeeping. In no time there's the beginning of a grumbling affection between us. The money is a terrific incentive. In a week I might take in a couple of hundred on top of my salary and tips. When Crunch gets out of the slammer, we'll need the extra cash.

Aesthetically speaking, my life is about as slanted in my direction as it has ever been. I've finally learned how to fuck, not just be fucked, and with privilege. If it keeps up, the weight might prove not only too much for the mattress of my bed, but for the floorboards under it as well. I'm just waiting for the night when the floor gives way and a John and I find ourselves locked in embrace in the scullery downstairs. I don't trust good luck anymore. It's always followed by locusts.

The lack of transportation services in this outback provokes me into buying a used red Bug to get around in preference to a dogsled or snowmobile.

In a small provincial area you may just as well forget trying to hide except under a big rock, where only a snake from Internal Revenue can get to you. I'm here two months and already I'm notorious and I don't even have a publicity agent or a hairdresser. On the main street the women in this hicksville trash me out in front of Woolworth's as the carrier of some rare form of hoof-and-mouth disease. Or they stand in the doorway of the bakery like a knot of Mrs. Grundys, giving me glowering glares. I make myself as disagreeable as possible by wearing short skirts, halter tops, and tall boots and take pictures of their mail-order hypocrisy with my cheap Kodak, a trick which always sends them scurrying for sanctuary in fear that I'll steal their souls with my little black box. The men are amused at my antics but gutlessly wary of me in the presence of their worst halves. In private conversation they make crude remarks or cute ones, depending on whether they've had their morning Wheaties or not, but in public mum's again the word, especially when Mom's around.

My misalliance with Willie continues weekly. Sometimes he shows up on Sundays and I treat him to brunch at the best restaurant in town, where we're just in time to entertain the after-church crowd and cause a sensation. I continue to take pains to dress as vampily as possible just to give them an eyeful. Later he takes me up in his red-and-white Piper Comanche and we touch down on a quiet lake and camp out under the stars for the night. I discover that Willie is not all full of hatred but rather full of want and as such he turns into a wanton animal—like me.

Back at the hotel it's only when one of my Johns whispers in the middle of heated foreplay, "You're awful soft-skinned for a whore," does it suddenly occur to me that I am one. Then I stand before the mirror in my room and repeat the word until I get a mental picture of Eve's one-acre plot. And what do you know, the clothes fit like my skin.

Maybe, as Simon said, I'm here strictly to please the Philistine tendency in man: to take, conquer, and claim. But it's still a five-letter word of puzzlement. I can't understand the animal in my nature that gives it so freely without conscience or conscious anxiety. Maybe there's an Oriental odalisque creeping around in my psyche somewhere.

I relate to each John the same way. My third eye homes in on one particle of gold dust buried in the ash of human experience, through the combination of bone, muscle, fat, and memory, and expands upon it until it glitters and clouds both his vision and mine.

After all, isn't it Everyman's secret dream to hit a strike? Even the earth is a whore waiting to be exploited and now that she's being exploited she's fighting back with earthquakes, hurricanes, and eco-logical germ warfare. As for myself, like any self-professed libertine I expand on my knowledge as well as the territory by conquering each John's tendency toward cunnilingus, Cupid, and the Curia. According to my Book of Genesis, I'm bringing John, John, the piper's son back to the womb of everlasting boohoo and flummery.

My answering service in Toronto rings up with a real heart-stopper. Long-lost Vincent is back in the country on a self-imposed furlough. Anxiously, I call him back in Quebec and he says to expect him shortly. Officially, I'm supposed to have two full days off a week but in reality I take only one. Now I'm suddenly shaken at the thought of demanding three days in a row.

As Norma always says, the first thing she should've done when she married Pottypoo was get him pregnant. He gives me one hell of a time, standing at the bar in his bare feet with a double rye in his hand and his belly coming out of his shirt, weaving, burping, and farting. "What the hell do yeh want time off for anyways? You'd only spend it on your back and not get paid for it."

"Mind your own damn business."

"But it is my business." He guffaws with a belch. "Every time you get fucked I make another dollar. You're not going off to fuck for nothing. I won't have it."

"I'll do what I like. I don't belong to you."

"No, *you* don't—but your cunt does!"

Enraged, I go over the counter after him. By the time Pinky and Norma pull me off him, Pottypoo is bellowing like a stuck pig on the floor. "Did you see that?" he wails pathetically. "The little slut tried to strangle me!"

"She should have punched you out and done us all a favor," Norma says flatly, taking the glass from his hand and ordering Pinky to trundle him up to bed.

Later, she gives me the green light on my three-day sojourn but adds an extra John to my schedule in the meantime to make up for it.

A few nights later on, I come downstairs and see Vincent at the bar having a drink, and immediately a warm and elemental memory surges through me. He's put on weight, his hair is short, he's as brown as a nut and wearing khaki army fatigues, a T-shirt with a denim vest overtop, and a buck knife strapped over his shoulder underneath. His reaction upon seeing me is disciplined and unemotional, a simple once-over glance and offhand "Hi" before guiding me toward the door.

"Ready to go?" he asks restlessly as soon as we're in my room.

I throw myself into his arms and he kisses me hard but without heat, then pushes me away. "We have lots of time for that later. Hurry and get ready. I want to get out of here."

Everything is always a panic with him. When I return from bathing, he's lounging in the window, smoking a cigarette and playing with Piddles. "I thought you gave up smoking?" I ask, packing a rucksack.

"Some things you give up. Some things give up on you."

Don't I just know it.

We board his Harley, which he's had in storage since he left Canada, and head up north a good thirty miles and make camp by a peaceful lake. The moonlight throbs on the water and the silence is broken only by the quavering shrieks of the loons. We stretch out on our sleeping bags by the fire and sip on a bottle of Scotch. He's as contented as I've seen him. "This is what I came up here for—you and the peace," he reflects, folding his hands behind his head.

"Peace is only a state of mind. It never really exists."

"That's because people like you and me won't let it. We're too busy fighting it for some kind of obscure truth."

The wind penetrates the trees like an oboe. Vincent never seems to change—the smell of the jungle is still on him. There's one distinct change in him but I can't put a name to it. He won't talk at all about Angola; a few scars added to his body speak for him. There's so much I want to get off my chest I don't know where to begin. It seems to be an unspoken agreement between us not to touch. This is not the appropriate moment. So I say anyhow, "Why did you buy a home in Switzerland and not here?"

"I've outgrown Canada. The clothes shrank on my back the minute I left for Nam. I wouldn't be content here now. It's like walking back into the 1950's. That's the way other countries see us. It's just too goddamn backward and the people so goddamn shallow and provincial. They've got no comprehension what's going on out there, nor do they care. I've adapted well to Switzerland. It's clean, pretty, and neutral."

Doesn't the bastard ever fail at anything? Maybe surviving is what he's really good at. He's managed to outrun the hangman this far. He's smarter than I am. He accepts the one and only true reality—the constant state of chaos. Vincent doesn't kid himself about anything. I kid myself about everything and well-wish the disgusting away in a blink.

"Say," he asks suddenly, which one roped you into the oldest profession, that overweight jackass at the bar or his dragon of a wife?"

"Nobody did. It was all my doing."

"Bullshit. What the hell's been going down while I've been up to my ass in elephant grass?"

I begin with Crunch and end with Pascal. An hour later he flicks the ash from his cigarette and grunts, "Wish to hell I'd been here. I would have hunted the son of a bitch down and wasted him. But I'll pass his name through the underground grapevine in Europe. Maybe somebody else will get lucky. I'll give you a box number in Zurich so you can write me."

"Do you think I've got nothing better to do than squeeze my brain just to entertain a mug I only see every leap year?"

Suddenly he reaches for me and we consecrate the battleground between the sexes. Then we strip down, wade out into the cold water, and thrash about until the light breaks the top of the pines. Vincent can't understand why I needlessly bounce from one extreme to the other in life without incurring more dust and rust.

He calls me a tongue-twisting sensationalist.

I call myself a sensualist.

He pooh-poohs my sexual greed.

I call him an emotional iceberg.

He laughs at my limited psychometry.

I climb on a high horse named Rejection of Him.

He pulls me down with a slap in the head.

I stay down and unzip his fly.

He calls me a sensationalist and orders me to swallow him.

After a repining round of lovemaking Vincent seems taut and oddly agitated. Finally he offers to set me up in an apartment if I'll move to Zurich for a while. "Then we'll see," he says, very noncommittal.

"Is that all?"

"For now isn't it enough?"

"No, it's not enough."

He gets angry and insinuates that I'm using excuses as heavy artillery and reason as cannon fodder. Then he pours himself a stiff drink and at the freezing point explodes. "I always liked your natural unpretentiousness. Now all you want to do is play mental chess. I'm getting too old for games. I don't give two shits what you've done with your body. I've done worse with an M-sixteen. We've moved against the norm—we understand each other. If we give it a shot, maybe we'll find we belong together, too."

"The timing is all off. I can't."

"I'm scaring you, aren't I?"

"Give me time. I need time."

"Why? You never give anyone else any. You don't want anything in life but lust in fluid form. Too bad it doesn't come in returnable bottles."

My mood shifts to the offensive. I slap his face. He backhands me to the ground, takes a belt of Scotch, and pins me to the sleeping bag. Now that he's a hero's trophy on the mantel, he wants to be his own tennis partner as well.

I confess to him that Crunch is getting out of jail soon and I promised him we'd give providence a chance. He gives me hell for not telling him in the first place. Then he gives us his best wishes. As an afterthought he says I have a year to make up my mind about Zurich. While he's never been essential to my life, Vincent has never been outside it either. Being with him has been too much of an experience. Today's waste often becomes tomorrow's chase. Has the eleventh hour arrived for us yet? Or the twelfth?

26

've had Deliverance Day marked on the calendar now for months. At the end of the summer I ask Norma for a week off and she gives it to me, knowing that if she doesn't, I'll quit. With mixed feelings of joy and shudders of cold fear D-Day is finally here. Crunch is getting out.

I drive my Bug over three hundred miles south to a motel near Queenston. In the morning after a bath, a farmer's breakfast, and a prayer I take a cab into the city. Crunch doesn't want me to pick him up in the VW—something about it being bad luck. And he always laughed at *me* for being superstitious.

It's a cloudy, humid day with the threat of an impending storm. I've been waiting outside the Queenston penitentiary with the cabbie for over an hour. I don't know which is worse, assuring him that I'm not Bonnie Barker waiting for Clyde, or pacing and littering the ground with butts. The tall gray walls give me the creeps. It's a violation against the human condition, reeking of pointlessness.

Crunch comes chugging out the door. He's reading the ground in front of him and carrying a brown paper shopping bag. I'm more shell-shocked at seeing him than he is at seeing me. Before, he was a raging voice in an envelope. To shut him up I could shove him in the drawer. Now that he's back, I'm up the proverbial creek if he ever finds out what I've been up to the last few years. Worse, I still haven't been able to account for the six months I spent incommunicado with Pascal. Crunch has been pressing me for the truth ever since, planning to put the squeeze on as soon as he got out. As Vincent once said,

"A hero is Everyman's fool." Now I'm back at square one, trying to play the heroine in a fool's game. And I'm damned skittish.

Crunch hesitates and lifts his head, staring straight over my shoulder as if he doesn't see me. Then he ambles closer. Did his letters, like mine, become merely a flagrant show, a flimflam sham to keep us both buoyant?

He gives me a quick mechanical hug, springs into the backseat, and pulls me in after him. "Let's get to hell out of this town." He grunts, rubbing his jawline fitfully. "Where are we going anyway?"

"I did what you said. I left the car at the motel."

"Have you got enough money? I can't get to the bank today."

"Money is the least of our worries," I assure him, seeing that he's still locked in stirlag.

We swing out onto the 401 Highway. He eases up a little and loses some of that harried-hare quality. Fishing a bale of prison tobacco out of his pocket, he fumbles with the papers. I try to help him but he slaps my hand away. "I can still roll my own goddamn cigarettes, for Chrissake."

I press up on my haunches and knead his knotted shoulder muscles. He prods a cigarette between his lips and grabs my arm. "Don't do that! Do you wanna drive me crazy?"

Now the recovery has got to be recovered. I light up a cigarette and pretend to ignore him and he grabs my arm. "Hey, I'm sorry, rabbit. I didn't mean that—but I'm—Jesus, I'm hungry. I missed lunch."

"Then we'll stop and eat."

I tap the cabbie on the shoulder. At the next town he veers off the freeway and onto the scenic route along the riverfront.

"Christ, I almost forgot," Crunch suddenly gasps, leaning forward and thumping the cabbie on the shoulder. "Pull over—right here! Do what I tell yeh, pull over!"

Expecting to be either robbed or killed, the cabbie's face turns chalk white in the rearview mirror. He wipes his forehead on his sleeve and pulls over to the shoulder. Crunch gets out, walks along the gravel a few paces, picks up a stone, and throws it as far as he can. Then with a smile of relief he gets back into the car. "It's something I promised myself I'd do as soon as I was sprung," he explains briefly. "I wanted to be able to throw a stone without having it strike a wall and talk back. C'mon, let's go."

An hour later we pull into a steak house. As I don't want to feel rushed, I offer the cabbie a free meal. Under the circumstances I put him at a table across the room.

It kills me to watch Crunch eat. Three meals packed into one sitting. He puts it away as if at any minute I'll swipe his plate. Every so often he scans the room warily.

"Did you scrape me up some clean duds?" he asks in a fog.

"Uh huh. There's a whole suitcase full in the trunk."

"Good. I wanna get rid of this shit as fast as I can."

When he's finished, he pushes his plate away and gets to his feet. "C'mon, let's go."

Trying to slow down the motor in his brain, I pick at my trout. "I want another Bloody Mary. Sit."

"Okay, but hurry." He sighs irritably, clasping his hands at his mouth.

"Why not have some dessert?"

He gives me an incredulous look as if he's never heard of the animal. I order him a piece of strawberry shortcake and he eats without a word. A few minutes later he drops the fork in the plate. Comfortingly, I grab his hand. "What's the matter?"

"Nothing," he says hoarsely. "I'm at the top of the world looking down."

"And how does it look?"

"Flat—flatter than shit on the road." What he means to say is that he feels one-dimensional, incapable of throwing shadows. "C'mon, let's go, rabbit. I wanna screw your ass off and I'm half crazy. You understand, don't yeh?"

I give him a nod and wonder how many times he'll have to vindicate himself before he'll find that second dimension outside of himself. On the way to the motel he's in a different frame of mind completely. I'm fairly looped myself. We drool and hold hands like a couple of

high-schoolers on a first date. He has the cabbie jack up the volume
on the radio to screen our private panderings.

We arrive at our destination ready to relax and indulge in each
other. I pay the cabbie the flat rate I promised him and Crunch and
I are on our own without a chaperone. The motel is a comfy little
hamlet, homespun on a river surrounded with trees and the sound of
the current mooing past the window of our room. The first thing
Crunch does is tear down the streamer I've strung across the wall.
Welcome home, JAILBIRD.

Immediately I run him a bath and throw in all kinds of soaps and
surprises, including a battery-operated Mickey Mouse boat to help
him unwind. Meanwhile he switches the TV on and off and fingers
the chocolate cake and party bric-a-brac I bought for tonight's celebration. Then he flops on the bed and watches me through his arms
folded across his eyes. He's all edges and corners with hidden places
within spaces, and pits. Mainly pits. Dwelling in his own shapeless-
ness, he's soaring a thousand miles above a flat surface, afraid he'll
never be able to land.

After stripping down, he gets into the bath and I chuck his clothes
into the garbage bin outside. He'll never wear them again. When I
return, the toy boat comes whizzing through the air and lands at my
feet. I take it back into him. "You didn't like it?"

"The goddamn thing is busted."

"That's funny. This morning it worked fine. What did you do to it?"

"What do you think? I sat on it."

He won't let me wash him down and instead soaps himself up like
mad, trying to remove months of dirt and desperation from his body.
I sit on the floor beside the tub watching him. "Maybe you'd rather
be alone?"

"Don't start telling me what I want. If I said I want you here, then
that's exactly what I mean," he grumbles hotly. "Get us a drink. Then
you can tell me one of those wacky stories you make up out of your
head."

I pour him a double shot of Canadian Club, open a beer for myself,
and begin.

* * *

"Once upon a rainbow and over it, right to the bottom of a bucket of gold, lived Orgasmo.

"One day he woke up, had his breakfast of gold dust, and said to himself, 'I'm sick of the same meal day after day. And I'm tired of being alone. I have many questions to ask and nobody to answer them.'

"He crawled to the top of the bucket. The Goopers were busy hauling sacks of gold dust across the rainbow and dumping them into his bucket. 'Where does the gold dust come from?' he asked them.

" 'The Gold Diggers on the dark side of cloud nine,' one of them piped up.

"After the next storm the rainbow came out again. So Orgasmo put a sack of gold dust over his shoulder on a thunderbolt, tucked an umbrella of sunbeams under his arm, and trudged over the rainbow to cloud nine.

"The Gooper sentries on the other side immediately covered their noses and fell to their knees, crying, 'Ohhhh—it's him! It's him!'

"Orgasmo was taken aback. 'What's the matter?'

"The head sentry stepped forward to explain. 'We've never come face-to-face with a germ before, much less the King of Germs himself.'

" 'Is that who I am, what I am? Exactly what is a germ?'

" 'So as not to offend you, I'll only say that for me it's not a healthy state of being.'

" 'That's funny,' Orgasmo puzzles. 'I feel just fine.'

" 'Tell me what you're doing here.'

" 'I want to find out why I've been doomed to live at the bottom of a bucket of gold.'

"The sentry has a big belly laugh. 'What nonsense. You haven't been doomed—you've been saved. Being a germ, you can do anything.'

"Orgasmo suddenly feels hungry and hauls the sack from his shoulder and discovers with horror that it contains only ash.

"The sentry explains the phenomenon. 'If gold dust is returned to this side of the rainbow it is reduced to its original state.'

" 'But why?'

" 'It's a mystery of the universe. All we have here to eat is ash. Can you live on ash?'

" 'I've never tried it before,' Orgasmo replies, putting back a mouthful. 'Why, this doesn't taste any different from gold dust.'

"The Goopers guide him to the edge of a shaft of white light cut right through the cloud like a screwnail. Orgasmo opens his umbrella of sunbeams and floats down into the mines of the Gold Diggers. It's dark and musty but his umbrella lights a pathway between the piles of ash.

"The Gold Diggers working in the tunnel ahead hesitate in their labors. One of them speaks up. 'Who are you and what do you want here?'

" 'I'm Orgasmo, King of the Germs. I live at the bottom of a bucket of gold dust at the other side of the rainbow. I'm trying to find out why I was doomed to live there. Can you help me?'

" 'Sorry, but we've never been on the outside. We're born blind and never see the fruits of our labor. We're only miners of ash from human suffering. One thing we do know—if it wasn't for us, you'd starve to death.'

" 'What would happen if *I* didn't exist?'

" 'We'd be back working on earth in the rock pile of human endeavor. The rainbow would no longer stand as a pathway to paradise. A speck of gold dust in a handful of ash could no longer be supported in the human imagination. There would be everlasting darkness.'

" 'I must find out what my destiny is.'

" 'What a fool of a germ you are, Orgasmo. Your destiny is here where your power is uncontested.'

" 'But I wasn't even asked if I wanted to be a germ.'

" 'What right do you have to question anything? You're nothing but a fat little amoeba who had the luck to be born on the right side of the rainbow. You're inconceivable to the human imagination and a mystery to medical science. Go home, Orgasmo.'

" 'No. I will go among the mortals of earth and find an imagination big enough to fit me and a branch of science to accept me.' "

* * *

Crunch has to shake me several times before I register his presence and snap out of this dream world. "You'll never shut up if I don't stop you," he growls with a grin.

"Let me finish," I argue, full of inspiration and idolatry.

Ignoring this, he slides over the side of the tub and pins me to the bath mat. "You're leading me into a goddamn sequel, rabbit. Or maybe it never ends."

"But this is absolutely larcenous," I squeal, soaking wet and playfully struggling against him. "I'm just coming to the good part where Orgasmo encounters the germ called the Hong Kong Flu on a beach in Victoria, B.C."

"You're even crazier than I remember," he says, impatiently relieving me of my underwear.

We get it on without even taking the time to really get it off and I discover that the strange physical chemistry that chained us together before is still alive and shaking the apple tree.

Now that we've christened the day, we move on to the bedroom and place a sacrificial lamb on the altar of our altered states. I pull out the food and the tweeters and the party hats and we have our celebration and after food and drink and another round of lovemaking we hit the sack, zonked out.

In the middle of the night I wake up to hear Crunch in the bathroom hunched over the toilet, throwing up his guts. I know he's had too much, too fast, too soon.

Embarrassed, he tries to ward me off. "Get outta here. I don't want you to see me like this!"

"But I caused it! I know the name of the germ we've both got. Let me in!"

He's in no condition to argue and I'm in no mood for anything but taking extra-good care of a germ named Orgasmo.

The beast purged, I clean him up and we have a cigarette. Later in his sleep he tosses and turns and cries out something about a riot.

When I awaken in the morning he's not in bed. In a panic I whip open the door and with a surge of relief see him on the pavement, playing handball with the motel proprietor's young son. After watching him for a few minutes I get this prickly sad sensation. What will ever become of us two lost germs?

We stay on at the motel for another two days to wind down and relax. The only bad rumbles between us occur when Crunch questions me about those six lost months in my life which seem to drop out of the bottom of space and time altogether. I still refuse to tell him anything about Pascal.

The morning of the fourth day we begin the long pilgrimage back up north but all the way west first to Niagara Falls so that Crunch can close out his old bank account. While we're there, we stop off at the Rendezvous and have a nostalgic meal with Vito.

From there it takes us two days to go north to Big Rock. I let Crunch take the wheel the whole way. He doesn't need two pillows to sit on to see through the windshield and gets listless and bitchy sitting like a lump in the passenger seat.

Finally I ask him about his fat bank account.

"There are some things you're better off not knowing," he said.

During the entire trip I'm trying to figure out how to tell him that I'm a stripper and not merely a barfly. But it doesn't seem important or relevant—or is it that my conscience is masked with cold dread about what I've really been doing? I'm still in a fret over the scrap I had with Norma about quitting my whoring night shift and moving out of my room at the hotel. Anyway, Crunch is only too happy to have me off the Strip in Toronto, so why provoke him? As usual I'll just let things sort themselves out.

After we arrive in Big Rock we combine our resources and book into a motel outside of town. Crunch buys a secondhand Jeep Cherokee and nips off with Chase, a worker with the John Howard Society, which helps ex-cons, to purchase a chunk of land with water passing through it. The latter stipulation was mine entirely. Born on an island in the stream, I have to be close to water to feel comfortable. As soon as the land deal goes through, we pitch a large tent like pioneers on our fifty acres of woodland on the edge of a small lake. Then Crunch hires two local boys to give him a hand putting up a log house. He's been drawing up the plans for it in the carpentry shop in prison for the last year. He's so busy laying the foundation, he doesn't take too much notice of my comings and goings. Thankfully, he's usually sound asleep when I slip in at four o'clock in the morning from work at the Wampum Room. Only once does he grab me as I vault into the sleeping bag. "Where were you?" he asks groggily.

I crawl into his arms, giggling from fatigue. "Working. I have a job. Remember?"

"What work can you do that I can't do better?"

"I can hustle up better bad news. Now go back to sleep."

Life on the lie gets pretty crazy. I'm in a constant flurry, worried that Crunch will find out the nature of my past and present job. It's like jiggerbugging around a lamppost in the rain. I'm not sure whether to fear the lightning or the lamppost falling over. Either one will bring the whole world crashing down upon my unworthy head. So why not quit my job? The security is too comforting and Crunch and I need the extra money.

One night I'm right in the middle of my bumps and grinds onstage, right down to where my fake grin is bigger than the G-string I'm wearing, when I have this terrible double vision that quickly solidifies into familiar flesh and bone at the edge of the stage.

"Come here!" Crunch shouts, his face a mask of anger.

Acute embarrassment overcomes fear and I crouch over, desperately trying to shush him down. "Go away . . . please, I'll talk to you later!"

Seething with white fury, he grabs my ankles, yanks me over his shoulder, and stomps through the crowded room toward the door. The audience loves it. Figuring it's part of the act, they thump their glasses on the tables, yipping go-boy incentives. The uproar is deafening.

I'm yelling like the driven rain as he dumps me bare-assed into the passenger side of the Jeep. Jamming the engine into gear, he seizes the steering wheel as if he means to rip it out of the floor.

"I forgot the laundry," I sputter. "It's in—"

"Fuck the laundry."

The night air is bracing. Chills start rippling up and down my spine, as the song says. But it's due to my state of undress. Crunch reaches into the back and fires a green plaid lumberman's shirt at me. "Put it on!"

With churning stomach I try desperately to regroup. "Have you got any cigarettes?" I ask testily. "Mine are back at the hotel."

He flings a package at me. "Light one for me while you're at it."

I strike a match. He takes the cigarette without a word. Pissed right off I get that old reliable urge to open the door and jump into the ditch—except there isn't one, only endless forest. I take hold of the door handle anyway, trying it out for size. Suddenly it gives way and flies open. Crunch grabs my arm just in time, holding me like a vise, and we skid to a stop sideways on the shoulder, inches from being hurled through the windshield and into a tree.

He shakes me until my teeth rattle. "I goddamn love you, you little fuckup, but I'll kill you if you ever try that again!" He shoves the engine into drive and spins the wheel as we fly back onto the highway. "Goddamn little whore," he curses under his breath.

"How the hell do you know?" I scream, scared shitless about just how much he does know.

"A guy at the garage told me," he says blackly.

"Exactly what did he tell you?"

He looks me right in the eye a second before changing gears. "Everything."

"Why, the miserable little rat!"

"Is that all you've got to say?"

"What do you want me to say? We needed the bread."

"Bullshit. I could've gotten a job to make it up."

"Sure. They're all union at the mill and their relatives get all the jobs. The employers in town will keep giving you the runaround. You're not from around here. They don't hire ex-cons. To get what you want you've got to be prepared to do anything to get it."

"Still making excuses for everything, aren't you? That's the only thing you're really good at. Twenty years old and you've got it all worked out. You can't make up the rules as you go along, rabbit. It doesn't work that way." I refuse to answer, so he rants on. "And I suppose you don't enjoy fucking either?"

"It's only a job," I lie. But it's not truly a lie.

"You've made a fucking fool out of me. I can't start fresh here. You've blown it for me. Everyone in town is having a good laugh at both of us."

"So let them laugh. What does it matter? What the hell do *they* matter? I hate them. I've always hated them. What do you think keeps me on the street?" I'm on the defensive and it's driving me into hysterics.

"It matters to both of us. We're gonna live here."

"That's no reason to kiss their ass. Are they paying our way?"

"Everyone, no matter who he is, has gotta do it. Indirectly, they *do* pay our way. You'll learn to like kissing ass whether you like it or not."

"No, I won't, you rotten bastard!"

"You're the one who should have been doing time in jail!"

"Go to hell!"

He lashes a hand at me that crashes me almost to the floor. My head's reeling. I stay in a sobbing crouch until he pulls into the yard. Full of dumb insolence, I jump out of the cab and head for the tent. "Stay out here!" he shouts after me. "I'm not finished with you yet!"

I mosey on back and silently watch him build up a fire until it's crackling wood chips and spitting live ash. A moon blots up behind the trees, thickening the midnight shadows. On bended knee he throws a final log into the orange flames that jab and tear at the dark. "When I left you were only a stupid kid. What's happened to you since?"

"Lots."

"Tell me."

"No. Besides, it doesn't matter now. I'm going back to work at the hotel tomorrow—on both shifts."

He pokes at the fire again, fiercely. "Over my dead body. You really love living dangerously, don't you? After working in that joint in Toronto you can't stop."

"I've got the rest of my life to stop."

"But only one day to grow up in. And that day's today. Can't you see I'm doing you a favor? There's more in you than that."

"There's more to shit than flies and flies don't make it top-grade manure."

"Another crummy excuse . . . you're incapable of looking after yourself."

"I am, too!"

"Not when you use self-sufficiency as a trade-off for everything. You aren't gutsy enough to gamble on anything, including decency."

"What makes you think you deserve someone decent anyway?" That came out dead wrong but it's too late to take it back. Bluntness is one of my worst traits. "I didn't mean that—I'm sorry."

There's an interminable pause. He picks up a live wood chip and hurls it across the yard to the lake. Then he circles the fire toward me, glowering. "For the last ten years I've had to live with my own sorries. Now I've got to live with everybody else's. But I won't put up with it from you."

He lunges toward me and my feet take instant flight. In seconds I'm scrabbling over the slippery rocks on the edge of the lake, intent on drowning myself. I trip and fall into the shallows, scraping my knees. Crunch is right behind me. He hauls my body up and drags me back to the fire while we have a screaming, struggling wrestling match. He sits down on a tree stump, pulls me over his knee, and wallops my ass until I'm choking on bile and tears. Then he throws me roughly into the tent and zips up the flap. "Go to bed!"

When Crunch comes in for the night I'm writhing on a swarm of bees and I tell him straight. "It's over—finished—everything. Write me out a check for my share and I'll leave."

He pours himself a whiskey and sits down on one of the trunks. "You left your Bug at the hotel. How are you gonna get into town?" he asks with amusement in his face.

"I'll hitchhike. Then I'll come back with a gun that fires bazookas so I can blow you to Pluto where you belong." His ironic laughter drives me into a fury. "I mean it, we're through—I hate you!"

"You hate nobody—you're not capable!"

"First I'm not capable of taking care of myself. Now I can't even hate. Who the hell do you think you are, a white slaver? And anyway, what's so damn funny?"

"You tell me. You're the one who taught me to laugh."

oo confused to be angry and too hurt to be consoled, I burst into
tears. He puts a Scotch into my hand and I glide from his lap
to the sleeping bag, where he joins me, hot, smelling of damp
pine and woodsmoke. Thus begins an unraveling of our psyches during
what turns out to be truth sessions over the following months. It's a
sappy time for spilling our guts and releasing our frustrations and fears.
At first we find it awkward to lower our defenses enough to talk about
ourselves because we're naturally (if surprisingly in my case) introverted
and secretive but gradually it becomes easier and easier, especially
when we realize that self-preservation need not be a negative, solitary
occupation of the ego. It can also be an interchange of strengths and
weaknesses. We have nothing to fear in each other and since we need
each other, we hide nothing that is crucial to both our individual and
mutual well-being.

That first time I tell him about my life on the roll in Toronto. He
tells me about the horrors of prison life. Though we don't cover all
the bases and take care not to dig too deep, it's a step in the right
direction. Then we have another drink and for a few minutes are lost
in our own thoughts, swallowing up the darkness of the surrounding
woods. In being honest with ourselves and each other, it feels as if
we are kindling a new life together.

Crunch props himself up on one elbow and faces me. "A couple
of times I thought about doing this, having my own setup, working
for myself. But the women I was with were all wrong for it. They
wanted what I couldn't afford. I never got around to figuring out what
I *could* afford. I made a hell of a mistake by marrying once. I don't

remember the ceremony, that's how drunk I needed to be to go through with it. A few months later she ran off with the guy next door. She even took the ten grand I'd saved working the pipeline. If I had caught them I would have killed them both. But I learned. Now I don't get drunk either on whiskey or women. When you came into my life I had squeezed myself to the wall like a leopard who'd lost his spots. Now that I've found my spots, it's time to learn how to use them."

In the morning we drive into town. I pick up my belongings and Piddles from the hotel. Quitting my job is like cutting myself from an umbilical cord and setting myself adrift. And I almost reconsider. Then I remember Crunch's last words to me before I got out of the Jeep. "I can look after you better than the street. Give me a chance to prove it."

Pottypoo is rangy at the news. "Good riddance to yeh, cunt" is about all he can muster before his liquid lunch.

Norma's more sedate and cool. Underneath she's as mad as a hornet. She pulls me into the office for a good-bye whiskey and water. "Trust you to upset the applecart," she announces. "What you're doing is wrong. You've heard me say it so I won't waste spit by repeating it in this lifetime. But you'll be back."

In the days that follow, I learn to cope with a strange electrifying silence that covers the air like a shield of ice and affects my nervous system like raw sugar. To someone used to lots of noise and action, it's a corruption of nature itself. A chronic insomniac, I'm up all night wandering around our property, as if waiting for a storm to break. I usually end up reading until dawn, when the air is broken by the comforting whirr of chain saws and chipped voices.

I soon adapt to the tranquil pitchblende by adopting the conscious-ness of an odalisque extraordinaire. I purchase another, smaller tent and begin stockpiling it with crockery, pots and pans, cookbooks, bedding, and all sorts of household effects which might come in handy in a siege. . . . I'm still that insecure. Then I set up a miniature nursery of plants, herbs, flowers, vegetables, and even a couple of saplings which I will move into the cabin. Meals must be prepared on time for Crunch and his two helpers, who're now going full-steam to get the cabin up before the snow flies. His helpers have even put up their own tent near ours to save the traveling time from town. The root cellar's been dug and the cement footing poured in. Now the walls are going up. I've never had a house before so it's all a rather frightening prospect.

My new emotional state is a pictorial wash in luminous halftones, a dreamy watercolor waiting to solidify into an earthy Rubens. I'm forever expanding my knowledge of Crunch through the little things I either forgot or which were neatly deleted from our caulking correspondence over the past years. He doesn't like his food mixed together on the plate, the corn mashed up with the spuds. In clothing he won't wear anything loud and refuses to wear a suit at all. When deep in thought he paces in short straight lines and reads the ground. He's reserved with the word and doesn't waste time on idle chatter. As he is shy and reserved about demonstrating affection, our sexual calisthenics are not heralded by any romantic lead-in, verbal or otherwise. Often his biological urges catch me unawares first thing in the morning or in the middle of the day, which I suppose is about as exciting as exciting can ever get in the outback. The ball is always in his court and after he hits it, the play's in mine, and it's my job to exploit the advantage as a pregame warmup.

Instead of tea and fruit juice, he drinks water by the gallon. Something profound is always "a caution" and something foul "a crock of shit." Often he'll pick up a spider from the floor of the tent and set it outside rather than step on it. He despises me creeping around softly at night, trying to be quiet. "Stop pussyfooting around!" he thunders. "What do you think I've got ears for?"

We have the same inheritance and are blood-bound to reap the same harvest. He, too, is a lower working-class crouton who got left out of Caesar's social salad. But while he raised his consciousness in the clink, I worked on mine in fits and starts between the cracks in the pavement on the streets.

Just after he was sent up I read *Crime and Punishment* for the first time and immediately identified our lodestone with Rodya and Sonya. Ever since, I've kept a hard-cover edition in my luggage for inspiration.

Now it's no longer a link but a witness—a portent and polestar to guide us. The best line he's come up with to support his claim on me is "I could never deny you anything you didn't already have."

Since we're so isolated out here in the bush, Crunch buys me, as an early birthday present, a fully grown great Dane. I call him Rasmus. Then he decides I should learn to shoot a gun properly. So every day while the men are having lunch I try to blow a line of beer bottles off the top of a sawhorse with either a snub .32 or the .22 rifle.

As this rock-ribbed country is not fit for farming, Crunch has made a deal with Marcel, a local trapper, to take him out on the lines to see if he has the stomach for the fur trade. As for myself, I've already missed the planting season. I'll have to wait till spring to put in a garden.

The inevitable happens one morning when Willie's red-and-white Piper Comanche circles overhead and passes low over the cabin before sloshing down on the lake, floating on its heavy rubber pontoons toward the dock. I'm both peeved at Willie for having the nerve to show up here and terrified that Crunch will find out about our affair. Obviously Willie showed up only out of sheer curiosity mixed with a tinge of revenge, eager to check out the man I ended up with. He introduces himself to Crunch, shakes his hand, and gives me a sly grin loaded with cynicism. "Thought I'd drop around and say hello. Say, she's turning out real nice," he admits by way of a greeting.

"Good enough," Crunch sighs, thinking Willie's talking about the cabin.

"We shouldn't be getting any snow for another few weeks—so the weatherman says."

Crunch smiles back at him evenly. "At least heaven is with me then."

And that's the thing—it is.

They meander to the tent, exchanging small talk. I poke around and make myself anonymous and useful, pouring out strong coffee and dishing out goodies. Crunch has a natural knack of getting along with people—until they cross him, that is. Nobody up here has bothered to bug him and he intentionally keeps out of temptation's way in order to avoid confrontations. But he's clearly nobody to mess with.

Crunch doesn't take to Willie at all. He's unnaturally quiet throughout Willie's high-profile monologue in the "me, myself, and I" syndrome, and keeps giving Willie suspicious, almost snarly glances as if he can hardly wait to get rid of him. He never could stomach a born braggart.

When Willie finally hits the sky, Crunch lingers near the tent watching me clean up the dishes.

"I don't mind knowing about the others, yeh know," he says suddenly, gravity in his voice. "But I don't like them showing up at my door and laughing in my face."

I whirl around with a gasp, my cheeks on fire. "How'd you know?"

"I've got eyes, rabbit. Any guy who shows up right out of the blue to say hello and then spends his time goading and watching your old lady is playing a fool's game."

"But you don't understand Willie," I argue. "Let me explain him to you."

"You don't have to. I might not know who he is, but I know what he is. I heard about him in town. Since when have Nazis appealed to you?"

"Don't be silly. Willie never told me he was a Nazi."

"That's the worst possible kind. He doesn't know that he is one. The whole time the bastard was here I was wondering . . . what you'd do if I refused to fuck you again."

His anger is spinning off into vulgarity. I *must* be in trouble and I *must* pretend I'm not. "Simple," I reply deprecatingly. "I'd be gone tomorrow."

"Yeah—you *and* the excuse will be gone. You've been looking for one since you moved in. Congratulations, rabbit. You just screwed yourself."

For the following week he works on my sanity by avoiding me, being aloof at meals, playing the enigmatic eunuch in bed. Who says that love is sex and the rest is pure plumbing? Horny, confused, and wounded, I count venomously each day as the last . . . and yet still I hang on, waiting for him to communicate again. Every night I lie beside him in a sweat, ravaged by an all-consuming heat worse than any I've known. Finally I can't stand it anymore and when he wakes in the middle of the night with a hard-on and finds me under the covers making love to it he heaves me up and across the tent as if I were a leper. "Fuck every man in Big Rock if you like, but don't ever touch me again!"

"But you promised to take care of me." I am on the brink of hysterics, sure I've just snuffed the perfect relationship.

"I am—I'm taking care of your bad angel."

Unfortunately, my bad angel doesn't see his reasoning. I tear out of the tent, and reeling about in the dark barefoot in my nightgown, find the road and start running like a crazy fool. Goddamn, I should never have trusted an ex-con. Will I ever learn? Will Norma forgive me and take me back?

Feeling sorry for myself and hating the world in general for peopling it with devils dressed as saints, I stumble toward town, crying up a storm of recriminations and making a whole string of new-life resolutions. About a mile down the road Crunch's Jeep pulls up and he approaches me. I'm so relieved that my first impulse is to jump in beside him and throw myself in his arms. Then he speaks to me. "C'mon, quit being an ass. Get in and I'll take you home."

This does it! Something in me cracks . . . something that's been neutralized for over a year. I see a stranger before me and not Crunch at all. In panic, I freeze. "I don't trust you. Stay away from me. Go away."

The minute he puts his hands on me I transform into a screeching banshee, wriggling and squirming, biting and kicking. My voice belongs to a demon. *You're like him, that French schizo in Montreal. One minute you want to make love to me and the next minute you want to kill me. I won't put up with it. Leave me alone. Don't kill me. No, no, no, no, please. Aaaaaieee. Get away, get away from me! Please don't kill me. I'll do anything you say.*

This really frightens him. Finally, to shut me down he smacks me out cold, puts me into the Jeep, and takes me home. It takes him until dawn to wheedle the worm out of the woodwork with a simple confession. "I only wanted to give you a dose of the hell you put me through in stir. I never meant to hurt you, rabbit."

Even then Orgasmo won't come out to play without two double Scotches and an hour of confessions on the raunch, when I tell him the details of my interlude in Montreal. Crunch comes out of it afraid *for* me and I come out of it afraid *of* me. But it's given me a pretty good look into myself. People aren't what they hate. They are what they fear.

Now that the populace roundabout has been warned about our move-in I expect every nosy parker within twenty-five miles to invent an excuse to drop by. I don't want them here consecrating my hallowed ground. They resemble an open window to the past that I would prefer to have closed. But when strangers show up I suddenly can't see the hypocrite in myself and like the perfect hostess I'm all exuberance, laying out a red carpet and a full country spread.

"They don't like me," I complain later, drumming my fist on the pillow at night. "I can tell they don't. They only came to see what we have."

Crunch kisses my breasts and mumbles. "You see devils that aren't there," he says, falling to sleep. "And angels that should be chopping last year's tinder."

The game I've been playing with Mother Nature the last two months has been successful. A visit to the physician in town proves I've never been able to cheat Her. I've been caught and fricassee-fried. I'm knocked up and knuckled under—in joy. Now that I'm hitched to a newel-post I can only respond with a Mohawk war cry: *Harraaskwah!*

I give Crunch the news in the middle of an orgasm—the only way to give a man precarious news on a slim budget. He's ecstatic and starts to follow me around the yard with a warm but stunned expression on his face.

When the roof's on the cabin, Crunch launches me up onto his shoulders so I can wield the hammer that symbolically drives the last nail into our shingled Shangri-La south of Hudson's Bay. For good luck he climbs up and bolts an orange weathercock into the roof.

The good luck is poorly packaged. For the next month I'm sick from one day to the next and can keep nothing in my stomach. Crunch, like the steadfast ram of my universe, is always on hand with a bucket and mop to catch everything I throw up. Eventually my system evens out and my body physical makes a truce with the goddess of childbearing.

When I'm feeling more myself, we hire a U-Haul and take a trip to the next big town and buy primitive furniture, a wood and electric stove, and a fridge that grizzles ice cubes and grows beards on innocent baby cabbages.

Twice I rearrange the furniture in our two-bedroomed cabin before it's a cozy confrontation around the fireplace. Then I'm terrified that symmetry will outdo me altogether. First thing you know I'll have a subscription to *Good Housekeeping* and be using an egg timer.

A week before Christmas we drag a pine tree into the house and trim it up with all kinds of chintzy winks and blinks it took me two weeks to make out of felt, Styrofoam, pinecones, and angel hair. On Christmas Eve, Crunch goes into town. For our good deed of the season he brings back the Whoopsey Gang, Larry, Minnie, Norma, and Pottypoo. The Gang get one of their presents as soon as they arrive: one after the other, they're chucked into the bath for their yearly baptismal into the human race, and then suited and booted in remedies I purchased from the nearest Sally Ann. But my sanitizing service draws a few complaints. Pissy McCoy bitches about the water being too hot. Joe the Rat is afraid of drowning when he discovers he's not submerged in something other than bubbles from Labatt's Distilleries. Morgan the Pirate won't remove his headgear. Crazy Jack says he must bless the water before getting into it and the appropriate words of divine inspiration won't come to him. When they insist that I be blindfolded before bathing them, I throw up my hands altogether and let Crunch take over.

Norma and Minnie help me prepare dinner. Crazy Jack attempts to say grace. It turns into a strung-out eulogy for a dog he lost under the wheels of a Ford when he was five years old. He sobs into a handkerchief and gets so beside himself he falls right off his chair. Then Larry chokes on a pickle and his glass eye drops into the mashed potatoes and Pottypoo retrieves it with a shot glass. At times I try in vain to bring dinner to order by rapping my spoon against the Woolworth crystal, as Joe the Rat eats the entire dish of sour cream for dessert, Crazy Jack recites his latest poem, "Ode to a Snowflake," Cornish the cat climbs to the top of the tree to play with the angel and Pissy McCoy falls to sleep in the cranberry sauce.

After dinner Morgan straddles a chair backward by the window and marvels at the wonder of the northern lights. Norma has come out of her shell and is waltzing around the floor to fiddle music with Crazy Jack, who thinks he's a celebrant at Oscar Wilde's wake. Minnie, turned out in her best scarlet lace undies, clings tightly to Pottypoo, who tries to eat her 38C cup before passing out. The party winds down a bit in the bathroom: Pottypoo is at the toilet and Norma is slapping his back, Pissy McCoy is lying in the bathtub sucking on a bottle of whiskey, Crazy Jack is talking to the ghost of Dorian Gray in the mirror, Minnie is washing her lovely undies in the sink, Morgan is shooting at everyone with a water pistol that came out of his Christmas sock, and Cornish is diligently unraveling the toilet paper. Crunch and I stand in the doorway, laughing our heads off.

All in all, this lunatic night and the following day turns out to be a rip-roaring success. Despite the fact that Crunch wanted to spend Christmas alone with me, he says he had a hell of a good time—the best ever.

Now the wordlessness of each day personifies itself in a lyrical literacy of sounds—a door banging, a floorboard creaking, a gun going off in the distance (Crunch is out shooting rabbits), and always the wind, the harbinger of good and bad news.

I thought this Madeira-in-the-Main would liberate me from the world. But now I'm feeling trapped inside of a milkweed, more enslaved than ever by time and the past. Yet this feeling, I know, is merely transitory.

Once in a while Chase, our friend from the John Howard Society, pops in to boost our spirits. In private he butters me up with references to the change in Crunch's life since he met me. But I know butter and truth better than he does. Change has nothing to do with conformity—one just rides the other's back and they both keep praying the other doesn't stumble. For Crunch and me it's all been patch and certify. To some extent I take well to my billowing state. It's very *domus divina*. I wallow in woolly headiness by cutting down to five ciggies a day and drowning my system with milk and exotics and eat like a Roman on the rampage.

In late spring we have the kitchen littered with incubators and can't sleep at night for the squawk of the baby chicks. Crunch bought them for the henhouse he's currently putting up. I lay in a massive garden and erect a fence around its perimeter to keep out the coons. Then I brush up on the history of China so I have some marvelous new stories to tell Crunch over dinner.

Somehow, deep in my gut, I know I'll never know contentment like this again; and every time the north wind batters the side of the house and the windows rattle, I pray that it is not warning me of some disaster to come.

On the appointed day of my deliverance from Haggard Hall, I ignore Crunch's advice and show up at the maternity ward of the nearest hospital, suitcase in hand and defiant to the crisp. According to the date circled on my doctor's calendar, I'm supposed to have a baby today. According to the nurses on duty, I'm supposed to wait for a dam to burst. I blow a fuse and trundle outside to the Jeep, where Crunch's laughing himself silly.

Instead, my son arrives in July—slowly—in grids and grinds and screams to Hera to transfer the air in the lining of my uterus to the line of saliva at the side of my mouth. After twenty hours of traumatic labor with Crunch holding my hand, the bloody little glycerine ball gives up and slides out from between my legs into the nightmare of light, sound, and touch. He's a seven-pound butterball, blond-haired, with big brown eyes the color of Crunch's, and his angry little cries echoing in the delivery room remind me that I may have committed an outrage. Only when he's been wrapped up and put into my arms does he cease to complain and I wonder if my arms will always be strong enough to hold him. The responsibility he's given me is crushing. Meanwhile I require extensive stitching and a blood transfusion, which keeps my green eyes greedy and my stomach empty and elastic.

I've never had a child before except at the Saturday afternoon movies. The heroine, coiffured and perfumed, is always propped up against a bank of pillows flashing a Cecil B. De Mille smile and cradling a cameo-perfected bust of a peaceable and impeachable Hymen. How very facile.

My state is less than haut monde. I look like the morning after I was dropped in the passion pit in a straitjacket and my son resembles a shriveled-up Siamese. Poor Crunch! He's emotionally drained and flushed and came out of this in worse shape than either I or the baby. He looks like he's just attended the miracle of the Nativity in Bethlehem and is waiting for the Star to guide him.

In honor of Alexander the Great and the Graham Bell wafer who invented depressing two-hundred-dollar phone bills, I decide to call my son Alexis.

At home I realize just how pathetically vulnerable this Alexis baby is and I try to harden myself into a cocoon of protection around him. I breast-feed him and air him, bathe him and air him every morning. I'm so afraid he'll stop breathing in the night I put him in bed with Crunch and me. While I pamper and fuss over his care, I wonder whether he'll inherit any of my defective genes or, worse, my damnable karma. Will I someday be guilty of selling him short or selling him out? It's like I'm knitting him a Jovian-Joseph coat of every color in the human imagination to help launch him to the promised land's greener-than-green pastures.

Another Christmas snows and goes. Then in March I have a hankering to visit cronies in town. Crunch agrees to watch Alexis for the afternoon so I jump in the Jeep, which has a new foghorn beeper and wide-track tires. I have a meal with Larry and Minnie in the kitchen of the hotel, a rap with Norma in the office, and a cigar and a beer at the bar with Pottypoo and Pinky. As a chaser to my day out, I spend the afternoon shopping and then drag the Gang back with me for a pre-spring overhaul of a bath, clean duds, and a few square meals.

Returning at dusk and miles up the road from home, we notice a pillar of smoke slowly billowing its way above the snow-laced tree line into the darkening sky. There's something prophetic about the way the huge winter sun is bleeding orange behind it. Then a cold devastating fear impales me like a stiletto—there's hardly a trace of wind! In a mad panic I jam the Jeep into fourth gear and grind the gas pedal to the floor. The closer we get to that stack of black smoke, the closer I know that day is turning to night . . . maybe permanently and the closer we go I know I'm teetering on the abyss of doom. I'm shaking and sobbing so bad I can hardly keep my hands on the wheel as we tear down the road at a frightening clip, bouncing in and out of the potholes, skidding on the ice patches, and being knocked around in our seats. Thank God I've got the Gang with me, yelling to cool down because everything's all right and holding my sanity together, or I'd lose control of the Jeep altogether and go right off the road.

When we screech onto the property, that pillar of smoke has already solidified into a grave marker and I get a sudden jab of pain in my chest that takes my breath for a moment. The cabin is burning wildly, and hungry flames are pouring through the roof and I go out of it entirely. Instead of braking, I blindly hit the gas and we plunge forward toward the burning cabin and Crazy Jack rams his boot onto the brake and grabs the wheel just in time and spins it in the opposite direction and we crash sideways into my red Bug parked nearby. Without even turning off the motor I scramble from the Jeep, screaming Crunch's name, whispering *Alexis*, madly searching the outbuildings—but nothing. Oh God, only ear-shattering silence and the flames and smoke and locked in overdrive like a maniac I race around the cracking hissing fire bowl trying to find a vein of entry through this forest of fumes and there is none, so I whirl toward the woodshed stumbling and falling over my own feet, grab an ax from the corner and hellishly slash at the glass in the front window of the cabin and smoke gluts out in black gaseous gushes and flames lick at me, hungry for air. I have to get in—in—my child, my savior, my life is in there some-where! Frantically I roll in the snow, take my coat off, and wearing it over my head for protection, attempt to force my way through the window. I'm trying to mount the ledge when Crazy Jack and Pissy McCoy come up behind me and grapple with me, dragging me back, back, back to the sidelines and they have to tackle me to the ground and sit on me in order to restrain a hysteria that knows no bounds while Piddles plaintively clips about the yard in circles. Then a section of the roof crumbles in and the last thing I remember before screaming myself into unconsciousness is the weathercock turning into a torch and toppling into the inferno. It was pointing east.

come to in the back of a police cruiser, wrapped in blankets, surrounded by officers and firemen all talking at once. Suddenly it hits me and I completely lose control of my limbs and go berserk, thrashing out in all directions. Two officers have to hold me down and a doctor administers an injection.

By midnight half the town has arrived to view the calamity and the yard has been transformed into a melting pot of garbled voices and whirring lights and I'm powerless to destroy them and myself in the bargain. The cabin is a charred heap of glowing live coals, Alexis and Crunch dead among them. Nobody and nothing could have survived such an inferno. The police wait around until the fire burns itself out entirely so they can search for the bodies in the rubble.

After which I self-destruct.

I'm blinded by a great white light which shows me all my failings in one throw of the dice. Too shattered to move, all I can do is kowtow and kiss the devil's ass.

I'm driven back to the hotel, where Norma takes charge of my affairs. She makes the necessary arrangements with the undertaker, consults my bank manager, and puts our fifty acres up for sale with a real estate agent.

For the next week I'm kept on sedatives and tied into bed so I won't harm myself. I sign documents without reading or understanding them and refuse to eat. Since nobody from the hotel staff can be spared to baby-sit and I won't let strangers come near me, the subdued Whoopsey Gang is pressed into service. Joe the Rat tells me Gray Owl fables.

Crazy Jack quotes and misquotes from the Books of Job and Lamentations, coming up with gems like "You've been spared for a divine purpose." Morgan the Pirate rides the bed railing and rages about the immortality of the heavens ("Sow wind and reap whirlwind"), while Pissy McCoy tries to make me put down a spoonful of Minnie's best homemade pea soup.

The official word from the fire inspector is that the 110-voltage aluminum wiring in the cabin was to blame and the finger points directly to a local electrician who lives inside a whiskey bottle. Thankfully, Crunch, Alexis, and Rasmus were smothered by the smoke before the flames reached them. For years afterward, wherever I am, I cannot return to my lodgings without experiencing a twinge of hysteria. I either carry my valuables around in my handbag or stash them in the icebox.

The funeral, performed by a United Church minister, goes according to a patterned nightmare. The Gang are outfitted in clean suits and, along with Minnie, Larry, Norma, and Pottypoo, stand in attendance giving me moral support. Chase and other members of the John Howard Society act as pallbearers. At my request Crunch and Alexis are buried in the same coffin a few yards from the remains of the cabin, a wish sanctioned by the new owner of the property. Rasmus is buried right beside them.

My poise threatens to return when the sod starts to fly. I collapse.

Over the course of the next few weeks I keep badgering Norma with the same line. "What am I going to do now that Alexis is . . . now that Crunch is gone? He was going to save me!"

And she keeps giving me the same reply: "Now I guess you'll have to save yourself, sweetie."

Snowballed into a dark *I don't give a damn, Mr. Man*, I try to beat grief down to the dregs, the way I've always dealt with anything I cannot face—I pretend the tragedy never happened.

My first impulse is to pack up and run away. But I have nowhere to go and the thought scares me silly. Besides, I need the security of my friends right now to keep stable. When some people are fighting grief, they bury themselves in their work. Except for the fact that my work involves hormones and sensuality, I am no different. Ravished with torturous pangs of guilt—I am a Jonah and am in some way responsible for Alexis's and Crunch's deaths—I leap with self-destructive gusto back into my former occupation, nighttime stripper and early-morning whore at the Moosehead Hotel. It's as if I can prove that I'm a bad seed and annihilate myself in the process.

One night, about two months later, I'm just down from a sweaty set maneuvering a loaded tray around the floor when this cockabully grabs me by the G-string. "I'm working, soldier—catch me later," I say, trying to shake him off.

"I'd rather catch you now. Sit down, Toots. Norma won't mind. I've cleared it with her."

He's well over six feet, muscularly slender, moustached, with gray-flecked black hair, a suited smoothie just off the cocktail circuit who doesn't look like he belongs in these parts. The finishing touch to his makeup is a low-key cockney accent. I wonder if it was bought or stolen.

Without asking my permission he turns my arms over, checking for track marks. Then he relaxes and gives me a salesman's smile. "I'd like to be your friend."

"I don't like people who talk with marbles in their mouth."

He places fifty dollars in sawbusters down on the table. "How much of a good time will that buy, Toots?"

"What do you want from me, friendship or sex?"

"Both—if I can get it."

"Oh, I see—you're an undercover nark," I add, knowing that the only asset I haven't been robbed of is my indifference.

He smiles thinly and pulls a crease into his pant leg. "I have a tidy little operation on the road you might be interested in. The money's double what you make shaking your buns off in this dive."

"Doing what?"

"What you do off hours upstairs for chicken feed."

"If Norma knew you were trying to hustle me she'd throw you out."

"Screw her. She's strictly small-time. Keep the fifty. There's plenty more where that came from." He hands me a business card, drains his glass, and gets to his feet. "I'll be back Thursday. Think about it. It's not every day you get the chance to work in a classy setup—you won't be young forever."

This final dollop of intelligence isn't lost on me. I'm ancient now. After he pushes off, Norma pulls me over to the bar. "He's checking out mighty quick, considering he already paid for you for the night."

"Twice," I confess, showing her the bills in my hand before shoving them into my elk-skin bag. "He offered me a job, Norma."

"The son of a bitch," she seethes. "I might've known. Hasn't stuck his nose around here for a while. Been laying low, I guess. The last time he run off with one of my girls I warned him I'd get him for it."

"Should I take the job?"

"It's up to you." She shrugs. "You've got a brain—figure it out."

"But who is he? What is he? Is he safe?"

"Cosmos is a business buckaroo from Toronto. Owns a few hotels and Christ knows what else. On the side he's what you might call a high-class pimp. As far as being safe—no man's safe, sweetie."

My nightmares about Crunch and Alexis have gotten so bad lately that I'm unable to sleep without sedatives. As long as I remain here, I won't be able to shake the past. Maybe a change in locale as well as work would do me the world of good. This scuzzy place is starting to get to my head. I'm talking like Dutch Schultz and thinking like John Wayne. My itchy feet won't stand in one place for long. If I didn't jump at this job, I'd jump at another one in another couple of months. Besides, I'm getting sick and tired of running my ass off in the Wampum Room. Usually I'm so wacked out by the end of the night it's all I can do just to service the Johns Norma sends up to my room. Why should I have to work so hard? Maybe it's time I lived in style for a change. I thank the gods for sending Cosmos to me.

O Athena, I relent and wholeheartedly repent everything—except for taking this bend in the road. Crunch's and Alexis's ghosts are too familiar here!

My second meeting with Cosmos is frostier than the first. How can

I tell him that I hate his guts because he's a way out, not a way up? Instead of playing the eager beaver, I pretend that I haven't made up my mind about working for him yet. To rub his ego I let him make the decision for me. Now I have someone to blame if it doesn't work out. He asks me a slew of questions about myself, most of which I ignore or refuse to answer. When I don't kowtow to him, he kowtows to me—with the deference of a sugar daddy. He makes all the arrangements with a slick professionalism that makes me tremble with excitement and relief. When he leaps into his Lincoln Continental, Norma gets her revenge by taking the back lights out with one ear-shattering report from Buster.

On a hot day in June I find myself standing on the sidewalk in front of the hotel waiting for my ride to Girls' Town. The Whoopsey Gang are sitting on my luggage, giving the flies a feast. I have a handbag over one shoulder, an army canteen over the other, a steel washtub, and Piddles on a red leash at my feet. I cause such a sensation that a young boy stops to take a picture and his mother furiously pulls him away. "You're not taking a picture of that hussy!"

This's the first time I've been called "that hussy." And from now on anytime somebody says I'm archaic, I simply hide behind my shades and glance over my shoulder toward Sodom. No, I won't turn into salt. I've already turned from salt into live ash.

A big Jeep Cherokee pulls up to the curb. One crusty, ornery old cuss with grizzled cheeks gets out and dawdles over at a modest pace. Then he stands there, parked in neutral himself, chewing a toothpick contemplatively. "I see you're already waiting for me," he rasps.

"For over an hour," I complain. "One o'clock is what's written on my calendar. It's now two-fifteen."

"Ain't that too bad," he sneers in a scratchy voice. "Maybe I should've come in a fancy limo-zeen."

"Thanks, but this heap will do just fine."

"Oh, it will, will it? I'm glad." But he doesn't seem convinced. Keeps staring at my luggage and scratching his head thoughtfully. "I'm Poppy. You are as hell got a lot of stuff for one person. Is that fryer going, too?"

"Cosmos said I could bring him."

"Well, he's too small for seven stomachs. Still, he might do for a midnight snack."

"What're you talking about? He's my pet."

He curses under his breath. Sounds like his stomach growling. The toothpick works from one side of his mouth to another. "I wasn't told nothing about no goddamn fryer."

I heave a glandular sigh and grit my teeth. Typical fare for worms in the outback who're just trucking along. Angrily, I make up his mind for him by kissing the Whoopsey Gang good-bye and hauling my gear into the back of the Jeep. He watches me and makes a face. "Now I suppose you'll go and tell Colette I wouldn't give you a hand—just to get me in shit?"

"You got that right. Who's Colette?"

Ignoring me, he leaps into the driver's seat. "Trouble. Youse women is always trouble. Never met one that wasn't."

Holding Piddles in my lap, I pull the door shut. He throws the toothpick away, pulls a fresh one from his shirt pocket, and jams the Jeep into drive and it's *Good-bye Big Rock's bad news and Hello Oblivion's fresh blues!*

"Hey, what's the canteen for?" A self-satisfied smile rides his face. "Where the hell do you think you're going, the Yukon?"

"The carburetor in this thing might blow its top."

"Shit bricks—she's only two years old."

"Actually, the water's for Piddles," I confess. "He needs cooling down from time to time."

"Oh, well, excuse me," he mimics in a squeaky voice. "I should have brought servants and bellhops with me too."

"Thanks anyway, but I do my own hopping."

"Yeh, I'll just bet you do. One of those women's lippers, too, eh? I could be dying of thirst and you'd give it to that goddamn fryer, wouldn't you?"

"Yup, that's me."

I let him stew a minute before offering him the canteen. "I ain't gonna touch it after some goddamn fryer's been at it. Might be contaminated."

Angrily I screw the cap back on. "Congratulations—you've gotta be the biggest son of a bitch I've ever met, bar none. What makes you so ugly, or is that too ugly to talk about, too?"

"You ain't seen nothing yet, you little mouthpiece."

"Flunky!"

"Floozie!"

Driven into a grudging stalemate, we endure the sixty-minute ride in silence, which takes us from a paved main road to an unpaved bush road, and to bug my ass Poppy intentionally hits every bump.

This godforsaken area must have been used for logging, which explains why this half road is here in the first place. The surrounding bush is carpeted with green foliage wildly wrapping itself between and around the stubs of tree trunks that poke up through the rich loamy surface like thumbs. Here and there a strong sapling struggles its way upward. Nice place, I guess, if you like petrified forests.

Miles farther on, the forest again rises up to its natural height and seems to swallow us. Finally, to the relief of my numbed buttocks, we arrive in a man-made clearing on the shore of a picturesque lake. I discover that lumberjacks once had a base camp out here until the company they worked for moved on. Now all that's left are a few piles of rotting timber and pieces of wrapping wire littered about. An extra-long red-and-white trailer is parked under some pine trees near the water. The ground out front is dotted with a few umbrella tables and some lawn chairs, along with an expensive gas barbecue. Again, the calm stillness stuns my senses where the human is the intruder and nature's all.

So this's Cosmos's Babylon Backwater.

"Go on in." Poppy spits the remnants of a toothpick out of his mouth. "I'll take care of your stuff."

I put Piddles back on his leash and get out. At the door of the trailer a plumpish copper-haired coquette about forty years old embraces me, crushing me against her ample bosom. I can smell wine and licorice on her breath. She's well done up but, oddly, not too overdone. Chic's the proper word. Poised as if she's about to give an informal luncheon for an entourage of glass sniffers, she introduces herself as Colette. I envision a French teapot in a Chanel cozy, pouring noblesse oblige. Inside the trailer, while giving me the once-over, she pours a glass of red wine, her musical chuckle tinkling like wind chimes. Her accent and aura warm me to the marrow.

I introduce her to Piddles. "This's my dog but he looks like a duck. He's no bother. He doesn't bark, lay eggs, migrate, dig holes, or bite the postman."

She touches her bobbed hair in a gilt mirror. "Oooo . . . I think maybe the duck can stay but the dog must go." Then she gives Piddles a pat on the head, a sign he's been accepted on the lawns of Versailles.

Poppy bumbles in and rustles himself up a couple of ham sandwiches in the galley kitchen. Colette tells me that the girl I'm replacing ran off with an engineer from a mine farther north. "We stayed up there too long," she sighs. "Love waits for no one."

"Neither does a flat tire," Poppy muses, sitting down at the table like a saddlesore cowboy just home from a roundup.

"You will meet the other girls later," she continues. "They must have their afternoon nap, you see, because they're up so late at night. Are you hungry, chérie?"

"Famished."

"Fix her up something, Poppy," she tinkles.

He gets to his feet, cursing.

Colette chuckles and kisses him on the head like an errant child. "Don't mind Poppy. He makes friends with nobody and hates everybody. But he's basically quite harmless."

Cosmos obviously hired this old badger as a bouncer-protector-caretaker-whatever because he won't have to worry about love and triangles turning the trailer into a clawing cathouse.

Taking my arm, she draws me through a screen of beaded curtains into the congested parlor. The decor is early bordello, late fiddledee-dee, with a small bar, two sets of atrocious gold-gilded lamps with shades dripping iced raindrops by the bucket, a velvet kidney-shaped couch in oxblood on fake mahogany legs, and matching armchairs. Behind it all I can see the hand of Cosmos decorating a dance hall in London's East End. His taste buds are in his feet. The only thing bigger than a big shot is always his publicity. But I suppose the illusion's fun.

Apparently the trailer gets its electricity from a sophisticated break-down voltage regulator and a power cable taps us into the hydro lines feeding a nearby mine.

Colette unravels my hmms and huhs and caters to my yes-no-maybe-huhs by giving me another glass of wine and some imported toffee from a gold bonbon box. Then she gives me the grand tour of the trailer. Outside of the modest-sized kitchen, complete with a chrome dinette and a blue budgie named Amour in a cage, and the spacious parlor, the other side of the trailer has been ingeniously chopped up into seven cubicles. One is a walk-in closet posing as a bathroom and the other six are merely walk-in bedroom cupboards posing as closets with just enough room to juggle golf balls. Each one is outfitted with a single brass bed with a shelf and storage drawers underneath and overtop, furry carpeting on the floor, and matching gold-trimmed white combination vanity and chest of drawers in wood and particleboard with a mini oval mirror and synthetically furred stool. I'm beginning to think I'm walking inside of a crazy contemporary Aztec's brain cell. It's an illusion inside of an illusion inside of a nutshell. The glare of artificial opulence is blinding.

I start to unpack in the cupboard assigned to me and Colette sits on my bed, leg over leg, elegant, smoking a cigarette through a three-inch holder, watching me. Then she explains the house rules and how we are paid. When I'm finished finding a place for my two suitcases of books and one of clothing, she takes me into her room for a fitting.

Naturally, my working costume is two sizes too big and has to be taken in from the black lace straps on the shoulder to the scarlet bodice with its tit underwires. I make do with the matching fanlike hair dohickie and the garter belt and black fishnet stockings.

According to Colette, when men crawl out of the bowels of the earth or wander out of the emptiness of the forests, they deserve more than the standard mundane fare of blue jeans and a dirty T-shirt. Not only do they appreciate the privilege of stepping into a Walt Disney production of *Désirée Pawing Irma La Douce* to music from *The Moulin Rouge*, but they're willing to pay well for the voyeuristic trip.

Later on, my comrades wander in to give me the once-over and Colette does the introductions. Freda's a tall, lanky brunette with a lovely face who I'm told in an off whisper is very slow upstairs. Green-eyed black-haired Cassie is a bosomy fireball with an impish pout, and Terry is a strawberry blonde who's constantly painting a smile on her snippy face in the reflection of her nail polish. Then there's Lena, a pale, auburn-haired, freckled bookworm. A real mishmash of extremes.

Then there's me. And since I'm the smallest by a notch I'm quick to realize I'll have to speak up or get shoved to the back of the line.

Everyone has to contribute to the household chores. Colette posts a weekly schedule on the corkboard in the kitchen which she regularly rotates. Lena and Terry are on meal duty tonight.

During supper the girls ply me with questions about the outside world. I assure them it's right where they left it—polluted, upside-down crazy, and ticking like a time bomb. We all lend a hand with the dishes. Then, on my way to the bathroom, I tear open the big door of the hall closet and step on top of Poppy, who's having an after-supper lie-down. Wrong door! Nobody told me this was his kiddy-sized kennel. Cursing thickly, he brooms the other girls and myself toward the door.

Outside, we fall into mild horseplay and banter. I've been constrained by pain for so long that at first it's hard for me to join the festivities. Then the fun and games lead us to building a roaring fire by the lake and we roast marshmallows, and a ghost from my adolescence rises up inside of myself and demands attention. All at once there seems to be no reason to hold it all in. Now is the time for letting it all go. Little by little, I can feel the chains loosen.

Once away from Colette's stern eye, Cassie lives up to her tab of "house bootlegger" by passing around a cache of beer and whiskey she has hidden in the shallows of the lake. Freda's only allowed a small ration of beer. "Straight hard liquor makes her go bonkers," Cassie explains.

When it's dark we strip down and wallow in the lake. Cassie surfaces at my elbow like a blowfish. "How'd Iron Pants suck you into this?"

"Simple—I let him think I needed sucking."

She hoots with laughter. "Terry got nailed while waiting for a bus in Temagami. Lena was lining up at a welfare office in Cobalt. Freda—well, Freda was walking the streets in a stupor in some two-bit hole when Colette picked her up. Freda's her pretty pretty baby."

"Knock it off," Lena scoffs.

"Well, it's true," Cassie counters. "Wanna know how I got to this sinbin? I'm hitching it to Toronto when Cosmos rolls up in this far-out Lincoln and picks me up. When I push a button and the friggin' windows start going up and down and he passes me a mickey from the glove compartment, I know what's going down. I'm not stupid. So I get ready for action. Leg bent to knee him, old dukes ready to fly—the whole bit. What's he do? Pulls into a truck stop for a bite. Me? I've got five bucks to my name. So I figure—okay, big shot, you want to invite me to lunch, you get stuck with the tab. Then we're eating and he's fishing around for information—where am I going? where am I gonna stay? Hell, I'm glad he let me order the most expensive thing on the menu. I just keep shoveling in the grub, hoping I'll get it all down before he gets the check so I can vamoose out the bathroom window. Then he feeds me a line about this operation to see if I'll take the bait. Talks a blue streak. I order another piece of blueberry pie and let him. Then I figure, Why the hell not? I like to eat like I like to fuck. May as well get paid for doing both. When I get up to leave I'm so stuffed I feel as if I just got fucked anyway. Hell, I just pulled my first trick for eighteen bucks 'cause that's what the tab came to."

Lena makes a face. "Don't listen to her. Every time she tells that story she tells it different."

"Bullshit—it just comes out different," Cassie argues. "Hey, I'm here, aren't I? Anyway, I can't stomach the city. Out here I can get home now and then with lots of bread to boot. The winters are a hell of a drag but if you can handle frost on your frillies, you're in."

"Did Cosmos ever offer you money for sex?" I ask her.

"I guess not. I would've given Iron Pants a bust in the chops. You don't like him, do you?"

"He's a bona-fide beef jerky."

Everyone laughs. "Hey!" Cassie hoots. "Let's call him that. I'm getting tired of Iron Pants."

A truck rumbles into the clearing and pulls up behind the trailer, thus ending our pillow talk. This rowdy army of backwoods yahoos tumbles out the back. Poppy clips across the yard with a .22 rifle and Colette trips behind in a satin robe and high-heeled silver slippers, playing ambassador.

I give Cassie the nudge. "I thought we weren't expecting any business tonight."

"We weren't. But around here you expect the unexpected. There's always a wolf pack coming out of the woods."

Suspended in an excitable high, we wait in the shallows, partially submerged. After a word with the Johns, Colette steps onto the dock and claps her hands as if she's calling a kindergarten class to attention. "Girls. Girls," she coos. "We are working tonight." Linking arms with the pick of the litter, she leisurely strolls back into the trailer, leaving us on our own.

Freda begins waving her arms and whirling uncontrollably in the water.

"Stop splashing!" Terry cries. "My hair's getting wet. I just spent the afternoon setting it."

Before we can close in and give her a proper dunking, one jumping yahoo hollers from the shore. "Hey, boys—look what's in the water! Let's do some night fishing!" Stripping off his clothes, he dives in and slathers toward us like a shark.

Teasing him, we swim farther out. When he converges on us, we playfully try to drag him under. His fellow yahoos onshore are undressing so they can join the jam session. Freda, who's easily the strongest one of us, grabs him from behind in an armlock around the neck and pushes him under. He tries to surface but she won't let him. It's clear to all of us that the game is over.

"Code red!" Cassie hollers, grappling her from behind. We tackle her other appendages. It's like prying apart a death grip. By the time we have her subdued, three yahoos are bobbing beside us, helping to hold her. Cassie and I float the victimized yahoo to shore, pitch him on his stomach, give him first aid, and he throws up half the lake. Though he's quite shook up and still panting for breath, he's all right.

Now everyone's assembled on the lawn outside the trailer. The fracas has triggered a shouting match.

"Okay, who gave her the lousy booze?" Cassie rants. "She's got eighty proof on her breath!"

Taking immediate charge, Colette claps her hands and orders silence. Quietly she talks to Freda, who's been in hysterics for five minutes, while stroking her forehead and cooing to her like a child. In minutes Freda calms down completely and breaks into muffled sobs in her arms. She's given a sedative and put to bed. Then Colette calls the girls into a private huddle. She's spitting mad. Freda filched a bottle of Canadian Club from Cassie's room while we were pretending we were water sprites in the lake. She found it while rooting around for a crystal paperweight of Cassie's which particularly fascinated her since last Christmas.

"I knew I should have given her that damn thing," Cassie grumbles, kicking at the ground.

"You know you are not allowed to keep liquor in your room!" Colette says. "I will talk to you in the morning!"

"Goddamn French cow!" Cassie's cursing under her breath as she pulls me back toward the water.

Colette rounds up the Johns with a chorus of smiles and come-on cozies. "Everyone, the evening is not lost. Come now. Enjoy— enjoy."

Out in the lake Cassie mocks Colette outrageously and I break out laughing. She continues her foul mood until one of the yahoos swims up from behind and takes two handfuls of tit. Then she swells up with sass and ass again.

We decide to play touch tag as a foreplay forerunner. One of the yahoos tags himself as It and zooms in on us, his grinning face posing like Jaws above the surface of the water. Shrieking with laughter, we playfully splash him and dive and surface in an attempt to escape. Suddenly, the other yahoos, bored by having only one protagonist, announce that they're clones of It. The water is soon sizzling with sexual sauce. Fatigue finally drives us into pairing off for the evening.

A prairie Polack from Saskatchewan is one hell of a way to break in new ground and your first night at a new job, especially when he decides to get it on right in the goddamn lake. He swells up inside of me underwater and the walls of my vagina close up around him and suddenly we're together in a hot, vacuum-suctioned embrace, body-locked. Stuck together and embarrassed as hell, we're finally forced to call out for help.

Our dilemma turns into their big joke of the evening and provides a comic if crudely pathetic chaser to Freda's earlier outburst. Everyone is in hysterics, until with Colette's verbal instructions we finally get uncoupled onshore.

Then we go back in the water for a refreshing midnight swim and after a while Poppy appears, dumping a pile of towels on the dock. "Her highness wants yeh all inside—pronto!"

"And what's *his* majesty want?" Cassie pipes up sharply.

"For you to go to hell in a handcart. I'll pay the freight bill."

Everyone sends him back a barrage of catcalls and whistles.

"Is that guy for real?" shoots the Polack at my ear.

"If he didn't cause a draft every time he opened his mouth, we'd never know he was alive."

My first night of sashaying around the parlor full of oomph and froufrou with a tray of drinks is a success, and though Piddles later finds his way into my bed and clips my partner's pecker, the Polack proves a bucking good way of opening another can of beans—out of water.

My daily routine goes something like this: Every morning I spill out of bed to the Big Ben alarm at ten o'clock. Then I follow Piddles's waddle down the hall, pull the cloth off Amour's cage, and after feeding her, set the coffeepot on to perk and heat up a plateful of Colette's homemade croissants. By the time I've had a quick shower, everything is ready. I take a continental breakfast tray into Colette, and while we eat, drink, and talk, I help her set her hair with steam rollers and manicure and polish her nails. My awe of her boudoir is total. Her vanity is covered with mysterious crystal vials of perfumes and lotions, containing everything from linden flowers to *Rosa damascena* to witch hazel and ylang-ylang, plus potions from major Paris perfumeries. She's the classiest woman I've ever met and the warmest and I can't understand why she's marooned herself here in the Canadian backwoods. In comparison to French women, I've always found, English women are archaic, dull, characterless, and their souls seem cold enough to give you hypothermia. My pet name for Colette is Mamoshka. She calls me *mon petit chou*. And this little cabbage soon learns that although this basilica in the bush is Cosmos's fief, it's *our* stomping ground and Colette's sweetmeat.

During these fleshed-out tête-à-têtes, she tells me things I already know, things I wish to hell I didn't know, and things I don't want to know. But it leaves me with an inkling as to what toppled the French monarchy and devaluated our dollar along with the English pound. She also teaches me that artless passion is a fool's game.

Then at eleven I load the tray and go banging on doors. Colette's now ready to hold court. Everyone descends on her room with yawns, groans, and grimaces. Here's our sanctum sanctorum.. We laugh, air our grievances, and wash our dirty linen as well as everyone else's.

Piddles gets more attention than I do. He's so overfed he gets sick. The problem isn't with the night crawlers and worms he consumes outside but with the junk food everyone sneaks him behind my back. In no time flat he has his own toy box and he's established himself as house mascot.

As we have a rigorous work schedule most evenings, sometimes handling as many as four Johns each in one night, we're lucky to be able to grab a few hours' relaxation in the afternoon by stretching out in chaises longues in the sun. Colette dabs a concoction of elder flowers and orange blossom on her face and sips at a cup of chamomile tea while I massage coconut oil into her back. Then I read to her from her favorite novel by Simone de Beauvoir.

The only hassle we have all summer is with a troublesome three-some who keep showing up for dinner without being invited, a family of black bears.

Cassie becomes my best friend. She's the mouthiest, the bawdiest, and probably the toughest of the crew. But I love her wild laughter and she's the only one to horse around with when I'm bored. The others are usually too lazy to join our revelries. Cassie's afraid of nothing. I'm afraid of everything. Anything I'm not afraid of is an even more horrid proposition. And I'll do almost anything to prove I'm corruptible.

29

Cosmos has a bush pilot fly him and five of his big-shot buddies in from Sudbury. From the parlor window I watch him trudging up the dock, swinging an impressive-looking attaché case. It's probably made of rattlesnake skin, containing a half-eaten chicken sandwich, an outdated copy of *Time*, and three stale Chiclets. City slicker hooey-phooey doesn't fool me for a minute. By the look of his buddies, I think I know the type: so far in the hole, multinationally, that they'll have to live through three life cycles just to be able to pay for a small share in their own karma.

I hide out in my room while he's having a business conference with Colette in the kitchen. According to Cassie, he always asks her for a report on each of us and apparently has a little book where he keeps intimate notes on us—our sexual preferences, etc. Cassie and I make a pact to find and destroy the contraband.

Around suppertime Terry knocks on the door. "Cosmos wants us all in the kitchen—now!"

"I'm sick," I titter, lost inside the pages of George MacDonald Fraser's *Flashman at the Charge.*

Three minutes later there's another knock. I don't answer, so Cosmos strides in. His tone is pontifical and irritable. "Uptight about something, Toots?"

"How would you know what uptight looks like on me?"

"What I don't know about any one of you wouldn't fill a thimble. When I drop in I like to see all my girls."

"I have a natural aversion to meat inspectors and dogcatchers—but here I am."

He lights a cigarette. "Why not tell me what you really think of me."

"Okay, you're a prick."

"But you came to work for this prick anyway, didn't you?"

I can't fault him there. That I did. I can feel the blood coming up behind my face.

He slides his suit coat off and tosses it over the vanity stool. "Supper's on. So I'll have to settle for one of your Nanookie specials," he says, with such ease I'm sure he's joshing.

"I hope you haven't gone and put money down on this race." I'm trying to be excruciatingly cheerful.

"Listen, Toots," he says with grit in his voice. "I don't pay for something I have rights to."

"Then I won't put your rights in jeopardy by paying in counterfeit currency."

He glares at me for a split second, then snaps his suit coat up and flips it over his shoulder. "I could fire you for this."

"Sure—if your ego could stand it."

Angrily, he takes two quick strides to the bed and sits down beside me. Then he blows smoke in my face and fingers my scoop neckline. "This conversation isn't finished, Toots. It just got going. In future keep that in mind. And the next time I ask for you, move your tush. Prick or not, I'm the boss here. You're setting a bad example and I've got better things to do than chase errant children. It makes me think you're not happy . . . that worries me. I don't like to be worried. Comprehendo?"

"Sì, señor."

"Another thing. Colette tells me you're a little overzealous on the job. I realize you had a nasty piece of luck last spring, so I'll give you time to adjust. Just remember, this's a business. They get what they pay for—nothing extra for sentimental reasons. Not every John who shows up for a piece of ass is a convict. . . ."

Damn him! I fire my Big Ben alarm at his head, miss, and hit the wall instead. "You're not fit to kiss his footprint in the snow!"

"Pick it up," he says, a chill in his voice.

I pluck it up and hand it to him. He slaps my face and grabs my arm as if he means to break it, his eyes jetting white flame. "I won't force you into giving me sex but don't ever do anything like that to me again!" Then he yanks the door open and prods me through it. "Let's go and eat dinner."

In the kitchen he changes his mood dramatically. Since he's brought back the heat and the meat in the forms of new Johns *and* a supply of lobsters and they're being boiled up in three big aluminum pots, he's king of the flesh pile. His big-shot buddies have already made themselves at home, found a chair along with their tongues, and are sitting around shooting the shit with the girls. One of them is an MP, which could mean either Mediocre Pervert or Minor Pushover, depending on your politics. He's feeding Terry salad with a spoon, a clear indication that whatever his job, he'll have a new one when he gets back. A guy like this changes his portfolio this week so that he'll have an excuse next week for failing to receive last week's portfolio in the mail. That's why he'll surely soon be at the UN with a minister of this-and-that name badge, still carrying his old minister of such-and-such attaché case, his degree in agriculture tucked inside.

To keep my ego in the hot seat, Cosmos guides me into a chair beside him at the head of the table. Then he doles everything out and butters everyone up with compliments, bad jokes, and petty puff pieces. Though it's hard to resist his hearty repartee, I volunteer nothing throughout the meal. He keeps giving me stiff over-the-wineglass appraisals and I keep wanting to kick him under the table. For the first time since I arrived, I'm out of synch with the surroundings. I've just declared war on a solvent state of affairs.

After supper Cassie and I clear the table. While the others are outside taking a nature walk through the woods, Cosmos disappears with Terry into her room. Cassie makes a sour face over the dish suds. "He's got a weakness for blondes, wouldn't you know?"

"Most insecure sons of Johns do."

"Better not let him hear you say that. He'll give you a rap in the mouth."

"He already did. But I forgot to enjoy it and say thank you."

In England, where they have a flair for metaphors with an occupational hazard, Johns are called punters. In layman's terms, a punter is a shortsighted golfer with his lust concentrated on the first hole and his credit rating buried in the ninth. He's a sucker who knows he's the ball you're punting around the surgy side of the green, and you both celebrate human hypocrisy in a teacup. All for the sake of greens fees. Cosmos is a punter circumventing the sand trap.

By eight o'clock in the evening everyone's plastered enough to try building a Tibetan temple of human bodies on the lawn outside the trailer in honor of Narcissus. But the acrobatic stunt never really gets past the weed line.

Cosmos, with his sybaritic tastes for debauchery and sorcerer's sense of chi-chi, suggests a game of sexual snooker instead. The grass is used for a pool table and eggs and broom handles are used instead of balls and cues. Cosmos delegates Cassie and me as the booby prizes, no doubt to get even for giving him the brush-off earlier. So we sit back on the grass in our bras and panties with our legs spread open, using our hands to improvise side and end pockets. The table stakes are a kiss-an-egg and the eight egg takes all.

The game turns out to be a rip and I don't know who looks more foolish, the Johns down on their stomachs shooting for their breakfast or Cassie and I blotting egg yolks off the insides of our legs.

Just when it looks like the Mediocre Pushover will take the pot to bed tonight, Lena and one of the Johns, who strayed off for a private party of their own, come charging out of the woods, screaming. They've just come across a black bear rummaging through our garbage dump.

Drunk enough to panic—and enjoy the jump it gives your bio-rhythm—everyone converges on the lake like lemmings in season. When Colette throws us a basketball from the dock, the night winds down with a pool-party version of water soccer.

Two days later the Johns and Cosmos fly out and I couldn't be happier. Things between Cosmos and me hadn't improved. He continued to goad me and I continued to pretend to ignore it.

One morning Poppy takes the girls into town to pick up supplies and shop for trinkets at the five-and-dime to keep themselves and our house adorned the year round. To me, shopping for shopping's sake is a tedious waste of time and energy, a vice for young hens and old roosters in search of a place to lay eggs. Colette and I remain behind to soak up some needed rest and solitude. No sooner have the others left when the sky opens up and a torrential rainstorm unleashes its fury on the trailer. While Colette has a nap and a soak in the tub, I catch up on my reading in the parlor. Eventually, Colette emerges from her room in a silk kimono and prepares lunch for us. Afterward, she invites me into her room for a drink and switches on André Gagnon. Over a bottle of Château Margaux we slowly slide into a rap session which begins with the chill factor and ends with Henry Miller.

Colette kicks off her heels, stretches out on the bed, and encourages me to lie beside her. In a light voice she trippingly shares memories of a short modeling stint in Paris when she sold Chanel No. 5 from advertisement boards in the Métro to her conversion to the oldest profession, compliments of a shady Hungarian artist with gold teeth and a bad case of kleptomania whom she met on the Champs-Elysées. To support him she took a job in a Pigalle restaurant that served as a contact point for establishing a regular clientele. When she returned to her digs and discovered her Hungarian lover in bed with another man, she stopped patronizing the arts and decided to patronize herself instead. She packed her belongings, withdrew her savings from the *caisse d'épargne*, set up shop in an apartment with a girl from Dupont in the Latin Quarter, and went into business servicing a higher-classed clientele. Sometimes she hung out in a café down from the Moulin Rouge where the music was slow and jazzy and there were mirrors on the walls and phones on the tables so you could dial-a-trick discreetly. When she took her one-woman show on the road and experimented in hotel rooms on the French Riviera with various recipes of congress from the *Kama Sutra of Vatsyayana*, she was able to raise her prices considerably.

Then at a Monte Carlo casino came her tumultuous meeting with a French-Canadian gangster playing the bank at baccarat. He brought her back to Canada and their affair ended suddenly in a bloodbath on the floor of a Montreal tavern when he was gunned down. She was forced back into the skin trade, this time as the madam of her own brothel, until street politics pressured her into giving up the business and seeking her fortune in Ontario. Colette's lilting lyrical voice and the picaresque world she lived in seem to be just as much of a dream play as this one. She's exquisitely polished and makes me feel as if I've spent my life as a yashmaked Arabian water-bearer always caught between the well and the sheikh's tent.

The game shifts to show-and-tell when I reveal a vaccination mark at the top of my right leg put there in the 1950's to keep this baby-boomer in long skirts and short-sleeved blouses. In turn, she removes her silk kimono, revealing an ample cleavage in all its waxed radiance. She shows me an ugly scar on her abdomen put there by a tight-assed pimp in Paris who tried to buy her rebelliousness back from her self-image and lost. Colette politely panders to that cold Germanness in my nature that must have every emotional confrontation identified, labeled, and locked in a separate room. She works toward possessing the key to these rooms while catering to that curious contradiction in my sex I left buried in my mother's womb. I trust her because she lets me play child at the breast, not allowing reason to disturb my sense of security. Even when she lets me have a puff of her Gauloise cigarette between sips of wine and playfully kisses my face while pretending to arrange my hair in an upsweep, I refuse to treat her mothering as anything but camaraderie in the buff. Yet I'm still all bastions, turrets, and fear in the cellar, my nerve ends tightening in defense of the home firm.

To relax my body physical, she turns me over facedown on the bed, pulls my nightgown down to the waist, and works her magic hands from the base of my skull up behind my ears, then downward toward the base of my neck, massaging the provincial quirks out of my nature. As she unknots the muscles in my cramped shoulders, she also releases me to the nymph of the afternoon.

The session has scarcely begun when she suddenly stops and giggles something sinfully sizzling in French in my ear. I roll onto my back and watch her pour another glass of wine while listening to the rain pelt the tinny roof overhead in perfect rhythm with the piano concerto emanating from the stereo. Breaking the hypnotic spell I'm under, Colette switches off the bedside lamp, plunging us into another, darker one. She concentrates on my conscious self by addressing my sub-conscious fears and strokes my face like a pet cat, asking me questions about myself. It's like having my mind felt up in the backseat of a spaceship en route to Mars. Dully, I read the ceiling I can't see and answer her in monosyllables tied together with a need I haven't felt deprived of since infancy. Now her fingers are moving in small circular motions around my breasts and then she's captured one in her hand and you'd think it was a baby bird, she fondles it so gently. I'm no sooner uncomfortably fighting the desire to push her away when her attention turns oral and I'm fighting a bigger, more dreaded desire to have her continue. Cool, mature, she seems almost oblivious to the inner melee she's creating in my erroneous zones until my secret wish is granted and I find her hand petting my thighs. Immediately, Col-ette's image changes from earth mother to sister in the cloister. With her mouth she initiates a voyage of exploration to the baby-powdered *bonne bouche* at the apex of my senses, where the kittenlike minis-trations of her tongue have my vagina palpitating like a second heartbeat.

This is the *dark* at the end of the tunnel called love.

As my mother superior at work, so far Colette has never played either the male aggressor or the female lay-me-down in her associations with either the clients or the staff, always allowing passion to take a backseat to propriety. I'm trying to see her here as an asexual wet nurse. But it's impossible. She's too poised in intent and her act too stylized. She knows no mercy whatsoever in the art of lovemaking and keeps the scales tilted in her favor. Did I say lovemaking? I'm feeling too good to be normal. It's just occurred to me that Colette's changed her image again—to Sappho. When I break the interlude by mentioning the word lesbianism, she ceases and shushes me quiet with "You think too much, mon chou. I'm not a lesbian. There are some things the English haven't invented a word for yet."

Although she hasn't given me the French equivalent for what we're doing, I'm appeased for the moment because it's been sanctioned by some advanced philosophy I'm not yet developed enough to understand.

The rest is a narcoticlike sensation of being tied down and having my cunt coiffured like a toy poodle. Because I'm inexperienced at tangling with soft flesh with a feline dexterity, I feel guilty at not being wholly able to give anything back—at least not yet. I'm waiting for her to notice that my clitoris is misplaced but she doesn't seem to to notice that what she's holding in her mouth is . . . driving me out of my mind. I want to regress with her to childhood and romp with her in a field of flowers but she keeps dragging me back by the adolescent cunt into a field of mud, in spasms, until I'm controlled by the cunt and it explodes and has destroyed me and she's kissing my face and I'm past cunt altogether, *mine*, and into a mad tangle with another, *hers*, and I'm past cunt altogether, *ours*. When was I ever in the practice of comparing anyway? It was enough shame to own one in the first place.

This confrontation with my own sex has given me a kaleidoscopic closeup shot of my own femininity, which is a shade on the frigid side. My *affaire de coeur* with Colette becomes very *tête-bêche* and continues as a fleeting proposition. Yet our encounters must never be mentioned outside of this, the back room of the Women's Institute, where the female's history is always recorded side by side with her anatomy and anything touching her Mary, Mother of Jesus psyche must never be referred to as anything but the final Christian taboo.

On further reflection it's significant that one of the most frightening confrontations of my life and one of the most tender were orchestrated by a Frenchman and a Frenchwoman.

Although I despise any form of sexual politics, in the ensuing weeks harsh words are exchanged between Cosmos and Colette on my account. Ass-sucking Terry told Cosmos that she found Colette and me in bed together one night. When I ask Colette about it, she merely laughs it off by explaining that Cosmos is jealous and angry that she got to me before he did. I think we've both just deflated Cosmos's Hugh Hefner sense of self and I'm delighted.

But despite this, Colette remains my sometimes bed partner and full-time guru. She instructs me in the art of *amma*, a traditional therapeutic method of Oriental medicine, using rubbing and pressure massage to exercise and restore the body physical to its normal functioning. She teaches me how to inspect and disinfect a penis and how properly to inflate a limp one. She shows me exercises to help control the sphincter muscles of the vagina, which will not only arouse a half-interested prick but extend the ecstasy of a stiff one without ejaculation—a form of *karezza*. She shows me how to mix everything in drinks from a Jack Daniel's to a Manhattan. Finally, she tries to impress upon my mind that a cunt must not grovel to its own self-image or it runs the risk of becoming one in the true sense of the word. She wants the word *fuck* deleted from my vocabulary. As she sums up, "*Fuck* is for the unfucked underling but definitely not for me." She's the most liberated woman I've ever met and I love her.

Every day of Indian summer is gold-tinged, an hors d'oeuvre for the feast to come. But the color of the woods gives me the shivers—fire, in all its subversive ordinates. To counteract the ghosts of the godly, I get up before dawn every morning, put on my Indian moccasins, and dress and sprint three miles along the old Voyageur trail in the woods, screeching up a storm. The only way to subdue old furies is by outrunning them with new ones.

Later I stand under the shower tired and sweaty, hoping I've just won another battle in the war I declared on the gods last spring. Secretly I pray for the death pall of winter, my favorite season of the year. I don't want to have to match the moving elements anymore. I want them to match and devour me—ice me in.

One morning when I'm running it finally hits me—why I came here in the first place. I wanted to get buried. Here I can do both, by writhing in other people's gold dust and ash. But what comes next? Where do I go from here?

30

Right through to the middle of February's annual drearies, we're enumerating snowflakes in an unnavigable ocean of barrens, buried in a tomb within a tomb. Johns come and go when the weather permits and the girls get on each other's nerves. Fights flare up over nothing and our disparate personalities rub and grate.

Lena reads and does crossword puzzles, Terry polishes and repolishes her nails, Freda plays with Piddles and learns the alphabet, Cassie drags us outside for snowball fights and gets into everybody's way, and Colette locks herself in her room with a bottle of wine and sometimes cries.

I put *Cavalleria Rusticana* on the phonograph and mooch around the parlor, pressing my nose against the hoared-up window, trying to penetrate the sound barrier of my own thoughts and the swirling lacework on the glass. Am I waiting for something to happen or hoping some old ghost will suddenly appear—like Crunch perhaps? I can't seem to free myself from this snow-smothered corner of the universe. I can't seem to lay down plans for the future. I can't seem to find a future worth my consideration.

Things perk up again when four high rollers from Stateside, up here to do an inspection tour of the nearby mine, blast in for a three-day bender before their return jaunt to Chicago.

At first they're awed by our little setup in the bush. I suspect they think they've been kidnapped and taken to Bora Bora by a bunch of Eskimos in a catamaran. The head honcho is Lord Jim, a burly, good-natured redhead who's constantly laughing and eating jelly beans. The other three huskies are pumped up with as much hydrogen but fail to reach the same altitude. As usual, Cosmos must put on the ritz and turns into a pernickety fishwife by checking the glasses and Sheffield silver for spots and snapping his fingers at us as if we're toy poodles jumping through hoops of fire.

The first night of our guests' sojourn is a roughhousing bang-up and it lasts until well into the next morning. But after a few hours' sack time, a quick shower, a hearty breakfast of pancakes and eggs, and a game of volleyball in the snow outside, everyone is raring to go again.

To satisfy Lord Jim's love of gambling, the action shifts to the kitchen table, which is set up in the parlor, which offers more player and spectator space and adds to the theatricality of the event. The name of the game is five-card stud and the joker is the harlequin in the deck. After each player is dealt one card up and one card down and the holder of the highest card initiates the betting, the girls start to lose interest in the mechanics of the game and concentrate instead on the stakes and the studied expressions of the players as they examine each other coolly, featherbedding the eventual Irishman's bluff we call Bless the Shovel that digs and piles the bullshit.

The men do not lose interest. At the tenth round of betting, the stakes have gone up to over five thousand dollars.

By nightfall, when supper is on the stove in a soup tureen, they're still bivouacked in the parlor with glistening faces, sweaty armpits, fatigued constitutions, and a slight asthmatic condition due to the smoke. We girls can do nothing but empty overflowing ashtrays, replace empty glasses, speak in whispers, and pretend to walk on eggshells. When the French-Canadian pea soup is dished out, ten games have been played, each one a card-riffling *mise en scène* in its own right. After supper the play resumes.

Though Cosmos has won only four of the preceding games and has written out a check to the tune of twenty thousand dollars, he has no intention of quitting.

When midnight rolls around, the marathon finally starts winding down with puffy faces, dilated pupils, inflammable tempers, aching-all-over bodies, and loser's lethargy. I keep waiting for the Cincinnati Kid to arrive and clean up.

Cosmos has now finally drained his petty cash, and since he's unwilling to go into any more bank accounts, he puts our operation as the stake in the final game. Lord Jim pops another jelly bean in his mouth, scratches his head, and accepts.

The cards go down and up and Cosmos is immobile, doll-like, flaring his nostrils, his voice degenerated to a series of guttural monosyllables. The end comes early in the third round, when, sure that he's on the roll to a winning finish, Cosmos slaps down a full house of three spades and a pair of nines.

Lord Jim, whistling through his teeth, splays down four of a kind—in jacks.

Whomp!

Poor Cosmos. He looks as if he's been dealt the death of the thousand cuts. For one brief moment we girls are thrilled that the son of a bitch got his clock cleaned. Then we're staggered at the prospects of foreign ownership and the Stars and Stripes flying above the trailer and our hearts miss a beat.

But Colette takes Cosmos's place at the table and our spirits begin to lift. Having just spent two hours in the bath and boudoir, she's as fresh as a cucumber, scented, bright-eyed, and saucy with her glossy auburn hair swept up into a soft bouffant. Setting a hand-carved wooden jewel box decorated with jade on the table and challenging Lord Jim to a return bout with the operation again on the line, she puts a few pieces of expensive jewelry up as collateral. Fascinated, Lord Jim laughs with good humor, orders another drink, and accepts. Cosmos meets her move with a slight snub, and when she informs him that if she wins she wants a 50 percent share of the operation, he angrily scribbles out a note to that effect.

Giddy and strung-out, we huddle around Colette supportively. She's not only doing this to save her own ass—she's trying to save ours as well. With a cultivated snap, she blushes, sighs, purrs, and displays her cunningly wrought charms to the limit throughout the ensuing game to distract Lord Jim from the hand he's about to play. It's almost as if she's trying to seduce Lady Luck herself. With the exception of Cosmos, the men warm to her and Lord Jim doesn't even seem to mind when she blows him away in the fifth round with a straight flush of hearts.

We whoop it up for joy and dance each other around the parlor until Lord Jim's buddies join us for cocktails and comeuppance. Colette escorts the sporting, jubilant Lord Jim off to her room and we're left to comfort Cosmos, who's in no mood for anything short of screwing fate up the ass.

The cold weather finally breaks into a glorious thaw. The snow shrinks away in stunted swaths around the trees and the creeks sputter and gurgle and then gush, breaking free into torrents. The spirit of rejuvenation throws us into a tizzy of rambunctious restlessness and Colette finds an outlet for it by putting us to work. As we'll soon be on the move again, she oversees a vigorous spring cleanup. Every square inch of the trailer is scrupulously scrubbed inside and out. Then Colette makes out a shopping list and sends Poppy on a series of errands to town. Glasses and towels have a high mortality rate. The kleptomaniac sons of Johns must carry them out under their coats. The first-aid cabinet is refurbished, the freezer filled, and Clay, the local bootlegger, restocks the bar.

On a day when steady V-lines of geese are whooping overhead, four men in a transport arrive from town with Cosmos to move our trailer out. The hydro is disconnected, the plumbing dismantled, the garbage dump filled in, and the trailer hooked up to a flatbed. We're off for another sinful season that will stretch loosely from the beginning of May to late September. Periodically, we hole up on lakes at prearranged pit stops near mines, lumber mills, hunting lodges—anywhere populated with a scarcity of women and a glut of men.

Cassie and I pool our money and buy a canoe from an Ojibway at a nearby trading post. We get the animal strapped onto the top of the Jeep while Poppy stands nearby, chewing toothpicks to pieces and giving benediction. "Youse need that damn thing like youse need another hole in your snatch."

"What makes you an authority?" Cassie yips back with a grin. "You probably never seen one up close in your whole life."

Restored to her natural high, Cassie drops me a menacing wink and whispers in my ear. "How about getting another notch on your research belt? Tonight we're double-dating Ronnie and Joey, two Ojibway boys from the reserve. I've already set it up so you can't refuse."

"But what about Colette?"

"So what about her? Look, we're not even working tonight. We'll be back before morning and won't even be missed."

Feigning a bad case of fatigue, we retire early, remove the window in Cassie's room, and crawl out the trailer just after dark. Luckily, we've got a full moon to light the way to the nearby river. We paddle the canoe out a piece in the shallows and, playing it safe, try to keep close to the shoreline. But a sharp turn in the river catches us unawares and we're snapped like metal to a magnet into the wild sloshing current and find ourselves riding surge and froth at an alarming speed. The river takes a jaunt to the left and we're out of danger and quickly skimming along the inlet at the opposite shore. To calm myself I take a pull at the sealskin flask around my neck and pass it back to Cassie. When I about-face, there's no time to duck as a branch from an overhanging tree zaps me smartly in the face. Thrown off balance, we capsize in a shot and with a heavy splash I sink right under the cold water. For a second I'm in shock trying to find my sea legs and fighting for air and buoyancy. I surface, sputtering and blowing water out of my nose, and I can feel the force of the current whisking me along at a frantic pace. Cassie's head is bobbing nearby. "What the fuck happened?" she screams.

Happy to be alive, I become my nauseous giddy self, choking on water and humor. "I got attacked!"

We have no hope at all of catching our canoe. It's probably a quarter of a mile down the river by now.

"If we don't get to shore, we'll get pounded to smithereens at the rapids," Cassie snorts, breathlessly.

My optimism is short-lived. Willing myself not to panic, it's all I can do to keep my head above the waterline. Little by little I draw from a reservoir of strength I never knew I had, and with desperate labored strokes we elbow in toward the treed shoreline in a slant and manage to haul ourselves aboard an ice-aged boulder of granite marooned in the shallows. Like two drowned rats clinging to each other for support, we wait to stabilize, then stagger into the woods seeking warmth.

For about half an hour we backtrack along the shoreline in the hope our dates will be waiting for us up the river. We're so cold our blood is running purple. Cassie curses a blue streak and dumps the whole load in my lap. It's my fault we capsized, lost the canoe, almost drowned, and will probably die of pneumonia before reaching home. I can only shiver in retaliation. It keeps my metabolism gyrating.

Thankfully, we spot a glow in the trees ahead and come upon a fishing camp where two Jeeps and a tent are wedged into the trees. This is no time to question providence. Four husky-looking middle-aged men in their lumberjack togs are hunched around a fire, drinking. At our approach they give us a go-boy rally cry. Cassie explains our situation but by the grins on their pug faces I don't think they care how the hell we got here. Ignoring our soggy appearance, they invite us to join them. "Come on, girls. Come on over and have a drink."

Stupidly I ask for something warm to put around me. Immediately a burly arm encircles my waist and I'm squeezed against a muscular thigh. Cassie asks for blankets in a "Keep your hands off my crotch" tone of voice and gets them. We peel off our threads in the tent, hang them in the trees nearby to dry, and wrap our bodies up in the blankets.

Ignoring the whistles and slick hick winks, we relax Buddha-style at the fire with a beer. The one called Phil performs the introductions. And here's the stunner. Phil can't remember our names but he's got our game in the bag. I can't recall his visit to the trailer some months back. I only know I wasn't the one who turned his crank. Having unmasked our identities, they're sure our trembling has everything to do with itchy tails and nothing to do with elemental exposure. It's open season on the Goldilocks twins. For once, Cassie doesn't seem to be in the mood to either parley or party. "I don't trust them," she warns in a whisper. "For Chrissake stay sober and don't pass out on me."

Two beers later and each of the four wolves has had enough time to lift a hind leg and draw up a territorial imperative. Their grammar-school linguistics have hit the barroom and the meatily macho is on the road to hard core. It's clear by this time we won't be allowed to leave without a fight.

Then, as if spooked, the buck called Hank blunders to his feet. "Well, what the hell do we have here?"

I wheel around, starting.

Two Ojibways in blue jeans come hiawathing into the firelight with knapsacks on their backs. Quickly, Cassie identifies them as Ronnie and Joey, our dates for the evening. Tall and slender with hawkish good looks, they have long black hair to the shoulder and headbands across their foreheads. They heard our screams on the river over an hour ago and have been searching for us ever since. Phil's not thrilled about their untimely arrival. Nevertheless, he invites them to stay for a drink and makes the mistake of staking his claim on Cassie without her approval. "I'm first for some free fucking, honey. Let's go."

Cassie brings him to heel fast. "Knock it off, King Stud. I don't give nothing out for free."

"Don't give me that shit!" he shoots back, grabbing her by the hair. "You two didn't come out tonight to go canoeing. You came out to get fucked by an Indian. You'll settle just for getting fucked."

Joey springs to his feet, flinging his knapsack to the ground. "Hey, man. Cool it. Why not leave the girls alone and let them decide what they wanna do."

When Hank produces a shotgun, I'm expecting a full-scale massacre. But he merely gives the barrel a loving pat. "Sit down and shut up. If you're lucky, there'll be some ass left over for you."

Joey settles back on his haunches, reaches for a beer, and appears to concede. Cassie does the same and allows Phil and the bulldozer named Ray to manhandle her into the tent.

The last big bad wolf pushes me down, tears the blanket down to my waist, and goes to my tit. Cassie must be getting sweet revenge because I can hear Phil howling like an animal caught in a trap. And this is having a hell of an effect on the wolf grinding away at my cunt, trying to reach godhead. I'm ruminating on-the-squirm on the religious experience of sex when Cassie returns. She's wearing an oversized plaid flannel shirt and jeans and while opening beer bottles gives me my marching orders. "In five minutes make an excuse to have a piss. Then meet me at the Jeep. I've got the keys."

My dehydrated brain tries to accommodate. Five minutes doesn't compute because I'm not wearing a watch. The wolf between my legs won't release me for anything insignificant. And which Jeep and which keys?

I could use some help in the form of accomplices. But Joey and Ronnie are still welded into the backbone of the forest, their faces expressionless and impenetrable as wooden totems, their black inchoate eyes focusing on the darkness beyond. I'm sure they're both in a trance until Ronnie catches my glance and nods his head toward Hank. Even then it's several minutes before I take the cue.

Handicapped by the still-lunching wolf, I can only motion Hank over and hope that the swelling in his pants will permit him to get this far without a spill. He crouches before me. "You better not be funnin' with me, girl."

I tickle his fly encouragingly. The minute he loses control of himself he loses his grip on his Remington and the boys put the breakaway in motion. Hank and Hank's shotgun wind up in the river. My big bad wolf gets a kick in the head. Cassie has brought the tent down around the ears of the two naked wolves inside and is already in the driver's seat of the second Jeep, impatiently gunning the engine, when I arrive. Ronnie and Joey hop in beside me and Cassie burns mud.

The old mining road ahead is a four-wheel drive's dream of a good time. We plan to ditch the Jeep far enough ahead so the big bad wolves will have a hell of a time finding it. But we've only gone about three miles when Ronnie draws our attention to the wind getting up in the trees and the shifting cloud masses overhead. The sky is puffing itself up into a bruised arabesque.

With a heavy storm brewing, the boys suggest we drop the Jeep.

Cassie slips the keys in the glove compartment and leaves the distributor for the other Jeep on the front seat. Then the boys take us on a short but exhausting trek through the woods until a suitable spot to camp is found. No sooner have the boys hacked branches from nearby bushes and begin to erect a primitive lean-to between two trees when the rain starts slashing down in solid sheets. Cassie and I crawl inside and bed down with the boys in their sleeping bags.

The storm shatters the atmosphere most of the night—lightning splitting the sky in half and thunder pounding away at our senses. The four of us are so fatigued that sex isn't even considered. Joey is so smooth of skin and adolescent to the touch it's like sleeping with my brother. To keep warm we cling together like bear cubs in a den enjoying the security and serenity that closeness brings. I don't understand the native's grim pagan gods with their animal senses, wild empty spaces, and biological tie to nature but I suspect they're not as complicated as they appear. I'm used to the Olympians with their flair for archery and family feuds. Lulled to sleep by the leaves dripping overhead, my last conscious thought is that man was nature's only genetic mistake.

Ronnie and Joey wake us shortly after daybreak and while they're fishing for breakfast, Cassie builds a fire and I dress in the other clothing she stole from the fishing camp. A good meal and a healthy touch of sex prompts Cassie and me into fantasies of digging in and setting down roots. It's a fantasy I toy with every day of the week.

We spend the day with the boys and late in the afternoon they accompany us part of the way back to a place near the trailer so we won't get lost. After leaving them, Cassie and I bounce along in a high carefree mood, pretending we're self-sufficient Voyageurs on the path to discovering a new world. Despite our optimism it's after dark when we reach the trailer. With torn, muddy clothing and scratched arms and legs, we shuffle inside and run smack into a heavy pall of silence, like walking in on a funeral.

"Where the fuck were you two?" Cosmos demands from the parlor doorway, his face flushed with liquor and rage.

"Ask *her*," Cassie says, zipping off to her room to avoid a scene.

"We went canoeing and got lost," I explain hesitantly.

"You left without getting permission from Colette or telling anyone where you were going. I was about to call the police."

"What more can I say? I'm sorry."

"Get cleaned up, I'll deal with you later."

I'm bathed and sitting in my room in a towel, blow-drying my hair, when Cassie bursts in. "Do you know what that bastard did? He gave me the ax. I have to be out of here tomorrow!"

She falls into my arms, dissolving into a hysterical crying jag. Quietly, Colette slips in and calms us both. "I will speak to him," she promises, taking Cassie back to her room.

Without knocking, Cosmos strides in and I fly at him. "Why didn't you give me the sack, too?"

"The clientele finds you a better piece of tail, Toots. Individually you're both manageable. Together, you're uncontrollable. I'm running a business, not a halfway house for jailbait."

"You make it sound like I'm a criminal or something."

"Well, you have all the right tendencies." He continues on my emotional extravagance and sexual excesses; and struck by the hypocrisy, I laugh in his face. Why should I feel sorry for losing something I never had in the first place?

"It's not enough you get it here. Now you've got to go balling in the woods with the Indians, too!"

"Maybe they do it better."

He slaps my face, and losing my balance, I reel backward into the vanity. "Do they?" he sneers hotly. "We'll see about that!"

Before I can properly defend myself, he hauls me to my feet, pitches me facedown on the bed, and placing one knee against my spine, puts me in a helpless position. Hearing the zipper on his fly I try to wriggle my way out while cursing him thickly. "Why fight me?" He laughs caustically. "I'll win anyway—and you know that. Why not be disgustingly submissive and save us both the time."

"Nobody owns me."

"I own you so you don't have a goddamn choice. This's the end of the conversation we had last summer."

"How about paying me first?"

"I told you before—I don't pay for it."

"Well, I won't work free gratis. It's apolitical and against the capitalist norms that say, Don't give up a dime of sweat unless you've got a quarter of somebody else's in your hand first."

"Your foreplay is as fucked up as your sense of autonomy," he grunts, gripping my thighs and pulling my buttocks upward.

"Aren't you a big shot—having to resort to rape," I rage stupidly, knowing what's coming next.

He answers me by suddenly jabbing his enormous erection into me in one thrust, screwing my closely pressed muscles open, and I siphon his heavy hardness up to the hilt with a cry of release, and he heaves and plunges and I rock and buck, knowing I'm lost and caught in the paroxysms of pain that are sending electrodes to every part of my trembling body and if he stops I know I'll die of anguish. I'm nothing but an object of feeling and life itself is reduced to that pumping prick. Then in one power thrill of tremulous emotion the devil is shocked out of both of us and Cosmos rolls onto his back in a narcoticlike daze.

The heat's back in my life and it's worse than never. With his alfresco sex style Cosmos is a paradigm for the fall of Rome. Once again I've fallen for a beast with two horns and a tail who offers me sanctuary, employment, a sandbox to play in, and the chance to live up to the cunt's image I have of myself. Though we're both corruptions of nature and have nothing but contempt for each other, we feed off each other's weaknesses, picking at the carcasses of our emotionally dead souls. It's a regular storm in a teacup, lust in a locust's summer.

I wake in the morning wearing only leftover luster and a lopsided grin. The contretemps of the night before is terrible. The room looks like a brigand's breakfast.

Out of the devastation comes a stinging slap of warnings and a caress of good news—Cassie can stay on.

As soon as Cosmos hits the road and my libido calms down, I get permission from Colette to extend an invitation to Simon to come up for a visit. Up until now he's had to take a rain check.

A bush pilot flies him in the very next weekend. The minute he steps onto the dock in his beige safari suit, we're dancing attendance on him. Cassie grabs his flight bag and I take the big wicker picnic basket packed with all sorts of exotic goodies. He kisses me on the cheek like a schoolgirl. "Darling—on the spot and as plucky as ever."

Colette takes his arm and strolls toward the trailer while the rest of us giggle behind like coolies.

To make room for Simon, Terry willingly gives up her bed and shares mine.

Once Simon settles in, Colette calls him outside and they spend the afternoon lounging at the umbrella table, watching us behave like water sprites in the lake while they partake of the wine and caviar he's brought, pretending they're brunching at a café on the Seine.

He has presents for each of us, plus his own stock of Earl Grey tea, which he brews up, driving us into gales of laughter with his ribald theatrics. After dinner he ties on an apron and instead of helping us dry the dishes he juggles them, smashing three in the process. Then he stuffs his mouth, ears, and nose with lit cigarettes and tells us naughty jokes and limericks while they burn down to butts.

Poppy doesn't know quite what to make of him. When he discovers that Simon's a blue blood related to the Queen, he spits the toothpicks out of his mouth and addresses him as "your Honor," to which Simon replies, "That's right, with your honor and my pleasure, we'll save the day."

He allows Freda to lead him by the hand into her room to view her treasures and play with Piddles. He sits on the end of the dock with Lena, dipping his feet in the water, and encourages her educational pursuits. He gratifies Terry's sense of self by showing her how she should wear her hair and how to properly highlight her cheekbones. He meets Cassie's tough exterior head-on by skinny-dipping with her after dark and then screwing her in the woods.

Cosmos and Simon wouldn't hit it off. Simon represents everything he secretly envies and openly despises, what he left England to escape. Now that Cosmos's decidedly nouveau riche, he's developed a distinctive elitist's posture. He hates the class of blue blood he cannot buy into and is at the same time contemptuous of those below his station.

At midnight Simon tiptoes in and shakes me awake. Quietly we slip back to Terry's room, light a candle, open a bottle of wine, and hold vespers. "The northern air agrees with you, darling," he admits. "It's the first time I've seen color in your face that wasn't synthetic."

He pours us glass after glass of wine and we have a heart-to-heart rap for three hours. Racked with fatigue and frolic, we laugh so hard we're nearly sick. At one point he gets to his feet, trying to compose himself. "Darling, I have to leave you now. I have an appointment in the room at the end of the hall."

"Why, you devil," I tease.

"Come, darling—you'd be the last one to deny a man absolution in the divinely abstract."

"First Cassie, now Colette."

"I always finish off with a sublime chaser. That woman is far too exquisite for the Canadian wilds."

"If you're not back in your coffin by dawn, Zeus only knows what you'll turn into."

"Pray for me, little mother." He kisses me on the cheek and disappears.

Hours later I hear the bedroom door open and close. The mattress under me sags and Simon hugs me from behind. "Well, did you learn anything?" I say, grasping his hands.

"Decidedly. I now know what divided this country. Perhaps in future I'll discover what can bring it back together again."

"Probably the animal that divided it in the first place."

I ask him what he thinks I should do in the future and he admits that a change is definitely in order.

"What would I ever do without you and your brand of cutting counsel?"

"Self-destruct."

"But why is that?"

"You expect it, darling. Your own best enemy is always yourself. You have an affection for Colette, don't you?"

"Sure—I guess I love her."

"Good, then I'll put a bug in your ear. Learn everything you can from her—she's tops."

The next morning Cassie, Terry, Lena, and I take Simon for a two-day camping trip, which's rather like the Four Musketeers taking Cardinal Richelieu through Alice's looking glass for brunch. One by one, we break every rule in the book on Surviving in the Woods. Lena gets a dose of poison ivy, the blackflies have a field day with Cassie, Terry gets a bad cold, I get so constipated I can't walk, and Simon comes back with only a burr on his sleeve.

The night before he leaves for Toronto we get in a truckful of Johns. Simon adapts admirably, putting on a French accent and pretending he's Colette's brother François, a down-and-out gay artist from Paris. He keeps us in stitches the whole evening.

Everyone's heartbroken when he goes. Before he gets into the plane he gives me a final morsel on a Ritz cracker. "Everything you'll ever need you can find inside of yourself. Remember that, darling." He shuts the door, then calls through the glass, "Be a good fucking girl and keep those cards and letters coming in."

In April a new recruit at the local cop shop refuses to jeopardize his mother's morals and his father's ego by accepting under-the-table bribes from Cosmos, so the police pull a raid on our full house—in the middle of the night. Without warning, a tremendous banging at both doors. Lena sets off a smoke detector in the hallway. The trailer is suddenly surrounded by skidoos and flashing lights, and some nincompoop is announcing "Last call" through a foghorn.

Before Colette can collect herself and get to the door, the trailer is pressurizing with us girls and the Johns caught in the middle of a thumping, shrieking, door-slamming bubble burst.

The John in bed with me leaps into the closet to dress and is immediately bombarded by a shelf of the complete set of Winston Churchill's *History of the English-speaking Peoples*.

While he's brushing up on his history, I'm tangling with geography alfresco. Clothed in nothing but a bed sheet, I break the double glass in the window with a lamp, and dive headfirst in the nearest snowbank. An O.P.P. officer with blue lips and burnt cheeks sprints around the side of the trailer and chases me into the woods and one, two, three,

I've fallen into our garbage pit! He hauls me out kicking and screaming obscenities. I try to tear the moustache off his face. He gives me a whack on the butt and carries me inside.

In the parlor I nick a bottle of vodka from the bar to warm up. There's so much noise that nobody even notices.

Colette is trying to make herself understood in English while philosophizing in French. Freda is crying and clutching Piddles so he won't bite anyone. Lena is sitting on the couch glaring over an *Esquire* magazine. Cassie is being physically restrained by two officers after giving one a nosebleed. Terry is on her knees salaaming for a warm cell with running water and an on-call manicurist with a lisp. Poppy is explaining how he was shanghaied and brought here for purely pornographic reasons. The hysterical Johns are publicizing their religious denomination, credit rating, and political party affiliations with references to everyone's paternity. Is nothing sacred?

Finally, to establish order, one of the cops blows a whistle. We're put in lineup formation to help sort out this mixed bag of tricks and chicks. Since they won't trust the females to dress without further muss and fuss, we have to go as we are. Colette hands out our coats and boots. Meanwhile, the Johns scramble into the bedrooms to hyperventilate. Luckily, I'm able to tie my bed sheet into some sort of toga.

We're eventually hustled off through the yawning void to the local lockup in carriers towed behind the police skidoos. The night air is blue-cold and snaps against our faces in creases. There's a chip of a moon posted like a sentinel over the pines. Quietly raging, Colette refuses to speak and keeps tapping her boot and chain-smoking. Freda calms Piddles with a bedroom story about a princess and a frog prince but there's no punch line and none of us is amused. Lena reads the night ahead and grits her teeth. Terry whines about leaving her cosmetic case behind and holds her mitts against her cheeks so frostburn won't make her look like an overdone tart. Cassie verbalizes everyone's pent-up anger, and slipping her my bottle of vodka, I laugh at all of them.

At the nineteenth-century lockup, Colette makes the essential phone call to her lawyer, Sam Potter, who says he'll transmit our SOS to that SOB Cosmos.

We're held until noon the next day. After lunch we're released into Cosmos's hands. With the exception of Colette, who gives him a frosty reception, we service his ego by groveling before him like little gnocchi. Having the edge, he gives us the bad news. Our operation has been temporarily put on ice. We may not be back in business until sometime in the summer. Which means that I'm not only out of a job, and out of a house, I'm out of a home as well.

PART V
GONE

31

he other girls experience a momentary rush of adolescent hysteria over the news. Then they gravitate toward a put-your-best-high-heel-forward optimism. Feeling a little lost and helpless, I alone can see nothing progressive about change. At twenty-four, I'm getting set in my ways. I must be getting old.

I'm thankful that the cops let us back into the trailer to collect our belongings. Colette books us into the hotel in town to collect our wits and make plans for the future. As far as I'm concerned, the future can't be planted or fertilized like a garden. Like the past, it's best left to fallow into a weed bed.

Now that Lena has completed her high school by correspondence and stashed away enough money for an education, she decides to bus it to Toronto and take an aboveboard waitressing job until commencement of college in the fall. Colette has a monetary interest in the business and refuses to leave the north. Instead, she rents a small house for herself and Freda. Terry and Cassie decide to accompany Lena to Toronto for purposes of speculation. Cosmos offers to set them up in an apartment. I decide to go along for the ride.

Our preparations to meet civilization head-on are frenzied. Colette plays mother hen. She gives us advice, helps us arrange our wardrobes, and makes us feel like baby chicks leaving the nest for the first time. Our good-byes at the bus depot a week later testify to the emotional bonds we've developed over the last few years. Though Cassie, Terry, and I promise Colette we'll be back in the summer, we know we won't. This's the end of one chapter and the beginning of another one. Colette realizes we won't be back, too. Her last piece of advice is not to make commitments we can't possibly honor.

Lena leaves us at the bus depot in Toronto. She's adamant about making it on her own. I admire her for making the break so quickly, cleanly, and finally—until I realize she's talked me into doing it myself.

In theory the decision seemed a cinch. But after renting an apartment near the University of Toronto, I'm ready to hit the panic button and move in with Cassie and Terry. The city itself is the problem. Like a fish out of water I'm paranoid and restless, penned in by concrete, glass, pollution, and overdrive; I'm dazed by the noise and blinded by the lights. I can't survive on my own. I can't change professions. I've been a holding tank of suck-ass servitude and stall too long.

I give myself another week to make the transition. But the joke's on me. Fate's decided to give me only a day.

In my line of business it's normal to attract weirdos of every description but I always try to weed the dangerous deviants out of the lineup. That very night I'm picked up by a middle-aged John in a Buick on College Street. He smells like a government backbencher but says he's an art entrepreneur. He has practically no lips at all, chews his nails, and reminds me of a king crab with his 250-pound payload, pasty complexion, and bored countenance.

Back at my apartment he opens an attaché case on the bed. It could easily double as the Marquis de Sade's travel kit, complete with a whip and handcuffs. Too late I realize that I've goofed up. We won't be playing tonight's game by the Marquis of Queensbery rules. The mark of a queen, maybe. Some girls will chance letting a trick tie them up and play voodoo witch doctor. But I won't.

Instinctively, I reach for the knife in the sheath on my leg and order him out. He laughs at me with such grunting rancor I'm put off balance. He slaps my face, and takes the knife out of my hand. "Pulling a knife on someone without knowing how to use it is almost as bad as not using it at all."

My hopes that Sir Sangfroid is a masochist are dashed when he manhandles me to the floor, binds and gags me, and ties me to a kitchen chair. When he uses a surgeon's deliberate precision to cut the clothing from my body with my knife, I'm past terror, somewhere in a dead zone of insensibility. Unable to invoke any response from me, he cuts the insides of my arms, just enough to draw blood. I grit my teeth and he's the one who reacts. "You're not playing the game," he says, his voice rising an octave.

That part of myself still functioning waits for the next attack. It comes quickly with the sharpened tongue of his sex pistol. The moment the whip hits my back I realize that I have found yet another way to die. I wriggle, I buck, and I weave from side to side, and I make a mistake—I scream. So he hits me again, and again I scream. And every time the sting of the needle tears at my flesh, I keep making that mistake and each time I make it I pray I won't make it again. But I do. The blows come one after the other, burning, until I run out of prayers and somewhere I'm drifting farther and farther away. . . .

I don't know when I pass out but eventually I come to, groggily, hugging the chair, my hands suddenly freed. I feel as if I have a vicious sunburn, the kind that cracks and bubbles into blisters. Sir Sangfroid has left and taken his instruments with him. He might have cut me worse. But once I fainted I was no longer a fun victim.

Still, I sit in the kitchen chair, shaking spasmodically from an inner chill, unable mentally to articulate the word *safe*.

Slowly my sensibilities gather threads. If I get up out of this chair, I'll be committed to some sort of action. *First, I must lock the door in case he has a change of heart and returns. Secondly, he might have tricked me and might still be in the apartment so I must not lock the door. Thirdly, I must forget locks and doors altogether. They can't keep him out or me in. Now get up and get out of here!*

I act on this single nugget of thought. I watch a specter of myself cross the darkened hall to the bedroom. I watch her switch on the light, remove a dress and coat from the closet and underwear from the bureau. I watch her shuffle in and zip up and reach for a shoulder bag. I watch her carefully lock the apartment door behind her. I won't be back.

It's a typical winter's night for Toronto. A little rain, a little snow, and a helluva chill in the wind barreling up University Avenue from the harbor. I hit the street and find it hitting back at me.

At the next corner the light changes to green. All I can feel is the nails raking my back and the fear throbbing in my guts. All I can see is the black nothingness in the pavement beyond as if I'm being shot down a tunnel. . . . I can't pass go. I'm still waiting for the light to change to red when I remember Uncle Teddy's old line of inspiration. *Deal yourself another hand, mate. There's always a fresh deck of cards in somebody else's pocket.*

By the time the light switches to green again, I've set my course. I'm on track. My next play is into *somebody else's* pocket. At twelve years old I made a similar decision to survive. I put my psyche in a Moses basket. I left that basket at the door of the powers that be. I had myself institutionalized. What goes down must come around— again.

When I reach the terrestrial tarmac of the Yonge Street Strip I don't have to advertise. The short Persian lamb coat I'm wearing over the purple prickteaser and the three-inch glow-in-the-dark pumps say it all: STREET MEAT FOR SALE.

I sashay a while, watching the action, having the action watch me light a cigarette, window-shop as an excuse to see who's about to climb aboard my own reflection, and slip into a fast-food eatery to get warm and grab a bite, giving potential Johns the bum's rush when I sense their *modus operandi* doesn't match my consumer price index.

I take up the cause at a no-parking sign. Another John on the pickup patrol approaches the parade route. A cocker spaniel with a cop's badge in his pocket, pretending he's a hound dog. "Waiting for someone?" he says, moving within soliciting range.

"Maybe."

"Maybe it's me you're waiting for."

"Maybe I'm not your type." I cruise on ahead at the speed of a glowworm. I could make my pitch now but why make it easier for him than it is for me? He follows on an angle behind my shoulder. The choreography says we're a married couple on the brink of divorce. I let him play me all the way from Gerrard to the lights at Dundas.

Then I give him the prime rate for oral sex on the love-without-interest insurance plan. He whips out a shield. I get a knee into his groin. In a flash he has me on the ground, my hands behind my back, reading me my rights. Mission accomplished.

I'm whisked off to the 52 Division precinct. I'm questioned briefly, then booked for soliciting, resisting arrest, and assaulting a police officer under the bogus name on my fake ID.

I have to make a scene in order to be allowed my one phone call out. Now that I'm on the inside, it won't hurt to have a helping hand outside just in case I need it. Naturally, there's no answer at Lena's or Biscuit's, and Cassie and Terry's line rings busy.

Next, I'm put into a clean, warm cell and given a coffee and a blanket. For the first time since arriving in the city I feel safe.

In the morning I'm loaded in a paddy wagon with ten other prisoners. The door is slammed shut. The transferral takes a good hour. The smoke builds in solid layers as cigarette after cigarette is fired up. The lack of fresh air brings an assault of fists on the cab. The guard switches on the fan. Minutes later the temperature drops below freezing. Another assault ensues until the heat is turned on.

Hello, Toronto West Detention Center. A cubist's conception of low expressionlessism. I'm photographed and fingerprinted, my personal belongings searched, recorded, and stashed in labeled plastic bags. The process takes two hours of musical cells.

The cuts on my arms look suspiciously suicidal. The head psychologist performs an interview to see if I'm animal, mineral, or vegetable. She looks frigidly friendly and asks me how I feel. I plan to slit my wrists or hang myself from the bars of my cell. I expect help. She doesn't know what to expect, and commits me to the psych ward—solitary confinement.

Two frontline bulldykes order me to strip down and bend over. They want to check the crack of my ass. I might be carrying peekaboo plastic tampons that contain drugs or razor blades. I give them a voyeuristic eyeful, shower, and dress in a denim shift of double thickness that can't be turned into a hangman's noose. I'm pitched into a yellow-bricked cell containing a cot with a mattress, a sink, and a toilet. The window has been blacked in. There's no view to the world. The body must live but the spirit must die. That's the law in Shangri-La.

Soon my rage erupts from the inside out. My brain cells are burning, my stomach muscles are doing the St. Vitus dance, and I'm sobbing. I sit on the floor in my own vomit. I wait for a quick release from the gods of mercy. They can't get in because I won't let them. Emotionally, I can't function anymore on the street. I'm not allowed to function here at all. Numbly I pinch my cigarette butts all over the floor, grinding them into the concrete with my bare foot. Ashtrays aren't allowed. They can be broken and the pieces used to slice veins. Jobs can be lost because of such an oversight.

My stir time begins with lost time. For the first time in my life I'm really at the mercy of society and its goon squad. Even if I had a hotshot Bay Street lawyer, they'd still have me by the ass. Nobody can get to you here. I'm dependent solely on the staff for the basics of self-sustenance. Don't they just love rubbing my nose in my own vulnerability.

To beat time back to the wall where I can kick it, abuse it, put it on a leash, I sing every dirty song I know and play head games. During the day the light is blinding and opens up every gritty corner, every scrap of graffiti on the walls and ceiling: CONGRATULATIONS SUCKER— YOU'VE JUST REACHED THE ARSEHOLE OF THE WORLD!

I won't see myself like this—with those seedy eyes of a screw staring at me through the grille in the door. They won't even allow me a piss in privacy. I've become government property with a number and a chart. My anger curls into a ball. It buries itself under the heavy denim blanket, where there are anonymous layers of darkness to hide under and devils to play with. Hopefully, I'll drift into a sleep that will last into the next millennium.

The dinner cart is trundled down the corridor. I can't eat. There's no longer any reason to feed a vanity that isn't. My body is an empty shell. I manage to gulp down the weak tea the kitchen staff has washed their socks in. The last act of aggression has to be against the body physical. The toilet is the last seat of assignation.

Sounds and thoughts hit the wall and ricochet back. I'm being attacked by the very vibrations I create. Maybe if I create enough noise within I can shut out the noise from without. My cell becomes a think tank of revolution. The unspeakable will speak and be heard. Crime is not a social riddle anymore but a simple equation on the blackboard. Guilt + depression = crime.

Now what is it I'm really guilty of? Am I responsible for Crunch's death? Is my life-style the culprit? What's wrong with escaping society's Monday-to-Friday sitcom? What's wrong with living each day as grab-bag Saturday night? Am I a sociopath or an emotional misfit? Where are the good old days when sanity was monitored as nothing more than being true to your school?

A screw walks by my cage, making a quacking sound at the back of his throat. Is the jerk trying to amuse or confuse? I ask him if he's Donald Duck from the entertainment committee.

He says I can call him Rick.

I ask Rick for a cigarette.

Rick asks me how badly I want one.

I see. It's to be a war of attrition.

"Tell me how badly I want one."

Five minutes later a bale of tobacco and a package of papers are thrown in. Rick says I can vindicate myself by making rollies for my comrades in Cell Block P. That's the secret. Play the criminal and their conscience loves you. Play the innocent and they don't trust you. Play the citizen wronged by the system and they downright hate you.

At ten years old I made candy money by kissing the village idiot boy behind the school door for a quarter. I would have kissed him for nothing. I loved his soul. He was the ugliest boy in the village. Would he have kissed me for a dime? You betcha.

I'm the ultimate joker. I keep offering myself to the world as a fool. The world keeps accepting my offer. I keep celebrating by kissing the cold concrete.

The screws keep notes on my disintegration on a clipboard outside my cell. Day 3 into my hunger strike. My *cri de coeur* for a pen and paper finally brings a compromise—if I attempt to choke down supper I can have both plus a trashy novel. Hungry to pen grott, I agree.

To christen my pen, I draw a skeleton on the wall doing the *danse macabre* on the coffin of Moses and beside it graffiti a ditty from the Depression that Crazy Jack once taught me.

> As you ramble on through life
> Whatever be your goal or strife
> Trust only in a doughnut.
> Keep your eye upon the dole
> But trust in nothing but the hole.

I'm allowed another phone call and manage to contact Cassie. She hires a lawyer for me. The overachiever drops by the next afternoon with encouraging news. If I plead guilty to the three charges against me, he'll arrange to have them reduced. To be a lawyer all you have to have is a working knowledge of shuffleboard.

On the fourth night a new prisoner is brought into Cell Block P. She's going up for stabbing her boyfriend to death. She keeps beating at the door of her cell, calling my name. "Anybody—somebody— please answer me!"

Slipping onto the floor, I creep along the wall, searching for that plaintive voice. It's coming from out of my childhood somewhere. To touch her mentally, I roll five cigarettes. The night guard passes them along to her. "How do you feel now, my baby?"

"Mummy!" she sobs again.

For the remainder of the night I sit on the floor wrapped in my blanket, talking her to sleep. I don't dare let her go. If she lets go of me, I'll let go of myself.

On the fifth day I'm awakened for court at seven o'clock. After breakfast we're transported by paddy wagon to College Park downtown. Twelve of us are stuffed with twenty others in the Pigpen. A dirty congested cell with a toilet and sink, smelling of urine and cigarette smoke. There's a big glassed-in partition at one end of the room with a two-way mirror. The cops can watch you have a piss without asking your permission. Two girls are standing on a wooden bench along the wall. They're calling their boyfriends through the ventilating shaft to the Bullpen, where the male prisoners are kept.

An emaciated Puerto Rican girl mumbles inaudibles and roams around the pen looking for a cigarette. No one will oblige. She shimmies over and knocks her leg against my knee. I roll her a cigarette. She tells me she's an illegal en route to New York City from San Juan. I slide a cigarette between her fingers. In a doper's daze, she slumps on one hip and lazily strikes a match. Then the unforgivable— a bloody menstrual pad falls to the floor between her legs.

Nothing that happens here is an accident—it's a omen, a psychological turn-off or turn-on. She's just committed the worst crime imaginable. She's just betrayed her sex.

"Why don't yeh burn yourself up, yeh fucking ratshit!!" one of the hardknockers hollers, instigating a go-girl rally cry that turns into a pagan war chant.

Dreamily, she puts the match to the hem of her dress. Immediate silence drowns the room. We're suspended in an ahhhful trance. The sizzling cotton suddenly connects to flame. The girls burst into a wild cheer, encouraging the flame up her body.

Hysterically, I jump to my feet. Another girl and myself leap toward the Puerto Rican. We wheel her back into the toilet to put out the fire. The door bursts open. Stormtroopers rush in. The three of us are thrown up against the wall. Given no time to explain, we're hustled off to separate cells.

I'm still shaking from the incident at my hearing an hour later. It's not until meeting with my lawyer back at the slammer that I'm aware of being granted bail.

That very night I'm pulled out of solitary to make room for others in worse shape. The promotion is accompanied by a new set of jail threads scavenged from the highways of the 1960's—blue jeans, a T-shirt, and runners. I thought I'd be buried in anonymity and regimentation. But it seems I'm to be buried in nostalgia. My hitching thumb is on the twitch.

I'm turned loose on an overcrowded range. A range has twelve two-bunk-apiece cells. They half-moon a communal washroom and recreation room with four long steel picnic tables and a TV in a cage. Meals are eaten in the cells to avoid food fights. Showers are prescheduled to avoid gang rape. I have no problem identifying with the philosophy of sorority living. *What is yours is yours and what is mine is mine unless I want or need yours.*

Now I'm allowed visitors other than lawyers. Cassie shows up the next afternoon. She's determined to put up the thousand-dollar bail. I'm determined that she not. Instead, I ask her to have my apartment cleared out and my belongings put in storage. "It's the least I can do." She laughs. And that's the grit of it. The *least* I get from others, the better I'll be. The *most* I'll get for myself.

My lawyer hires a psychiatrist to do an assessment. The two-hour session begins like a rehearsal in search of an opening night. It ends like a burlesque that bombed out. I refuse to abrogate my individuality by trying to appear normal. At the same time I'm *not* trying to be tabbed as neurotic, psychotic, or schizophrenic. Because of my fake ID and the precarious professions of my friends and associates, it's essential for reasons of personal security that my past life remain under wraps. As the courts can have files produced on demand, I can't even fall back on doctor–patient confidentiality for support. So understandably this "I'm okay—you're okay" psychodrama never really advances past the catch-me-if-you-can call to arms.

According to the doctor's prognosis I have a chemical imbalance called the manic-depressive syndrome. Translated into layman's terms, I have a brainful of buckshot. He prescribes a drug called lithium. It's guaranteed to neutralize my highs and lows. Though skeptical, I'm willing to accept his judgment—for now—until I do some assessing and researching on my own. I'm in no position to argue.

The following month I keep my nose clean, my eyes open, and my ears on. I learn that epileptic fits are as natural to jails as the guards themselves. They're caused by drugs and the stresses of confinement. I learn that justice is all in the price of the lawyer and that bail is injustice's big night out on the town. I see old women humiliated, sick women ignored, and young women abused. I see girls using menstrual blood as a cosmetic and women using nihilism as a wonder drug. I see guards using everybody as guinea pigs for their off-campus university courses on criminal psychology. Ten percent of the population don't belong here and are merely the products of a screw-up in the system that uses the human being who can't afford a lawyer as a made-to-order suppository.

North American society is divided into three groups: those already perverted, those learning how to become perverted, and those who can't afford to be perverted because they must pay for the perversions of the other two. For all this you need two cars for your hormones and one chauffeur for your conscience.

I started smoking at thirteen. One night in the theater I dropped an ash and set my seat and my pants on fire. By the time the fire department arrived I had single-handedly wiped out the seats front row center and smoked out the balcony. Rome's been burning ever since.

I'm still riding the fast machine, melting saddles and feel chased by a heat-seeking missile. I was so busy digging holes to crawl in, I never used one to crawl out; so busy getting it on in the backseat, it never occurred to me to take the wheel. I never wanted the hands-on responsibility. There's security in darkness—and dampness. I could never see myself as a '60's child because I never stopped being its late bloomer. I loved the petting, the pawing, the nuzzling, the squeezing, the hugging—the needing to, the poking, the prodding, the having to. I couldn't stop foreplaying it. I couldn't stop depending on those five U's of survival: being untouched, uninvolved, uncontrollable, and ultimately unavailable for comment. But somehow I always managed to find the back door. The women's room was always right beside it.

I don't think I'll ever grow any older than I am today.

Things look up considerably five weeks later. At my trial I'm put on probation for a year. Lena offers to recommend me for a job at the restaurant where she's currently working.

At nine o'clock in the evening on the day of my release, I'm escorted down the straight and narrow hallowed halls of silence. The big steel door squeals into the roof. The man in the guardhouse beckons me forward. Back on the street, the red light changes to green and all I can feel is the fear throbbing in my guts . . . and I'm running on empty.

EPILOGUE

And so here I am back at the dawn of civilized madness where the whole mess started with nothing but a finger and a head to scratch.

It has taken me a quarter of a century of scratching to change from caterpillar to butterfly.

Thankfully I'm still praying to the Olympians. Every morning I open my eyes to Zeus and go to sleep snuggling with Orpheus. I've got Orgasmo, the germ, stashed in my suitcase, along with his leash. Not a word comes out of his dirty little mouth that I haven't scribbled.

There's a book of profundity and profanity in everyone and a library of anachronisms, old and new, many unexplained and unrealized irreconcilables and unvoiced complaints from the mouths of both the quick and the dead.

This one's mine.

Sorry that it didn't come with coupons or recipes for happiness. . . .

ABOUT THE AUTHOR

CATHERINE ROMAN is the pseudonym of a young woman living somewhere in the province of Ontario, Canada. She is currently working on yet another "literary outrage."